THE CASH MACHINE

A TALE OF PASSION, PERSISTENCE, AND FINANCIAL INDEPENDENCE

BY DAVE AND CHANA MASON

What is this page doing here? Simple, it's about money.
You know, dough, greenbacks, moolah, loot, cash.

Some of us worship it. Others call it the root of all evil. Either way, we all use it. We all need it. But how often do we take the time to truly understand it?

Most readers skip over this page like they skip over other money matters. This book aims to reverse that. Shoving money issues under the rug doesn't make them go away, and it certainly won't help you make smarter financial decisions. What it does is pass control of your financial future to people who rarely have your best interests in mind.

This novel aims to help you step up and claim ownership over your financial future. So fittingly, it begins with this page, where we assert our ownership over our intellectual property.

Cover design by the amazing Juan Hernaz.
Check out his other amazing works at JuanHernaz.com

Interior layout by the ever-reliable Zoran Maksimović,
www.macsimovic.com

To Stephen and Barbara Mason

You tried so hard to set Dave on a solid financial path…

It's not your fault we had to learn our lessons the hard way.

INTRODUCTION

There's an old adage in writing: *Write What You Know*. This is why so many money books focus on just one narrow area of finances, because they're written by an experts in the field.

Our adage is slightly different, it's: *Write What You Want To Know*, or perhaps, in this case, it's better stated as *Write What You Need To Know*. Before writing this book, we were not money specialists, and we soon realized that what we didn't know about money was hurting us.

We've had periods when we've earned tremendous amounts of money. How much? Enough to set ourselves up for life without ever having to work again. That is, it could have set us up for life had we understood how to properly spend and invest it. But we didn't. So instead of being set for life, we found ourselves in massive debt. To keep our heads above water, we had to sell our house, the one we thought we'd raise our family in.

So there we were, broke, with nothing to show for our great earnings of the past (which had, alas, mostly dried up by this point). We realized we needed a serious money education—not just in one or two areas—but across all major domains.

When we want to understand a subject, we find no tool so effective as researching and writing a novel about it. That's the birth story of *The Cash Machine*. We wrote this book for ourselves and have already seen tremendous impact from applying the lessons you're about to learn. We hope you will as well.

Dave & Chana

NOTE TO READERS

A few notes to readers before you begin:

1. We've done our best to make all of the information in *The Cash Machine* up to date and accurate at the time of publication. However, financial regulations change so quickly that sooner or later, some of the information will become dated. Should you spot anything inaccurate, out of date, or (Heaven forbid) a typo, please let us know at **BuildMyCashMachine.com/feedback** so we can update the text.

2. There's only so much detail a novel can go into before the story starts to unravel. In writing *The Cash Machine*, we've sought a balance between offering tons of useful information and not overwhelming our readers. This means that with some financial lessons, we're just giving you an introduction and an overview, not spelling them out in exhaustive detail. We thus consider the book just one half of this project. The other half lives on our website and within our online community. To get plugged in, visit **BuildMyCashMachine.com**.

3. Most of the lessons in this book are universal and apply anywhere in the world. For a minority of the lessons, non-US based readers might have to research how to apply the strategy in their home countries. Fortunately, most of these provisions have international parallels. For instance, while only the US has the ROTH IRA, many countries offer tax protections on retirement accounts. So if you're not the US, don't worry, this book is for you too.

CHAPTER 1

DRIFTWOOD

With the grace of a beached whale, I plopped on the sand next to my ex-boyfriend Dylan. "I think I'm finally drunk enough to ask you the question I've wanted answered for the past seven years." *Seven years*. Had it really been that long since we were college freshmen? "What the *hell* happened to you in Mexico?"

Dylan didn't answer me straight away. He gazed at me the way only Dylan could, with quiet blue eyes that took in more than he let on. He strummed his beat-up, second-hand guitar as the sun set over his shoulder. "You may need to be drunk to ask, Amber, but I need you sober to understand."

All that courage I'd drummed up balled itself into my fist. "I think I'm entitled to know what happened, given that you dumped me over it."

"I didn't dump you, Amber, I—."

"Come on, Dylan." I pounded my fist into the sand; speckles flew into the air. "You told me you were going to Mexico for a week's vacation and never returned. What would you call that?"

Dylan's hands fell silent on the guitar. "I asked you to join me there, if you'll recall."

"Yeah, right." I shrugged him off and watched the sun mark the wistful end to yet another day. "As if I'd also tank my entire future to party in some Mexican backwater."

Dylan sighed. "I didn't stay there to party, Amber."

"Then why were you there?" My jaw clenched with a rage I hadn't felt in years. "Tell me, dammit."

"I tried telling you."

I should have been over it by now, but facing those blue eyes, I was a heartbroken teenager again. "What, in that stupid letter you sent back with Kyle?" Kyle was Dylan's best friend, and the two of them had traveled to Mexico together for winter break. A week later, Kyle returned alone, bearing nothing but an envelope. The letter went on and on about how he'd discovered something amazing in Mexico and how I should come down there to join him, but I recognized it for what it was: a sign that the greatest relationship of my life had somehow crashed and burned.

Dylan's expression tightened. "I called you when I got back into the country if you recall."

He had called. At first, I'd been prepared to let him grovel and then take him back. But Dylan hadn't groveled. He hadn't seemed the least bit sorry about his choice. Even that I could have forgiven, but there was more. Within five minutes of starting the conversation, I realized this was no longer the guy I'd loved a few months earlier. Dylan left for Mexico a fiery, ambitious college freshman. He came back empty. Rather than returning to school, he moved back in with his parents and took some manual labor gig.

Now, seven years later, our college friends and I were finishing grad school and starting our careers, and Dylan was still scraping by doing the same dead-end work. I knew this from Kyle, who, after three years attending law school out of state, was now back and engaged to my best friend, Libby. Dylan and I set them up, just a few weeks before the fated Mexico trip. Now in some desperate attempt to return the favor, they'd convinced each of us to join them for an afternoon at the beach, no doubt hoping we'd fall back in love. Didn't they understand that even if I could forgive Dylan for abandoning me, I had no interest in dating a loser? Dylan no longer crashed with his parents, but had only managed to upgrade to a tiny basement apartment Kyle called The Coffin.

I ought to have kept my mouth shut but couldn't hold back. "Look, Dylan, I know this is the wine speaking, but that doesn't make it any less true. You need to get your life together. I mean, look at you."

Dylan lifted his thick arms. "Something wrong with the way I look?"

That bastard. He knew I wasn't referring to his physical appearance. Even worse, he knew how attractive I'd always found him, how I'd melted over his sandy-blond hair and dimpled chin. The years had treated him well. His jaw had squared out and now sported a trim beard that hid the dimple but gave him a manly look he'd lacked. He'd been almost wiry in college, but seven years of manual labor had filled him out nicely, a fact I'd tried not to notice since there was *no way* I was getting sucked in again.

Fortunately, he wasn't the only one the years had been kind to. Whenever I look back on old pictures from middle school to college, I always saw the same thing, a girl hiding from herself. My shoulders were rounded forward, my dark hair pulled back, my face devoid of makeup, and I carried an extra ten to fifteen pounds of *security* fat. Ironically, Dylan was the first one to draw me out of hiding, to show me the beauty of my curves. Even getting dumped hadn't sent me scurrying back into my shell. Now, seven years later, I was no longer embarrassed by the woman I'd become. I stood straight, shed those unwanted pounds, let my hair grow out, and wore just enough makeup to shine. In other words, that girl who had been so infatuated by the first handsome boy to notice her was no longer starving for attention.

It wasn't only physically that I'd matured. I knew what I wanted in life and could no longer be swayed by an easy smile and a dimpled chin. Handsome though he might be, the new Dylan was no longer enough for the new Amber. I knew that, and it was time he accepted it too. "You and Kyle used to be on the same track. Yet, he drove here in a new BMW while you rode your bike."

"So…" Dylan's eyes narrowed.

He probably considered this shallow, but I was no longer just looking for companionship. I wanted someone I could build a life with. That didn't necessarily mean riches. It might be a different story if Dylan was poor because he devoted his life to pursuing his dream and building a non-profit or something. But I wasn't about to make those same sacrifices for a guy stagnating in his life. No, thank you. "You had such potential."

"He still does," Kyle called from up the beach. He and Libby walked over hand in hand. "Potential is Dylan's specialty."

My head fell into my palms. I never would've brought this up if I knew Kyle could hear. "Let's drop it, OK, Kyle?"

"Not a chance. The fact is, while I was slugging away in college and law school, Dylan here was building his potential." Kyle jabbed Dylan's side. "Weren't you, Dylan?"

"You could say that," Dylan replied with an easy grin.

"I do say that. If potential is what you're looking for, Amber, Dylan's your man."

"Amber's right, Kyle," Libby said. "You talk too much."

"That I do, my love." Kyle bent over and kissed her hand, then patted Dylan on the shoulder. "If the girls don't want to talk, then let's sing. Play us some Janis, Dylan."

"Bobby McGee?" he asked.

"Yeah, right. You know the one I want."

Much as I hated Dylan, I couldn't believe Kyle would be so insensitive. "Dylan, play us something else. How about Yellow Submarine?"

"We've got all night," Kyle said. "You can make the next request, Amber."

Libby came over to my side. "Kyle, don't be a jerk."

But Dylan ignored us both and struck up the chords for Janis Joplin's *Mercedes Benz*. I couldn't bear to sing along, but the two men belted out:

Oh Lord, won't you buy me a Mercedes Benz
My friends all drive Porsches, I must make amends
Worked hard all my lifetime, no help from my friends
Oh Lord, won't you buy me a Mercedes Benz

Why must Kyle be so cruel? Despite all the pain Dylan had caused me, I was a mother bear at heart, and the wine brought out a ferocious need to protect. "Come on, Dylan. Let's take a walk."

From the speed that Dylan dropped the guitar and rose to his feet, I knew he'd been waiting for just such an opportunity. Poor, clueless Dylan. Couldn't he see I just wanted to look out for him? Of course he couldn't. He followed me down the beach like a puppy, and then, once we were out of earshot, came the inevitable. "I was wondering if you're free next weekend, Amber?"

A mixture of butterflies and squirming maggots filled my stomach. "Dylan, I think it's best we just stay friends."

"If you give me a chance, I think you'll like me."

"Like you?" I stopped walking. "You think that's my concern, that I won't like you?"

Dylan's arm reached out. My heart raced, and I felt the heat of his solid hand as it landed on my shoulder. "Give me a chance, Amber."

The setting sun's orange glow danced in Dylan's deep, blue eyes. There was a presence about this guy. I'd never felt so safe as I did in his company. I'd put my trust in him like I had with no other. And then he'd smashed me and my trust on the rocks. There was no way I was going there again. I threw off his hand. "It's not happening."

Dylan's head sank. "Can't we ever put the past behind us?"

"I could forgive the past, Dylan, if I believed in your future." I searched the sky for words. "This isn't college anymore. I'm looking for something more."

Dylan sat down on the edge of a jetty. "You mean a guy like Kyle?"

Part of me wanted to sit beside him, to enjoy the sunset on the water. Instead, I turned my back on the scenery. "You say that with such scorn but look where Kyle is today." I pointed toward the bonfire. "You can't blame a girl for wanting to be with a guy who's going somewhere."

"All you see is our past and present, Amber." Dylan's voice grew louder, and he dug his heels into the sand. "You have no idea what awaits either Kyle or me."

"Come *on*, Dylan. I don't need a crystal ball to see where each of you is headed."

"True." Dylan crossed his arms. "All you need to know is where to look."

"Oh? You think I'm looking in the wrong place, do you?" I planted my hands on my hips. "Kyle's an attorney at a top firm. He's making a great living, and if he makes partner, he'll make a fabulous living. He's got a gorgeous car, a gorgeous apartment."

"And…" Dylan punctuated each word, "a big fat, gorgeous rock on his gorgeous fiancé's finger?"

Was he making fun of Libby or me? "Yes, that too!"

"You realize Kyle works over 60 hours a week at a job he himself calls 'soul sucking?'"

"Grow up, Dylan! A career doesn't have to be all butterflies and rainbows." As a fifth-grade teacher, I spent half my time stopping my class from bickering. But out here, I wasn't Miss Romano, I was Amber, and Amber was a traditional Italian girl raised to *never* back down from a fight.

"You're saying *what*?" Dylan stood, and his voice boomed. "That you need to *sacrifice* for financial stability?"

"Duh. It's part of being a responsible adult."

"Responsible? The only things Kyle's sacrificing are his time and health." Dylan's hand thrust toward the bonfire. "He's not making himself a living; he's digging himself a grave."

Was he proud of being a loser? Did he really have the audacity to spit on a friend making something of himself? I should have kept quiet, but the heat in my chest was boiling over. "Big deal! So Kyle has to put in long hours and do grunt work for a while. Look at the lifestyle he's building."

"That's your definition of success?" Dylan's hands flew into the air. Maybe he had a little Italian in him after all. "An exorbitant lifestyle?"

Was he daring to call me shallow? Is that what this was about? Was he expecting me to fantasize about living in a dump for the rest of my life? "Is it so wrong wanting some nice things and a little financial stability?"

"So that's your goal? Nice things and stability?" Dylan's gaze bore through me like an X-ray, throwing me off balance.

I teetered from one foot to another, uneasy, unsure, but mad as hell, nonetheless. "I want to be able to afford a home. I want options."

"So which is your goal?" Dylan stepped up to me, challenging me to think straight, which his gaze always made it difficult to do. "Options? Or stability?"

"My goal?" What did he want from me? He was the one who was supposed to be all lazy and clueless. My gaze fell to my toes, which were easier to face than his eyes. "I can't say that I've ever sat down and formulated a goal. But... but that doesn't mean that I don't know what I want."

"That's exactly what it means. Without a goal, how can you possibly know if you're moving toward it or not?"

I studied Dylan's ratty shirt, the grease under his fingernails, his disheveled hair. I never saw him doing drugs, but I always suspected that he'd gotten sucked into the Mexican party scene and never got his life back together. I couldn't help but hate him for being such a bum. And here he was lecturing *me* about *my* goals. "Wake up!" Rage seethed in my belly like bubbling acid. "You asked me out, and you don't even have a car to pick me up in."

"Not all of our parents buy us cars and pay our way through college, you know." Dylan's nostrils flared like a raging bull. "Every dollar I spend, I need to earn myself, so you better believe I need something before I buy it."

Now he was calling me *spoiled*? The *nerve*. "I'll have you know that I make my *own* car payments and pay my *own* grad school tuition. And is it such a bad thing that my parents wanted to help me out until I got on my feet? Don't you want to provide for your own kids someday?"

"Trust me, I'll be able to provide my kids exactly what they *need*."

I caught the way he stressed the word *need*. Would he throw his kids out into the world with nothing but the shirts on their backs to learn from the school of hard knocks? Did he think poverty was some badge of honor? "Look, Dylan, if it brings you comfort to tell yourself you're doing great, then so be it. But don't expect me to come along for the ride."

I waited for Dylan's next blow, to hear him come roaring back about how well he was actually doing. We Romanos knew how to fight, and I stood braced to fend off his attack. But the retort died on his lips. He must have seen that it was a losing venture because he exhaled toward the heavens, shook his head, and walked away, back toward the fire, with his head bowed.

I took a long walk to cool off before returning to the bonfire. I scanned the scene but didn't see Dylan. His guitar was missing too.

"So you let him down easy, I see." Kyle poked at the coals with a piece of driftwood.

"I was a bitch and a half." I poured myself another glass of wine. "He left?"

"Oh yeah. We barely got a goodbye."

"I didn't want to hurt him." Despite the pain he'd caused me all those years ago, Dylan had never been malicious, just clueless. "But maybe it's for the best. Maybe a bit of reality will wake this guy up."

"Wake him up to what?"

I collapsed next to the log pile. "That Dylan's 25 and doing nothing with his life."

"Oh?" Kyle broke apart a glowing coal. "Is that reality as you see it?"

Dylan was his best friend, but did Kyle have that much of a blind spot for him? "Come on, Kyle, you told me he's living in a basement apartment the size of a coffin."

"You're behind the times. I said that about his old apartment. Now he's living in a slightly bigger basement I call The Crypt."

"Glad to hear he's moving up in the world." I rubbed my hands together in the heat of the flames. "But he's still awfully far from being able to afford even a normal lifestyle."

"I assure you, he can afford it now." Kyle threw on another log. "He just doesn't put the same value on normal that you do."

"Come on. Why would a guy live in a basement if he could afford better?"

"Why not ask *him* that?"

I thought surely Kyle, who'd worked so hard to build a career, would see things my way. Was there something I'd missed? "After our last conversation, I doubt he'll be eager to speak to me again."

"Fine, then I'll tell you what he told me. He lives in the basement because the mortgage rates are better if he lives in the building."

Mortgage? "Wait. You're saying he owns the entire building?"

"That's right." Kyle leaned back onto his elbows, enjoying my flustered state.

I searched Libby for answers, but she seemed as clueless as I was. "Then why live in the basement if he could live anywhere?"

"The basement has the lowest rental value. By taking the least expensive apartment for himself, he builds his financial foundation that much faster."

Something didn't add up. "You said Dylan just moved. Is that's what he's been doing all this time? Living dirt cheap in The Coffin to save up and buy himself a building?"

Kyle's grin was pure mischief. "Oh no, he owns that building too."

CHAPTER 2

HANDS OFF

The following Saturday at 6 am, I pulled up in front of Dylan's place, an old Victorian house with four mailboxes. Why was I here? Simple. I was too stupid to learn from my mistakes. After Kyle's guilt trip the previous weekend, I figured I owed Dylan an apology. A text message would have done it. A voice message would have been overkill. But in my stupid, inebriated state, I called him. I blubbered on for a good five minutes about how I'd been unfair and judgmental and over the top and a good twenty other things. Dylan kept quiet the entire time, never berating me, never interrupting to defend himself. When I finished my endless soliloquy, I had to check if he was still on the phone. He was. And when he finally spoke, I wasn't prepared.

"Does this mean we can see each other again?" he asked.

"Uh…"

"How about we go hiking next Saturday?"

Hiking? When was the last time I did that? After all my blubbering, my defenses were down. "Um. Ok."

Still, waking pre-dawn was not my idea of a first date. OK, technically, it wasn't our first. But it felt that way. We'd been together in college for less than two months when he disappeared to Mexico, and we didn't really "date" much in college anyway. We more "hung out" the way college students do. But I hoped he understood that we were no longer 18. At 25, I was done "hanging out." Yet here I was. 6 am. Picking up my date because he didn't have a car of his own.

I didn't want to honk and wake the neighbors, so I pulled out my phone to write him a text. Before I hit send, Dylan came running out, carrying a backpack. How the hell had I gotten myself into this? "You know," I said as he climbed into the car, "if one of my friends is on a date pre-sunrise, it means they hit it off with the guy the night before, not that the date is just beginning."

Dylan shut the door. "Your friends aim too low."

"At least we don't have to worry about traffic at this hour. Unless a herd of cows tries crossing the highway." I pulled onto the road. "It's your job to keep me awake the whole drive, so you might want to brainstorm scintillating topics of conversation."

"I could tell you about Mexico."

At the very thought of Mexico, a wave of anger pulsed through my veins. I'd never felt so abandoned in my life as when Dylan ditched me for whatever he found south of the border. At the beach last week, I'd wanted to hear about it, not only because I was drunk, not only to satisfy my morbid curiosity, but also to bring closure on a painful chapter of my life. Now I was no longer drunk and no longer positive I wanted closure. I didn't want to start our first date in seven years by bringing up anger, resentment, pain, and frustration. I shook my head to clear the haze of emotions already forming. "No, not Mexico. Not yet. Not today. You'll have to find some other way of keeping me awake."

Dylan opened his backpack. "I brought us a thermos of Neapolitan roast."

That was more my style. "Let me guess, you roasted and brewed it yourself?"

"Just brewed it," he said, slapping the thermos. "I splurged and bought the beans from Peet's."

"Impressive. What's that, an investment of sixty-five cents an ounce?"

"Not quite. I buy in bulk."

"Of course you do. Fill me up, Romeo."

A little after 7 am, we pulled into a parking lot dotted with a half dozen cars. "See, it's not so early," Dylan said. "We're not even the first ones here."

"The existence of other crazies doesn't make us any saner."

"Doesn't it? I swear we're constantly surrounded by insane behavior, and the only thing that stops us from recognizing it is that everyone's doing it." Dylan lugged his backpack over his shoulders.

"It's too early for a philosophy lecture. Come on, let's hit the trail."

My crabby, early morning attitude dissipated once we got moving. "I haven't hiked in ages. It's beautiful out here."

"Sure is. I keep dreaming of this place but haven't made it out here in years."

"Why not? No car?"

He lifted a sagging branch high above my head so I could easily walk under it. "No, I get rides or rent a car when I need to. Hiking just isn't something I love doing alone."

"Why alone? You're a friendly guy."

"Hiking isn't a priority for Kyle or my other guy friends. They'd rather watch a game. When they do take trips, I rarely want to shell out enough to join them."

"No girlfriends?" I slapped his shoulder, trying to lighten the question, but I cringed at the image of another girl in his arms.

"Nothing serious."

"Why not?"

"Well, for one, the only girl I wanted to be with flatly refused to see me."

I blushed. *The only girl?* Did that mean in the past seven years there hadn't been anyone else? I'd erred on the other side. With Libby's encouragement, I got right back out there and started dating guy after guy, hoping to find someone to fill the void Dylan left. None of them made a mark on my heart the way Dylan had, but at least the dates distracted me. I'd assumed he'd done the same. Had I been too hard on him by never giving him a chance to explain? "You need to learn to chase a little, Dylan. I was angry at you for leaving me, but I still had hopes that we'd get back together when you returned to college."

"But then I never returned to school."

No, he never did. The trail split. A sign hung over the branch to the right that read:

Widowmaker Gulch
Caution: For serious hikers and climbers only.
Casual hikers are advised to take the Daisy Trail.
Both trails lead to the top.

Dylan turned left onto the Daisy Trail.

I stopped at the trailhead and dug my hands into my hips. "Where the hell do you think you're going?"

"To the top." Dylan pointed ahead. "It's a beautiful hike."

"On the Daisy Trail? I don't think so." I wagged a finger at him. "Unless you don't think you can't hack Widowmaker?"

"Look, I just thought…"

"Yeah, I know what you thought. You thought your dainty little date couldn't handle the big boys' trail. I didn't wake up at 4:30 this morning for some walk through the daisies."

"4:30? You picked me up at 6:00."

Why are men so clueless? Did Dylan think I was going to pop out of bed and hop into the car? Show up on our date with bedhead and pillow lines on my face? Even if I wasn't yet sold on this second go-around with Dylan, I still wanted that boy to swoon. "I'm going this way. If you're man enough to handle Widowmaker, you're welcome to join me."

I turned my back on Dylan and headed up the trail with a sly grin on my lips. I just hoped I hadn't bit off more than I could chew.

Dylan came running up behind me. "I wish I'd known you'd want to hike Widowmaker."

"Why, to give yourself a little more time to Man-Up?"

"No, I would have brought my climbing gear."

Climbing gear? That didn't sound good. How much trouble had I gotten myself into? I suppose we could always turn around if it got too hairy, but until then, I'd be damned if I was going to show any fear. "There were no other girls all this time?" I braced myself for the answer.

"A few, but my lifestyle choices were so different that dating was never easy."

"You weren't willing to compromise for a relationship?" I'd certainly compromised plenty for my own. In the past seven years, I'd never fallen for a guy like I had for Dylan, but I still had a boyfriend more often than I didn't. How often had I spent time with a guy who I wasn't crazy about rather than be alone?

"I compromised some, but I never felt great about it. We'd go out to dinner and a club. I could easily blow enough in a night to feed myself for a week."

"You never eat out?" That was so not going to fly with me.

"Now and again I'll go out for business purposes, but it's been four years since I ate at a restaurant for fun."

"Four years?" When was the last time I'd gone even four *days* without eating out?

"I tried limiting it at first, but then every time a friend wanted to go out, it brought up a fresh debate. I wasn't saving that much, and I constantly felt like I was missing out."

"Sounds like in high school when I tried to lose weight by *cutting back* on dessert. Each day I'd convince myself it was OK to have just a little, then a little more. My weight stayed the same, and my stress levels went through the roof.

You're saying it's easier to draw a line in the sand. So you went Cold Turkey on restaurants?"

"Restaurants and quite a few other things." The dirt trail ended, replaced by a field of boulders. Dylan leapt onto the first boulder and extended a hand to help me up. I ignored the hand and jumped onto a second boulder, not quite as nimbly as he had, but at least I'd managed it on my own.

If Dylan was trying to sell me on why we should get back together, he was doing a horrible job. No restaurants. Presumably, no movies, concerts, or other entertainment. What did he hope we would do? Sit around The Crypt and watch videos together? Not my idea of a relationship. "But why? Why all this deprivation?"

"To build myself a strong financial foundation."

My face flushed with the memory of the lecture I'd given Dylan at the beach. I'd accused him of lacking the maturity to make sacrifices for his future. I was right about him lacking maturity, but I had the direction wrong. He wasn't one of those guys who couldn't *save* money; he came from the more depressing breed who couldn't *spend* it. Periodically, I'd read an article about some poor old fart who died and his family discovered he had millions stuffed away in his mattress. Having all that money and never enjoying a dime of it was so much worse than never having it at all.

Dylan pulled out a bag of trail mix he'd made, and I took a handful. As I ate, I thought about my own expenses. So much of the money I spent was social. When looking for apartments, I insisted on one with a nice big kitchen, where I could work my magic, and with a large enough living room to host a pack of friends. It also had to be in the right part of town, close to my favorite restaurants and clubs. I went out to eat plenty, but seldom alone. It hit me how incredibly lonely Dylan's journey must have been. "You think all this has been worth it?"

"Has what been worth it?"

"All the deprivation you've subjected yourself to."

"I've made tremendous strides these past few years." He grabbed a handful of trail mix and shoved the bag into the side pocket of his backpack. "They'll pay off in the future."

Would they? Would he ever allow himself to enjoy all that money he was hoarding away? Somehow, I doubted it. "I bet it's been tough in the meantime."

"It hasn't been too bad." Dylan studied the seeds in his hand as though they were tea leaves. "Until now."

"What's changed?"

"Seeing you at the beach. Like God says about Adam, 'It's not good for man to be alone.' I'd shut down a part of myself that can't remain dormant forever."

I couldn't help but grin. "It was beguiled by my feminine charms?"

"It came roaring back to life." I felt his eyes on me but dared not look up to meet them. "It reminded me we had unfinished business."

I chewed on the sweet yet tart mix of chocolate chips and raisins. Dylan's business might have been unfinished, but I was more certain than ever that I'd made the right choice in keeping my distance. Why couldn't he have just gotten himself a good degree, landed a solid job, and enjoyed the fruits of his labor like the rest of us? Sweet and handsome as he was, I wanted more for my future than living in some basement and writing off all social life as "too expensive."

If we'd been out at some café, I'd probably make my excuses now and slip away. As it was, we were on a beautiful hike, and Dylan was pleasant enough company. I decided to finish the hike with him as a friend, then let him down as gently as I could.

The boulders ended at a rock outcropping. This was some of our easiest hiking yet, and we followed the bare rock until we came to a cliff that hovered over us like an enormous beast waiting to pounce. Off to one side of the trail, the mountain sank into what must have been Widowmaker Gulch. The other side of the trail was full of thorn bushes. That left two options. We could wimp out and turn around, which would add hours to our hike, or we could scale the cliff.

I'd climbed cliffs like this in the past. A decade ago. At summer camp. Wearing a helmet and strapped into a harness, with a counselor feeding me the belay rope. I supposed that was the equipment Dylan referred to.

I turned to Dylan. "You want to go first?"

"No, I think you should go first."

"What's wrong? You chicken?" And yes, I did the whole chicken-wing thing with my arms and made the chicken noise.

Dylan didn't bite. "No, I want to be able to catch you in case you fall."

Oh. Good idea. I swallowed hard, shrugged my shoulders, and started up the cliff. It wasn't vertical, but it was pretty darned close. There were several small ledges in the cliff face, and these—plus other cracks and crevices—gave me the hand and footholds I needed. That was, if I could get high enough to use them. I slipped my hands onto a solid hold, but I didn't have the leverage to hoist myself up.

"You want a boost?" Dylan asked.

I looked over my shoulder to see Dylan poised beneath me, his hands six inches beneath my butt, ready to push.

"You keep your gorilla hands away from my ass," I said in my sassiest voice. "There will be no free feels today."

Dylan pulled back. "I was just trying to help."

Poor guy. He was too clueless to tell when he was being teased. "I know you were. I'll tell you what. Bend over and make a basket with your hands." He did, and I put my foot into it. "Now lift."

Dylan hoisted me to the point where I could get myself nice and secure on the cliff face. "I really have to do 40 feet of this?" I called down.

"The top half is easier than the bottom, once you get past…"

Eager to be up at the top, I didn't wait for Dylan to finish his sentence. I reached up and got my fingertips over some handholds. The rock felt strong, but I didn't yet have a firm grip. If I could get a decent spot to plant my foot a few feet up, I'd be alright. There was a small crack in the rock, I dug my left foot into it, and felt some support. It wasn't as much as I liked, but if I could get a decent push off, I'd…

"Wait, Amber, slow down."

I pushed off hard with my right foot, hoping my left would support me while I found a strong foothold. My left held OK, but the angle I was climbing at put too much pressure on my fingertips. I tried to adjust them, to get a better grip, but it was too late.

The fingers of my left hand gave way, and my body swung like a pendulum. I twisted around and lost my footing. My right hand clutched the rock, but not securely enough to handle all my weight. I lost my grip and fell. I hit the ledge beneath me. If I could hold on there, I'd be OK. But I didn't have the body control I needed. I got a foot on the ledge slowing my fall, but couldn't hold it. I banged an elbow, then a knee against the hard rock before losing all contact with the cliff.

Dylan grabbed me. Awkwardly. Painfully. My head hit his shoulder. One of his hands grabbed a leg, the other an arm. But he stopped my fall. He protected me from smashing myself against the rocky ground.

"Are you OK?" he asked.

I tried to tell him, 'yes, I'm fine.' I tried to thank him for catching me. But it's not what came out. Instead, a ball of fire rose from my insides, and I screamed, "Dammit, why weren't you there for me?"

Dylan's eyebrows twisted in confusion. "Amber, I'm right here."

I hit him. My pathetic blows must have felt like raindrops against his muscular back. "How could you do this to me?"

"Amber," Dylan whispered into my ear, "I caught you." He lowered me gently to my feet.

Tears flooded my eyes. Dylan stood as a blur before me. "Not now," I cried, "then." I thought I'd made peace with him leaving years ago, but in my terrified, hysterical state, a load of baggage came pouring out. "How could you desert me like that?"

Dylan backed up. "Amber, I..."

All the pain in my knee was channeled into Dylan. "You tell me you love me," I jabbed his chest with my pointer finger as I blubbered like a toddler, "then you go off on this two-week trip, and all I get back is some stupid letter! Seven years, Dylan. You left me alone for seven years."

"Woah!" Dylan's hands shot up in protest. "I came back after three months."

"What a load of crap! You came back from Mexico. But you didn't return to your life. You didn't come back to me."

"I called you as soon as I got home."

I ignored his feeble retort. "You know who I went to the Winter Formal with that year?"

"Who?"

"Brian O'Dell. The six-handed groping machine. He didn't give a damn about me. He just wanted a hot date who would put out. When I didn't, he ditched me and went home with some floozy. I had to hitch a ride home with Kyle and Libby, who obviously wanted to be alone but took me anyway. Do you have any idea how humiliating that was?"

"What does that have to do with me?"

"You should have been there." I smacked his chest with one hand after the next. "You should have been my date. You should have protected me from all those slimy guys."

"Amber, I..."

"You had so much going for you. You went to a good school. You got good grades. You had this bright future. And you had *me*. I loved you so much. I used to dream about our wedding, about having kids together."

Dylan's eyes grew wide. "You did?"

"All I ever wanted was to be with a good guy. And there you were. You were so sweet. So present. You weren't like those other guys who just wanted to score and could care less about the emotional wrecks they left in their wakes."

"Amber..."

"And what do I get? A letter!"

"That wasn't supposed to be—."

"You hurt me so much more than the Brian O'Dell's of the world ever could. Because I let you in. I trusted you with all my heart. And you tore out my heart and stomped all over it." I stomped up and down, now completely out of control.

Dylan rested his hand on my shoulder. "I'm sorry I hurt you. I never wanted to lose you. And I tried to get you back, but you wouldn't take me."

I turned up to face him. "I wanted you back. I wanted you back in the worst way. But the Dylan that left, the one building this amazing life, never returned. You could have had a great degree, a successful career, and an incredibly loving wife. Yet you gave it all up for what? To move back in with your parents and get some dead-end job."

"Amber, that's not…"

I swatted his hand off my shoulder. "Why did you do it? Why didn't you come back to me?"

"You know, when you were on the cliff, I tried to tell you to slow down." Dylan crossed his arms, and his tone grew stern. "I saw that you didn't have strong enough footing to get yourself up."

"What does that have to do with anything?"

"You didn't want to listen. You were moving so fast. You thought you were so close to a place where you could get a secure footing. You failed to see that each move you thought would bring you closer to safety actually put you in more danger."

"And…"

"I was just like you. Only when someone pointed out my risk, I stopped and listened to the warning. It took me three months to fully grasp how much danger I'd put myself in and to understand there was a much safer route up the cliff."

"The path of staying at the bottom and not reaching for anything in life?"

Dylan shook his head, and tears welled up in his eyes. "For the first time in my life, I understood the impact of the choices I was making. Or so I thought. Because I thought I could have it all. I thought I could show you where I'd been off and how I'd finally gotten myself on a course I could believe in. I thought you'd come to understand it as I did. I thought you'd accept my choices. Even be proud of them. I thought you'd continue to love me."

Now it was my turn to backpedal. "Dylan…"

"Had I known how much I'd have to give up, had I known that taking the smarter path would cost me the only woman I'd ever loved, then maybe I wouldn't have done it. Maybe I would have continued to blindly climb the cliff. And maybe, just maybe, I would have gotten lucky and made it to the top despite my stupidity. But I couldn't so easily ignore the warning. I couldn't unlearn the better way. So I carried on alone."

"I'll take responsibility for leaving you for three months." Dylan's eyes blazed, and he pointed hard at my chest. "But you need to own the last seven years. Those were your choice." Dylan walked away. I thought for a moment he was ditching me here, but he only went a hundred feet or so and sat down on a boulder, staring off into the distance.

I cried my eyes out until I had no tears left. Once my eyes were dry, I inspected the damage. I had a couple of cuts from where I'd hit the cliff, and my neck was sore from hitting Dylan's shoulder, but all in all, it could have been far worse.

I walked over to where Dylan sat. He still stared off into the distance, but when he felt my presence, he turned. I didn't want to delve back into the emotional maelstrom, so I just focused on the immediate problem. "If you're ready, I'd like to keep moving. Where do we go from here?"

"We have two choices. We can take another shot at the cliff or backtrack to the car."

"We can't hike back to the Daisy Trail and get to the top that way?"

Dylan shook his head.

"You sure? Daisies are my favorite flower, you know."

"There won't be time. We've come too far for that. The Daisy Trail is longer than this one. By the time we get to the trailhead, we won't have time to summit on that trail and still get back by sundown, when the park closes."

"But if we summit now, we can go back on the Daisy Trail?"

"We could, but it's not my first choice."

"You want to go back down the cliff?"

"No, the trail is a loop." Dylan pointed up the cliff. "From the top, we'd climb down the far side of the mountain and along the river bank to the parking lot. There's a nice little spot over there I'd wanted to share with you."

"And we can't get there if we head back?"

"Not this trip."

I didn't have the heart to tell him this would be the only trip we'd take together. As long as I put in the effort coming out here, I wanted to reach the top. "Forward it is then."

"I don't want you getting hurt again."

"Then it sounds like we'll both need to slow down and think through how to do the climb together. I'm willing to give it a shot if you are."

Dylan looked me up and down, not in that creepy way that guys sometimes did, but as if assessing just how badly hurt I was.

"I'm OK, Dylan. Some of these cuts may continue to sting, but I'm a big girl. I can handle a challenge."

"Then let's try." Dylan got to his feet and handed me his backpack. "Put this on."

The pack weighed twenty pounds, at least. "Yeah, right. If I can barely climb this damned cliff with nothing on my back, you think I'm going to be able to do it wearing your backpack?

Dylan didn't pull it back. "Put it on," he repeated.

This time I listened. I put on the backpack. It was huge on me. The long straps made the pack hang a good eight inches from my back. Dylan reached over to tighten the straps, but they hung next to my chest, and I shrank back. Sweet Dylan, he was never one to invade a girl's space without permission. He withdrew his hand and said, "Tighten the straps. Pull there and there."

I pulled where he showed me, and soon, the bag was tight to my back. We headed back to the cliff face. "But I still don't think I can climb the cliff with this on my back."

"You won't need to." Dylan squatted. "Climb on."

"You're not serious?"

Dylan looked at me over his shoulder. "You don't want to turn back, and I don't want to see you fall again. What choice do we have?"

"You can't really make it up there with me on your back, can you?"

"We'll find out."

"No, we won't. I'm not riding on your back, hoping you make it to the top. If you slip, we'll both fall. Not only won't you be there to catch me this time, you'll come crashing down on top of me." I slipped the backpack off. "No, thank you."

"Then what do you want to do?"

"Let's be smart about this. You're the more experienced climber. You tell me what to do, I'll listen, and we'll get to the top together. OK?"

"OK." Dylan strapped on the pack.

"What's the first step?"

"Getting you back up to that first ledge." Dylan bent over and made a basket with his hands as he had before, but this time, I didn't put my foot into it.

"Dylan, you know what I said before about not boosting me up by putting your hand on my ass?"

"Yeah."

"I was teasing. You know that, right?"

Dylan's face remained blank. He didn't quite shrug, but I could tell he was anything but sure.

"I know you've always been cautious about respecting a girl's boundaries. That's one of the things I appreciated about you. I never had to worry about you pushing me too far."

"Amber, I promise I won't—."

"No, no, I want you to listen. I don't want you to do that here. I trust you; I really do."

"Even after everything that's happened?"

"I'm not talking about trusting you with my heart." I was never making *that* mistake again. "For now, just know that I trust you physically. The last thing I want is to fall because you were afraid to put your hands on me to support me. So if you have to touch me in any way to help either one of us get safely up the cliff, do it, and don't think twice. You understand?"

Dylan nodded. "We don't have to do this. We can go back."

"No. We're going to do this. Together." I faced the cliff. "Now, push me up."

This time, as Dylan helped me up, I held my tongue while he pushed his strong hand against the seat of my shorts. He thrust me upwards until I could get myself into a secure position on the first ledge. "Now hold still right there," he said.

He climbed up after me. "Can you move your left foot six inches to the right and lean into the rock?" I slid my foot over, and he put his into the vacated spot. I leaned in to make room, and he came up behind me, enveloping me, like a soft hug. "OK, you're going to let go of the handholds. Don't worry. I've got you."

I let go, held securely in place by Dylan.

"Now, reach up and grab the handhold right over there." Dylan indicated the same place where I'd slipped the last time.

"I don't have enough leverage there."

I felt his hot breath against my neck. "You will; you just need better support for your feet."

"But there are no good toe holds."

"You won't need it. Put your foot here." Dylan bent at the knees, turning his thighs into shelves.

I licked my lips. "I don't want to push you backwards."

"Don't worry. I've got a strong grip."

I reached up and grabbed on as tightly as I could. There was no way I could slip again with his body serving as a fence. I put my right foot on his thigh and pushed upward. That got me high enough to propel my left foot into a secure notch.

I climbed further, into a crevice in the cliff. I hadn't been able to see this from the ground, but if I followed the crevice, I could move forward without fear of falling all the way down. "It gets easier over here," I called out to Dylan. "I can make it forward on my own."

"You sure?"

"Yeah, I'm good." I climbed a few feet, then stopped. I secured myself in a strong position, turned back, and reached down. "You need a hand up?"

Dylan was already climbing, but he took my extended hand, and I pulled him up next to me. "We're through the hard part," he said. "Once we get through that crevice, it's just a short hike up to the peak."

We ate a picnic lunch on the peak, which had 360-degree views over the valley. Dylan's cooking skills weren't in my league, but were surprisingly good for a bachelor. He'd baked sourdough bread that morning and made sandwiches using heirloom tomatoes he'd grown in his garden. Somehow, I'd pictured him spending his days in some dark basement, eating ramen noodles to survive. How many other aspects of his lifestyle had I misjudged?

After lunch, we started our descent on the far side of the mountain, which opened into a lush river valley. "Something hit me during our little *discussion* at the bottom of the cliff," I said.

"Really? Two things kept hitting me." He was referring to my fists, of course, but I wasn't taking the bait.

"What hit *me* was it sounded like you gave your choices intelligent consideration."

Dylan's eyes rolled in that you've-got-to-be-kidding way. "That's a surprise to you?"

"Actually, yes. When you didn't come back, I figured you couldn't hack it anymore. I thought you'd lost all ambition, that you'd given up."

"Why would you think that?"

"Come on, Dylan." I grabbed hold of a tree branch to ease my descent. "You drop out of school, move back in with your parents, and get some manual labor job. If that doesn't sound like an express train to Loserville, I don't know what does."

Dylan shook his head. "You are all so blind. Your stories are so deeply embedded that even when the facts are staring you in the face, you can't see them."

"What's that supposed to mean?"

"What I was actually doing was cashing in my first-class ticket to Debtville and getting onto the slow, steady road to Assetville."

"But why hoard money if you're never going to use it."

Dylan's hands flew in the air. "What makes you think I'm never going to use it?"

"Well, you're not spending any of it now, so why would you—."

"That's not forever. It's just until I hit my goal."

His goal? At the beach, he'd asked me what my goal was, as if it was perfectly obvious everyone had one, but of course, I'd had no answer. "What is your goal?"

"Financial independence."

I laughed in spite of myself. "Really? You hope to go from living in poverty to mega-riches."

"Mega-riches?"

"Isn't that what it means to be financially independent? That you have so much cash, you never have to worry about money again?"

Dylan snorted. "No amount of money can ever make you financially independent."

"That doesn't make any sense. Surely if you make enough money…"

"Oh? Mike Tyson made 400 million dollars boxing. He went bankrupt. Michael Jackson made billions, yet his estate was 500 million in the hole when he died."

"Well sure, but I heard Tyson owned two white Bengal tigers, and didn't Jackson try to buy the bones of the Elephant Man?" I'd read about both in an article on dumb celebrity purchases while waiting for my last dental cleaning.

"Exactly, that proves my point. The fact is, people tend to spend every dollar they get, regardless of how much they make. Hell, Kim Basinger went bankrupt after thinking it was a good idea to buy an entire town in Georgia." We headed down rocky terrain, and with my bruised legs, I wobbled over the uneven footing. Dylan found a branch at the edge of the trail, cleared it of twigs, and handed it to me. "Here, use this."

"Thanks." I planted the branch on the ground and immediately felt more stable. "But Dylan, in all seriousness, I'm no Kim Basinger."

"Granted, you're cuter than she is."

I couldn't help but blush. "Last I checked, I wasn't looking to buy a town…"

"It's all relative. How you deal with money doesn't change with how much you make. Haven't you ever felt like money was burning a hole in your pocket? When you had more than you needed, you were pulled to buy something idiotic?"

A string of bad purchases ran through my head: the fountain pen I thought would finally get me to write in my journal; the seat warmer for my car that made me sweat; the espresso machine collecting dust on my kitchen counter. "You're saying it's bad to have more money than you need?"

"Not at all. It's great to have money. But you have to understand what money is and how it works." Dylan pulled out his water bottle, took a gulp, and handed it to me.

"Which is?"

"Picture an athlete—let's say a marathoner—a guy who runs twenty miles a day for fun. One day he wakes up to a hurricane outside. He has no choice but to stay inside. His girlfriend suggests that instead of working out, they sit on the couch and watch a movie. What's he feeling?"

"He's probably bouncing off the walls. He's got all this energy he wants to get out, and he's stuck sitting there, not using it."

"Money is also energy." The veins in Dylan's arms pulsed as he stretched them above his head. "It has the power to build skyscrapers or jumbo jets. It can fund schools or feed the hungry. If you have too much money in the bank, you're going to bounce off the walls just like the athlete who can't exercise."

Too much money in the bank was not a problem that plagued anyone I knew. Most of my friends were squeaking by, even those with high-paying jobs like Kyle. Between school loans, car payments, rent, and socializing, that didn't leave much to burn a hole in our pockets. But Dylan would say the opposite, wouldn't he? He'd say those expenditures were a result of having more money than we needed. "What's the solution?"

"You've got to put that money to work. It wants to be productive." His hand soared through the air as if taking flight. "Let it."

"How?"

"Investments."

I stuffed the water bottle into the side pocket of his pack and continued down the trail. "Like in the stock market?"

"That's one option. People invest in stocks hoping they'll grow. But to me, growth should be the secondary objective, not the primary."

"What's the primary objective?"

"Income."

I ought to be beyond my anger by now, but at the mention of income, my temperature rose. "If income is your objective, then why drop out of school? Don't tell me you think you'll make more in construction than Kyle will in law."

"Calm down, Amber. I'm not talking about active income. I'm talking about passive."

"Passive income?"

"Income you don't have to work for."

I stopped in the middle of the trail. "If you stop working, you stop making money. Isn't that the definition of income?"

"That's the definition of active income. If I stop working tomorrow, my active income will dry up, but my passive income will continue coming in."

My eyebrows furrowed in confusion.

"Think of a stock dividend," Dylan said, starting to walk again. "The dividend money just shows up in the account of everyone who owns the stock. No need to work for it. Like these flowers." He stepped to the edge of the trail, where a gray-green bush with purple flowers grew. "No one's planting them, fertilizing them, or trimming them. They just grow." He tore off a sprig, returned to where I was standing, and bowed. "Lavender for the lady."

I closed my eyes to take it in the earthy scent. When I opened them again, Dylan was smelling the flowers as well. His eyes were so close to mine, so focused on mine. Then I remembered I had to keep my head straight. I literally shook it and started hiking again to regain my focus. *What had we been talking about? Right, dividends.*

I swallowed hard and asked, "So is that where your passive income comes from? Stock dividends?"

"Mine comes from rent on my apartments. But there are a hundred ways to make passive income."

"You said your goal is financial independence. You rejected my definition, so what's yours?"

"It's simple. You're financially independent when your passive income exceeds your cost of living."

I climbed up and over a boulder as I chewed over his words. "Let me see if I've got this. If my monthly budget now is $3000 a month, then I'd need to make at least that much from dividends or real estate or some other passive source to be financially independent?"

"Not necessarily. You'll need to generate some passive income. But if you can reduce your cost of living at the same time, you can become financially independent that much faster."

"I guess if your passive income was more than you needed to live, you wouldn't need an active income at all, right?"

"Exactly." Dylan snapped his fingers. "That's not to say that I wouldn't continue to work. If I sat on my butt doing nothing all day, I'd bounce off the walls like the athlete in the hurricane. But once I no longer need to make money to live, I'll be able to do whatever I want with my time. I could focus on my passions rather than on someone else's agenda. I could live wherever I want, travel, volunteer. The thing I'm most excited about is the ability to take bigger risks because I'll have a safety net."

This wasn't sounding like Loserville talk. "That's some goal."

"Frankly, I think it should be everyone's goal. At least initially."

"Initially? What comes next?"

"You can live in abundance. You can have more than you need." Dylan offered his hand to help me down a steep decline.

"Isn't that greedy?"

"It doesn't have to be. The most generous people in the world live in abundance."

"Like who?"

"Like Bill Gates. He's spending billions trying to eradicate polio and cure malaria."

"He's spending some of it closer to home as well. Some of his educational initiatives have even reached my small classroom. OK, I see what you're saying. Like those foundations with grant programs. Someone has to donate all that money, right?"

"Yes and no. Someone certainly donated the seed money. But the strongest foundations don't use that money for grants. If they gave away their seed money, no matter how much they started with, sooner or later, it would all be gone."

"Then what do they do with it?"

"They invest in assets that generate passive income for the foundation. Since they only give away the income generated by their investments, theoretically, these foundations can exist forever."

Something clicked in my head. "It's like a Cash Machine."

"A what?"

"A Cash Machine. You insert your money into the investment cogs which churn out cash on the other end."

His eyes narrowed. "You mean like some Dr. Seuss contraption?"

"Exactly. I'm an elementary school teacher. If I want to teach my kids about the environment, I don't lecture about air pollution. We read and discuss *The Lorax*. If I want to teach about discrimination, I read them *The Star Bellied Sneeches*."

"You want to lump together all these investment vehicles as some—."

"Cash Machine. Exactly. Much easier to understand."

"You ready for the real gem of this hike?" It was mid-afternoon, and Dylan stopped just as he rounded a bend of trees. "See where people have piled up rocks to make a small pool by the edge of the river? Know why they did that?"

I followed his gesture to the roughshod pool. The wall wasn't tight enough to keep in the water, but it at least blocked the river from flowing quickly through. "Why?"

"It's a natural hot spring. The water seeps out at 110 degrees."

"I wish you'd told me. I would have brought a bathing suit."

Dylan's eyebrows rose like Groucho Marx. "Out here in the mountains, hikers normally go in without."

Skinny-dipping on the first date? Was he kidding me? Even in college, we never got that far. More than once, I wondered if all that crap in his letter had been a cover-up, and if he hadn't met some party girl who put out more than his prude girlfriend back home. "There's something we need to talk about," I said. I knew this issue would come up, but I hadn't expected it quite this quickly.

"You're not horribly deformed or anything, are you?"

I whacked the back of his head. "I'll leave you horribly deformed if you don't shut up. This is serious. You know how I was hesitant to date you because I was afraid of getting my heart into a relationship that wasn't going anywhere?"

Dylan leaned down and cocked his head to meet my gaze. "You're not having second thoughts about giving me a chance, are you?"

Of course, that morning, I'd already decided that there was no way I was dating him again. But something shifted at the cliff. I still wasn't sure where he was going, but I didn't want to let this great guy slip away a second time until I had a better idea of the life he was building. "No, but all I'm doing is giving you a chance. I'm not ready to jump in with both feet." I forced myself to look away. "Until I know this relationship is going somewhere, I'm saying no to intimacy."

"You're saying we'll have to bypass the hot springs?"

"There's no way I'm driving all the way out here, hiking for eight hours, and skipping the hot springs. I'm going in dressed, and if you're OK doing the same, you're welcome to join me."

Dylan held his hands before his chest in a pleading gesture. "Can I at least take off my socks and shoes?"

"Fine." I crossed my arms. "I'll avert my eyes."

Fabulous as the hot springs were, going in dressed made the last leg of the hike less than comfortable.

"So I should never expect to go out to eat with you?" I was still struggling to accept what I'd gotten myself into.

Dylan shrugged. "I need to learn to compromise. I can't expect you to make the extreme decisions I did."

"Must have been hard missing out on all those times with friends."

"You know the hardest part? It's not like they were rich, and I was poor. It was the other way around; I was making money while they were in school.

Each week, I'd watch them spend money they didn't have, digging themselves further into debt, while I sat home alone. It would have been so much better if we'd all hung out together and watched a movie or played cards or enjoyed some other inexpensive activity."

"Like hiking?" I shot him a grin.

"Yes, like hiking." Dylan tightened the straps on his backpack.

"What you're saying resonates on the flip side. I was one of those people spending money I didn't have so I wouldn't be left behind. I couldn't stand the thought of being left out."

Dylan jumped onto an outcropping of bald rock. "It wasn't too bad. I can be obsessive, and I made the savings into a sort of game, seeing how little I could spend. But it would have been a lot more fun if I had friends doing the same thing."

I followed the lines of Dylan's sturdy shoulders. He was never one to back down from a challenge. Yet, when he wrote to me, telling me he'd discovered something amazing in Mexico, and encouraging me to join him, I hadn't given him the benefit of the doubt. Watching him now, it struck me how hard these past seven years must have been. I'd been so angry he hadn't returned; I'd barely spared a moment for what he must have been going through. Despite all of his friends writing him off, he carried on alone. I jumped onto the rock outcropping beside him. "It's hitting me how little I know about your life since you left college."

Dylan turned back to me. "What would you like to know?"

I wanted to know how much he suffered, but he would shrug off any more questions about struggle. Dylan didn't complain; he just went through whatever he had to, silent and alone. I thought to ask him about all he'd learned, but when I opened my mouth, what came out instead was, "Did you think of me in Mexico?"

"Oh yeah." Dylan gazed towards the horizon as if revisiting the small coastal town. "During the day, I was always busy, but at night, I slept alone on this old fishing boat, and my mind would wander. You were a favorite destination."

"So you'd dream of me while sitting on deck, playing guitar in the moonlight in this quaint Mexican port?"

"You make it sound more romantic than it was. Throw in the stench of fish guts and cheap Mexican beer, and you'll be closer to the truth."

A girlish grin took over my face. "The point is, you thought of me?"

"Yeah, and I kept thinking of writing to you. But when I didn't get a response to the letter I sent with Kyle, I figured you wanted nothing to do with me."

I bit my lip. "That's pretty spot on. Sorry, Dylan."

"It's OK. The truth is, some paths are easier to walk alone."

My expression fell. "I thought you wanted me to join you?"

Dylan shrugged his shoulders. "It was a pipe dream. College was too important to you. Had we continued dating, I would have felt like an outsider. Either that or I would have given up and returned to school. It was better the way things worked out."

"You make school sound like such a mistake. You think it was a bad idea for all of us?"

Dylan picked up an acorn and tossed it up and down. "Not everyone. Remember my old roommate Tim?"

"That's Dr. Tim now. He recently graduated med school."

"Tim knew he wanted to be a doctor from the time he was ten-years-old. While Kyle and I were rushing our fraternity, Tim was hunkered down studying biology."

"I remember."

"You know how long I spent in high school debating whether college was the right place for me?"

"How long?"

"As far as I can recall, the thought never passed my mind once." Dylan threw the acorn over his shoulder. "All of my friends went; my parents expected me to go. It was such a given, I never questioned it. Sure, I debated which school to go to, but whether to attend school at all? Never."

"You finally thought it over in Mexico?"

"Exactly. It was the first time I ever sat and thought about what I wanted out of life."

I studied his face. "And what answer did you come to?"

"I realized that I had absolutely no clue."

I giggled. "That was your big revelation?"

"It was a huge revelation. Here I was spending years of my life and getting myself hundreds of thousands of dollars into debt, and I didn't even know what I wanted from my education. Had I been a guy like Tim, with a clear reason for being in school, I would have stayed."

"But school's such an amazing place to experiment and figure out what you want to do." My hands danced through the air the way only an Italian's can. "Hell, I didn't know I wanted to teach until Junior year."

"That's another question I asked in Mexico: was college the best place to figure out my path?" Dylan bent over to tighten the laces on his hiking boots. "It certainly offered an environment to explore, but I decided the opportunity costs were just too high."

"Opportunity costs?"

"Whenever you do one thing, you give up on the opportunity to do something else."

"Like by coming out here with you in the wee hours, I missed the opportunity to get my beauty sleep."

That line gave Dylan the perfect setup to tell me how beautiful I looked anyway, but of course, he missed it. "Exactly."

"You just moved back home? I'm sure your parents *loved* that." Why was my voice dripping with sarcasm?

"They were relieved. There are opportunity costs with time and others with money. My folks had taken out a fair amount of college debt in their own names. And not just for me. They were in their mid-fifties and had more money tied up in student loans to send three kids to school than they'd saved in their retirement accounts. Meanwhile, my older brother couldn't find work in his field and wound up taking a retail job he could have gotten out of high school."

I thought about my parents and all of our school expenses but quickly brushed it off. As a successful attorney, my father didn't have the same financial struggles Dylan's parents did. "What about your sister?"

"She studied education like you."

"Did she ever teach?"

"Oh yeah. For five years, until her first kid came along, and she decided not to go back to work. Guess how much of a dent she made in those educational loans during those five years of working?"

I didn't have to guess. I barely got by on my own teacher's salary.

Dylan stepped off to the side of the trail and started clapping his hands.

"What are you doing?"

"Snakes hang out near raspberry bushes." He pointed out dark red berries I had missed.

"Snakes eat raspberries?"

"Snakes eat creatures that eat raspberries. I want to make sure I'm not one of them." Dylan slipped his hand into the dark green leafy mess and picked a bunch of the plump berries. He reached out and passed me a handful, then went deeper into the bush for more.

I popped a raspberry into my mouth and moaned the way only a food-obsessed Italian can. Dylan moved slowly through the thorny bush, getting pricked every so often, but remaining stoic. He didn't mind a bit of suffering to get what he wanted. I, on the other hand, would have settled for only the berries in easy reach rather than risk getting cut by the thorns.

When Dylan emerged, we sat down to enjoy his harvest. "What happened after Mexico?" I asked.

"I got myself a construction job with a remodeling company so I could learn to fix and maintain houses."

"You didn't find it hard to find work without a degree?"

Dylan flicked a fly away from his face. "Not at all. For all the talk of underemployment these days, the construction industry struggles to find enough skilled workers."

"What kind of skills?"

Dylan fingered off each word. "Welding, plumbing, electricity, carpentry."

"You got yourself a certification in one of those?"

"Just some basic training in each, not a full certification in any."

I popped a berry into my mouth. "You wouldn't have made more as a specialist?"

"I would have. And if I wanted a long-term construction career, that's probably what I would have done."

"What did you want?"

"Lacking any clear life vision, I figured the best thing I could do was work on building a solid financial foundation, so by the time I figured out what I wanted, money wouldn't be a barrier."

I guess that sounded smart, but wouldn't a higher-paying job be a better bet? Blue-collar work seemed beneath a smart guy like Dylan. "What does learning welding have to do with that?"

"The more I learned about money, the more I realized real estate would play a role in building my wealth. Short term, I thought it would be smarter to manage my apartments myself rather than pass them on to some property manager. I took night classes to flush out my skills and soon got a job refurbishing houses."

"You just did whatever tasks they gave you?" A raspberry burst in my hand, turning it reddish-purple.

Dylan dug into his pack and fished out a napkin. "At first, I did all the lowest level jobs, then my responsibilities grew with my experience. After a year, I was elevated to foreman even though I was still the newest guy on the crew."

"Impressive."

"Not really." We'd gorged on berries until our teeth looked like they belonged to vampires. Dylan helped me up, and we continued on the trail. "The owner needed a foreman who could communicate with him, the workers, and the homeowners. Virtually everyone else on the crew was Mexican, and most of them barely spoke English."

"But thanks to your time in Mexico, you could communicate with them?"

"That and my first year working with them on the crews. I'd get stuck for words now and then, but between Google Translate and the experience the guys had on the job, we got through OK. Luther always told me that each additional skill I acquire adds exponential value, and that was certainly the case with Spanish."

"Luther?"

"The guy I met down in Mexico."

So Luther was his name. When Kyle came back from Mexico alone, he'd told me about some crazy old fisherman who captured Dylan's imagination. But it wasn't Dylan's imagination I'd missed. I'd blamed Luther for stealing away his heart. Late one night, I'd called down a string of curses on this old fisherman that would have made my Grandma Mona blush with pride.

"So even with that first job, you were already preparing for a career in real estate?"

"I wouldn't call it a career, but I wanted to position myself to invest." He offered me a hand as we climbed up and around some steep boulders.

"My cousin worked a remodeling job one summer. It paid better than minimum wage, but not a ton better. At that salary, it must take years to save up enough to buy even a crummy property."

"It took me nine months."

"Get out of town!" Why did I keep slapping his arm? "You bought your first property only nine months after coming back?"

"No, I had the down payment money after nine months, but the bank wanted to see that I had a full year's worth of stable income before they'd make the loan."

"Where did you get the money? You couldn't have been saving enough for a down payment with that job."

"I moved back in with my parents, which cut my expenses to almost zero, and I waited tables on the weekends to get extra cash."

"Even so, real estate costs a fortune." A log lay over a small stream that crossed our trail. With my arms out, I teetered across as though it were a balance beam. "Look me in the eye and tell me you saved enough money to buy an apartment after only one year."

I jumped off the log and faced Dylan. Those blue eyes locked onto mine. A girl could get lost in those eyes. Finally, he looked away and said, "You've got me. I didn't buy an apartment after one year."

"Ha, I knew it."

His lips curled up. "I bought four apartments."

"You are so full of crap!"

He stopped and held my eyes again, but this time he didn't look away. "I swear."

I had to swallow before I could get back my voice. He wasn't lying. That much I could feel. But still… "That makes no sense."

"It made no sense to me, either."

"Then how'd you do it?"

"By taking advantage of government loan incentives. At the time, they felt like loopholes. I couldn't understand why anyone would write the laws that way."

"Does it make more sense to you now?"

"A bit, but mainly I stopped trying to make sense of it all."

"You want to tell me about them?"

"Sorry, Amber, maybe another time." Dylan headed up the trail towards a lush canopy of trees. "I have no interest in spending our first date in seven years going through technicalities of tax and banking law."

"Hey, look!" I pointed up. Only a few feet ahead of us, a huge bird sat atop a nest on an oak branch. "Is that an eagle?"

"You got it. You can tell by its beak."

"Is it nesting?"

"Right again. You know, eagle eggs take five weeks to hatch. The pair will sit for that whole time, even if it's a bad egg."

Futile as that sounded, I sympathized with the mamma bird, with how heartbreaking it could be to give up hope, especially when now and then, one you'd written off as a bad egg showed signs of life. I blew the eagle a kiss and continued up the rock face.

"Pull over here." Dylan pointed to a gas station on the side of the road, halfway through our drive home.

"You need to use the restroom?"

"No, I want to fill you up."

"That's OK, Dylan, I'm fine covering the gas."

He shook his head. "I asked you out, and you were nice enough to drive, which saved me from renting a car. The least I can do is take care of the gas."

"I don't mind paying for it, really."

"Amber, don't think that because I'm this guy who doesn't spend much money that I think others should pay for me. It's the opposite. The things I refuse to pay for are things I don't think *anyone* should pay for, at least until they're financially independent. Which I assume you're not. So there's no reason you should take the hit."

Why was I arguing with a guy who wanted to treat me? "Fine. Go on, be a gentleman." Dylan pulled out his wallet and drew out a gas card. "Hey, is that an actual credit card you've got there?"

"Did you think I'd pay cash?"

"Isn't that what all those financial gurus say to do?"

"Don't confuse your gurus." Dylan inserted his card into the machine. "You're referring to the guys who teach people deep in debt how to get out. They're speaking to an undisciplined audience who struggle to control their spending as long as they've got plastic available."

"Lack of discipline isn't your problem, is it?"

"Nope." Dylan filled the tank and got back in the car. As we turned back on the road, he swallowed twice, and I knew he was bracing himself for something. "I've been thinking a lot about what you said back at the hot springs about… you know, the intimacy thing."

"Sorry if that was hard for you." He had been alone for so long. 'Don't touch the girl you're in love with' couldn't have been an easy thing to hear.

"I'd be lying if I said I didn't want to get physical, but I respect it."

"I appreciate that."

"What hit me was how focused you are on marriage. That's what you mean when you say you want to figure out if this is going somewhere, isn't it? It's marriage or nothing, right?"

I pulled onto the on-ramp back to civilization. "That's the stage of life I'm in, Dylan. Is that freaking you out?"

"Not quite freaking me out." He fidgeted with his credit card.

"You're not one of those guys who's afraid of commitment, are you?" I gripped the wheel as I sped up to merge onto the highway.

"Not at all. But if that's the direction we're going, I've got a concern of my own to raise."

"Uh oh." I wasn't expecting this.

"You can give it but not take it, eh?"

I sat taller and puffed out my chest. "I'm a big girl. Go on, lay it on me."

"Divorce rates are through the roof in this country. You know what's one of the biggest causes?"

"Infidelity?"

"Other than that."

I bobbed my head like a clueless party girl. "Substance abuse?"

"Besides that."

I tapped the wheel. "Men being dirty, beer-guzzling, misogynistic pigs?"

"Amber!" Now it was my turn to get slapped on the arm. Only Dylan was way gentler than I.

"Yeah, yeah, I know. Money."

"Right."

"I gave you my line in the sand, and this is yours? I need to adopt your whole money thing for us to move forward?"

Dylan rubbed his knee. "I'm willing to compromise to some degree. All I'm saying is that we need to be on the same page."

Yeah, right. "How much compromise are we talking about?"

"At the rate I'm going, I expect to hit financial independence in as little as five years and no more than ten. That's even with my plan to relax my standards in three years."

"Why are you planning to relax your standards?"

"As disciplined as you think I am, even *I* struggle with living like this indefinitely. Luther emphasized that the earlier you start building passive income—."

"Your Cash Machine," I corrected him. For a guy who acted like a financial whiz, he really could be slow sometimes.

"Right, the earlier you start building your Cash Machine, the easier the whole process is. So I committed at age 18 to spending ten years living frugally and laying the foundations of my Cash Machine."

"A decade of deprivation?"

"You could call it that. Once the decade is over, I'll continue to build my Cash Machine, but whether I'm financially independent by then or not, I'll allow myself a few more luxuries."

I switched into the fast lane to pass a Mack truck hogging the highway. "Like living above ground?"

"For one."

"And the last thing you want is some spendthrift wife ruining all you've worked to build, right?"

"Exactly."

"So you say compromise, but it sounds like I'd have to shift a lot more than you'd be willing to. Right again?"

"I guess so. At least when it comes to the money I'm bringing in. I won't try to tell you how to spend what you earn."

We drove on in silence as I chewed over Dylan's words. I'd never been this greedy, materialistic girl like some of my cousins. But there were still things I wanted. My car must have slowed because a rusted jalopy whizzed past. Or maybe it just felt that way because my vision had blurred.

"You OK?" Dylan asked.

"Yeah… it's just…I've got this friend Joanna. When she first started dating her husband Dennis, Libby and I couldn't fathom what she saw in him. He was this geeky guy who'd rather read a dissertation about the mating habits of the lungfish than watch the Super Bowl. But he was a good, stable man who owned his own dental practice, made a strong living, and was home every day by 5 pm.

"Then, six months ago, Joanna gave birth to Ethan. All she ever talks about now are the new foods he's eating, the clothes he's growing into, how he's starting to crawl, and all the smiles and giggles and play they share. I asked her recently how long she was taking for maternity leave. Joanna said she wasn't sure if she was ever going back to her agency. Dennis makes enough to support the family, and she wants to throw herself into being a mom with all she's got. Later on, she'll decide if she'd rather be home full-time raising her kids or go back to work." I wiped my eyes with the back of my hand. Why was this making me so emotional? "If I went on this journey with you, that would never be an option for me, would it?"

"Are you kidding?" Dylan laughed. "Do you have any idea what I'm building?"

"Truthfully, not really."

"Don't think of me as some lazy bum who wants to quit work and live poor for the rest of my life." He cupped his hands into the shape of a megaphone. "I'm building a Cash Machine."

"I still don't really know what that means."

"Look, you want to know about being a stay-at-home mom? Let's say we were a normal couple. At this point in our lives, we'd be doing great. We'd have two full incomes, and we could easily live in a one-bedroom apartment. We'd have plenty of money to pay our school loans, eat out, go to shows, you name it. We'd make our retirement fund contributions but otherwise spend just about everything we make. A few years out, the first kid would come along. Now we'd need a larger apartment. We'd need diapers, and cribs, and strollers, and new clothes every three months. We couldn't afford to maintain our lifestyle on one income, but if we both continue to work, we'd need to pay for daycare. This is when most couples get squeezed."

"But not if they have a Cash Machine?"

"Right. Since I'm not spending the majority of what I make now, I'm able to build resources for the future."

"Wait." I turned to look at him, but not so much that I couldn't still see the road. "You save the majority of your income?"

"Over 70% of my post-tax income goes into building my Cash Machine."

I did the math in my head. I was making a little over $50,000 pre-tax and a bit under $40,000 post-tax. I only managed to invest a couple thousand of that into my 401(k) retirement account. I spent all the rest on covering school debt, housing, food, and entertainment. My eyes bulged when I realized how my wee 5% of savings shriveled like a prune next to Dylan's 70%. But I couldn't imagine how that would relieve him of having to work forever. "Still, if expenses will go up so much in the future, won't you burn through that eventually?"

"It's not like I'm sticking it in my mattress to spend later. The idea of the Cash Machine is that you never spend any of the money you put into it."

"None of it? Then what's the point?"

"The point is that the money gets invested in income-producing assets. It's what I said about foundations. The original investment is like the goose that lays the golden egg. You can spend all the eggs you want, but if you make a goose stew, you're screwed."

I laughed but couldn't get past the fact that this guy who didn't even own a car thought he could build this gigantic income machine. "You *really* think you can make enough from your Cash Machine so only one of us would have to work?"

"One of us?" Dylan's head fell back in amusement. "When I finish my Cash Machine, neither of us would ever have to work again unless we chose to."

My eyes narrowed. "And we won't have to live like Charlie Bucket to do it?"

"Absolutely not." Dylan spread his arms wide. "Financial independence is our Golden Ticket! We can travel the world, settle anywhere, and buy as much chocolate as you can sink your teeth into."

"You make it sound like we'd have unlimited cash." Why did I keep saying *we*? "How's that possible?"

"It won't be unlimited. Just the opposite. The Cash Machine will produce a certain amount of money each year, and as long as we don't spend more than that, it'll give us the freedom to build the future of our dreams."

I hit the gas and pulled into the empty oncoming traffic lane to overtake the jalopy. "It still sounds delusional to me."

"Look, I'm not telling you to make any changes now. We've only been on one date. You can wait to see how things develop."

I shook my head. "That isn't going to work."

Dylan stiffened. "So that's it? You're dumping me?"

"It would serve you right for that letter you sent me all those years ago. But no, I'm not dumping you. But I'm also not going to wait and see. It's not like I even have a philosophy around money; I just do what my friends do. You've put more thought and dedication into this than I've put into anything in my life.

It's not realistic to force you into some wishy-washy fifty-fifty compromise. You claim you're willing to shift, but it's clear this project of yours is non-negotiable. I've either got to be all in, with both you and your Cash Machine, or all out."

"You can take your time on this." Dylan lay his hand on my elbow, and I forced myself to ignore the heat radiating up my arm. "I'm not pressuring you."

I shook my head and lifted my arm to prepare for another lane change. Dylan's hand fell to his lap. "I can't take my time. The longer we're together, the more emotionally attached I'll become. I need to know now, while I can still walk away, whether I can handle going down this road with you. And I can't decide on something I don't understand."

"So what do we do?"

I couldn't believe it. Was I seriously giving the guy who caused the greatest heartbreak of my life another chance? "You're going to walk me through building my own Cash Machine. Where do we start?"

CHAPTER 3

LATTES AND LETDOWNS

"**B**efore we create the blueprints for your Cash Machine," Dylan said as we continued our drive home from the hike, "we first need to make sure we're building it on a solid foundation."

"What a beautiful analogy." I turned the radio down and switched to the classical music station. I could tell this was going to get heady and wanted to make sure I had Mozart's full support. "Unfortunately, I haven't the slightest clue what you're talking about."

"We're going to collect all your financial data: your bank accounts, credit card statements, student loans, retirement plans, whatever you've got. We're going to import them into a single app so we can get a look at the big picture."

"Well, why the hell didn't you say so?" I slapped my hand down hard on the wheel. "Collect all my statements? I can do that. That's my first assignment?"

"It depends. Do you pay off your credit cards in full each month, or do you ever carry a balance?"

I squeezed my thumb and index finger together almost to the point of touching. "Maybe I carry a wee bit of a balance."

"At what interest rate?"

Hot patches of pink rose up my neck. "I'm kinda not really sure."

"In that case, your first assignment starts now. Is the credit card with the balance in your purse?" Dylan reached over to grab my purse from the backseat, then stopped. "Why are you pulling over?"

"I'll get the card out." It was a bit too early in our relationship to have a guy digging through my purse. Especially this time of the month. "What are we going to do with it?"

"We're going to call your credit card company."

I grabbed the card and clenched it with an iron grip. "You're not going to cancel the card, are you?"

"That all depends on what we find out." Dylan yanked the card out of my hand.

So much for my iron grip. I fought down the urge to grab it back. Nonetheless, I wasn't willing to relinquish all control. I gave him my fiercest schoolmarm look. "You're not canceling my card."

Dylan held up his hands in defeat. "Fine, I promise I won't cancel it." He pulled out his phone. "At least not today. I'm just going to call and see what I can find out. OK?"

"You drive." I unbuckled my seat belt. "I'll call."

Dylan went around to the driver's side, and I slid over the middle. An eighteen-wheeler drove by, and Dylan pulled in behind it. The oncoming traffic lane was soon empty, but Dylan made no effort to pass. It drove me nuts to drive this slowly, but I had the haunting feeling that if I told Dylan to floor it, he'd give me some lecture about fuel efficiency.

At the sound of the automated service, I entered my digits and asked for a representative. After about five minutes, the road widened as it went uphill, and Dylan finally eased past the truck. Just as the road narrowed back into a single lane for the downhill, the representative finally picked up. After a long, canned introduction thanking me for my business, she said, "This is Candice. How can I help you today?"

I turned to Dylan and shrugged; I didn't know the purpose of the call.

"What's your balance?" he said.

I asked Candice, but before I got a response, Dylan said, "Put it on speakerphone. I want to hear."

The woman's voice boomed out of my phone. "As of today, your balance is $6849.71." I quickly turned down the volume.

"At what interest rate?" Dylan called out.

"I'm sorry," Candice said, "but I need authorization before I can discuss the details of the card with anyone but the primary cardholder."

"It's OK, I authorize," I said. "You can answer his question."

"Yes, ma'am. Your current interest rate is 23.99%."

Ouch. I had no idea it was so high.

Dylan lifted his eyebrows. "What's the lowest possible rate you can give her today?"

These reps were too well trained to lecture or laugh at us, but I pictured Candice rolling her eyes in her cubicle. You can't just call up a major bank and negotiate with the phone representative.

"One moment while I check on that for you," Candice replied.

Wait. Was she looking into this?

"My records show that you have been a loyal customer for five years and have never missed a payment. In thanks for your loyalty and perfect payment record, I'm authorized to reduce your interest rate to 12.99% today. Would you like me to go ahead and do so?"

Hell yes! I regained my composure and politely said, "Please, that would be wonderful."

"Your new interest rate will go into effect as of today. Is there anything else I can help you with?"

I was about to say, 'no, thank you' when Dylan spoke. "Are there any membership rewards on this card?"

"No, sir. It is not currently enrolled in our reward program. Would you like me to enroll you today?"

Yeah!

Dylan said, "What are the terms of your reward program?"

"On this card, one point will be accrued for every dollar spent. Points can then be redeemed for cash back, purchases, or travel."

"Is there any cost for the program or an annual fee on the card?"

"No, sir. There is neither."

Dylan winked at me. "Then yes, please enroll the card in the program."

I turned to him with my jaw hanging low enough to clean the floor of the car.

"The card is now enrolled. Is there anything else I can do for you today?"

Again, Dylan jumped in before I could refuse. "Yes, what is the credit limit on this card?"

I heard the click of Candice's keyboard as she searched for an answer. "It's currently set at $14,500. Would you like me to check if it's eligible for an increase?"

Dylan nodded toward me. "Please."

"One moment, sir."

My face contorted in confusion. "Why do I want that?" I whispered. "I figured you'd want me to lower my balance, not increase it."

Dylan's fixed me with a hard gaze. "The extra money isn't for spending, so don't get the increase if you think it will tempt you."

"I'll be a good girl," I said, smiling as innocently as I could. "But why get it if I can't spend it?"

"It raises your credit score."

"Really?"

"One of the factors they evaluate is the percentage of your available credit you're using."

I cocked my head. "So raising my available credit lowers the percent I'm using, is that it?"

"Exactly." I found the confidence in Dylan's voice incredibly attractive. I liked how he was taking charge, but wasn't going to let on. I was still beyond hesitant.

"And my credit rating is important because…"

"Because it can determine whether you'll be approved for a mortgage and under what terms."

Candice came back on the line. "Your card has been approved for an increase to $22,000. Would you like me to put that through?"

"Yes, please," I said.

"Your new credit limit is available immediately. Is there anything else I can help you with today?"

Dylan jumped in again. "Have there been any fees assessed against this card recently?"

"Yes, sir. Last month there was a $29 return payment fee."

I shrunk against my seat. "I didn't have enough in my checking account at the time," I said, only loud enough for Dylan to hear.

Dylan ignored me. "Are you able to waive that fee, Candice?"

I sat up again. "Are you serious?"

Candice, of course, took it all in stride. "Yes, sir. As a courtesy, we're able to do a fee waiver once every six months. Would you like me to go ahead and put that through?"

"Yes, please," I said

"The fee has been waived, and you will see the credit on your next statement. Is there anything else I can do for you today?"

I sat in stunned silence, waiting to see what else Dylan was going to pull out of his hat, but he just shook his head. "No thanks."

"Thank you again for being a loyal customer and have a great day."

The line cut out, and I lifted my chin from the floor. "Holy crap. You just cut my interest in half. Do you mean I could have been doing this all along?"

"Absolutely." Dylan sat taller. "Plus getting 1% cash back."

My tush did a little victory dance in my seat. "That's awesome."

"Not really. I wouldn't recommend you stick with this card. For now, I just wanted to show you the power of asking. This woman had to hit a single command on her computer, and it spit out a new interest rate. But the bank has no incentive to offer it to you on its own. As long as you're happy paying the higher rate, they're content to let you do so."

"Why are they willing to reduce it at all?"

"Because the type of people who ask for lower rates are also the type who compare cards. You pay on time, so you're a low-risk client, and 12.99% interest is still a fortune. They'd rather have that than lose you." Dylan eased the car toward the exit.

"You think I can do better than the deal you just got me?"

"Far better. That's your other assignment for this week. I want you to research available cards."

"Got it. So I'm supposed to figure out the best one to move over to?"

"Not one." Dylan lifted his index finger, then opened his hand wide. "Ones. I expect we'll start you off with at least five."

"Five cards? Is that also to raise my credit score?"

"No. Getting new cards might even hurt your credit short-term. It's only on existing cards where raising your limit can pad your credit rating with no downside." He gave me the don't-mess-with-my rules look my father used to throw at us when he and my mother would leave us home alone. "Unless you're tempted to spend the extra money, of course."

"But if not for the credit rating, what's the advantage of all these cards?"

"You have to consider credit from the bank's point of view. They're watching out for *their* bottom line, not yours. They'll give you massive incentives in one area to draw you in, but there's always another area where they're hoping to make their cash."

"So either way, they screw you?"

"No, you screw them!" Dylan banged on the dashboard. "Once you know the rules, you can turn the game in your favor. I have twelve cards myself."

Twelve? "Why so many?"

"To maximize incentives. Some give me a huge bonus for joining. Others give me cash back in one category or another. Last year alone, I made over $2000 in credit card sign-up bonuses and over $3500 in cash back rewards."

My mouth fell open again. "$3500?"

"Yep. I get between 2% and 5% back on every dollar I spend. All financed by those undisciplined folks who pay 23.99% interest on their cards."

"Hey," I said, slapping his arm, "That's not nice!"

"I thought there was no physical contact until you were 'sure' about me?"

I had to purse my lips to keep from grinning. Dylan was beating me at my game as much as he was playing Visa and Mastercard like financial fiddles. I quickly turned the subject back to money. "How did you possibly spend enough to get $3500 cash back?"

"Remodeling houses." Dylan turned into his neighborhood. "Some of that stuff isn't cheap."

"That's all for the houses you own?"

"No, most of it came from work projects. My boss reimburses me for expenses for the places we're working on. He offered me a company card, but I'd rather use my own and get the rewards."

"So when researching cards, what should I be looking for?"

"First off, we need to deal with your current card balance. The cards that have strong rewards programs won't be a good solution for that. Those cards probably have at least a 3% balance transfer fee. Instead, you'll transfer your balance to a card that offers 0% balance transfer fees and gives you a 0% introductory interest rate. That card won't offer you any rewards, but it doesn't matter. You won't be making any purchases through it anyway." Dylan turned onto his street.

"Are you saying I'll be able to get the interest on my current balance down to nothing?"

"Absolutely. As a general rule, you never want to pay credit card interest."

"A general rule? That means there are exceptions, right?"

"Oh, yes." He slowed the car to a stop in front of his place.

"Like when?"

Dylan got out of the car and grabbed his pack from the back seat. He leaned down so he could look me square in the eye. "Like when you're a hell of a lot savvier than you are now. Until you know exactly what you're doing, stay away from credit card interest."

Dylan biked over to my apartment early the following Saturday. I hadn't seen him all week, which left me feeling antsier than I cared to admit. Between his work schedule and managing his own properties, his time to see me was limited. He was never far from my mind, though, especially as the assignment he'd given me kept me in Cash Machine mode.

I opened the door, and my heels bounced with excitement to share my news.

Dylan wore an old t-shirt from a Phish concert we'd seen together before his Mexico escapade. I felt a hint of nostalgia looking at the shirt, but just for a moment. It was so tattered and worn, I wouldn't have used it to clean my toilet.

"What's got you all jumpy?" he asked.

I pushed my revulsion with his shirt out of my mind. I had more important things to focus on, like gloating over my victory. "Guess what I did yesterday?"

"What's that?"

"I brewed my own coffee rather than buying a latte on my way into work."

Dylan snickered as he slipped past me into the apartment.

"I thought you'd be excited." I pouted. "I saved over three dollars."

"Three whole dollars?" He couldn't keep the sarcasm from his voice.

"OK, fine, it's not a lot. But think of it in percentages. I saved over 90% on my morning coffee expenses. Sounds a lot better that way, doesn't it?"

He stifled another laugh.

"You're still not excited." I stamped my foot on the floor like a five-year-old. "I thought I did so good."

"You're doing great." Dylan leaned over and kissed my cheek. My insides shivered, but I tried not to show it. Then he tipped his head and said, "That wasn't too intimate, was it?"

"Ordinarily, I'd say no." I pointed a finger at him as though he were a naughty student. "But even a kiss on the cheek is crossing a line for a guy who has the nerve to mock me."

"There's no mocking here, I promise." Dylan sat on one of the bar stools at my kitchen counter, looking a little too at home for his first visit. "I applaud the intention, but you're starting upside down."

"How do you mean?"

"It's like my boss always says, 'Don't sweep the floor when you've got a hole in the roof.'"

I crossed my arms. "I don't speak shop talk."

"Let's put it this way." Dylan twisted the lid off my cookie jar. I couldn't help but notice the grime under his fingernails.

"No, no, no, you don't!" I pounded my hand onto the lid. "You're not sticking your grubby hands into my cookie jar before washing them first!"

"Yes, Mom." Dylan headed to the sink with his tail between his legs. He scrubbed with a hearty helping of soap, but his hands didn't look much cleaner as he dried them on my freshly laundered towel. Construction guys had a level of grime that stuck to them like Krazy Glue.

"As I was saying…" He headed back to the counter, pulled one of my grandmother's biscotti out of the jar, and held it up in the air. "Imagine trying to lose weight by skipping the slivered almonds on the biscotti. It helps, but doesn't get at the core issue." He pointed the biscotti at me and added, "Tell me, if we were to rank your expenses from highest to lowest, where would lattes fall?"

"Somewhere between rent and toilet paper."

"And closer to…"

I rolled my eyes. "Toilet paper, obviously."

"It's not so obvious." Dylan took a bite. "I pay more for toilet paper than I do for rent."

"Funny you never mentioned these digestive problems on our first date."

Dylan didn't even give my lame joke a courtesy laugh. "Since you're probably paying far more in rent than you are for lattes and toilet paper combined, let's start there. Did you do your homework to track your expenses?"

"Yep, I loaded all my bank statements into that app you sent me."

"What did the results say?"

"I haven't looked them over. I figured we could do that together." I put my laptop on the counter and opened up the app.

"Let's see what we've got." He arranged my bills by category. "The first step is to track your expenses and see where your money's going. Any surprises here?"

"Ooh, there's a digital subscription JibJab I hadn't realized I was still paying for. That should have expired over a year ago."

"It probably auto-renewed. You'd be amazed at how many people still pay for things they've forgotten about. That's why I make a point to turn off auto-renew, especially for things on annual billing. If I can't turn it off, like with annual fees on credit cards, I put a note in my calendar to make sure I still need it before it's renewal date. Any other surprises?"

Dylan finished his first biscotti and went back for a second while I scanned the hundreds of line items from the past year, hoping I wouldn't find anything seriously wrong, like a flat-screen TV shipped off to Nigeria. My stomach lurched as I realized how little attention I paid to my bills each month. If there'd been any fraud, I could have easily missed it. I sighed when I got to the bottom and saw that all the charges were undeniably mine. "All looks correct. What's your prognosis, Doc?"

"It could be worse. You're making your payments on time. No one's going to come and repossess your car anytime soon."

"Good luck if they did. My lease is up next month. See anything else in the data?"

"You have a fairly normal expense profile."

"Meaning what?"

"Pretty much everyone's three biggest expenses are housing, taxes, and transportation. Food is normally fourth, but for you, food and transportation are pretty much the same."

I slumped. "I eat out a lot."

"There's no judgment here. We just want to see where you stand." Dylan pulled the laptop back over to him, and I grabbed a biscotti myself, a bit of sweet support to handle the blows he was about to send my way. "Let's start at the top, with your rent."

"Don't you go touching my apartment." I gazed toward the brick fireplace, which didn't work but still looked stunning. "I love this place."

"You're paying $1500 a month for it, and a couple hundred more in utilities."

"But I'm only six months into a one-year lease, so I couldn't leave it if I wanted to. Which I don't."

Dylan held up his hands in defeat. "Your next biggest expense is taxes."

"I won't give you a hard time for cutting those. But good luck. If there's anywhere I could save on taxes, my father's accountant would find it."

"I'm sure he would." He tapped the tax line item on the screen. "But your problem isn't an accounting issue. By the time the accountant gets your data, you're already stuck."

"Meaning what?"

"Mastering taxes is all about the way you earn and invest your money. Since that involves major life shifts you're not ready to make, let's put taxes aside for now and move on to transportation. Mr. Money Mustache says most people can make their biggest gains here."

"You're not seriously going to give me financial advice from a guy who calls himself Mr. Money Mustache, are you?"

"You want me to quote someone else? Every financial advisor I know agrees that leases like yours stink like skunk roadkill."

Now it was my turn to shove a cookie in Dylan's face. "You weren't complaining when I picked you up last week to go on that hike…"

"I'm not complaining that you have a car." Dylan bit right into the cookie I held in his face, which wasn't technically intimacy, because he didn't touch me, but felt mighty close, nonetheless. "I'm pointing out that your lease is sucking you dry."

"What's so bad about it? I get to drive a nice car at a decent monthly rate."

"You're currently paying $300 a month for your lease. How long is it for?"

"36 months."

"That means you're paying a minimum of $10,000 over three years, plus a wide range of possible fees depending on how many miles you drive and what condition the car is in when you return it. Not to mention that your insurance is higher because you're driving a new vehicle. All that money goes straight in the garbage, with no hope of getting anything back for your investment. That's reward-free risk."

"The reward is getting to drive a nice car." I shimmied my head with full-on attitude. "Rather than biking to work like some know-it-alls I've met."

"You need to weigh the pleasure of driving a new car against the other rewards you could get for your $10,000."

"Like what?"

"Remember that quadruplex I bought after living with my parents for that first year? I put less than $10,000 down on that property."

"You must have been left with a gigantic mortgage."

"True, but not all debt is made equal. My mortgage is high-quality debt."

"High-quality debt? Isn't that just some rationalization, like high-quality herpes?"

"Don't thumb your nose at debt. Debt can be good or bad."

"How can debt be good?"

"Good debt is leverage. In this case, my mortgage allowed me to buy a property 30 times what I could afford to buy in cash."

"But isn't that going to be a weight around your neck? How's it any different from a car lease?"

"The difference is that I didn't just acquire debt; I also acquired a passive income source. I moved into the basement and rented out the other three apartments."

"I think I see what you're saying. It's not that mortgages are good debt and car leases are bad, it's more how you use them, right? Like my cousin George got a decent paying job as a driver, but he needed a certain kind of car for it. So for him, his car lease was good debt because it allowed him to make a lot more money."

"Exactly. From the time I moved into my first quadruplex, the money I collected each month covered my mortgage payments plus taxes, insurance, and utilities. It also brought my housing costs down to zero. I made a profit really—most months, I had money left over."

"How long was your mortgage?"

"30 years."

"You must have been about 20-years-old when you bought that house." My eyes grew wide as hubcaps. "Are you saying that by the time you hit 50, you could own a four-unit building outright, without ever putting in more money than I've spent on my piece-of-crap car?"

"I thought you liked that car?"

"I did. But if you had three rental units and no mortgage, you could retire on that."

"Are you starting to see the power of the Cash Machine?" Dylan reached for another biscotti, but I snatched the jar, sealed it, and put it atop the refrigerator.

"You'll ruin your brunch," I said.

"Oh?" Dylan rubbed his hands together. "What's the chef cooking up?"

"You'll just have to wait and see." I tapped the tip of his nose and immediately regretted it. I quickly turned around—so he wouldn't see me blush—and opened the fridge to gather up ingredients for omelets. The hairs on the back of my neck tingled, and I knew Dylan was watching me. I had to get the conversation back to neutral territory. "I hear how you could buy real estate with the money instead, but I still need a car." I cracked six eggs into a bowl.

"Then get a used car you can afford to buy in cash."

I threw away the eggshells. "All I can afford is a piece of junk."

"Listen to yourself! If all you can afford is a piece of junk, then you have no business leasing a new car." He got up from his stool. "Put me to work. How can I help?"

"Chop these." I passed him a cutting board and a pair of onions. Let him shed a few tears for me—I'd shed more than enough for him. "Dylan, I don't get your logic. The whole reason I got the lease is so I don't have to come up with all the money at once. It's just a flat fee per month. I can afford that."

Dylan got to work. It was a rare guy that knew how to use a chef's knife. Aunt Marie would be impressed. "There are ways to break up the cost of a used car into monthly payments too. But you'll have more options and get a better price if you can pay cash. How much can you afford?"

I turned back to my cutting board and diced red peppers. "Nothing, really."

"Come on, Amber. You have no savings? No retirement accounts?" He peeked at the computer to look through my retirement information.

I slammed the laptop shut. "Hold on, we're not touching my retirement accounts."

"Didn't you just say you could retire on the money you'd save on a lease?"

"I meant that *one* could. Specifically, you." I chopped a sprig of fresh basil. "I wouldn't have the slightest idea what to do with some multi-unit property. That's way over my head."

"And being in a load of debt isn't? Better to use the money today to buy a good used car, which will save you money and hold most of its value, rather than leave it in an account you can't touch for the next 34 years. What kind of accounts do you have, anyhow?"

"Just a 401(k)." I pointed my knife in his direction. "You got a problem with that?"

"Whoa! Down, girl." Dylan's hands flew up like a criminal under arrest. "I've got many, many problems with the 401(k). It mostly exists for people who can't be trusted around their own money."

I returned to chopping. "How so?"

"The government knows you'll blow everything you make without saving for retirement, so they set up a system that takes money before it hits your bank account, then penalizes you for touching it early. It's the only way to get most people to save anything. But I have no problem with self-control, so for me, there's only one reason to consider a 401(k)."

"What's that?"

"If your employer matches your contribution, then you're turning away free money by not participating." The chopping of his knife ceased. "What should I do with these?"

I lit the burner under my frying pan and added a dash of olive oil. "Throw them in here and keep them moving." I tossed the peppers in as well and got to dicing a handful of cherry tomatoes. "Back to this 401(k) thing. My school will match up to 50% of my contribution, so that's good, right?"

"Do they give you the money right away?"

"No, it only vests after five years. If I leave my job before that, I don't get all the contribution."

"Sounds like a trap." Dylan lifted the pan and flipped its contents like a pro. "The small amount of money they'll add could keep you from moving to a better job or starting something on your own."

"What about the tax benefits?"

"They're negligible."

"Oh, come on." Rehabbing apartments might have qualified Dylan to manage real estate, but retirement funds were managed by MBAs, not college dropouts. "You want me to believe that no one gets tax benefits from the number one tax benefit program out there?" I added the tomatoes to the pan.

"I should say, they're negligible for anyone building a Cash Machine. The 401(k) is not tax-free, it's tax-deferred. That means that you'll eventually pay taxes on it, just not now."

I threw salt and herbs into the eggs and whisked them into foam. "Isn't that still a good thing?"

"It depends. For someone like Kyle, who'll make a ton of money but doesn't worry about investments, it makes sense. He should be in a far lower tax bracket post-retirement when he gets the money than he's in now. Plus he'll save on capital gains tax on the profits." The vegetables flew into the air as he spoke. He caught them with grace and returned the skillet to the fire. "But if you build a Cash Machine, your income should go up as you age, not down. I'd rather be taxed now at the lower rate and use the money to build my Cash Machine than have it sit in some fund only to be taxed at a higher rate later."

I poured the eggs into the pan, took over the spatula, and nudged Dylan over. "I still haven't decided if you're crazy or not. Until I do, there's no way I'm touching my retirement funds."

"If you can get your car money some other way, then you're best off leaving it, it's not worth paying the penalties. But is your 401(k) at least in an index fund?"

I grinned, knowing I had him on this one. "Even better. I have it in a mutual fund that beat the S&P 500 six years in a row. I don't know what the S&P 500 is, but I know beating it is good." I pointed to a baguette on the counter. "Can you slice some of that and put it to toast?"

"Sure. The S&P 500 is a portfolio of 500 of the largest stocks, as determined by a company called Standard and Poor's."

"Got it, so S&P stands for Standard and Poor?"

"Exactly. As of when was this mutual fund of yours doing so well?"

"When I signed up for it, I guess. That was two and a half years ago."

Dylan popped a few slices of baguette into the toaster. "It hasn't beat it since."

"You know, you can be so freakin' arrogant sometimes." I lowered the heat on the pan. "I haven't even told you what fund I invested in."

"Doesn't matter. The odds of it beating an index fund that tracks the S&P 500 are tiny."

I wagged the spatula in his face. "It's time to show you that you don't know everything." I served the eggs onto two dishes and gave him the heartier portion—he was in construction, after all. I sprinkled the fresh basil on as garnish, just like Mom always did. "You ready to put your money where your mouth is, Mr. Smarty Pants?"

"Sure am. I'll take care of the bread and set the table. Why don't you go check your mutual fund earnings for the past two years? I'm not talking about the top-line earnings. I'm talking about the actual amount you put in your pocket at the end of the day after fees. If, in either year, you gained more than you would have with an index fund tracking the S&P 500, I'll make you dinner tonight. But if it underperformed in both years, you make it for me."

I prodded him with the spatula. "What will you make?"

"You set the menu." He held my gaze and didn't even blink.

"And you'll buy all the ingredients?"

"If you win."

"Oh, good." I couldn't help but smirk. "Because it just so happens that I'm in the mood for lasagna, with a homemade marinara sauce."

"Any appetizers?"

I should have gone easy on him, but his cocky grin set me on edge. "Minestrone soup."

"And for dessert, my lady?"

"Tiramisu."

"Sounds delicious. You can make me that exact menu when I win."

"You realize this is a sucker's bet, don't you?"

"Of course." He leaned in until we stood only inches apart. I didn't know if I wanted to slap him or kiss him.

"Still, it's sweet of you to be a sucker for me." I tapped his cheek with the spatula, leaving a tomato seed in its wake. "I think I'll put on some Pavarotti and take a hot bath as you prepare my Italian feast."

"Oh, it's a sucker's bet all right, but not in your favor. You don't stand a chance."

"Are you kidding?" I opened my laptop. "My mutual fund already outperformed the S&P six straight years, and now it only has to outperform it one out of two for me to win. It's in the bag."

"It's in the trash bag, where all those mutual funds belong." He opened one drawer after the other, presumably looking for cutlery, and I was happy for him to scramble a bit. "Go on, look up your returns."

While Dylan set the table, I split my screen, pulling up my mutual fund on one side and the Vanguard S&P 500 index fund on the other. My chest sank. There it was, plain as day. The S&P 500 had averaged over 8% growth, while my mutual fund barely hit 5%. "You son of a bitch." I slammed the computer shut. "How the hell did you know?"

"I didn't. I just know the system's rigged." The toaster pinged, and Dylan quickly grabbed the piping hot slices, threw them on a plate, and walked over to the table. "There are ten ways you're getting screwed on this mutual fund you don't even know about."

"Ten?" I pulled spreads out of the fridge: butter, jam, Uncle Sonny's olive tapenade. "Now you're just bragging."

"Am I? Care to go double or nothing on dinner tomorrow night?"

"I'm going shopping with Libby tomorrow to look at bridesmaids' dresses. Next week?"

"Deal."

I joined him at the table and poured us each a glass of O.J. "So what are your ten?"

"I don't know."

I shot my hands above my head. "Yes! I win!"

"Not so fast. You never said I had to know them off the top of my head. I don't know squat about mutual funds, just that they're bad news. I'll research them while you prepare my feast tonight, and by the time we sit down to eat, I'll have my list."

"Fine, but they'd better be ten good ones. I don't want to come back to find you've packed your list with a bunch of lame distinctions that don't make a difference."

"Oh, they'll be good." He raised his glass in toast.

Our glasses clinked together. "They'd better be." I gulped down the cool juice. "If you have even nine and a half, you're making me pizza next Saturday."

"How can I have half a reason?"

"Shut up." I spread tapenade on a slice of hot toast and bit into it. "I'm just saying, they'd better be damn good."

We hit the produce aisle first. I picked out vine ripe tomatoes, red bell peppers, eggplant, carrots, portobello mushrooms, and zucchini. I headed in the direction of the freezer section, but Dylan stopped. "You're not going to buy me some frozen tiramisu, are you?"

"My Great Grandma Mona would roll over in her grave if she saw me buying frozen tiramisu, and she's not even dead yet." I shot straight past the freezer section toward the bakery. "Come on, we'll need ladyfingers."

We spent way too long in the dairy section debating over parmesano versus pecorino. I decided to let him pick his pecorino, gathered up the ricotta and mozzarella of my choosing, and turned towards the exit.

"We need noodles, don't we?" Dylan asked.

"Sure, I could buy you store-bought noodles if you prefer those to the ones I make myself. How about Spaghetti-O's?" I turned my back on him and headed to the register.

"I guess I shouldn't mess with an Italian."

"Not unless you want to be eating microwave lasagna tonight." I laid the groceries on the conveyor belt, and a now quiet Dylan raced to help out.

The total came to a whopping $68.59. "You know, for a guy who's supposed to be teaching me how to save money, you're doing a lousy job."

He offered me an awfully innocent smile considering he probably didn't spend that much on food in a *week*. "Not to worry. $60 is a bargain for one of the most powerful financial lessons you'll ever learn."

"It's almost $70."

"So far." Dylan waved his keychain over the checkout scanner, which registered his membership number. The price dropped to $61.09. "Membership is free, you know. There's no reason to pay full price when some of these items are on special."

I gritted my teeth. "It's still over 60 bucks."

"Not with credit card rewards. You should be getting at least 2% back. Didn't you research the cards?"

I grabbed one of the two shopping bags and walked out of the store without a word.

"I'll tell you," Dylan said, standing up from my desk, "you might not know the finer points of retirement accounts, but you sure know your way around a kitchen."

I already had both the soup and marinara sauce boiling on the stove. "You finally done with that list, slowpoke?"

"I kept pausing to watch you work."

I suppressed a grin. "Don't get used to it. Next week I'm planning on doing the watching."

"We'll see about that." Dylan slipped a ladyfinger out of its package.

I slapped his hand away. "They're for the tiramisu."

Dylan pulled back but still managed to steal one. "You always sing opera when you cook?"

"Only when making Grandma Mona's lasagna."

"In that case, I might have to request it again next week." He raised his eyebrows and bit the ladyfinger.

"Don't decide so fast. You don't know what I sing when I make burritos. Besides, this bet is far from won. What have you got?"

Dylan flourished a piece of paper. "The number 10 reason why mutual funds always get destroyed by index funds."

"Doing a countdown, are you?"

"Hey, I was almost a drama major."

"I thought you were pursuing business?"

"That's the great thing about dropping out of college after one semester: I was almost a lot of things. Now stop distracting me." He flipped over my wooden salad bowl and patted out a drumroll. "Number 10: All costs of researching investments get passed onto you, whereas index funds require no research and therefore have no costs."

Part of me wanted to see Dylan win this contest of ours, to show me that he really was savvier than he looked. A small part. A very small part. The other

99% of me despised losing bets under any circumstances. "That's a totally lame reason. I want my fund managers doing their analysis. A research budget makes perfect sense. Not counting that one."

"Oh?" Dylan didn't look the least bit discouraged. That's good. I like a guy with a bit of fight in him. "Next you'll say that you want the funds advertising themselves too. Do you know that they also pass that expense on to you?"

My eyes bulged like a cartoon character's. "You've got to be kidding me."

"Nope." He pointed to his list. "It's called a 12b-1 fee. They can bill you up to 0.75% each year for their advertising costs."

"0.75% of the profits?"

"Oh, no." Dylan tapped on the bowl. "0.75% of your total account balance."

"Their advertising costs should come out of their share, not mine." I threw the carrots into the soup. "That can be your new number 10."

"But I had it at number 3."

"Then it sounds like you'd better come up with a new number 3." I grabbed semolina flour for the noodles. "Either that or get busy building yourself a brick oven, because that's how I like my pizza baked."

Dylan cleared his throat. "Number 9, also under rule 12b-1, they can give out commissions and bill them to you, most often to whoever handles your 401(k) plan."

"Doesn't strike me as a big deal, but I'll give that to you." I turned down the soup to simmer. "Next."

"Number 8, management fees. They charge you between 0.5% and 2% each year for handling your money."

"Your index funds don't have that?"

"Index funds require next to no management. Vanguard charges 0.05% in management fees for its S&P 500 fund. Mutual funds charge 10 to 40 times more." He didn't wait for my response before moving on. "Number 7 is a purchase fee paid to the fund when you buy-in. Which perfectly matches with number 6, which is a redemption fee of up to 6% when you sell."

I was trying to knead the pasta dough but felt myself wanting to punch it. "That's a lot of fees."

"I'm just getting started. Number 5 is called a Sales Load, which is a fee paid to the broker when you buy or sell. This can be 5%, which means more or less the equivalent of a year's worth of gains goes up in smoke."

"Sounds like a load of—."

"Sure does," Dylan leaned over the counter and snatched a slice of red pepper. He bit into it with a Bugs Bunny grin of satisfaction.

"You're sure enjoying yourself."

Dylan shoved the rest of the pepper in his mouth. "What can I say? Being right is the greatest feeling in the world—well, other than…"

Time to change the subject! "So, you got any more fees up your sleeve?"

"They're not up *my* sleeve. I didn't make these babies up. I'm just the messenger." He looked back at his paper and said, "Number 4, mutual funds are buying and selling constantly, and they bill the fund for each transaction."

"As opposed to index funds that just buy and hold?"

"Precisely. But there's an even bigger consequence to all the buying and selling, which brings me to number 2."

"What happened to number 3?" I asked as I rolled out the dough.

"You made me use it for number 10, remember?"

"That just means you owe me a new number 3."

"I'll get to it, but right now I'm on number 2. Are you familiar with short-term and long-term capital gains?"

"No, what are they?"

Behind my back, Dylan sneaked into the cookie package again. "Well, say this ladyfinger is your initial investment." Dylan lay the ladyfinger on the counter. "And your investment grew over time." He pulled out a bunch more ladyfingers and made a pile out of them.

My hands were too covered in flour to fight him. I didn't want to make an even bigger mess. "So those are my profits?" I asked, pointing to the pile.

"Exactly. Now, when you decide to sell, the government won't tax you on your initial investment." He pointed to the one ladyfinger. "But they will tax your profits. By how much? Well, that depends on how long you held the investment. If you held it over a year, they tax it only a little." Dylan took one ladyfinger from the profits pile and bit off half of it.

"Hey!"

He ignored me and continued. "This is called a long-term capital gain. But if you held it for less than a year, they tax it at a far higher rate, called a short-term capital gain." Dylan ate the rest of the ladyfinger.

"Did you really need my cookies to get that point across?"

"I get hungry watching you cook."

As I sliced sheets of lasagna, I pondered this whole short-term versus long-term tax issue. "I don't get the problem. I've held my mutual funds for over a year."

"Mutual funds aren't one entity, they're a collection of stocks and the portfolio is constantly changing as the fund managers buy and sell. So they're always taxed as short term capital gains."

"That's not the case with index funds?" Whatever part of me that had wanted Dylan to succeed had long since been silenced. Now I just wanted him to crash and burn.

"Nope, because the stocks are just sitting there. They're not actively traded."

"Even in my retirement account?" I asked.

"No. In your 401(k), you won't be billed for short term gains."

I pumped my fist in the air, "Yes!" At least I'd beat him on that one.

"Your gains will be taxed as regular income, which is even worse. Of course, the same is true for index funds or anything else in your 401(k). Did I mention I hate those?" Dylan grabbed another ladyfinger. "As long as we're on taxes, I'll give you a bonus one for another cookie."

"Fine, but this is the last one, or I'm not making dessert!" At least I could still best him in the kitchen.

"Yes, ma'am." Dylan held the ladyfinger between his fingers like a cigar. "You can even get taxed on profits that the fund made before you bought it. Say they've held Apple stock for the past 20 years, and the week after you buy the fund, they decide to finally unload that stock. You owe capital gains tax on those profits."

"But I didn't profit from it."

"Doesn't matter. You're now a partner in the fund. So even if it goes down during the period you held it, you can get stuck with a massive tax bill."

I sighed in exasperation. I was so done with this game. "What's your number 1 reason?"

"Mutual fund managers make money whether the fund goes up or down. You could be losing your shirt while they're off buying a new BMW. Your interests are not aligned."

I didn't know whether to be more frustrated with Dylan for being so right about how screwed I was getting with my mutual fund or with the broker for never telling me any of this stuff. "You're still only at nine, by the way." I still hoped to save face on the bet. "So you'd better get back to your research or start working on my pizza. I'll take a Caesar salad on the side."

"And a bottle of red wine?"

"White." I laid lasagna noodles into my baking dish and spread a layer of ricotta over them. "By the way, how could you be so sure my fund would lose against the S&P 500 when it beat it so many years in a row?"

"Oh right, I forgot. I'll call that number 3, the mutual fund bait and switch. A bank might have hundreds of funds, and statistically, they're bound to have some that beat the S&P 500 a few years in a row. When it comes to advertising their featured funds each year to suckers who know little about the market, which do you think they highlight?"

I imagined my broker was the pepper mill as I cranked it over the cheese. "Obviously, the ones doing the best."

"Right, so even though on average they're getting killed by the index funds, in their publicity, they're always highlighting the small portion of their portfolio succeeding."

I handed him the pecorino and a grater. "But if a fund has a strong track record of success, shouldn't it be a strong investment?"

"If only…" The pecorino fell like snow over the lasagna. "The fund that was doing well may have been tiny in previous years, but now that it's featured, the amount of money it has under management goes through the roof. The bigger fund can't slip in and out of opportunities like it did before."

My body drooped like the roasted veggies I laid over the first layer of marinara sauce. "So the whole character of the fund changes?"

"Precisely. You may as well erase the history."

"And those fees add up to such a difference?"

"It's huge." Dylan rested the cheese and grater onto a plate, then pulled paper and pen from my desk. "Let's say you invest $100 each in a mutual fund and an index fund and they both went up at 8% a year, but the mutual fund charged 3% in fees, reducing your gains to only 5% a year. Guess how many years it'll take for your $100 to reach $10,000?"

"I don't know. How many?"

"No idea."

"Swift, Dylan." I took a ladyfinger and bit off the end.

"I thought you needed those for dessert?"

I threw him my mother's *don't mess with me* look.

He fled back to the laptop. "That's the great thing about the internet. You don't need to know something to have the answer within minutes. Give me a second."

I lay another layer of pasta into the dish while Mr. Librarian pecked at my laptop. I had to admit his geekiness about all this stuff was pretty cute.

Dylan entered his data into an investment calculator. "OK, the index fund would take 60 years to grow to $10,000. At the same time, the mutual fund would only be worth $1867."

"Less than a fifth as much?" I whistled. How could 3% add up to be so much?

"That's the magic of compounding."

"Is that what you aim to get? Around 8% a year?"

"No, that's what the stock market as a whole tends to return over time. Index funds can be great for those who want to park their money somewhere and not have to think about it. My Cash Machine is something different entirely. I aim to double my money every five years, which means I need to get at least 15% annual growth."

"And you've been able to get that?"

"I've averaged over 20%, partially because real estate in our market has continued to go up."

Any hopes I had of winning the bet had long since dissipated. Now that my competitive side had been reined in, I could start appreciating Dylan for what he'd done. Beneath the grimy fingers and tattered shirt was a guy who had given serious thought to his financial future. How strong could he make it? I still wasn't sure, but I intended to find out. "Let's say you can't keep up the 20% return, and over time you get exactly the 15% you're aiming for." I pointed to the laptop. "What does your little calculator say would happen to that same $100 investment over those 60 years?"

"Let's see…It says the $100 investment would grow to $438,399." Dylan swirled on his barstool. "Oh yeah, and 87 cents."

"Four. Hundred. Thousand. Dollars?" I crushed black pepper with each word. "How is that possible?"

"Einstein said, 'Compound interest is the 8th wonder of the world, he who understands it, earns it; he who doesn't, pays it.' That's why you want to start your money compounding as early as possible. It's also why you want to be extremely careful with debt. Your school loans and credit card balances are also compounding, just not in your favor."

I'd never given much thought to the interest on my school loans or even on my credit cards. Just about everyone I knew paid interest on these; I'd just accepted them as a normal cost of living. "At least my school loans are super-low interest. I'm only paying 6%."

"It may sound low, but it adds up over time. And the biggest cost is a hidden one."

"What's that?"

"All that money that's going into your loan payments is money you're not using to build your Cash Machine. You may only be paying 6%, but if you weren't paying out that money, you could be investing it and watching it compound in your favor."

There was nothing I could do at the moment about my school loans, and I'd found a new credit card that would allow me to transfer my current balances interest-free for a year. I needed to bring my focus back to the matter at hand: my retirement accounts. "So those mutual fund fees add up, huh?"

"Absolutely. Fees are a compounding killer. Taxes are an even bigger one. That's why it's crucial when building a Cash Machine that you know the tax implications of each investment."

"OK, Dylan, you win. I'm still not going to cash out my 401(k), but I'll switch it over to an index fund." I slid the lasagna into the oven and mustered a smile. "What would you like for dinner next week?"

"What did you say you sing when making burritos?"

"You're just going to have to order them to find out."

"I've got some big news," Libby said as I hopped into her car. We were headed to Calcott Ave to pick out bridesmaid dresses. "The party planner for Kyle's firm's charity gala backed out for medical reasons." She bounced in her seat, and her blond ponytail swung back and forth. "Kyle convinced the firm to give it to me instead."

"Nice. I'm sure your boss was thrilled when you brought her that gig."

She bit her lip. "I didn't bring it to her."

"What do you mean?"

"That's my other piece of news." Libby hit the brakes at a stop sign and turned to me. "I quit my job."

"You quit?"

"Kyle's been pushing me to do it for months. He says his wife doesn't need to work some 9 to 5. And as you know, party planning is hardly 9 to 5 anyway. I didn't get home from the Schwartz Bar Mitzvah party until after 2 am last week."

I shifted in my seat. "I'm confused. Are you giving up working or going out on your own?"

"A little of both, I guess. I mean, planning my wedding alone is almost a full-time job."

"But that'll be over in six months."

"True, but hopefully there will be kids before too long. From the time my parents got divorced, our house was always empty when I got home from school. I hated it. I swore I'd be home for my own kids when I grew up."

"Which could be years from now."

"That's the great thing about party planning." Libby turned onto Calcott. "You take on as many jobs as you can handle. For now, I'll do a few one-off jobs like the upcoming gala. After we get married, I'll ramp it up if I can find enough work. Then when the kids come, I'll either go back to part-time or quit entirely." Libby eased into the parking lot.

"So tell me about this gala."

"Oh, you've got to come. It's going to be the Sunday night before Halloween, so I'm making it a costume party. All the money will go to the center for at-risk youth the firm does pro-bono work for." She parked the car in front of a row of boutiques.

I reached for my door handle, and Libby said, "Wait! I want to give you something first." Libby handed me a box the size of my fist wrapped in purple paper. Libby jiggled in her seat as I unwrapped the box. Inside I found a pedant of an owl, my favorite bird. On the back was etched, *Thanks for being the best maid of honor ever!*

Libby had probably given me thirty little gifts since freshman year of college. Most of them had been small and inexpensive, since she'd never had much money, but even when cash-strapped, she always managed to find some little trinket to express her affection. This one was more than just some trinket, though. The owl was silver with inlaid stones, and it clearly cost a pretty penny. "I haven't even started being your maid of honor..."

"You've been by my side for seven years. I know now won't be any different." Libby teared up as she embraced me, and I started bawling like a true Romano. Our make-up was all smudged as we stepped out of the car and into *Les Fleurs*.

I called Dylan when I got back from Calcott. "How was shopping with Libby?"

"You're going to kill me." I hid my face behind my hand even though Dylan couldn't see me. "I spent way more than I should have."

"Amber, it's your money. Do whatever you want with it."

"Yeah, but I want to give this whole Cash Machine thing a chance."

"What went wrong?"

It ached to tell him, as though he was the priest at St. Joseph's. "We went out for bridesmaid dresses, but then it was lunchtime, so we stopped for a bite. Then Libby wanted to get her nails done. You know how it is."

"Manicures are one hurdle I've never had to face."

"You know what I mean. Anyway, there are two things I wanted to run by you. The first is that Kyle's firm is having a Halloween gala. The firm does pro-bono work for a center for at-risk youth, and all the money raised is going to them."

"Yes," Dylan's tone was flat. "I've heard all about this gala."

"What you might not have heard is that the original party planner had to back out. Kyle got them to hire Libby instead. It would mean so much to her if we came."

Dylan sighed. "Amber, you know I don't go out for things like this.

"But this is for charity. You don't even give charity?"

"I do. 10% of everything I make."

Wow. For all my talk, I wasn't giving anywhere near as much. "Then what's the problem?"

"I consider my charitable contributions like I do my investments. I want to get the most bang for my buck as possible."

Until Dylan spoke, it had never struck me as an issue that this event raising money for charity would itself cost a fortune. "I guess galas don't offer a very big bang for your buck, do they?"

"I'm guessing not."

"If we're both just guessing, then we should at least know for sure before I'm going to let you off the hook. We can ask Libby next week."

"Next week?"

"Libby wants us to double date next Saturday." I promised her I'd pass on her suggestion, but I braced myself for Dylan's response. "She thought we could go out for pizza and a movie."

"Aren't you making me Mexican?"

I loved that Dylan looked forward to my cooking, even if it was for a lost bet. "We can do that a different night."

"I've got a better idea. Instead of making Mexican, why don't we all *make* pizza and *rent* a movie."

I squinted. "I can't picture Libby and Kyle baking pizza."

"Me neither, but I can't wait to see them try."

"Don't worry, Libby." Kyle took a swig of beer and tapped his pocket. "I've got Domino's on standby in case this pizza tastes like ass."

"If you eat Domino's, you must like your pizza tasting like ass." I kneaded the dough on Kyle's granite counter. "My family's been making pizza since yours was swinging from the trees."

"We'll see, Amber, just try not to make a mess of the counters, OK?"

"You know," Dylan said, "we didn't have to do it at your place."

"What did you want?" Kyle folded his head under his hands as if in a tornado drill. "The four of us to watch a movie crowded around your computer monitor, deep in the bowels of The Crypt?"

"We could have done it at Amber's."

"No way. When Libby moved in, we upgraded to a 67-inch screen with surround sound. It's better than being in the theaters. And if the movie sucks, you can always make out on the couch." Kyle puckered his lips at Dylan.

Dylan shoved Kyle away. "Amber's got a stacked kitchen."

"Don't you worry, little buddy, we've got everything we need right here."

"This is going to be fun." Libby pulled two aprons out of a shopping bag. "I haven't made pizza since I was a kid. Check out what I got us, honey." Her apron said *Professional Chef*, his said *Professional Taster*.

"I think you have these backwards," Kyle said.

"Please. You could burn cereal." Libby peaked over at the floured countertop. "Amber, tell me what to do."

"You can start on toppings. I bought a ton, so find out what everyone wants."

"Make mine a double anchovy," Kyle said.

Libby looked at him out of the corner of her eye. "Then you can forget about making out on the couch."

I went to preheat the oven, then stopped. "Kyle, your oven is still taped up."

"What tape?"

I yanked at the strip of blue, which squeaked as it pulled away from the oven. "The packing tape they put on it when it comes from the factory. You've never used this thing?"

"Of course we use it. All the time. Why, my Libby is a genius in the kitchen. Aren't you, honey." He nuzzled up to Libby. "She's just careful to reseal the oven after each use to keep out the moisture. Once these things begin to rust, you might as well throw them away."

I opened the oven. "Wise of her to also reinsert the operating manual."

"That way, it'll never get lost." Kyle kissed Libby's cheek. "That's my Libby, always one step ahead."

"You know, Kyle," Libby said, "if your hands were as fast as your mouth, maybe we'd get the pizza done tonight."

"Nothing wrong with my hands."

"Hey!" Libby slapped his hand away. "Keep them to yourself."

Before this conversation got any more awkward, I decided to step in. "Dylan and I were talking about the Halloween gala. What's the charity it's going for?"

"Crossroads. They're a center for at-risk youth. They're kind of a pet project at our firm. We do pro-bono work for them whenever they need legal help."

"But a gala must be a pretty expensive event." I tried giving voice to Dylan's concerns. "How much money can you really generate from something like that?"

"The firm picks up the cost of the gala." Kyle flexed his muscles, as if he and his team were warriors for noble causes and not a bunch of beer-bellied corporate attorneys. "All the money from the ticket prices and the silent auction will go directly to Crossroads."

That was the answer I was hoping to hear. Even Dylan couldn't object to the gala now. Could he?

Then he spoke. "The event must be costing the firm a fortune, then."

"It is," Libby said. "But it's amazing PR."

"Exactly," Kyle broke in. "How often do you hear positive news stories about law firms? This little project helps us present a different narrative."

Dylan slapped Kyle on the back. "Makes you sound like a bunch of modern-day Robin Hoods?"

"Something like that." Kyle downed the rest of his beer and grabbed two more. "Come on, Dylan," he said, handing Dylan one of the beers, "I want to show you my new chess set."

Dylan followed him into the living room, but it was an open-plan apartment, so I could still see them. "That's not new," Dylan said. "It's the same one you've had since college."

Kyle examined the board. "You know, I think you're right." He sat down at one side. "As long as we're out here, we might as well play a game."

I rolled my eyes at Libby. "So much for the four of us cooking together."

"Trust me, you don't want Kyle cooking anyway."

Kyle grabbed two pawns and mixed them up behind his back. He held them out to Dylan, "Choose."

Dylan shot me a guilty look, as if asking if it was OK to play rather than help out. "Go ahead," I said. "You boys have your fun. I owe you a meal anyway."

Dylan pointed to Kyle's right hand.

Kyle opened his hand. "Ah, black. You always did like playing from behind."

"Shut up and move." Dylan focused on the board, even though there wasn't anything to see yet. "King's pawn, like always?"

Kyle lifted the pawn in front of his king and moved it two spaces. "That's right. I stick with proven winners."

I don't know what proof Kyle was talking about, since Dylan quietly beat him in three straight games. Libby jumped in before they could start a fourth. "Pizza's in the oven. Time to start the movie."

"Since you bums didn't help with baking, we're picking the film," I said.

"Great." Kyle rolled his eyes. "It's going to be some romantic comedy, isn't it?"

"You'd better believe it. The king of them all: *When Harry Met Sally*. Thought we'd stick with a proven winner." I sent Dylan a wink.

"Your call," Kyle said. "You two lovebirds want the big couch or the love seat?"

"We'll take the big one," I said.

"Hoping to go horizontal?"

Libby elbowed Kyle in the gut.

Dylan said, "Amber just wants enough room to leave some space between us."

That *had* been what I was thinking, but it felt awkward hearing it said out loud. Out of embarrassment, I didn't go to the far end of the couch; I sat more toward the middle. Dylan sat next to me, still leaving a gap between us. But as the lights went off and the movie started, I inched toward him, and he did the same. Before long, our legs were touching. Then Dylan made the oh-so-bold move (for middle school perhaps) of reaching an arm around me and placing his hand on my shoulder. The second he did, an alarm went off on my phone.

"Dammit, Amber, you got a chastity app on that thing?" Kyle said. Hot splotches rose up my neck—it was a good thing it was so dark in here.

Libby elbowed him again. "Shut up, Kyle, or I'll get a chastity app myself."

"It means the pizza's done." I shot up and straightened my sweater. "It's about time, too. It'll give you boys something harmless to do with your hands."

"Libby, you are the greatest cook in the world." Kyle licked a dollop of sauce from his fingers. "This pizza is fabulous."

The pizza was fabulous, if I do say so myself. And Libby had been a big help. She'd washed all the dishes and wiped the countertop. We'd made a total of four pies, three of them pizza, the fourth a cherry pie I brought out for dessert. Dylan and I never did get cozy again on the couch, but he attacked my cooking with abandon, which filled me up in a way food never could.

I'd seen *When Harry Met Sally* at least a dozen times. We were on our third pizza when we hit my favorite dialog:

Harry: *There are two kinds of women. High maintenance and low maintenance.*
Sally: *What am I?*

Harry: *You're the worst kind. You're high maintenance, but you think you're low maintenance.*

Kyle cozied up to his fiancé. "You see, Libby, that's what makes you so terrific. You're high maintenance, and you know it." He kissed her cheek. "It's a damn good thing you wound up with me, and Dylan got Amber. The other way around would have been a disaster. Though I'm not sure a girl low maintenance enough for Dylan has ever been born. At least not in this country. Perhaps some third-world refugee."

Dylan laughed this off. "Have you checked the scoreboard lately?" he asked.

Scoreboard?

"I try to avoid it." Kyle picked a cherry with his fingers. "Just leaves me depressed." He served himself a double slice of pie and returned to the movie.

A little after midnight, I dropped Dylan off at The Crypt. On our way there, I brought up the gala again. I hated the idea of going without a date.

He put a hand to his stomach. "The whole thing makes me nauseous."

"Why? All the money you give goes to charity."

"I'd be surprised if what they raise at the gala even matches the cost of the event." Dylan's body stiffened. "The firm could just write a check and have greater impact."

I stopped at a light and turned to ask, "Don't you care about the at-risk kids?"

"Come on, Amber. You think buying costumes and attending a Halloween gala is the best way to help these kids?"

"You have a better way to help them?"

"I sure do. If I know Kyle's firm, they're going to pass whatever money is raised over to some high-end contractor to fix up the center." Dylan's voice grew animated. "Think how much farther that money would go if we volunteered even one day of our time and did the work ourselves."

I could probably use my girlish charms to persuade him to come but realized he'd resent me for it. "OK, I'm in. I'll give you a day to fix up the center. But I still want to go to the gala." The light turned green, and I took a left.

Dylan stared into the distance. "Do what you want."

After a long silence, I figured I should change the subject. "What was that scoreboard you and Kyle were talking about?"

A mischievous smirk rolled up Dylan's cheeks. "Just a little contest the two of us have."

"I take it you're killing him?"

"Total destruction."

"Good."

When I parked the car in front of The Crypt, Dylan hesitated. I felt the heat of his gaze seeping into my cheek and dared not turn. I got the distinct impression he was debating whether to lean over and kiss me goodnight. But Dylan was nothing if not disciplined. I'd told him no intimacy, and he was going to respect it. He stepped out of the car and waved goodbye.

I drove away, cursing Dylan's discipline under my breath.

CHAPTER 4

WHEELS
AND DEALS

"**I** did it." I was practically bouncing as Dylan came in the following Saturday morning. "I got my car money."

"Awesome." Dylan put down his toolbox and hung his jacket on the coat rack. "How'd you do it?"

"Credit cards. Just like you said."

Dylan's excitement dropped, and his eyes narrowed. "I'll let you explain what you mean while I take a look at that leaky toilet of yours." He'd noticed the constant hissing coming out of my bathroom the previous week and promised to fix it the next time he came over.

"It's just a drip," I said as I followed Dylan and his massive toolbox to the bathroom. "It's no big deal."

"The toilet is your number one water guzzler. Even a small leak can cost you over a hundred gallons of water a day." He put his toolbox down next to the toilet. Despite my calling it just a small drip, there was no denying that the hiss of the tank was almost constant. "You must have noticed that your water bills were astronomical."

"Um…" I never looked at my bills. They were auto-deducted from my account each month. Even if I'd seen them, I doubt I would have detected anything wrong. It's not like I knew the size of the average water bill. "Is this another of your metaphors about debt?"

Dylan ignored the question. He removed the top of the toilet tank and flushed the toilet, watching for who knows what. "Tell me about this credit card business."

"Well, I've been signing up for cards like mad, just like you told me to. I got that one with the zero balance transfer fee and zero interest for twelve months, so other than paying the monthly minimum, I don't have to worry about that massive balance. Another card came with a $200 sign-up bonus, 2% rewards, and no interest for nine months. I've got a $10,000 limit on that card. So there's my car money."

"Careful now, Amber. Credit is a dangerous game." Dylan pulled out a wrench. "How expensive a car are you thinking of buying?"

"Really, I could use the whole $10,000 and still come out way ahead of the lease terms I'd get."

"Don't let an unused credit line confuse you into thinking you have more money than you do." Dylan rubbed his fingers together. "How much *cash* do you have in the bank?"

"Well, now that I don't have to worry about paying back my outstanding balance, after my next paycheck, I should have about $2000."

"Bear in mind, even that $2000 is not yours. It's still money you owe." Dylan leaned over the tank. "But I think you should be able to spend that much and still be OK."

"You're not suggesting I buy a car for only $2000?" I sat at the edge of the tub. "That's insane. I can't get anything for that amount."

"Have you looked?"

"Not at that price. I was looking in the $10,000 range. Would that be so bad?" I leaned in to watch Dylan work.

"Do you have a rag or something? This could get messy."

"Yeah, sure." I went into the linen closet, brought out a pile of old rags, and dropped one next to the toilet.

"For $10,000, you can get a great, reliable car." Dylan turned off the water and started detaching parts of my toilet. "It's the same cost as the lease, but unlike with the lease, you'll still have value left after three years, probably about $5000 worth. The problem is that for the next year, you'll be making payments even higher than your lease payments. That's a killer if you want to build a financial runway."

"What's a financial runway?"

"It's the amount of time you could go without income and still be OK." Dylan pulled a beige thing-a-ma-bob out of the tank and placed it on the rag.

"Why would I go without income."

"You could be fired. The teacher's union could go on strike. Who knows. More importantly, once you have a solid runway, you can afford to take risks."

"What kind of risks?"

"All kinds. Investments. Changing jobs. Starting a business. You never know when an amazing opportunity will come your way, but if you're living paycheck to paycheck, you might not be able to float yourself long enough to take it."

"How much runway do I need?"

"I think anyone who doesn't have access to three months' worth of expenses is crazy." Dylan grunted as he worked out a black thing stuck in the tank. "I prefer to have a full year. That's when you get the flexibility to take some real chances."

"I need a year's worth of money in the bank, just sitting there?"

"It doesn't have to just sit, but it needs to be easily accessible. I have very little in the bank. I put almost all my money into my properties. But I also have a line of credit that allows me access to over a year's worth of living costs in a matter of moments." Dylan jerked back and pulled out a thick black ring with cracks along the edges. "Here's your problem."

"That little thing?"

"Little? This is what seals the entire toilet." Dylan dropped it in front of me. It smelled pretty rank, but out of politeness, I didn't pinch my nose. "Thousands of gallons of water are seeping through those little cracks every month."

"This is another metaphor, isn't it? You're telling me I have to seal up the cracks in my financial foundation, aren't you?"

"Must you always think like an English teacher?"

"You're just going to have to take me as I am." I picked up the cracked toilet seal. "So to get this runway going, you want me to buy a car for *only $2000*?"

"You're free to do what you want, but that's my advice."

"Am I going to have to push this thing uphill?"

"Not if you buy it smart."

"Like how?"

Dylan shrugged. "Do I have a car?"

"Are you freaking kidding me?"

"We need a new ring. We can discuss it on the way to the hardware store." He washed his hands, dried them on a clean rag, and headed toward the door.

"Wait!" I ran after him. "You come across as Mr. Expert telling me I can do this, and you don't even know yourself?"

"I could guess." He put on his jacket and pulled my keys off their hook. "Are you driving, or am I?"

"Gimme those." I grabbed my keys out of his hand. "It's my car, and as long as I still have a decent car to drive, I'll drive it myself."

Once we were on the road, I said, "If you can't help me, I might as well go to a dealer. At least they can tell me what my options are."

"No, they can tell you what *their* options are. They're looking out for their interests, not yours."

"One of the ways they look out for their interests is by providing good service. You can't go through life thinking everyone is out to get you. You said the same thing about the credit card companies."

"You were awfully giddy this morning about your credit card results."

I gripped the wheel tighter. "But you admit you don't know anything about cars."

"Look, Amber, I'm not saying you shouldn't buy from a dealer any more than I'm saying you shouldn't carry a credit card. Just don't depend upon a dealer for your education, because they'll always pitch you the cars they have, whether they're the best fit for you or not."

"So how else am I supposed to learn this stuff?"

Dylan sighed. "Turn onto Oak, and pull up at Jensen's Hardware."

Dylan jumped out as soon as I pulled in. I thought to follow, but I'd barely turned off the car when Dylan came running back out, toilet ring in hand. When we were back on the road, he said, "Let's say Kyle calls you up one day and tells you his firm is desperate. They've got a major client they're pitching, and due to a computer crash, they've lost all the research they need for a presentation. Worse, one of their paralegals is getting married that day, and virtually the entire staff is at the wedding. He's about to go to dinner with the client and needs to make the presentation in two hours. The research will be mind-numbingly boring, but he knows you can do it. He's so desperate that he's willing to pay you $1000 an hour to get it done. Would you do it?"

"For $1000 an hour? Hell yeah."

"Good. Then when we get back, I'll finish fixing the toilet while you research how to buy a great used car dirt cheap. I promise you that by the time I'm done, you'll have figured out how to save yourself at least $1000."

A half-hour later, Dylan flushed the toilet. It hissed as the tank refilled, and then the hissing came to a complete stop. I'd gotten so used to the toilet hissing that I'd tuned it out, but I much preferred the peaceful silence. Dylan came into the kitchen, where I sat at the counter with my laptop. I prepared to share with him what I'd found, but he just walked past me and started pulling stuff out from the fridge and pantry. This was his way of telling me to keep at it while he took care of lunch. So I kept reading the blog post I was on, for almost an entire minute. Then I closed my laptop and went to join him. Dylan was a hell of a lot more competent in the kitchen than Libby, but I still didn't like the way he hacked away at my vegetables. I pulled a chef's knife out of the drawer. "I'll chop," I said. "You're making a green salad?"

"Unless there's something more exotic you'd like. But I don't mind cooking. You've made me two meals in a row now."

"That's sweet." I bumped him aside. "Why don't you make panini to go with the salad. You'll find bread in that drawer over there and take what you want from the fridge to put inside. In the third drawer below the cutlery, you'll find the sandwich maker."

"Aren't you supposed to be doing research?"

"I did." The research had been shockingly easy. Yet, without Dylan urging me, I probably would've just gone to a dealer without bothering. "I Googled how to buy a cheap, reliable, used car, and in no time, I found dozens of blog posts telling me what to look for. I stopped reading when I found the same suggestions coming up over and over."

Dylan pulled the leftover pecorino, a box of arugula, and a portobello mushroom out of the fridge. "What'd you learn about cars?"

"First, some brands are made to last longer than others."

"Like Honda and Toyota?"

"Yes, though those brands have such a reputation for reliability that they don't depreciate as fast. Other Japanese brands like Mazda, Nissan, and Subaru also have great track records, but their prices drop faster."

Dylan sliced a baguette. "What else did you get?"

"10 years and 100,000 miles."

"You want to stay under those numbers?"

"No, but so many buyers aim to stay under 10 years and 100,000 miles that cars over those numbers plummet in price." I diced a pair of cucumbers and slipped them into the salad bowl. "Apparently, good cars can easily do 15 years and 200,000 miles these days. I searched on Craigslist and found plenty of cars in my price range that fit those criteria."

"You searched for cars up to $2000?" He gently buttered the bread.

"$3000. That's another point I kept reading over and over. I should plan on negotiating, especially if I'm paying cash. So there's a decent chance that someone advertising for three will take my two if it's in greenbacks."

"Nice." He thinly sliced the mushrooms and layered them onto the bread. "So you're all set to start looking at cars?"

"No, I found several articles on the more technical aspects of how to inspect a car. Those will take a little longer to go through." I squeezed a lime into the salad.

"If you want, we can go through those together while we eat." He closed he sandwich maker and pressed down. "Have you gotten your $1000 worth yet?"

"I got more than that from the first article. It's a crazy thing. When you told me to do the research, I knew just what to do. But had I been shopping for a car on my own, I would've skipped that step."

"I've found that to be one of the most powerful lessons in building my Cash Machine. Ignorance isn't cheap. As Marie Forleo says, 'Everything is Figureoutable.' I can't count how many times an hour of research has saved me from making a colossal mistake."

The next Sunday, I pulled up at Dylan's place at 7 am. "I thought you liked to sleep in on weekends?" he said as he answered the door.

"No choice, today's the day. My car lease is up this week, so either I'm replacing it today, or the dealer will most likely talk me into getting a new car when I return this one."

"What's the plan?"

I handed him an envelope. "You get to be my big strapping bodyguard and protect the cash."

He peeked into the envelope. "How much is here?"

"$2000." A grin forced its way into my cheeks. "I've been pulling cash out of the ATM all week."

A morning chill blew into the apartment, and Dylan threw on a pullover. "Where are we going?"

"I've set up appointments to see ten cars today."

"Great." He closed the front door behind him. "I know how you ladies get when you shop. You'll probably buy five of them."

"You shut up and guard the money." I slapped his chest. "Just remember that you're the muscle and leave the negotiating to me."

"Well, well. Look who found her confidence."

"I must have read thirty articles on buying a used car," I said as I got into the driver's seat, "and skimmed 400 car listings before narrowing it down to these ten. I'm ready to go."

Dylan buckled in and sat with his hands on his lap like a schoolboy. "What's stop number one, Miss Romano?"

"You keep this attitude up, little Dylan, and I might not let you out of the car to see the 12-year-old Mazda 3 I've got lined up. And you'd miss out because it's cherry red."

"I promise to be good," Dylan said. "How many miles does it have on it?"

"154,000."

"That's no spring chicken. What's the price?"

"$2800. The owner told me three times on the phone that the price was negotiable. He sounded desperate for someone to make him an offer."

"She's a beauty, ain't she?" The owner slid his hands over the curve of the hood, but his eyes watched Dylan.

I cleared my throat. "He."

"What's that?"

"Guys always call their cars *she*, like they're buying themselves some surrogate girlfriend, which I guess is not so far from the truth. But this one's going to be mine, so it's a *he*."

Dylan started at this. "You looking for a surrogate boyfriend?"

"Shut up and guard the money."

The owner approached me, and the stench of his cologne left me gasping for oxygen. "Then he's a beauty. Happy?"

I ran my fingers along the hood. The car did have a flawless paint job. "He shines in the sun; I'll give you that much."

"How about taking him for a ride?"

I circled around to the side to get a better look at the tires. I slipped a penny into the tread, with Lincoln's head facing down, just like I'd read online. Then I reached in to do it again further back. "I'm thinking not. Like many older men, this one's starting to bald."

Dylan nodded his head slowly as if to say, *damn, girl*. I felt good to be the knowledgeable one for a change.

The owner ran a hand through his thinning hair. "There's still some tread on the tires."

"Now, don't get me wrong." I backed away from the car. "A well-groomed bald man can still be dignified. Yet, this particular gentleman is only balding on one side. That's not just age. It's neglect."

"What?"

"You have uneven tire wear. That could mean your alignment's off or worse." I shook my head. "At the very least, it means she was poorly maintained."

"I thought it was a he?" The owner crossed his arms.

"Not anymore." I winked at him. "I'm going to let you keep this girl all to yourself."

"I can go down to $2200."

"Sorry," I said, "but I don't intervene in abusive relationships."

He licked his lips. "$2000."

I sucked in my breath and took another look at the candy red coat. This guy might have skipped a few tune-ups, but there was no question he kept it well waxed. "There's no way I'd take this car without an inspection, but for $2000, I'll at least take him for a test drive."

"This is exhausting." I sank into the seat of my own car, and a quick look at the clock told me it was three in the afternoon. We'd already looked at six vehicles. I was relieved when two owners called to say their cars had already been sold before I got there—the fewer choices I had to process, the better.

"You're doing great, Amber." Dylan opened a bag of grapes he'd bought while I filled up the car.

"I was doing great in the beginning, but now they're all starting to blur together." I grabbed a few grapes and popped one in my mouth. "Let's face it, Dylan, any car in my price range is bound to have problems."

"All we need is something serviceable. What's next?"

I turned left onto a small residential road. "Honda Civic, 9-years-old, 122,000 miles."

"That's in your price range?"

"$2400."

"Why so cheap? You said Hondas maintain their value."

We pulled into a driveway next to a grey civic with a large dent on the rear passenger side door. "That's why." A tiny strip of rust outlined the dent.

"You knew about this?"

"It didn't look so bad on the pictures." I set the car into reverse. "I think we should just keep driving."

"Too late. The owner spotted us. We have to at least get out and say hello."

I parked the car and forced a smile.

An older man in a cardigan came out of the house. "Hi there, you must be Amber. My name's Joseph, and this is my wife, Meg." Meg stepped out, carrying two glasses of water. "This was Meg's car, but one of our daughters just got a new car from her work, so she's passing her old car onto Meg. I've got all the maintenance records right here. As you can see, we've had the oil changed every three thousand miles. We did a major tune-up and replaced the tires just over a year ago."

"How often do you rotate the tires?" I asked.

"Once every six months."

"Any mechanical issues?" I was so hoping he'd say yes.

"None." He smiled at the car with a glint of nostalgia. "Runs like a dream. The only issue was a minor accident two years ago. But we had it checked out, and the damage doesn't impact the safety of the car, or it's driving at all. The biggest downside is that the dented door no longer opens, but since we could access the back seat from the other side on the rare occasions we need it, it didn't make sense to invest the money fixing it up."

To me, the biggest downside was that the dent made the car an eye-sore, but I didn't say so. "You're the only owners?"

"Oh, yes. I bought it for Meg as a thirtieth-anniversary present." He took the keys out of his pocket and held them out to me. "Would you like to take it for a drive?"

With the other cars I'd looked at, the owner always came along for the test drive, but Joseph trusted us to go out without him. That gave me a chance to do something I'd been dying to try all day. I drove it slowly around the corner and out of sight. "Hold on," I said to Dylan. I floored the car, taking it to thirty, forty, fifty miles an hour, then slammed on the brakes.

"Whoa, girl. Where'd you learn to drive?"

"In the Walmart parking lot, but that maneuver I picked up from a blog post. It tests the acceleration and the brakes."

"Both seemed smooth. Let's face it. This car's in great shape."

"Mechanically, yes. But what about the door?"

"That's the best part." Dylan put a hand on my shoulder. "It's pre-dented."

"Pre-dented is supposed to be a *good* thing?"

"Absolutely. What would happen to your current car if you dented it before turning it back into the dealer?"

"They'd slap me with a huge fine."

"Of course, because a dented car has a much lower resale value. These guys already dented this little Honda. They've taken all that depreciation already. You could get into another accident in this thing, and, as long as it still drives well, it would hardly depreciate at all."

In theory, Dylan was right. At least five of the blog posts I'd read over the past week talked about the major bargains you can get on cars with cosmetic damage. But this was going to be *my* car, perhaps for years. "I keep thinking about that red Mazda we saw this morning." I handed my phone to Dylan. "Look."

"You took a selfie with it?"

"Stupid, huh?"

"That car's got trouble written all over it. From what you told me, this one could probably do another 75,000 miles without any serious mechanical trouble."

I nodded. But as I turned the car back toward Meg and Joseph's street, my insides tightened. Changing my credit cards was easy. Following Dylan's advice saved me a ton of money with no downside (other than the fact that my old card had my college logo on it). This situation felt different. I'd be driving an older, dented car that was so-not-my-color. Or I could walk into a nice dealership, where they'd serve me a cappuccino and lease me whatever I wanted at an affordable monthly rate. It was obvious which choice I was more comfortable with, but I looked over at Dylan and knew that this ugly, dented Honda would lead me on the path to building a Cash Machine, the path toward a life with this guy.

I held those soft eyes of his. I'd never known anyone so sincere, so without pretension. More than anything, what I wanted at this point in my life was to find a good man. Dylan was nothing like what I pictured, but there was no question he was a good man. The kind of man I could build a future with. "Let's go back and see what kind of deal we can get on this."

"Your car drives well," I said to Joseph and Meg. "I'd like to offer you $1900, contingent on it passing inspection."

"Well, we did leave a little wiggle room in the price," Joseph said, "but I'm afraid $1900 is too low for us. We'd be willing to drop to $2200."

I hated this part, negotiating with a sweet, elderly couple. I looked over at Dylan, and he gave me a reassuring nod. "I'm sorry. It's a great car, but that's still a bit above my budget."

"What is your budget?"

"$2000."

"That's mighty low." Joseph hesitated. "How would you be paying for this?"

"Dylan, show them what we've got."

Dylan pulled out the envelope and fanned out the twenty hundred-dollar bills. "Deal."

An hour later, we received a clean bill of health from the mechanic. "We should celebrate," Dylan said.

"You got it." I folded the paperwork from the mechanic into the car's user manual. "But I want to make one stop first."

"Where?"

"The dealership. It's time to turn in my leased car."

"Don't you have until Wednesday?"

"Yep, and if that car gets so much as a scratch between now and Wednesday, I'm going to go insane. I'm not taking any chances now that I've got a new set of wheels." I tossed a set of keys to Dylan. "You drive the ugly, dented Honda. I'll drive my old car this one last time."

CHAPTER 5

LEGACY

When I got off the phone with my mom, I blew my nose, wiped my eyes, and tried to compose myself. I thought about calling Libby—she was my best friend after all—but I was a little surprised to find that the voice I most wanted to hear was Dylan's.

"Amber, you sound awful. Is everything OK?"

"My Great Grandma Mona passed away." Tears started gushing again, and I pulled one tissue after another from the box.

"The one who taught you to make Tiramisu? I'm so sorry to hear that."

"I'm flying out in a couple of hours for the funeral."

"Do you want me to come with you?"

Was he nuts? Didn't he have a clue what it would mean in my family if I showed up at a funeral with a guy? I might as well send out a Save the Date card. "You're sweet, but no. When I introduce you to my family, it will be on my terms, not upstaging poor Grandma Mona at her own funeral."

"Can I at least take you to the airport?"

"Dylan, you don't have a car."

"I can take yours. That way, I can pick you up when you return."

"It will be easiest to use airport parking. With my old leased car, I used to be nervous about leaving it in a big public lot. I was always paranoid it would get dinged up."

"Another advantage of buying a pre-dented car."

"Yeah, with this one, I might not even notice. I'll call you when I get back, OK?"

To me, Great Grandma Mona was this sweet old woman who spent all day in the kitchen, baking treats for the entire family. We'd visit her twice a year, and I'd spend at least half my time cooking with her. She'd ask me about my life and always remembered the names of my friends and teachers, and later boyfriends.

Sitting at the funeral, it hit me how little I'd asked her about her own life. Grandma Maria's eulogy stretched for three-quarters of an hour, going on and on with details I never knew. Grandma Mona came to America with nothing. Her family had saved for years to afford her passage over. At first, they'd objected to the idea of a single woman making the journey alone. They only relented once arrangements were made for Grandma Mona to move in with her uncle's family in Brooklyn, so she'd at least be under the watchful eyes of family.

There she put her cooking skills to good use and got herself a job in the kitchen of an Italian restaurant. She saved virtually everything she made until she had enough to send for her younger brother. Then the two of them saved up enough to finally bring over their parents. Only once she was surrounded by her family did she marry my Great Grandfather Frank, who died before I was born. His first two businesses failed, and Grandma Mona kept working in that Italian restaurant, even once she had kids of her own, until Grampa Frank finally broke through with his furniture business. Even while raising her kids, Grandma Mona helped out in the back office of the business as much as she could, and when Grampa Frank passed away, she took over running the company until it could be sold.

I thought of my dented car sitting back in the airport parking lot. To me, that old car had been a sacrifice. Meanwhile, Grandma Mona didn't even have a car of her own until she reached her forties. What would she have thought of Dylan? To her, a man had to have gumption about providing for his family. I couldn't help but think she would've liked him. What would she have said about me holding back because he didn't take me out to eat? Grandma Mona had a sharp tongue and wasn't afraid to give any of us a piece of her mind. I'd have heard an earful from her if I'd dared bring up the hardships of sticking with a man like Dylan while he built a foundation for his family.

There was hardly a dry eye during the funeral, but the luncheon afterwards was a different story. Family reunions were family reunions, and no matter what the occasion, whether it was a funeral or a wedding, we'd sooner or later do what my family did best: gossip. My cousin Maria Rose sat next to me. Her dress was a shade too red and three inches too short for a funeral, but I supposed this was as conservative as she came.

"I didn't know half those things about Grandma Mona, did you? What are you going to miss most? For me, it's her cannolis. I swear I'll never learn to cook like that." She tightened her gaze. "Amber, what happened to you?"

"What do you mean?"

"You look different."

"Well, my eyes are a mess."

"Oh please, none of us could stop bawling during Grandma Maria's talk." Maria Rose blew off my comment. "I mean, you look good."

"Thanks. I guess —."

"What's his name?"

"What?"

"The last time you looked like this, you were head-over-heels for that loser who flaked out on you in college." She leaned in. "So. What's this one's name?"

If I didn't fess up, Marie Rose would recruit our other cousins to bully it out of me. "Dylan."

I watched for signs of recognition in her face, but there weren't any. None of my family met him in college, and even if Maria Rose had, she probably wouldn't have connected it. After all, at the rate she dated, she's probably gone through two Dylans since then herself. "And Dylan does…?"

What was I supposed to tell her, that Dylan worked on a home remodeling crew and still waited tables on Friday nights to make extra cash? Grandma Mona would have understood, but would the rest of the family? "He's in real estate."

"Oh yeah?" She leaned back. "What is he, an agent?"

"No, he owns a few apartment buildings."

"Not bad. Carina, come join us." Maria Rose waved over another cousin who was looking for a seat. "Amber was just telling me about this real estate mogul she's dating."

"Uh, he's not quite —."

"You're dating someone new?" Carina sat down on my other side and bit into a breadstick. "I swear, Aunt Sofia had us half-convinced you were going to wind up an old maid." She put a hand on my knee. "Tell us about the guy! When can we meet him? You're bringing him to Thanksgiving, right?"

"Uh…."

"Oh come on, Amber," Maria Rose piped in. "You have to."

"We haven't been dating for that long."

"How long have you known him?"

How could I explain? "Seven years, but—."

"You're so bringing him!" Carina hit the breadstick onto her plate like a gavel. "Discussion closed."

Dylan surprised me at the airport. He held a bunch of daisies that I'd be willing to bet he picked from his small garden behind The Crypt. I took the daisies from him and said, "I brought you something as well."

"From the funeral?"

"From my time with my family. Close your eyes." I reached my hands around the back of his neck, leaned in, and kissed him, our first kiss since college.

"Does this mean…?"

"Keep it in your pants, sport. It was just a kiss."

"Then why…?"

"Grandma Mona would have wanted me to." Butterflies danced in my stomach. "I can be too harsh on you at times. I want you to know: all this effort you're putting in, it's not lost on me." I pushed my suitcase forward. "And speaking of effort, I'll let you be a gentleman and take my bag."

He took my suitcase and rolled it behind him. With his other hand, he softly held mine. It felt…nice. "How's your family handling it?"

"Grandma Mona was 98, and her health had been going for years, so everyone was prepared." Again, my eyes grew hot with tears. "Still, it's hard to say goodbye to a woman like that."

"I'm sure." Dylan stopped, pulled a neatly folded tissue out of his shirt pocket, and handed it to me. I guess he came prepared. "I remember when my grandfather died. We sat around for days, telling one Gramps story after the next. Is that how it was?"

"Uh…" How could I tell Dylan that Grandma Mona was hardly in the ground when Maria Rose first asked me about my romantic life and that, from that point on, it was all anyone wanted to talk to me about? "Everyone's eager to meet you."

"You told them about me?"

"What was I supposed to do? Half my aunts already think I'm an old maid. They *insisted* I bring you to Thanksgiving." I gripped his hand a little tighter.

"Just how many relatives will I have to meet?"

"Um…a lot."

"Like 20?"

I actually cackled—right in the middle of the airport parking lot. "Yeah, right. Try 100 if we're lucky."

"100?" Dylan stopped in his tracks. "Your family get-togethers must cost a fortune."

"They do, but Grandma Mona was always willing to pitch in for whoever needed it."

"She could cook, *and* she was rich?"

"Well, my great-grandfather eventually did quite well for himself." I steered us deeper into the long-term parking area. "Which leads me to the other piece of news from this weekend."

"You've inherited a fortune?"

"Hardly. She had too many descendants to make any of us rich." At this point, we'd reached aisle G5, and I pulled the keys to the Honda out of my purse. "But I got enough that I could have gotten a new car rather than this old, dented one."

"Amber, it's just not worth it. New cars depreciate so fast. They're a killer to anyone striving for financial independence."

"I know, but still…"

"How much did you get?"

I popped open the trunk and faced him. "$20,000."

"That's great. You realize how much time your great-grandmother just saved you?" Dylan lifted the suitcase into the trunk and slammed it shut. "Even with all the changes we've made, it would have taken you years to accumulate that much cash. Now you're ready to start building your Cash Machine."

"Start? What about all the work we've been doing?"

"The Cash Machine is your portfolio of investments that generate passive income. So far, we've just been trying to curb your outflow, so you have some money to work with, but you don't yet have any income-producing assets."

"I don't have any assets at all—other than this thing." I tapped the hood of the car.

"This 'thing' is not an asset, but that's for another time. The point is, with Grandma Mona's help, you can now use the most powerful tool I know to start building your Cash Machine."

"What's that?"

"The House Hack."

CHAPTER 6

THE HOUSE HACK

Wednesdays were my shortest days at school, so I booked an appointment after work with a mortgage agent at my bank. I'm sure Dylan would've been willing to come with me, but I decided to do this step alone. He didn't even know I was going. I told myself that I kept it a secret to surprise him later, but deep down, I knew I wanted to verify his claims.

The loan agent, Gregory, entered data into his computer for a full five minutes before leaning back in his chair. "Based on your current income and credit score, I should be able to pre-qualify you for an FHA loan of up to $125,000."

I scowled. Just when I was starting to think Dylan wasn't full of crap.

"Miss, there's no reason to get upset. Many people come in here and hope to be pre-qualified for higher amounts, but I have to tell you that $125,000 is not so bad. There are plenty of properties in town that go for even less."

I sank into my chair. "Well, my boyfriend seemed to think I'd be able to afford more than that."

Gregory held his hands together on his desk, all proper-like. "Look, the Federal Housing Authority program is remarkable. Through it, the government greatly reduces the down payment you need to purchase a primary residence. But even though you can buy a home with as little as 3.5% down, you still need enough income to make the monthly mortgage payments. It's all a question of risk." Then he gave me that kind of pedantic grin I offered the kid in my class who thought it'd be a good idea to bring his pet snake to school. "We're not going to loan you the money to buy yourself a mansion and then sweat each month over whether we're going to get our payment."

"That makes sense." I swallowed my pride. "I'd just been led to believe I could get more, that's all."

"How much did you hope to borrow?"

I squinted my eyes, embarrassed to even say it. "Enough to buy four apartments?"

"Four?" A wide grin grew over the mortgage agent's face.

"Pretty funny, eh? My boyfriend called it a house hack."

"Ah, you should have mentioned." Gregory swiveled back to the computer and punched in a few numbers. "That changes our calculation, doesn't it?"

"It does?" I shot up.

"I'll have to see the exact rental values on whatever property you find to give you a final number." He faced me again. "But if that's your plan, I ought to be able to lend you $300,000 or more."

"Wait." My jaw literally fell. "What?"

"It's very simple, Miss."

Miss? Was he getting pedantic again? "Call me Amber."

He nodded and continued. "As I said, getting a mortgage is all about risk."

"But why should buying four units change the equation?"

"Because, unless I misunderstand your plans, three of those units will be income-producing. The more income you make, the more you can pay back, so the more we'll lend."

Part of me was excited at the prospect of such a big loan, but another part growled. Why did Dylan have to be right all the time? "I thought this FHA thingy was just for primary residences?"

"Precisely, so we won't be able to lend you enough money to buy apartments in four different buildings. But the government allows for one property to have up to four living units and still be considered your primary residence."

My head tilted in confusion. "But how can it be both a primary residence and income-producing?"

Gregory shook his head. "That's what we call a legal fiction."

"Legal fiction?"

"Yes, that's when the law defines something to be different than we all know it to be. The most famous is a corporation, which the law treats as a person, even though it's not. In your case, Miss, the law allows us to consider a building of up to four units as a primary residence, even though we all see it for what it is, a legitimate commercial income source."

"That's idiotic."

"I don't make the policies, Miss."

"Maybe not, but the government doesn't force your bank to write these mortgages, does it?"

"No, but we're in the business of lending money. The more we can safely lend out, the happier we are. As I said, it's all about the risk. If the government is willing to absorb more risk on a property of up to four units, we're happy to let them do so. There's a strong rental market in town. Based on the numbers I see before me, I'd say that having three decent sized rental units could more than double your income."

"But I'll also be paying a lot in interest, won't I?"

"Yes, especially in the beginning. But much of that is tax-deductible."

This was getting complicated. "So how am I supposed to know if I'm even making money?"

"I'm not an expert in real estate accounting, but I'm happy to connect you with a specialist in this area if you'd like to know more."

"Sounds like you guys are all in cahoots."

"We are. There are too many moving parts for any of us to go it alone, so real estate folk network like crazy."

"In that case, I should introduce you to my boyfriend, Dylan."

Gregory slapped the desk, and his face lit up. "Dylan's your boyfriend?"

I leaned in. "You know him?"

"We belong to the same real estate club. No wonder you're looking to house hack. That's his favorite tactic. I've written him three mortgages over the years."

"All for house hacks?"

"Yes."

"I thought the house hack only works if it's your primary residence?"

"It does." Gregory's whole energy had changed. He now leaned back and laughed. I half expected him to light up a cigar. "Still, that doesn't mean we force you to stay there for life."

"But Dylan said that the terms are better on a primary mortgage loan than on a commercial one."

"That's true. For instance, if you wanted to buy a five-unit building rather than four, we could no longer consider it a primary residence. Not only would you pay a higher interest rate, but you'd need a downpayment of at least 25% that we expect for commercial loans rather than the 3.5% we're discussing today."

"But once he moves out, the property becomes commercial, doesn't it?"

"We don't renegotiate just because your circumstances change. Once a mortgage is written for a primary residence, it stays that way for the duration of the loan, which can be up to 30 years."

"You can have multiple homes on primary mortgage loans?"

"Indeed. I have clients who come in for a new one every year. Dylan himself has mortgages through us for three homes and a total of 11 units."

"You wrote him mortgages on 11 units, all classified as his primary residence, even though he can only live in one?"

"You got it, Amber."

What happened to Miss? "You have no problem with this?"

"Why should I? The numbers for each mortgage worked out. All Dylan's properties cash flow. The risk was minimal."

"What do you mean they cash flow?"

"Cash flow is the amount of money left in your pocket after paying all your expenses. So not only are Dylan's apartments paying themselves back, they also put money into his pocket each month." Gregory's grin disappeared as he caught my eye. "Is something bothering you?"

I crossed my arms. "It just seems so unfair."

"What's unfair, Amber?"

"That you've got all these loopholes. Why should Dylan own 11 primary residences, when most people can't afford even one? Isn't this just another example of how the rich get richer?"

"Not this time. I'll give you that it's a loophole, but primary residence policies, and especially the Federal Housing Authority program, don't exist for the rich. The amount you can borrow under the FHA program is capped, so you can't buy mansions with it, and you have to live there, so the rich can't just use it for investments alone. Besides, the real benefit of the FHA program wouldn't help them anyway."

"What's that?"

"The ability for those who don't have standard down payment money to buy a home with almost no money down. The flip side of doing this is that the government requires mortgage insurance for such loans, which is an extra expense. The rich can put down a larger downpayment and spare themselves this cost. Sorry to burst your rich-get-richer bubble, but this particular loophole exists solely for the poor and working class. Like Dylan." Gregory lifted his eyebrows. "You don't consider him rich, do you?"

"Dylan?" I couldn't help but giggle. "Who doesn't own a car and won't even go out to eat? No, I don't think of him as rich."

"There you go. In my experience, there are financial regulations that benefit the rich and others that benefit the poor. The only ones that consistently lose out are the ignorant. In this case, the law benefits the poor. That's fortunate for you, for based on the numbers I see, you're anything but rich yourself, so there's no reason you can't use this program to buy yourself a nice home and a significant source of side income at the same time."

"Can I go out and buy four apartments with $300,000?"

"Oh, yes. It might not be in the exact location you want," he leaned back in his chair again, "and it might need some work, but there are quite a few properties available at that price."

"Come on, Gregory. If it needs work, I'm right back where I started. I need my money for the downpayment and closing costs."

"The FHA program allows you up to a 6% seller assist, meaning that the seller can absorb closing costs of up to 6% of the property's value. So with the right seller, you can avoid most or all of those fees."

"That's still not going to free up enough cash to renovate four apartments."

"No, but if you can come up with 3.5% of the money for the rehab, we can finance the rest and add it into your mortgage."

My jaw went slack again. "You're kidding."

"No, Amber. It's called a 203(k) loan. It's a subset of the FHA program."

"And I can use the 203(k) money to fix up all four apartments?"

"Yep. As we said, all four are still classified as your primary residence."

I shook my head. "Unbelievable."

"I think we've covered all we need for now. Your next step is to find a property. When you do, come back, and I'll be happy to arrange financing."

"Another glass?" Dylan asked me.

"Only if you're willing to drive me home." When I left the bank, I made two stops. The first was to a liquor store to pick up a bottle of my favorite *muscato*. The second was to grab Dylan after work. I told him to bring his guitar and then drove us straight to the beach.

My head was still spinning from all I'd heard from the mortgage agent; the wine only sank me further down the rabbit hole. "I feel like I've entered this bizarre alternate universe. It's not about reality anymore; it's about legal fictions and loopholes." I gulped down what was left in my glass.

"Believe me, you've just begun to scratch the surface of the loopholes." Dylan filled my glass with the last from the bottle.

"None of this bothers you?"

"It used to." Dylan picked up his guitar and strummed quietly. "I used to expect everything to harmonize, as if one hand created all."

"You do realize I'm Catholic, right? I actually believe that one hand created all."

"I'm not talking about the creation of the world. I'm talking about our economic system. I expected the disparate parts to dovetail, but it was a pipe dream. Our laws are compromises, made by different lawmakers, in different eras. Some of them I like, some I don't. I could either spend my energy fighting against it or figure out how to thrive in the system we have."

"You don't think all this just helps the rich get richer?"

"It's not about rich vs. poor; it's about the savvy vs. the non-savvy."

Gregory had said much the same thing. And though Dylan himself was anything but rich, and he seemed to thrive with these loopholes, I still couldn't shake the idea that this whole system was a scheme of the wealthy. "Don't you think that the rich should contribute their fair share?"

Dylan laughed. "Try listening to the political discourse in this country sometime. The Democrats scream that the rich should pay their fair share. The Republicans scream that the rich should only pay their fair share. See the problem?"

"So everyone agrees that the rich should pay their fair amount, but everyone disagrees on what *fair* means." I wanted to be as cool about this as Dylan, but my insides wouldn't stop squirming. "You don't think the rich take advantage of the poor?"

"Of course they do. But the poor also take advantage of the rich. Many of those who scream the loudest that the rich screw the poor pay nothing themselves, even while collecting free housing, education, and health care. Where do you think the money to provide for that comes from? The rich bear the cost not only of providing for themselves but for the poor as well."

I suddenly felt like my student, Lisa, who whined anytime someone got a cupcake with more frosting than she did. I could even hear the squeal in my voice but was powerless to stop it. "But aren't most loopholes there for the rich?"

"No, it's just that the rich are usually the only ones sophisticated enough to know how to use them." Dylan played a riff that sounded like the opening of a gameshow.

"Where do you fit in?"

"I'm in the most powerful category of all." Dylan ran his fingers up the scale. "I'm one of the so-phis-ti-ca-ted poor."

"If you guys are so powerful, how come I've never heard of the *sophisticated poor*?" I tapped his guitar. "Let me guess, you're like a modern-day *Illuminati*, this ultra-powerful underground society, and you use your influence in the media to wipe out all mention of your existence?"

Dylan laughed. "The reason you never hear of the sophisticated poor is that we don't stay poor for long. You always hear the pundits on TV and talk radio clamoring about the top 1%, as if this is some static group. The fact is, people move in and out of the top 1% all the time. Many of the wealthiest people in our nation's history started dirt poor and pulled themselves up by their bootstraps."

An evening breeze rustled the water and chilled my skin. I cuddled up beside Dylan and wrapped a blanket around my shoulders. "How'd you get to be so wise?"

His lips softly landed on my forehead, and he whispered, "I listen a lot more than I talk."

Warmth tingled my skin. I could have sat there, enjoying that moment for hours, but curiosity got the best of me. "Listen to whom?"

"I'm listening all day long. Even while I'm working, you can usually find me listening to one podcast or another, trying to learn skills that will help me build my Cash Machine." He put down his guitar, pulled out his phone, and scrolled through hundreds of episodes he'd downloaded on his podcast app.

"So that's where you get it from? Podcasts?"

"Not only. About the only time I ever spend significant money on myself is when I buy a course or a seminar."

"Like what?"

"Like my first year back, I attended a seminar on buying distressed houses. I used what I learned there to buy my first house out of foreclosure. But really, it dates back to Luther in Mexico."

"Ah, yes, my old friend, Luther."

"Sorry for mentioning Luther. I know you don't want to hear about him."

"Actually, I do." This time, I felt no anger at the mention of Luther, only curiosity. "I know he was the one who first told you about building your Cash Machine, but I never got the full story."

"It's a long one. Might call for stargazing." Dylan leaned back onto the sand and gestured for me to join him.

"Go on." I nestled my head into the nook between his shoulder and chest. "Spin me your tale."

CHAPTER 7

A FISH TALE

The first thing Kyle and I discovered when we got to Mexico was that the resort looked nothing like the brochure. The pool was drained, the rooms were full of roaches, and the so-called club was a dingy bar.

Kyle thought this was hilarious. "If we're stuck in some hole-in-the-wall fishing village, we might as well fish."

We went down to the dock and found a boat with a sign that read *Fishing Charters*.

An old man stepped out of the boat's cabin. "You boys looking to catch some fish?" He adjusted a ratty, old baseball cap to block out the bright morning light. "If so, you've come to the right place."

"You're no Mexican," Kyle said.

"And you're not Japanese, but if you're looking to fish, we can talk business. Name's Luther," he stuck out a thick hand, "born and bred in Mississippi if it matters to you. Same Gulf, different coast, so I reckon I've been fishing these waters all my life." He looked the two of us over. "Now, you boys want to listen to an old man ramble, or do you want to fish?"

His boat was old but immaculate. We negotiated a rate, hopped on, and in five minutes, Luther had us on the water. Half an hour later, he pulled into a deserted cove. "Careful not to put your hands in the water," he said. "The fish bite so hard out here, they'll take your fingers off at the knuckles. Let's get you boys hooked up with some rods and bait."

Luther pulled out a pale white fish that wrangled in his hands. Kyle grimaced. "What is that?"

"Pucker up, boys and say hello to Miss Ruby Red Lips." Luther pulled open the fish's mouth, being careful not to get bitten, to show the crimson interior. "She's our secret weapon for catching Gulf Snapper."

"You don't use worms?" Kyle asked.

"You want a worm, Kyle? I'll give you a worm. Just don't be disappointed when Dylan and I bring in the big game, and you're left with squat. The first thing to know with fishing, as with life, is what game you're going after. Only then can you choose the right location and bait."

"In fishing and with life, eh?" Kyle sent a wink in my direction, clearly amused at the idea of this old, hick fisherman viewing himself as a sage. "I guess fishing leaves you plenty of time for philosophizing?"

"True, but it's hard to keep up my boat on a philosopher's salary. So it's good to know something about money as well."

Kyle sent me another wink. Now the old hick was a money expert too? "So what game are you going after?"

"In life?" Luther stuck a hook through Miss Ruby Red Lips' back, just ahead of the dorsal fin. "That's easy. I'm aiming to be *The Old Man and the Sea part II*, though this time with a happy ending. I plan to spend as many days fishing the ocean and as many nights in bed with my wife as I can muster."

"Sounds like a lovely goal for you." Kyle rolled up his sleeves. "But I'm guessing your wife is hardly my type."

"Too bad, Kyle; she'd whip your snarky ass into shape fast." Luther cast the rod and handed it to Kyle. "But life goals are as unique as we are. I'm afraid you've got to find one of your own."

"Can't you say that about all goals?" I asked.

"'Fraid not, Dylan. Take financial goals. As far as I can see, 99% of people ought to have the same goal. At least initially. Old Luther's no commie; I have no problem with you going farther once you hit it."

"Let me guess," Kyle said, "you think that goal should be to buy a boat?"

"You could do a fair lot worse than own a boat, Kyle. But no, the waters are crowded enough without every landlubbing idiot coming out here to disturb my peace. Your goal should be financial independence."

"What's that?" I asked.

Luther shook his head. "You know, it's amazing. 80% of what you learned in high school, and at least that much of what you're getting in college, you'll never use again. Never understood why they don't deep-six all that crap and teach you kids financial literacy." Luther leaned over the side of the boat and hauled in a floating beer can. "Stupid tourists."

"What's financial independence?" I asked again.

Kyle nudged me. "That's what they call people who are so rich they never need to work again."

"It has nothing to do with riches, Kyle." He dug a hook into another Ruby Red Lips and cast it into the water. "Even a simple fisherman like me can get financially independent if he knows what he's doing."

"You're financially independent?" Kyle asked.

"That's right." Luther tipped his hat at Kyle. "I hang up my sign and take a few charters for variety and a little extra pocket change, but I don't need to work another day in my life."

"I'm guessing that's only because you live in some Mexican backwater."

"You're not far off, Kyle. Old Luther may look like a crazy old fisherman, but I'm not down here by accident. Wasn't that many years ago that I had a job, and when I got my two weeks' vacation each year, you know what I'd do?"

"Let me guess," Kyle said, "you'd fish."

"Smart boy. I used to think I'd retire someplace near the water where I could fish all the time." Luther stared off into the distance, as though watching a movie. "Then, my friend Buzz told me I was thinking about life all wrong. I shouldn't ask what I'd do when I retire. I ought to ask myself what I'd do if I knew I could never retire. The answer hit me like a lightning bolt."

"You'd fish?" I asked.

"Righto. So why was I working fifty weeks a year so I could fish for two?" Luther passed me the second rod, and his hands grew animated. "I began putting Buzz's advice into motion, and within two years, I was able to quit my job, move down here, and get myself a small boat."

"You call this boat *small*?" Kyle asked.

"I'm talking about four boats ago, when I started. I keep trading up as my financial position grows stronger."

"And how is that happening? Let me guess, you're probably using this old boat to run drugs or shuttle illegals over the border." Kyle winked at Luther. "Smart move hiding out here in some podunk fishing village."

"Sorry to disappoint you, Kyle," Luther said, "but I like to keep my hands clean."

"Not from fish guts, you don't." Kyle waved his hand in front of his face to ward off the stink of the boat.

"Shut up, Kyle," I said. "Seriously, Luther, how'd you do it?"

"You might not guess looking at me, boys, but old Luther wasn't born into riches. Nor did I have some Wall Street job where I could run off with a hundred million after a couple of years buying and selling. Before implementing Buzz's advice, I had nothing but my PWA."

"PWA?" Kyle asked.

"My Poor White Ass."

Kyle wasn't wrong about the smell of fish guts, but if what Luther said was true, there was more to him than we could see. "You went from nothing to retired in two years?"

"That's right, Dylan. Buzz taught me the secret to lifelong wealth, and I've used that to sustain myself ever since."

I felt a sharp tug on my line. I leaned back hard and reeled it in. But the fight didn't last long. The line came in light and easy, and the hook came out of the water clean.

Kyle popped open a beer. "Let it go, Dylan. 'This guy's just toying with you like that fish that stole your bait. Can't you see he's just stringing us along but not saying a thing?"

"Not true, not true." Luther gave a scout's salute. "I'm honor-bound to tell any who want to listen."

"How are you bound?" I asked.

Luther grabbed my hook and dug it into another live bait fish. "That was one of Buzz's conditions for telling me. I give the same two conditions to everyone I teach."

I recast my line. "Why do you have conditions?"

"The world doesn't need another taker. If I'm going to teach you the tools of acquiring wealth, it's to turn you into a giver."

Kyle leaned into me. "You know what they say: If you give a man a fish…"

I pushed Kyle back. "What are these conditions?"

"Number one is charity." He held out a stubby finger. "You must agree to give 10% of your after-tax income away to others in need."

"That's once I become financially independent, right?" I asked.

"That starts now. Giving is like a muscle; you need to build it over time. A man who won't give ten cents on a dollar won't give a hundred thousand on a million."

Something inside me tightened. Kyle asked, "What if I need the money to live on?"

"Give anyway. When you give while you're still poor, even though it hurts, you'll come to know the power of charity in your bones. You'll understand you're not just building wealth for your greedy little self; you'll see that the more you earn, the more you can contribute."

I hadn't the slightest clue what Luther meant about the power of charity. If anything, charity seemed like giving power away. It was a noble thing to do, I supposed, and all well and good for those who had excess cash, but powerful? "What's the second condition?"

Another thick finger went up. "You must teach others what you learn. Knowledge, like money, is not meant to be hoarded."

Kyle took another swig of his beer. "OK, let's hear this big secret already."

Luther shoved his two fingers into Kyle's chest. "You agree to my conditions?"

"We haven't heard what you're going to say yet." Kyle pushed Luther's fingers away. "I'm not going to agree to give away 10% of my money for life when I don't even know if I'll take the advice."

"The conditions only apply if you accept the path I lay before you. And Kyle, you have nothing to worry about," Luther patted Kyle on the back, "you're not going to follow my advice anyway."

Kyle squared his shoulders. "How do you know?"

"Two giveaways." Luther tugged on Kyle's Polo shirt. "One, I see from the way you're dressed that you've got a love for the finer things in life. You're not going to want to give that up."

Kyle wiped his shirt where Luther had touched him. "Why should I have to? I thought this was the path to riches?"

"All great accomplishments require sacrifice. You won't be willing to pay the price."

"And the second reason?"

Luther grabbed himself a rod. "You think I'm a crazy old man."

"Nah, I don't think you're so old."

"You've got a sharp tongue, Kyle. I like you." Luther hooked yet another Ruby Red Lips. "That's why I haven't thrown you off my boat."

"If we're not going to listen, why are you wasting our time?"

"I'm not saying it for your sake, fool." Luther cast his line in the water. "I'm saying this for Dylan." The old fisherman peered into my eyes. "He's quiet, but deep. Like the ocean. I reckon he mulls over what he hears. An acorn planted in that soil might take root."

"Being quiet doesn't mean he'll listen to crazy." Kyle laughed, then went silent when he caught my gaze.

"I want to hear," I said. "Luther, I give you my word on your conditions. What's your secret?"

"Spend less than you make and invest the difference."

Kyle laughed so hard, beer sprayed out of his mouth. "That's it? Any idiot knows you should spend less than you make."

"Any idiot knows it, but not every idiot lives it." Luther cranked his reel. "Take you two idiots, for example. You're on a two-hundred-dollar boat charter right now, and I'm guessing neither of you makes a bent nickel."

"We worked all summer painting houses," I said.

"I see." One of Luther's brows went up. "You're still living off this painting money all these months later?"

"More or less." I squirmed. "We don't have so many expenses, but that money's covered beer all semester, and what's left over paid for this trip."

"I see. So both of you boys are on full scholarships?"

"What, you mean tuition?" My line grew taught again, and my back stiffened. "That's different; that's for school."

"Oh, silly me, I hadn't realized tuition was a different category." He pointed to my rod. "Keep it steady. There now. Hold your grip tight and slowly reel in the line, so the fish doesn't even notice you're bringing him home."

I reeled in, my rod getting more and more bent as I worked.

Luther turned to Kyle. "Fine, let's put tuition aside. Now, I expect both you boys are living at home to save on housing?"

"We're in the dorms for now," I said. "Next semester, we're moving into the fraternity."

"Oh, a fraternity. Fraternities are great because they're usually in nice, big houses, and big houses have great big kitchens. That'll allow you to save money by cooking your own food, right?" The fish broke the surface twenty feet from the boat.

"I know you're just trying to wind us up, old man," Kyle said, "but I'll play along. As I'm sure you've guessed, we're both on the school meal plan. Like tuition and housing, meals just get rolled into our student loans."

"Of course, student loans. No problem then." Luther leaned over the side of the boat with his hand net and scooped up the fish. He pulled it off the hook and threw it back into the water. "Afraid that one's too small to keep."

I looked down at my now empty hook. "You don't have a problem with student loans, do you?"

"Certainly not, Dylan. It was just a temporary lapse of memory on my part. I'm afraid it happens more often as we age." He set me up with another Ruby Red Lips. "You see, boys, I'd forgotten you paid off student loans with fairy dust and not *real* money."

"You're real funny, you know that, Luther?" Kyle reeled in his line to check if his bait was still on the hook. "Sitting on this boat all day must leave you plenty of time to think up jokes."

"You want to hear a real funny joke, Kyle?" Luther popped himself a beer. "Student loans aren't like other debt: they're exempt from bankruptcy law."

"What does that mean?" I cast my line back into the water, further this time.

"Bankruptcy gives protection from debt. So if you ring up crazy high credit card bills and then go bankrupt, much of that debt goes away. Not student loans." He held up his beer as if toasting the debt gods. "Those are yours until paid off, or for life, whichever ends first. The real tragedy is that they're being accrued by kids who have no concept of what they'll be able to earn with those fancy diplomas."

Kyle gripped his rod with both hands. Something was biting, that was for sure. "Wait," he said, straining. "Are you saying we shouldn't be in school?"

"What I'm saying right now is that despite your assertion that any idiot knows to spend less than he makes, you two are spending a fortune and making squat."

"That's just the price you pay for being in school," I said.

"Oh?" Luther locked his rod in the gunwale so he could stand behind Kyle. "Are there no ways to be in school without paying that price?"

"I guess I could have gone to the local school and lived at home." I shrugged. "But the education wouldn't have been the same."

Luther wiped his brow with his sleeve. "And is school such a given that there are no alternatives?"

Kyle tried bringing in his line, but whatever monster was on the other side wasn't coming up easy. Luther grabbed onto the rod, and the two of them grunted as they pulled. "Don't try to fight him. When he swims toward us, reel it in quick. When he swims away, just try to hold on." The line went loose, and Kyle reeled it in as fast as he could. "Now, this is *fishing*! You couldn't learn a real skill like this in some ivory tower—I can tell you that."

The fish swam away from the boat, and Kyle hung on for dear life. "The point of the degree is to help us make a living."

"If you stopped and ran the numbers, I think you'd be surprised. A guy who becomes a plumber right out of high school and manages his money well will slaughter just about any doctor who went through school on loans."

"Slaughter, how?" I asked. "In income?"

"It's not what you make that counts—it's what you keep." Kyle and Luther fell back as the line suddenly went loose. The remaining line billowed up on the rod. "Well, I'll be. He didn't just take our bait; he made off with our entire hook."

"You're saying the plumber will keep more?" I asked.

Luther pulled out his tackle box to find a new hook for Kyle's rod. "Compare their assets at age 65, and you'll see it's not even close."

"The plumber's still stuck fixing toilets." Kyle leaned back against the gunwale. With no rod, there wasn't anything for him to do. "You got something to eat?"

Luther jerked his head to a small cooler near my feet. "Actually, Kyle, a plumber who knows how to handle money can retire before the doctor even finishes residency."

I pulled out two sandwiches, keeping one for myself and tossing the other to Kyle. "That can't be true."

"Of course, it's not." Bits of tuna flew out of Kyle's mouth as he spoke. "Even if it is, who cares? Most pre-med guys I know have dreamed of being doctors since they were kids. They should give up saving lives for a few more dollars in the bank? Or so they can retire early by living in some Mexican backwater where tacos are five for a dollar?"

"If you've got a dream to be a doctor, you fully understand the costs, and you're willing to pay the price, then more power to you. Old Luther's in the business of making dreams a reality, not squashing them out. Me, my passion is fishing." He held up the newly tied hook with pride. "But guys with a mission at your age are the exception."

"Yeah?" Kyle said. "What's the rule?"

"You studs are. You're in school because you think you ought to be, even though you have only vague ideas of where it will take you. While you're figuring it out, you're amassing mountains of debt."

The two of us fell silent for the first time that day. Luther said, "How much are you going to rack up in loans for undergrad, Kyle?"

"I have a partial tuition grant, so that's not too bad, but room and board is all on loans. I'll probably have $125,000 in debt when I get out."

"Then grad school?"

Kyle chomped the last of his sandwich. "Probably another $125,000."

"Better than some. Had a guy on my boat last month who was over $400,000 in the hole by the time he finished his law degree. But $250,000 is hardly peanuts. You realize your parents probably spent less than that on their first house? You know how long the bank gave them to pay it off?"

I swallowed hard. "How long?"

"30 *years*. All that time, the interest continues to accrue. That $250,000 will cost you almost twice that to pay off. And that's with post-tax money. Pre-tax, you'll have to earn the better part of a million dollars just to cover your school loans."

Kyle waved him off. "But I'll be making so much more."

"Perhaps, but most don't make enough to compensate. It's like this fishing trip. You're enjoying yourselves, but you could have done more valuable things with your time."

My rod bent so far, I thought it was going to snap in two. I cranked the reel, but it barely moved. "Luther," I grunted.

The fisherman wrapped his hands around mine and took over the reel. I was kind of embarrassed, but mostly relieved. My back and shoulders were burning. "All that time sitting in a classroom has made you wimpy, boy. Some real man's work might do you good."

"So that's your thing, old man," Kyle said. "People shouldn't go to school?"

"Actually, I'm a huge believer in education. I just can't stand the way most of you kids are doing it these days, like it's some rite of passage."

"What's that supposed to mean?"

"It means that the majority of you will never work in your field of study, and almost half of you will take jobs that don't even require degrees. Meanwhile, you're burning through valuable years and racking up crazy amounts of debt."

"Degrees open doors." Kyle rolled his eyes. "I'm never going to get a job at Skadden Arps if I'm just a dropout who smells of fish guts."

"Only a small percent of you college kids ever get high paying jobs like that." He turned the reel a couple more times, and a massive pink fish slipped out of the water, thrashing in every direction. "But who knows? Maybe you'll be lucky. If so, I hope you enjoy that work as much as you think you will, because you're going to be stuck there."

"What does that mean?"

"What if the job isn't all you thought it would be?" Luther grabbed a net. "What if at age 25, you suddenly realize what you were meant to do with your life?"

"So I'd switch tracks, no big deal."

"Oh, really? You'd just switch?" Luther leaned over the side of the boat and netted the fish. "And what if your dream doesn't pay as well as corporate law? What if it pays enough to get by, but not enough to live on and keep up with your loan payments?"

"Then, I guess…" But Kyle's voice trailed off. Even he didn't have an answer to this one.

"Beauty. That's a blackfin snapper. A twenty pounder, I'd say. We'll be eating well tonight." Luther carried the fish onto the boat. "Fact is, Kyle, debt is a dream killer. You may think that the high-paying job you're going after is some prize. But it's a prison sentence. Once you're in it, you're going to have an awfully hard time getting out. Especially after you start getting used to the lifestyle."

"Actually, old man, I can't wait to get used to the lifestyle." Kyle popped another beer, put his feet up on the gunwale, and checked out of the conversation.

The next morning, while Kyle slept off the beers from the night before, I went down to the docks to talk to Luther alone.

"Well, well, if it isn't my young collegiate. I figured you'd be sick of fish by now, with all you ate last night."

I rubbed my swollen belly. "Quite sick of it."

"You sure?" Luther offered a mischievous grin. "The Mrs. made some mighty fine fish balls from the leftovers."

"Positive. I came down to talk to you, actually."

Luther patted my back. "Let me guess, you want to learn more about money?"

"Yeah, I do."

"You ever waxed a car?"

"Yeah, so?"

I waited for Luther to give me the analogy between money and waxing a car, but instead, he gave me a rag and a jar of wax. "I'll tell you all you need to know while you polish the rails to a bright shine."

Considering how much I'd paid him the day before, I didn't see why I had to work to get my questions answered, but I did what he said without protest. As soon as I started working, Luther kept his word and began what would be the first of many of our cash chats, as he liked to call them. "I'm going to make it real simple for you, Dylan. Tell me, when you get this big career of yours off the ground, how many hours do you expect to be working per week?"

I opened the jar of hard wax. "If I go to work for a big law firm like I'm thinking, then probably sixty or so."

Luther filled a bucket with soapy water, picked up a scrub brush, and hopped on the boat. "So how many hours will you work in your career?"

I started working the railing on the far side of the boat, rubbing hard as I did the math in my head. 60 hours a week times 50 weeks a year made 3000 hours a year. I'd start after law school, so I'd be around 25, and I'd probably work until I was 70 or so, like my grandfather. That would be 45 years. "135,000 hours?" Was I really going to be working *that* much?

"Not a small number, is it?" Luther fit a long handle onto his brush and scrubbed the boat floor. "Tell me, how many hours do you plan to spend learning about money?"

I rubbed the rag into the wax. "What kind of learning?"

"You know, how to spend it, how to invest it. Tax strategies. How to keep more of what you earn in your pocket?"

I shrugged.

"Did you take calculus in high school?"

"Yeah."

"Tell me three ways the calculus you learned is relevant to your life?"

"Truthfully, I hardly remember any of it." I smeared the wax onto the near railing and worked it until it shone.

"And it's been what, six months since you graduated? That, my friend," Luther slammed down his brush and suds flew into the air, "is a waste. Let me guess, your high school didn't even have a class on the practicalities of money, did it?"

My high school didn't teach the practicalities of anything. "Not that I know."

"I bet your fancy college has thousands of classes on Greek literature, gender studies, and other equally impractical crap, but I bet they don't have one class on the practicalities of money either, do they?"

The muscles in my shoulder were starting to burn from the effort. "I mean, there's a whole economics department."

"I'm not talking about all that micro-macro theory crap." Luther hosed off the suds, which drained to the back of the boat. "I'm talking about how to spend your hard-earned dollars and cents to make sure you're not some corporate slave all your life."

"It's not slavery." I stood straight, stretching my back. "My Dad's worked for Hillord since I was a kid, and he's getting paid."

"And what would happen if he got fired tomorrow?" Luther paused to wait for my response, but I didn't know what to say, so he pushed further. "Does he have investments to fall back on, or would your parents quickly find themselves in the hole?"

"He could always find himself another job, I suppose."

"I'd hope so, but still, he's a slave to *having* to work. I only work how and when I choose to."

"Kyle might think you're some kook, Luther, but I'm not fooled by the whole hick routine. You're a lot sharper than you let on. But you've got to understand that those who don't grasp money concepts the way you do will still need to work to provide for their families."

"It's not about brains, Dylan, it's about discipline." Luther turned off the hose and pointed it at me. "You can be the dumbest peanut in the turd and become financially independent. Speaking of discipline, how 'bout you show me you can talk and wax at the same time?"

I got back to polishing the rail.

"Look, kid, I'm sure your dad works hard to take care of y'all. But the truth is, just like your parents, you collegiates trust that your degrees will provide, then you stick your heads in the sand and ignore the very finances that make up your future."

"What would you have us do?"

"Learn, dammit!" Luther stepped back on the dock and rolled up the hose. "I'll make you this promise, Dylan. Remember those 135,000 hours you're planning on working? If you spend 1% of those hours learning about money, you'll be able to eliminate 80% of 'em entirely."

"You think I'd make that much more?"

"It's not about making more." Luther sat down on the now gleaming gunwale. "It's about making your money work for you rather than you working for it."

Kyle came jogging over. "Thought I might find you here. Didn't get enough crazy talk in one day?"

I looked down to see that my shirt was soaked with sweat, but it was so hot, I didn't care. "Luther made some interesting points."

"That's the beauty of crackpots like Luther. They may not make a lot of sense, but you can't deny they're interesting. Come on, let's go. Daylight's wasting and the kayaks we've rented aren't going to paddle themselves."

Dylan paused in his story, and I lifted myself onto my elbow to face him. "What happened next?"

"We went kayaking, just like we'd planned. But the few bucks we spent on kayak rentals weighed on me like no other expense ever had. For the first time, I wondered if this was a poor use of my money. Was I being stupid blowing the little cash I had at a time in my life when I was already racking up massive debt?"

"So what'd you do?"

"Each morning, I went back to talk to Luther while Kyle slept." Dylan tucked a few strands of hair behind my ear.

"This is the man who changed your fortunes? This guy sounds like a kook."

"Yeah, he comes across as kooky, but that's just his shtick. That kook kept putting me to work, but it was the cheapest education I'd ever had, so I did whatever he asked."

"How could you be sure he was right?"

"I'm no fool. I checked up some of the stuff he said online. But most of it just required a bit of applied logic and basic arithmetic. The more I thought about what he said, the more it made sense."

"And you still think that, even after everything that's happened?"

"More so than ever."

CHAPTER 8

HEELS AND TALONS

Libby invited me to go shopping for costumes for the Halloween gala, but I didn't want to get sucked down another rabbit hole of crazy spending. So, I took the creative route and headed to the Salvation Army. I snagged a fabulous dress that was shorter than my father would ever allow me to wear in public. It fit tightly around my Italian curves, which worked out well for the costume I had in mind.

The gala was Sunday night. I spent the weekend helping Dylan and a few other volunteers paint the walls at Crossroads. We scraped off all the water-damage, spackled the walls, and painted them a bland white. I suggested using a bit of color, but the director told me the teens would be putting up a series of murals.

While I did grunt work, Dylan tinkered with the electric box, which he called 'an outdated fire hazard,' replaced a heating unit, and fixed a leaky sink. Once or twice, he came across some issue that was out of his league, but for the most part, he knew just what to do. Dylan might have dropped out of college, but he'd never quit getting himself an education.

By late Sunday afternoon, paint was splattered on every article of my clothing, in my hair, and somehow inside my ear. After stealing what must have been my tenth wink of the day, I kissed Dylan on the cheek and grabbed my bag to go.

"You never told me what you were dressing up as," he said.

"Nothing special, really." I shrugged and avoided his eyes. "I just snagged a cheap cocktail dress at a thrift store." I figured he'd be proud I'd only spent $19 on my whole costume, but I decided not to offer details. I knew it would just make him jealous. Before he could ask questions, I waved goodbye to the team and scurried out the door.

After the longest, hottest shower of my life, I massaged half a bottle of gel into my hair and wound it into curly cues along my hairline. I plastered a thick layer of mascara on my lashes and turned my lips into a veritable stop sign. I faced the mirror with a bend in the knee and a flirtatious pucker. Susanna Boop winked back at me.

"How was the gala?" Dylan asked me the next day. He'd called me during my lunch break at school.

"Libby did a great job on the decorations."

"The party itself was a bit of a downer?"

I avoided a direct answer. "The firm insisted that costumes were optional."

Dylan snorted. "I take it corporate attorneys are hardly known for expressing their individuality?"

"You got it. I was one of about ten people who showed up in costume. Most of the lawyers showed up in suits."

"Ouch."

It was a good thing we were on the phone. It was easier this way to tell him only what I wanted him to hear.

I didn't tell him the band was on fire. I didn't tell him the bartenders were dressed up as skeletons, and one had concocted a special drink for the evening called *Spook of the Night* with floating olives made to look like eyeballs. I didn't tell him how Libby and I had bid on an item at the silent auction labeled: *Ladies Spa Day for Two: Massage, Manicure, and Margaritas*. At first, we bid to drive up the price, but whenever we got outbid, it rankled me to the point that we always fought back. Our eventual victory set us back $185 each, but why shouldn't we pamper ourselves once in a while?

Mostly, I didn't tell Dylan about all the attention I drew in my Susanna Boop costume, particularly from a tall Italian who was a principal in a venture capital group Kyle's firm represented. I politely refused Anthony the first time he asked me to dance, but like a true hot-blooded Italian, that only spurred his interest. The next refusal was harder, by then, I was on my second *Spook of the*

Night. The third time he asked, I was *Spooked* enough to give in, and we hit the dance floor. Anthony moved across the parquet with the grace of an athlete, and whenever he twirled me, my little Susanna Boop skirt flew embarrassingly high. I drew a line when he offered to drive me home. Still, when the valets brought around our cars, I couldn't help eyeing his midnight-blue Porsche, and I cringed when he saw my dented Honda.

"What did you dress up as anyway?" Dylan asked, drawing me back to the present conversation.

I messaged him a shot of me as Susanna Boop.

"All of a sudden, I'm wishing I'd gone," he said.

I wish he had too.

Dylan was right: there was philosophy, and then there were facts. No matter what I thought of the banking regulations, the facts were that I was authorized to spend $300,000 on a four-unit building, and now I wanted to find one. Of course, I didn't *have* to buy a four-unit place. I could have house hacked with a triplex or even a duplex, but then I'd have less income from the house and accordingly could borrow less. And this wasn't like my credit card debt. This was good debt. It was leverage that could bring me more income over time, and I wanted as much of it as I could get.

As with the used cars, I went online and researched what I should be looking for in a multi-family house. The first thing I learned was that buying real estate was *nothing* like buying a car. I couldn't just go online and look up the price of an eight-year-old, cherry red Tudor. Each house is unique, so it's priced uniquely. That's not to say I couldn't find data. I found plenty of data. Mountains of data. I also found tips on what to look for. Thousands of tips. And did I mention buying strategies? Dozens of buying strategies.

When school let out early on Wednesday, I went outside to meet Cynthia, the real estate agent, who, along with Libby, waited for me in the parking lot in her white Lexus SUV. As I didn't quite feel ready to start looking for a house for me, I thought I'd accompany Libby on her search.

After brief introductions, I asked Libby, "Why the sudden urge to buy a house? You guys have barely been in your apartment a year."

"I think a little of Dylan is rubbing off on Kyle. His firm had a really good year, and they just announced a massive year-end bonus. Kyle said, 'Why the hell are we dumping all this rent money into the toilet? Let's use the bonus as a downpayment and start paying mortgage instead.'"

"Smart man, your fiancé," Cynthia said.

"He gave you the job of buying it?" I asked.

"Well, obviously, he's going to see any house before we buy it. But he doesn't have the time to go looking around at twenty places. I can't blame him. Cynthia and I have already seen three houses today, and I'm totally overwhelmed. There are so many variables, like number of bathrooms, the size of the kitchen, and the age of the house. Then, of course, there's price..." She reached back and squeezed my knee. "Thanks so much for coming with me, Amber."

"I assure you, I'm being entirely selfish. Dylan's been pushing me to buy as well, so I'm hoping to get myself an education."

"Well, if you want an education," Cynthia flicked on her left turn signal, "it's important to start with the three most important factors in real estate."

"Oh, I know." Libby bounced in her seat. "Cynthia told me this morning."

"What are they?" I asked.

"Location, location, location."

"That's right." Cynthia eased onto Park Lane. "A house isn't like a car you can take wherever you want. Where you find it is where it stays, so you'd better choose wisely. That's why I selected the next house we're going to see, Libby. It's a bit bigger and a bit pricier than you specified, but it couldn't be better situated. It's less than a block from the best primary school in the district, and as you'll see, it's just stunning."

Cynthia didn't lie; the house was gorgeous. The downstairs had all hardwood floors and an open plan kitchen that looked out on the back yard. The master bedroom, one of four on the second floor, had walk-in closets and a giant bathroom that had two sinks, a jacuzzi bath, and a separate shower.

"One of my favorite features of this house is this walkout basement." Cynthia led us down carpeted stairs. "This gives the children their own play space to make as much noise as they want without disturbing the adults upstairs."

Children? They weren't even married yet. Libby's face flushed, and she squeezed her hands into her chest. "Can't you just imagine our kids playing here?" She whispered into my ear.

I matched her body language and forced a smile, but before I came up with something sappy to say, Cynthia led us back up into the dining room and kitchen. Libby periodically opened cabinet doors to peek inside but was mostly quiet as Cynthia pointed out the features, including an office that would be perfect for whenever Kyle brought work home.

Libby said next to nothing until we came back around to the foyer, and Cynthia asked, "What do you think?"

"It'll need new curtains, and I'll want to repaint the living room and den to brighten them up." Libby always had a great eye for design. "But otherwise, I wouldn't have to change hardly anything."

"That's something to keep in mind." Cynthia slid her hand across the granite kitchen countertops. "Some of the other places will need work, especially that first one we saw. You'll have to add that to the cost of the purchase. And renovations aren't usually covered by your mortgage."

"I thought they were," I said. "My banker told me that with an FHA loan, I could get renovations covered by the 203(K) provision."

Cynthia ran her thumb across her manicured nails. She did a poor job of hiding the cringe on her face, the same one cheerleaders back in high school would give if you showed up in thrift store clothes. "Uh. Yeah. That might be true for low-income housing, but none of the estates in this neighborhood are eligible for such a loan." She turned back to Libby and reconfigured her lips into a dental poster smile. "So, do you want to make an offer?"

"I love it." Libby's arms entangled around one another. "I'm just concerned that it's above our budget."

"It is a bit above, and that's certainly something you'll have to discuss with your fiancé. But…," Cynthia pointed her pen like a schoolteacher, "bear in mind: your house will likely be the largest investment you'll ever make and the largest asset you'll ever own, so you want to choose it well." She opened her notebook to the listing of a smaller house with blue shutters. "That three-bedroom we saw today is more what I'd call a 'Starter House.' It's well within your range and should be fine for your needs for the next five years or so. Many couples choose to go that route, to start small and then upgrade later."

"You don't like that strategy?" Libby asked.

"Truthfully, I don't." Cynthia closed her binder again and faced Libby with a worried expression. "Moving is one of the biggest stresses in life, on the same list as divorce and losing a parent, and beyond the stress, it's expensive. I never like the idea of setting yourself up to have to move, not when you can buy a 30-year house right off the bat."

"Hmm…" Libby's face fell.

"But the bigger reason is that real estate around here is exploding. There's no guarantee you'll be in any better position to buy a house like this one in five years than you are now. And let's face it, houses like this, with everything a family could need, right next to a great school and down the block from the park, they just don't come up every day. If it were me, I'd grab it."

"How is the pricing relative to the other houses in the neighborhood?"

"It's a shade high," Cynthia said, tipping her hand back and forth, "but I know they're open to offers."

"OK. We'll have to think about it."

"Of course, but don't think too long. This one just went on the market, and I don't expect it to stick around. In fact, if your fiancé wants to come see it when he gets off work, I'm willing to come back and show it again tonight."

This all felt very pushy to me. We'd only been in this place for twenty minutes, and it was selling for a hundred times more money than I'd ever held in my hands at one time. Was Libby really supposed to jump so quickly?

My friend mirrored my sentiments. "Whoa, that seems fast."

"Don't I know it." Cynthia shook her head. "You'd think that with such a major life choice, you'd want to take your time, but real estate's a fast-paced game. Those who wait get beaten to the best opportunities by those who act."

"You're saying we should decide tonight?"

"I can't even guarantee it will be around that long. I'm showing it once more late this afternoon, and I already have two appointments scheduled to show it tomorrow."

Libby turned to me. "What do you think, Amber?"

"It's a great house. But I don't know. It does seem like short notice."

Cynthia gave us a sly stare. "You want to know my favorite buying trick? You make an offer, but you put in a contingency, like it has to have a clean inspection report, or your mother-in-law needs to approve it or something like that. That way, if the seller agrees to the offer, you've locked in the property and the price, but you bought yourself time to think. Then if you change your mind, you can always say there's something you didn't like on the inspection report, or your mother-in-law refused to give her consent. You could even make an offer now, and we'd make it contingent on your fiancé agreeing. What do you say?"

My trip with Cynthia had given me a lot to consider. All through my evening run through Granger Park, I kept thinking about that house. The shame was that the kitchen, with induction stove, dual ovens, and an island big enough to house a marina, would be completely wasted on Libby, but I would thrive in a space like that. My own kitchen felt downright cramped by comparison. Still, I put on a pot of fusilli and invited Dylan to join me after work.

"How's the house hunt going?" he asked as we sat down to dinner.

"I've learned quite a bit online, and I tagged along with Libby today. They're going to put in a bid on this gorgeous house we saw this afternoon. But I haven't seen anything for myself yet. Any advice to get me started?"

Dylan swallowed a mouthful of fusilli. "The first thing to know in real estate—."

"Yeah, yeah, I know." I puffed up my chest and pointed like Jiminy Cricket. "Location, location, location."

"You finished?"

I shrank back. "That's not what you were going to say, is it?"

"No."

"Sorry. I'm listening." I crossed my legs and folded my hands into my lap. "Just sitting here politely, not saying a word."

"Let me guess, you heard that location line from the agent today?"

"Yeah."

"What else did she tell you?"

I took him through all the tidbits I'd picked up. Dylan scowled every now and then but mostly attacked the fusilli with abandon. When I finished, he said, "I want you to throw everything you think you know about real estate into the garbage."

"So that whole thing about location?"

"Look, I've heard of retail businesses that invested millions of dollars to move one store over because being on a corner gave them that much more foot traffic." Dylan paused as he buttered a piece of french bread. "A retail store might go crazy for location, but that's not the type of real estate we're doing."

"What about the other things she said, like about your house being your biggest asset and investment?"

"That's a load of crap." Dylan pounded the table. "For Kyle and Libby, that house will be their largest liability."

"How can you say that?"

"It's easy. In addition to the costs of upkeep, they're going to have to pump a tremendous amount of money into their mortgage payments each month."

"But much of that money will be paying down what they owe, and they're in a hot area. The property should be worth more over time."

"If the property does go up, then on paper they might be making money, but paper profits are a myth. The only way they'll make anything from this house is when they sell it, and they have no intention of selling it for decades. Until then, it will be a financial drain."

"It's still an asset."

"According to the basic rules of accounting, yes, it's an asset. But I want you to start thinking in terms of Cash Machines. According to Cash Machine logic, anything that produces income is an asset. Anything that drains income is a liability."

I cut up my slice of beefsteak tomato as I processed his words. "Cynthia, their agent, told Libby another alternative was to go into a starter home but warned her that property values are going up so fast they might not be able to afford the bigger home when it's time for them to transition."

"Look, if they want to put all their money into real estate because they think the market's on the rise, that's fine. But this isn't the way to do it."

"How would you do it?"

"Let's say the most they can currently invest in real estate is a million dollars, represented by this salt." Dylan held up a salt shaker. "If they buy Cynthia's argument that the real estate market is going to explode, they might want to max out the amount they're allowed to borrow and go all in." Dylan opened up the salt shaker and spilled all the salt out onto the counter.

"Hey! I just cleaned that."

Dylan ignored me. "Cynthia would now have them put all their money into one giant home, that they hope will one day be filled with children, but for now will be mostly empty." Dylan pushed all the salt into one big pile. "Alternatively, they could buy a home that is just big enough for their needs right now."

"Perhaps they could move into a crypt, like some ghouls I know?"

"Knowing Kyle's tastes, let's say that their bare minimum would be somewhat more luxurious than my own. Let's call it $250,000." Dylan moved about a quarter of the salt into a smaller pile. "If they put that other $750,000 into rental properties…," Dylan used his knife to separate the remaining salt into lines like a coke addict preparing to get high, "then they could make income even in poor economies."

"But eventually they do want to have a big family."

"Eventually. Whenever they need a bigger home, they sell one of the rentals and upgrade." Dylan moved one of the salt lines into the big pile. "And they never have to worry about getting priced out of the market, because their rental properties will be appreciating along with the market."

Dylan's logic felt so cold and calculating. "You're only talking about financial sense. What about emotional? Don't you think it's comforting to move into a house and know that this is going to be the home you raise your family in? Like, I've done nothing to this apartment," I gestured to the bare wall above the fireplace, "because I'm eventually going to leave it. But once I buy, I want it to feel like *home*." My eyes glazed over as I imagined living in a place like the one I'd just seen with Libby. "I'm going to paint the walls; I'll give it my personal touch."

Dylan placed his hand on my arm, waking me from my reverie. "Touches like paint and decor aren't very expensive. It's better that you invest in those every few years then sink into debt to save yourself that effort."

"Every few years? Cynthia said moving is one of the biggest life stressors people go through."

"Moving's a pain. Especially if you have as much stuff as Libby and Kyle keep accumulating. But to avoid one stress, I'm not going to take on a bucketload of others. The stress of moving is intense when you're in it, but then it passes. The burden of making a living is constant for those without a Cash Machine. And the strain of keeping up their chosen lifestyle will keep Kyle working 60 hour weeks. It's nice that his non-existent kids will have a huge basement to play in, but something tells me they'd rather have Daddy at their ball games."

Dylan using the word "Daddy" pulled at my heartstrings. Was he thinking about Kyle and Libby or us? Still, the thought of moving from crypt to crypt felt not only sad but destabilizing. It's one thing for a bachelor to grab his five possessions and bike over to the next pad, a whole other thing to keep moving a family around every time you find a good investment. "Don't you want to put down roots?"

Dylan grabbed my hand and gazed deep into my eyes. "Of course, that sounds wonderful. But think hard about this decision Kyle and Libby are making. They think they're buying an asset, but they're actually buying themselves a giant liability because they'll already bear the costs of kids' rooms when they have no kids. They'll pay a premium to be next to a school their kids won't attend for at least six more years. They'll pay higher property tax for this place, higher utilities, they'll pay landscaping costs for a yard that no one will use, and the biggest thing is that they'll pay massive interest each month."

His voice grew in intensity as he added, "If the cost of securing my financial future is moving once every few years when I'm young, so be it. I never want to live in more house than I need. At least not until I'm financially independent. If I have the cash to buy a large house and I think it's a good investment, but I only need a small apartment myself, then I'd rather buy a multi-unit house and live in a piece of it."

His words sounded cool and logical, but the warmth of his hand told a whole other story. In the depth of his gaze, I saw him as a father for the first time. He wasn't just trying to get rich; he wanted to build a life where he'd be present with his family. How many dance recitals had my father missed because he had a big case at work? The word "Daddy" still reverberated in my chest. If there was any chance of being part of that future, I was going to have to jump into his way of doing things.

"Righto. A multi-unit house." I shook myself away from his gaze and brought myself back to the world of dollars and sense. "Which brings us back to house hacking." I got myself a pen and paper. "You didn't like my location answer. You didn't like anything I heard from that agent, did you?"

"She was right about one thing." Dylan sank back into his plate and layered a piece of mozzarella and basil atop a chunk of tomato. "If you see a property you like, you've got to move fast. Making your offer contingent is a way of protecting yourself lest there's anything seriously wrong. I know investors who make offers on properties sight unseen, then rely on their contingencies to get them out of the deal if they don't like it."

"Glad to hear you two agree on at least one thing." I wrote *Rules* at the top of the page and underlined it. So what do you consider the primary rule of real estate investing?"

"You make your money when you buy."

I held my pen over the paper but didn't write anything down. "That doesn't make any sense. Wouldn't you make your money when you sell?"

"There are people who try to time the market. They buy in cities and neighborhoods where they think prices will increase, and they make their money when they sell. They're called real estate speculators. But that's not us."

"So how do we make money when we buy?"

"Two ways. One, we buy properties at below market rates."

"Got it." I wrote down *buy at below market rates*. "So if we can buy a property at 20% less than market and then turn around and sell it at full market price, it's as if we made the difference in the value when we bought, right?"

"Yes. The people who buy and sell like that are called house flippers. But that's also not us."

Us? I didn't even own anything yet. "So who, my dear, are we?"

"We buy and hold. Mostly, we aim to buy cash flowing properties. A property cash flows when it brings in enough money to cover its costs and still generates a profit."

I wrote down his definition. I was such a good little student. "In essence, we're buying ourselves an income stream?"

"Correct."

I considered the difference between this type of investment and the speculating Cynthia was pushing Libby to do while I scooped up some pesto with my fusilli. "Since we know the rental value when we buy the property, it doesn't even matter so much if the market goes up or down. Is that what you mean?"

"If the market goes up, it can be a great thing for us. But you're right, the rental market is far more stable than the purchasing market, so even if the cost of homes goes down, our income stream on the property should be unaffected."

"But why would anyone sell a house for below market value?"

"There are quite a few reasons. I bought my first property on foreclosure. Banks are not in the business of buying and selling properties, so when they foreclose on a place, they often sell below market price to get money back as fast as they can. But it's hard to buy foreclosed places these days."

"Why is that?"

"The market's been going up for years. Most foreclosures happen when the market goes down." Dylan grabbed a piece of paper and wrote down numbers as he spoke. "Think about it. If you owe $240,000 on a house that is now only worth $200,000, you might be tempted to walk away from it and let it become the bank's problem. But if the house is worth more than you bought it for, if you owe the bank $200,000 on a house that's now worth $240,000, why would you default and let the bank take your profits? If you don't have the money to pay your mortgage, it's better to sell the property, pay off the bank, and pocket the difference."

"So other than foreclosures, how else can we buy below market?"

"I can take you through the basics if you want, but I'm no expert." Dylan cleaned up the last of the sauce with a chunk of french bread and popped it in his mouth. "How about if you put on another pot of fusilli, and I'll ask Jade to come over and explain it herself."

"Who's Jade?"

"She's my wholesaler."

Jade was the anti-Cynthia. Cynthia's hybrid-electric SUV glided up the driveways of multi-million dollar homes. Jade's Mustang rumbled down my street. Had this been a movie, the soundtrack would have blared *Bad to the Bone*, but instead, her radio blasted techno music that drowned out even her souped-up engine. Cynthia comfortably showed off marble-floored foyers in her matching pink blouse, skirt, and heels. Nothing about Jade matched. Her leather jacket screamed 80s punk rock, her jeans were ripped, her pitch-black hair was dyed with streaks of the same flashy red as her lipstick, tattoos with a tiger and Chinese characters ran up her neck, the makeup on her pale skin would embarrass most whores, and those candy-colored nails looked like talons. She was twenty-two at most and looked like she'd feel more at home at a rave than a real estate club.

She shook my hand with a polite "how do you do," then attacked the fusilli with an appetite that put Dylan's to shame. When she came up for air, she asked, "So what's the score?" I noticed green speckles in her deep blue eyes. Behind all that noisy garb, Jade was gorgeous.

"House hack." If Dylan was at all embarrassed by Jade, he didn't show it. "Quadruplex if we can find one."

"Not many quads around. Cash or charge?" She asked Dylan, as if I wasn't even there.

"Amber needs a full mortgage," Dylan replied. "FHA loan if we can get one." I just sat there, nodding like his sidekick or something.

"Bummer. That limits the options. Neighborhoods?"

"Preferably B. I'm willing to go down to C+. Maybe even C if it's a great property, but this is Amber's first deal, so I want easy. Definitely no D."

"Can someone please tell me what's going on?" I tugged at Dylan's shirt like a snotty kid. So embarrassing. "What the hell are those letters?"

Dylan turned to me. "Kyle and Libby are looking to buy in an A grade neighborhood. The scale goes down to D. You wouldn't feel safe walking at night in a D neighborhood."

"Why would anyone want to buy in a D neighborhood?"

"Cheaper purchase price and better returns." Bits of bread flew out of Jade's mouth as she spoke. "The people who want to live in A neighborhoods have good jobs, pay their rent on time, and rarely go on three-day benders that leave their houses trashed. The slum lords deal with a lot more risk, so they collect higher rent relative to the purchase cost."

I held Dylan's bicep with both my hands and forced my sweetest smile. "I'm sorry, Jade, but I'm still not even sure what it is you do."

"I'm a wholesaler."

"What's a wholesaler?"

"You ever seen those signs that say '*We Buy Ugly Houses?*' Those are from wholesalers. We find houses, cheap."

"And you do *what* with them?"

"I agree to terms with the owner." She pulled another hunk of bread and pointed it at me. "Then, I sell the term sheet to someone like you to make the actual purchase."

Something about this chick didn't add up. "If you're getting such great properties, why don't you just buy them for yourself?"

"Cash retention isn't my strength, and my credit is hardly what you'd call impeccable. Besides, property management isn't my gig. My deal is I get in fast and get out faster."

"Why does needing a mortgage limit the options?" I asked.

"There are hundreds of reasons that someone sells a house for below market," Jade said, "and none of them are good."

"Like what?"

"Some are just structural." She slipped a toothpick out of my ladybug holder and pointed to the ceiling. "Say you've got a hole in your roof, and you don't have the cash to fix it. It might only be a $3000 repair, but no bank is going to write a mortgage on that property until it's fixed. The law of supply and demand. Once a mortgage is out of the question, 95% of buyers disappear. The price comes crashing down."

OK, I could see the logic in this. "So a cash buyer could come in, buy the house, fix the roof, and then sell it at market?"

"That's one option." She picked at the basil stuck between her teeth as she spoke. "The banks are anal as hell. I did a property last month where the first floor was six inches too low. Six inches! The banks all cited some regulation about the water table and said they'd have to consider it a basement. Guess what that did to the property assessment? It put it in the toilet."

Now she was losing me again. "That seems harder to fix than a hole in the roof."

"Way harder. Not worth doing the work. Not a great fit for a house flipper. But perfect for someone looking for a cash flowing property on the cheap. Those six inches may have tanked the purchase price but don't do squat to the rental value." She gulped down a whole glass of water in one go, slammed it on the table, and asked, "You got anything sweet around here? My mouth reeks of garlic, and I've got plans tonight."

My fusilli had just the right amount of garlic in it, but I suppose it was natural for her to be sensitive to garlic, given her resemblance to a vampire. "Uh, sure." I gritted my teeth the whole way to the kitchen, where I pulled out a box of chocolates I'd gotten as a gift from the PTA. On my way back, I asked, "But there are also cheap places without structural issues?"

"Sure. I did a deal once where there was a deadbolt on the bedroom door. Who the hell has a deadbolt on their bedroom?" Jade nodded slowly as she spun her tale. "Turns out this woman was married to a real dirtbag. This guy would get drunk and beat the crap out of her all the time. When he could catch her, that was. The deadbolt was how she kept herself and her kid safe when he went into one of his rages." She picked through the chocolates, touching one after the other, but only took a dark one with white stripes.

"How do you know all this?" I grabbed three latte-colored caramel squares before she could get her talons on them.

"I'm a wholesaler. It's my job to know what's wrong with a property. People tell things to their wholesaler they'd never tell their therapist." She tossed another dark one into her mouth. "Anyway, she'd decided that she'd had enough. But you don't just calmly tell a guy like that, and you sure as hell don't put a For Sale sign on your lawn. I checked it out; the house was all in her name. The day of the closing, her movers got her out of there in three hours flat. The jackass came home from work to find a pair of bouncers from the local club waiting for him, one carrying a baseball bat."

I almost spit out my chocolate. "They beat him up?"

"Oh, no." A sly grin came up Jade's face. "These guys are pros. They gave him a letter from his wife explaining she was leaving him, had sold the house, and was filing for divorce. The new owner changed the locks and hired the bouncers to make sure the scumbag didn't go into a rage and wreck the place. The bouncers opened the door and escorted the guy from room to room while he gathered his things. Then they locked up and left."

"All this is legal?" I asked.

"Wholesaling is a grey area in the law."

While Jade downed yet another of my chocolates, I mouthed to Dylan. "What the hell are you getting me into?"

He perked up and smiled like a puppy. "Real estate."

My head tilted towards my shoulder. "Funny how none of my other friends risk jail time when buying a house."

"Chill out." Jade smacked my arm and rolled her eyes. "I'm the only one taking risks here. There's nothing illegal on your end."

"Why is that?" I asked.

"It's a question of whether wholesalers are brokers or not." She leaned in, and I almost gagged on her perfume. "I'd say no, I'm just going out and finding you a deal. But licensed brokers hate competition, so they argue we shouldn't be able to do deals without becoming brokers first, which none of us would ever do. Far too much time, money, and effort. So they harass us when they can, but it's no big deal 'cause most of what we do happens under their radar."

I turned to Dylan. "Why can't I just call a *normal* agent and go see a *normal* property? That woman I met today doesn't even charge the buyers a commission."

"Typical agent commissions are 6%," Jade said, grabbing my attention. "You're right they're on the seller, but that doesn't mean the buyer doesn't pay for them. Think about it. You sell a house for $100,000 with an agent. How much'll you pocket?"

"Uh…$94,000."

"So if before you get an agent, a friend comes up to you and asks what's the lowest you'd take for your house, what would you say?"

"I guess I'd say $94,000. OK, I got it. Still, I can't do a cash-only deal, so does any of this help me?"

"Not every wholesale deal requires cash. Needing a mortgage limits your wholesale options, but you still have a chance of finding a deal way better than anything an agent will show you off the MLS."

"What's the MLS?" I asked Dylan.

He rubbed my shoulder. "The Multiple Listing Service. That's where the online real estate sites get their properties, and where most real estate agents find them as well."

"The thing about limiting yourself to the MLS," Jade licked the smudged chocolate off her fingers as she spoke, "is you're competing with every other eligible buyer, so you're probably paying full market price or close to it."

"You don't go through the MLS?"

Jade rolled her eyes. "Hell no. There are no wholesale deals on the MLS."

"Where do you find your listings?"

"My deals aren't listed." She poured herself another glass of water and downed it in two seconds flat. All that chocolate must have dried her out. "Typically, I buy lists of homeowners and send them postcards saying I want to buy their house."

"And people say yes to that?"

"Some do. Then I've got to figure out why they want to sell and what stops them from doing it through the MLS. Sometimes there's nothing wrong; they just never thought to list it or couldn't be bothered. Looking for a property for you, I won't bother with a postcard, though."

"Why not?"

"I do postcards when I'm targeting thousands of homes and hoping to find a couple of dozen owners willing to talk. You're looking for a quadruplex. There aren't a ton of those around, and even fewer eligible for a bank loan. I'll narrow down the list, identify the owners, and knock on their doors. Either we'll get lucky, or we won't."

"What happens if we don't get anything?"

"Then I've wasted a few hours of my time, and you don't owe me anything. You can decide if you want to expand the search to triplexes and duplexes or wash your hands of me. It's not like we're exclusive anyway. You think I care if you look yourself or with an agent?"

It was abundantly clear that this girl didn't care. "What happens if you find something?"

"I negotiate the deal and get them to sign off on it. You'll get first dibs to buy it off me. You'll check out the place. If you want it, you give me $5000, and it's yours. If you don't, I'll sell it to someone else or let the deal fall through."

"You can do that?"

"Oh yeah, I always have contingencies in my deals. But I rarely need them. I've got quite a few repeat buyers who trust that if I bring them a deal, it's a good one. Some of them buy off me sight unseen."

My gaze went from Jade's thick eye liner to her jagged earrings to her three-inch heels. Did I really want to enter the real estate underworld? I felt squeamish as I turned to Dylan. His puppy grin was back, and he nodded. I didn't know about Jade, but I trusted Dylan enough to take the risk. "OK, let's try it."

The day after my meeting with Jade (after I scrubbed down everything she'd touched), I began my hunt in earnest. I wasn't about to seek out abused wives looking to sell fast and disappear in the middle of the night. That wasn't my kind of real estate. But if Jade could do all that, I could at least call an agent and browse through online listings.

My first call, during a free period in the school day, was to Cynthia. "Amber, I was hoping I'd be hearing from you. Did you hear that Libby's offer was accepted?"

"I heard. That's a great house. But totally out of my price range."

"No problem. Let's start simple. What neighborhood and price range are you looking in?"

I was proud of myself that I knew enough real estate jargon to tell her exactly what I wanted. "I'm looking for a B neighborhood, though I can go down to C+."

"I'm sorry, I'm not following you. What's your price range?"

"Up to $300,000."

Cynthia coughed, and her voice dipped a few notes. "Well, that's somewhat lower than I normally go, but I have some ideas that might work for you."

"That's for a quadruplex."

The silence on the line made me cringe.

"You know, Amber, I'm not sure I'm the agent for you. There's a new girl in my office who's willing to do some lower-end housing while she gets up to speed. Let me give you her number."

I wrote the number down but called Dylan instead. "I want to start seeing homes with an agent. A real agent." I took a breath to keep my voice calm. "They don't have to drive a Lexus, but I prefer someone who looks less at home on a wanted poster than Jade. Don't you have anyone for me?"

"Sure, hang on a second." Dylan put me on hold and was back a moment later with another guy on the line. "Phil, I'd like you to meet Amber. She's pre-approved for an FHA loan and wants to start looking at properties immediately."

"Fantastic, Amber. What sort of neighborhoods are you interested in?"

I felt like a fool repeating what I'd said to Cynthia, but I braced myself and said, "Ideally B, though I'd be willing to go down to C+."

"No problem," Phil said, and I immediately sighed with relief. "What have you been pre-approved for?"

"Depending on rental values, I should have a budget of around $300,000 for a quadruplex."

"That budget is fine." He spoke at an easy pace, which I found calming. "Quads aren't the easiest properties to find. Are you willing to consider triplexes as well?"

"Yes, but..."

"But the budget would be a bit lower, I understand completely." I could almost hear the soothing smile on his face. "Do you want me to send you pro formas and comps?"

My head jerked back. "Sorry, are we still speaking English?"

Dylan broke in. "All that's a bit above her head at the moment, Phil. Why don't you take her out and show her a few places?"

I nodded. "Yes, what Dylan said."

"Great," Phil said. "When would you like to start looking?"

"Any chance we can do it after work today? I'll be off at 3:30."

"Absolutely. I'll set up our first appointment around 4 pm to give you time to get there. Does that work?"

"That sounds wonderful. I'll see you then." My hand rested on my chest. "Dylan, please stay on the line."

"Is that more your speed?" Dylan asked once Phil dropped off.

"So much more. But he's experienced, right? I called Cynthia earlier, and she tried to push me off on the new girl in the office. She also didn't have the slightest idea what I meant when I asked for a property in a B neighborhood."

"That's what you get for calling Cynthia before me."

"What's that supposed to mean?"

"Look, in your school, the kids have art classes, right?"

"Yeah, so?"

"Let's say the art teacher gets sick one day. The normal substitute is unavailable, but they hear of this other guy who's extremely qualified. He's got a Ph.D. in Art History and is a professor at the University. He comes into class and starts lecturing the kids about Gaugin. Good fit?"

I laughed. "Obviously not."

"And it doesn't mean that either the art teacher in your school or the professor are bad teachers. There are different types of art teachers in the world. The same with real estate. Cynthia deals with high-end, residential clients.

She's all about location. She's going to take a handful of clients and a handful of properties, and really work them both. She's a saleswoman, and she'd going to do everything she can to make one of her clients fall in love with one of her properties. This is a whole other bucket of fish. The fact that Phil's willing to work within your purchase price doesn't mean he's anything like the new guppy in Cynthia's office. Phil probably sells more properties in a month than Cynthia does in a year."

"How can he do that?"

"He's swimming in a different ocean. He deals with investors. His clients don't fall in love with his properties; they buy when the numbers work out."

"So his clients aren't looking for a love affair. Why does that mean he sells so much more than Cynthia?"

"He casts a much deeper net."

"What's with all the fish talk? Is that more of Luther's influence?"

"Could be." I could almost hear him smiling on the phone. "Look at Libby's case. Now that she's bought herself the 30-year house, Cynthia will never hear from her again. Each time she sells a client like Libby, Cynthia has to go out and find another one to take her place. Phil has clients who buy from him multiple times a year. For some of them, seeing the property is only a formality. By the time they step in the house, they've already looked at the pro forma, so they know exactly what their income and expenses should be, and they've looked at the comps, which tells them what similar properties in the area have recently sold for. For them, it's all business."

That triggered a memory of something Jade said. "Will Phil's clients ever buy from him sight unseen?"

"Absolutely. He usually finds his properties on the MLS, so he'll rarely find outrageous deals. But when he does, it's a lucky client that gets first crack at the property. His more successful clients know enough not to hesitate, even long enough for a viewing, lest they lose out to someone else."

"This first property is a triplex selling for $275,000," Phil said that afternoon. "One thing that I love about it is that it's just a block down from the hospital."

"Dangerous neighborhood, is it?" I asked.

Phil looked confused. "No, why do you say that?"

"Why else would it be an asset being so close to a hospital?"

Now he grinned. So far, I liked Phil. He was a clean-cut guy in his mid-thirties and felt like a younger Morgan Freeman. He wore a blue polo shirt and drove a Subaru Forrester. Perfect. Not too high-end, not too scary. "Close to the hospital is good because that means there's a steady influx of high-caliber tenants. Doctors doing their residencies love to live close by."

"Got it." I needed to start thinking more like an investor.

We walked into the first-floor apartment, a spacious two-bedroom. "This house is sixty-years-old, has hardwood floors throughout, and is structurally sound. It doesn't look like there's been much work done to it over the years, so you might want to upgrade things like the electricity and appliances." He walked me through to the back. "There's one thing in particular that made me feel like this place could be a good fit for you. Look at that: a back door."

The door opened onto what could best be called a mudroom. Phil grinned as if he'd just shown me a piece of hidden treasure, but I just stared back at him blankly. "And that's exciting because…"

"Because you were hoping to get a quadruplex, and this one's only a triplex. You're looking to maximize the rental income you can get with a property that still qualifies for a primary residence mortgage."

I still didn't get it.

"The doctors who are most particular about getting a rental close to the hospital are those here on rotation. They come for three months and then they're gone. While they're here, they're working their butts off, and the last thing they want to think about is their housing. Granted, they're a bit more work than getting long-term tenants, but they'll pay a premium for places that are fully furnished and close by. "

"Is there a hidden invisible apartment I'm missing here?"

"Yes!" Phil gave me a high-five. "That's exactly it! This back door allows you to divide the ground floor apartment into two, one large, one small. The smaller one will be perfect for doctors passing through on rotation and should give a nice boost to the cash flow of the house."

My vision expanded. I saw where a kitchenette would fit right next to the bathroom and how I could add cute touches to make this place feel homey to a resident living far from home. I was still taking baby steps, but I was starting to get it.

Once we finished the walkthrough of the house, we left my car there, and I rode with Phil to the next place. It was time to get a deeper understanding. "Walk me through the numbers."

"The house is listed for $275,000, and I think you should be able to get it for $265,000. I expect the attic apartment will cash flow at about $75 a month. That's the least valuable, so you might want to take that one yourself. The middle apartment should bring in $125 to $150 a month. The bottom one should do the same, but if you divide it like I'm suggesting, I think that apartment could cash flow $400 or more."

"Slow it down for me, Phil." I pulled out my notebook and a pencil. Math demanded a freshly sharpened #2. "How did you get to those numbers?"

"OK, we've got about a ten-minute drive to the next place, so let me give you a real basic overview of real estate accounting. Cash flow is the amount of money you have left in your pocket at the end of each month after paying your expenses. Have you got that?"

"Yeah, that much I understand."

"OK, good. Coming up with the number is not quite as simple as taking your income and subtracting your expenses, though."

"Why not?"

"Because many things can go wrong and you need to be prepared. In reality, a quadruplex might have $2000 of positive cash flow one month and a $500 loss the next."

"Why?"

Phil stopped at a red light and faced me. "Because tenants move out, and it might take a month or two to replace them. Things break, and it might cost you money out of pocket to fix them. So when investors look at properties, they always leave a margin of safety by making conservative estimates and having cash reserves for when things go wrong."

"Like what?"

"You could get a tenant who skips town, or worse, a squatter who refuses to pay rent. The plumbing could go bust, or the roof could start leaking after a storm. Anything's possible."

My mind raced, thinking of all the repairs my parents had made over the years, the worst of which was a rat infestation that evaded the efforts of the best exterminators. My stomach sank as though I'd just swallowed three eggs whole. "That sounds like a lot of headaches to deal with."

The light turned green, and Phil stepped on the accelerator. "It's only a headache if you're not prepared. That's why smart investors buy properties that give them enough wiggle room to cover difficulties. Plus, we add extra wiggle room on top of that. In running your numbers, you'll be safer assuming eleven months of rent per year instead of twelve. Each month you'll want to put aside a bit of cash for repairs."

"I'm going to have to deal with all these repairs like Dylan does?"

"Not if you have a property manager. Adding a property manager will cost you about 10% of your rental income."

"But if I manage them myself, I can just leave that out, right?"

"I always encourage clients to leave it in." Phil made a right on Brookline Ave. "That doesn't mean you can't do the management; it just means when running the numbers on a property, run them with the assumption that you'll be paying a property manager. If the numbers still work out well, then go ahead and buy the property and feel free to keep that extra cash yourself. But if you buy a property where the numbers only work out if you do self-management, you haven't invested in a passive income source, you've bought yourself a job."

"So the numbers you've given me…"

"Are all after taking into account some fairly conservative assumptions."

"Where'd you pull out these assumptions, out of a hat?"

Phil laughed. "Let me give you an example. The apartments in this next house we're seeing have separate electric meters, so the tenants will pay their own electric bills. When there's just one meter for the entire house, that expense normally falls on the landlord."

"Shouldn't that expense just get added into the rent?"

"Don't I wish. I suppose if all tenants were logical decision-makers, they'd be willing to pay a $100 a month more for an apartment that includes electricity, since that's about what they'd be saving. But most tenants don't think that way. The next time you have friends apartment shopping, go on and ask them to break down the expenses of each apartment they've seen, and be prepared for the blank looks you'll receive in return. Oh, they'll remember all about the neighborhood, the number of bedrooms, the rental price, and I'm sure they'll go on and on about some favorite features, like the view over the park. But few of them will remember which places include electricity and which don't."

"What are these other assumptions?"

"Most of them are pretty basic, such as property taxes, gas, water, sewer, garbage, and insurance. Then there's property management, which will fluctuate based upon how much rent you take in.

This was getting overwhelming. "Can you just write all the numbers down for me so I can see them?"

"For sure. They're all in the pro forma. I'll email it to you when I get back to my office."

All this jargon was making me feel pretty stupid. "What's that again?"

"It's a statement that gives you all the numbers of how a property stands today and projections about the cash flow you can expect in the future."

"That's one of those files you offered to send to Dylan?"

"Exactly. The other is the Comps."

"Remind me what those are?"

"The Comps show what other properties of a similar size recently sold for in the same neighborhood. The Comps help you assess whether the asking price is within market range. The Pro Forma helps you see how much return you'll get for your investment."

Phil slowed down at a stop sign. "Bear in mind, these numbers are only for year one. In general, both property values and rents tend to go up over time while your mortgage payments will stay the same."

"Until they all magically disappear when it's all paid off." I waved my imaginary wand.

"Exactly."

"Phil, can you tell me honestly, is this really a good investment?"

"What do you consider to be good?"

"Well, Dylan says he looks to get at least 15% annual growth on his money. Will I get that here?"

Phil laughed. "Are you serious?"

"So it won't get that high, eh?"

He only laughed harder. "Do you have any idea what the cash-on-cash ROI is on a purchase like this?"

"I have no idea what you just said."

"Sorry, let me slow it down. ROI stands for return on investment."

I scribbled the definition in my notebook.

"So," Phil continued, "if you bought a house in cash for $300,000 that brings in a profit of $30,000, it would have a return on your investment of 10%. Do you follow that?"

"Yes."

"But few investors want to buy real estate with cash."

"Dylan said cash buyers can get amazing deals."

"That's true. Let me restate that. Few investors want to buy real estate with cash and *keep* their cash in the investment. Those who buy with cash get great deals, improve the property so they can get a mortgage, and take their cash back."

"Why take it back?"

"Because what makes real estate such a fabulous investment is leverage. You don't need $300,000 to buy a $300,000 house. Most of that money will come from the bank. You have $20,000 to invest. When you ask me what your return will be, you're not asking how much money you will make relative to the $300,000 purchase price, but relative to the $20,000 investment. That's your cash-on-cash return. The cash you get out, relative to the cash you put in."

"OK. I get that." Grateful to be using a pencil, I erased the $300,000 and replaced it with $20,000. "So if I want a 15% return, then I'd have to make $3000 a year, right?"

"Precisely, assuming that you put in the full $20,000." Phil drove us into a more suburban part of town while I licked my lips, ready to do some number crunching.

"So let me figure this out. So you said I should live in the attic and that the middle apartment could bring in $125 to $150…"

"Let's be conservative and assume $125."

"OK, so $125 for that one, and I'm not sure how much I'll make on this splitting thing, so let's go ultra-conservative and say I only make $250 on the bottom apartment. That's $375. How's that greater than 15%?"

We'd stopped at another light, and Phil reached over and pointed to the number I just wrote. "That's monthly. The cash-on-cash return we're talking about is yearly."

"Woah!" Of course, how could I have missed that? "But you said to only assume 11 months, right?"

Phil lit up like a father watching his kid smack a baseball for the first time. "You got it! But, in this case, I already took that into account when making the monthly cash flow estimates, so you can go ahead and assume a full year."

"You mean…" I bit my lip as I multiplied 375 by 12. "I'd be making $4500 a year. That's more than 22%. Pretty good…"

"It's way better than that. Let's not forget you'll be living there as well. When allocating the costs, I divided them between the two main apartments, figuring you'd keep the attic for yourself. How much are you paying right now in rent?"

"$1200 a month." I still remembered my times tables and knew that 12x12 = 144. Adding the two zeros meant, "I'd be saving $14,400 a year?"

Phil offered a thumbs up. "Add it together, and you'd be making closer to 100% return on your $20,000 investment."

I arrived at Dylan's before 9 am, but he was already breaking a sweat turning up soil. I'd agreed to help him weed his garden, or the jungle as I called it. He figured I should put my muscle where my mouth was and help civilize the place.

"So, how'd the house hunt with Phil go?"

"Pretty great." I tied my hair back. "He showed me three triplexes and a quadruplex. All four of them cash flow, or so he says."

"Which one did you like the most?"

"Like?"

"It's not just an investment; it's a house hack. That means you have to live there, so you might as well choose the place you'd most like to be."

"Since when did personal preference matter to you?" If he wasn't full of sweat and dirt, I would have kissed him right then. "I figured you and I would go over the numbers, and you'd help me choose the one with the best return.

"Let's just say that I know my customer. This whole process will be far easier for you if you find a place you can fall in love with." Just when I thought aliens had transplanted his brain, Dylan added, "As long as the numbers work out." He handed me a pair of gardening gloves and showed me how to yank the weeds strangling his pumpkin patch.

"There's a triplex not far from my school." I slipped on the gloves. "The numbers aren't quite as strong as on some of the other properties, but it's this cute Victorian and will be less than a five-minute commute."

"That's not an insignificant factor. There's nothing more valuable than your time. If you can save ten minutes a day in the car, just think of how much more tiramisu you can make me over the course of a year."

I threw a wad of weeds at him. "Perhaps I'll use that extra time to peruse online dating sites."

Dylan's phone vibrated. He pulled off his gloves and slipped the phone out of his pocket. "Just how much did you love that Victorian?"

"Why?"

He turned his phone around to show me the message from Jade:

Found a quad. Total steal. Mortgage no prob. Will hold for 24 hrs b4 shop around. 1639 Haber rd. House vacant. Key under mat. Go see.

CHAPTER 9

THE DEATH
TRAP

"**H**oly crap, it reeks in here." I pulled my sweater up over my nose and dared one more step into the threshold. The house on Haber Road bore signs of disrepair from the street: peeling paint, a few broken windows, beer bottles littering the yard. But that was nothing compared to the surprise that welcomed us when we opened the door. "I can't stay here. Let's go."

"Not so fast," Dylan said. "Do you know what that smell is?"

"Rotting corpse?"

"That, my dear, is the smell of money."

"No, Dylan, that's the smell of poverty." I spoke in a nasal voice to avoid having to inhale. "Rich people don't smell like that."

"Money comes from identifying value where no one else can." Dylan pulled me by the elbow further in "There's a reason this house hasn't sold before. I bet everyone who walks in here tears the hell out. Never forget, you're buying a house for 30 years. Don't let a little stench you can eliminate in two days deter you. Especially if it drives down the price."

"OK." I recoiled into his chest. "Let's discuss it in the car. But I've got to get out of here. I'm going to puke."

Twenty minutes and fifteen dollars later, we were back. We'd picked up two medical masks and a bottle of peppermint essential oil. I doused the mask in oil, pulled it over my mouth and nose, and could still just barely handle being in the house. We did the fastest walkthrough I've ever done, then got the hell out of there.

"We're going out for coffee." I got back in the car and took off my mask. "I don't want to hear a peep of protest."

We called Jade on the way to the cafe. She laughed off the objections to the smell. "Professional hazard. I always keep a pack of cotton balls and plenty of perfume in my glove compartment. Half the houses I enter, you'd rather not get a whiff of." Then she told us the deal. $210,000 to the seller, plus $5000 to her. "Once you fix it up, I figure it'll be worth 320K easy."

Dylan didn't object to stopping for coffee, but I was surprised when he ordered one himself. I was downright shocked when he paid for us both. It was as if we were a normal couple, sitting in a cafe, listening to jazz, and sipping $10 worth of coffees that probably cost $0.25 to make. The first sip of coffee soothed my nerves, and the aroma covered up any lingering odor I may have picked up from The Death Trap on Haber, as I nicknamed the house. I held the cup just below my nose and stared at Dylan through the steam. "OK, smell aside, what did you think?"

"Jade's right. It's a steal."

Of course, Dylan's mind went right to value. "Other than the money, did you like it?"

"I actually did. The house has character. How about you?"

It was hard to get past the image of the trash and bird poop covering the floors, but I closed my eyes and tried to imagine how, with a bit of love, I could transform that place. "Yeah. I did too. I love the arches in that second-floor apartment. I could picture painting them a cornflower blue."

Dylan laughed and almost spit up his coffee.

"What's so funny?"

"It's OK. It's your house, do what you want with it."

"Go on, tell me." I nudged his sneaker under the table.

"It's not a work of art—it's a rental property."

"It's still going to be somebody's home. Wouldn't you want it to be cozy?"

"Cozy? No. I want it to be easy to manage." Dylan smoothed his napkin on the table. "I use one shade of off-white paint for all my properties. It's a color that doesn't fade much over time, so I can go in and do touch-up jobs whenever someone moves out without having to do a whole new paint job or match past colors. Plus, I can buy it in bulk, knowing it's the only color I'll ever need."

Coffee aside, this was not a normal date. "Always practical, aren't you, Dylan? I suppose you have a point for the tenants. But that's my favorite apartment. I want to live there."

"That one?" Dylan's head tilted back, and his eyes searched the ceiling, as if trying to recall the details of the place. "It's a bit big for one person, isn't it?"

I sipped my coffee and avoided his eyes. "That's true. What about for two?"

"If you took on a roommate, the numbers for the house look a lot better. But I figured you were past the roommate stage of your life."

Dylan could be awfully thick sometimes.

"I am." I took another sip of my coffee, watching him as he sputtered.

Dylan leaned in, and his eyes narrowed. "Are you saying what I think you're saying?"

"Yep. What if we made this *our* place?"

A smile started riding up his face, but then it stopped midway. "Why the sudden shift?"

"It's not sudden. It's anything but sudden. But it is a shift." I leaned in to meet him and got so close I could feel the heat radiating off his skin. "I guess I keep wondering what I'd do if I weren't scared. The answer that comes to me is always the same: I'd open my heart up to you and this crazy way of thinking you've brought into my life."

"Wow." He reached out and took my hand. "If you can do that, I'll personally paint the walls any color you want."

I blushed and sank back into my chair. "How about you? You've never been scared of me, but there must be something that scares you. What would you do if you weren't afraid?"

Dylan sighed. "I guess I'd BRRRR."

"Sounds chilling. What's that?"

"You know what house flipping is, when you buy a house cheap, fix it up, then sell it at a profit. A BRRRR is like flipping a house to yourself. It stands for Buy, Rehab, Rent, Refinance, Repeat."

"Woah." I pulled out my notebook. "So that's B and how many R's?"

"Four. You buy a cheap place, fix it up, and rent it out."

I wrote down Buy, Rehab, Rent. "What are the last two R's?"

"Since it's now a nicer place and bringing in more rent, appraisers will give it a higher valuation. Your next R is to refinance it based upon the new valuation, ideally getting back the money you invested in the house. Then you take that money, and the final R is you repeat the process."

"And banks will just allow you to borrow more money on it?"

"Why not? Banks are in the business of lending money. They just have to know there's enough value there to support it. Within a year, we should have no problem refinancing The Death Trap on Haber. Once we fix it up and rent it out, the value will shoot up."

"You really think it will be worth $320,000?"

Dylan leaned in. "With one small change, I think it can be worth even more."

"What's the change?"

"Adding a bedroom to the first and second-floor apartments. There's space for it, I checked."

"Where?"

"Right here." Dylan drew on his napkin. My writing was neater, but there was no way I could have redrawn the house from memory, especially after such a short walk-through. I suppose all those years in real estate gave him an eye for details, for he drew out the full floor-plan. "See right there? We could build a wall down that line, make the living room a dash smaller, and add a whole extra bedroom. My guys and I could do this in a couple days. It's pretty standard work."

"How much value can a bedroom add? I mean, it's not going to make the place any bigger, we're just taking the space from somewhere else."

"It depends. If you went from a four-bedroom to a five, you'd gain next to nothing—you might even lose value. But there's a huge difference in value between a two-bedroom and a three."

"Why?"

"Families. Think about it, if we were looking to buy a long-term home and start a family," Dylan lifted his gaze to meet mine, "what's the minimum number of bedrooms we'd want?"

My mind flooded with images of us living in a house full of kids. I loved kids and always dreamed of having two boys and two girls. "I guess three. A boys' room, a girls' room, and a master."

"Exactly. And families are a big chunk of the market. Jade doesn't just go out looking for people in dire straits. She's looking for unrealized value. Most of her clients are looking to either flip or BRRRR. For it to be worth their while, they need to raise the value of the property by a huge margin."

My heart was still fluttering. I gripped my pen and refocused on my notebook to get my bearings. "How much exactly is *huge*?"

"There's something called the 70% rule. Ideally, investors want their costs, including the purchase, closing, rehab, all of it, to add up to no more than 70% of the after-repair value."

"After-repair value?"

"The house's market value when they're done fixing it up."

I wrote everything he was saying but wanted to make sure I understood the reasoning behind it. "What's so holy about the number 70%? Is that just considered a good profit margin?"

Dylan nibbled at the shortbread that came with our coffee. "It's more than that. A commercial loan might only lend you 70%-75% of the value of the property."

"So if you stay under that number, you can get all your investment money back?"

"Exactly."

"It sounds like a practical way to do real estate," I said. "Why does it scare you?"

"It's something I could potentially do after hours, but the longer a rehab takes me, the longer the apartments will just sit there, unoccupied, making no money." For the first time since that night at the beach with Kyle and Libby, I saw Dylan twisted up. He picked at his cuticles, and his eyes darted around as he spoke. "If I'm going to throw myself into this strategy, it makes the most sense for me to leave my job and make this my main income. The long-term rewards are greater, and I could build my Cash Machine that much faster."

"Why don't you?"

Dylan slumped. "I've never been much of a risk-taker."

I allowed myself a giggle. "How can you of all people say that?"

"You know what's risky?" Dylan popped right up, ready for a fight. "Taking on massive amounts of educational debt in the hope that you'll be able to find a good enough job to support yourself and pay it back. The only reason it doesn't feel risky is that everyone's doing it."

"Woah." I put my hands up as if under arrest. "Chill out. I'm just saying that it seems to me like you're not mister play-it-safe."

"Seriously?" Dylan's tone softened, and he sank back into that nervous posture I'd seen moments before. "Look at my life. I spend a tiny fraction of what I make and put the rest in investments that generate passive income. Can there be any more conservative a path than that?"

I reached out and raised his chin so that our eyes met. "You're wrong. It takes a bold man to go against the grain the way you did. You can do this too."

Dylan held my gaze and breathed deeply. "I can." His face tightened. "But I leave myself with less of a safety net. I'd go from being an employed guy with a steady, active income to a full-time investor."

"Didn't you tell me that once you're financially independent, you'll be able to take risks?"

"But I'm not independent yet."

"You must be. You spend nothing on housing, nothing on transportation, next to nothing on food. You must be independent."

Dylan pinched his lips, as if pondering what I said, and a twinkle lit his eye. "You know what else? Guess what my taxes were last year?"

"How much?"

Dylan's eyes danced. "Nothing."

"How's that possible?"

"That's for another time. What I'm saying is, you're right. I've measured financial independence based upon the lifestyle I want to lead in the *future*. I need to have enough to support not just me, but the family I want to have. But by the true definition of financial independence, I'm there. My passive income covers more than my *current* cost of living."

I knew Dylan. He wouldn't make the decision right away, he'd chew it over first, but I could see the wheels turning in his head. We walked out of the cafe hand in hand. "You see," I said. "I could have been yours all this time. All you had to do was shell out for coffee."

I grew up on plastic. One quick flick of the wrist was enough to purchase anything I needed. Now, even my credit cards were becoming outdated. More and more, I paid with my phone without even needing to pull out my wallet. But buying a house was a different story.

Before I could make the purchase, I needed an inspection, a title search, and dozens of other things. No doubt, every step would have stressed me out had Dylan not been through it all before. "Real estate is a team sport," he said. "The better the team you build, the better you'll be able to execute amazing deals." Fortunately, he already had the people he liked to work with, so it only took a few calls to get an inspector and an attorney working on the case.

Miraculously, this house that the Munsters would thumb their noses at passed inspection. Not on all counts, mind you. The electricity was a mess. Some of the piping needed replacing. A section of the roof had cracked shingles. Despite all that, the inspector said the foundation was solid, and there was no sign of mold (though how he would have even smelled mold over the odor of rotting corpse, I didn't know).

Dylan went with me to the bank the day after we got back the inspection report. "Now, when it comes to renovations," Gregory asked, "just how extensive is the work you're planning on doing?"

"The place is a total disaster," I said.

"Will you be repairing any structural damage?"

I had no idea how to answer and felt immediately relieved that I had Dylan by my side. "No, the structure is good," he said.

"Will you need over $35,000?"

"I'm not sure." I shrugged. "Why? Is that all I can roll into my mortgage?"

"There's technically no limit to the amount you can borrow under the 203(k) loan. However, there's a streamlined version for loans under $35,000 that don't require any structural work."

Even the loopholes had loopholes. "And the advantage of the streamlined version is…?"

"That you don't need an outside consultant, who will charge you to weigh in on your repairs."

Again I turned to Dylan. He said, "We're planning on doing much of the work ourselves. I think we can keep it under $35,000. But just barely. Let's borrow $35,000 exactly."

"Very well." Gregory typed in some numbers on the computer. "The money will be put into an escrow account where you can draw on it for renovation purposes only. The renovations must start within 30 days of closing and must be finished within six months. Any questions?"

CHAPTER 10

HOT CIDER

I didn't sleep at all the night before Thanksgiving. I was 25 years old, had never brought a boy home to meet the family, and Dylan hardly excelled at first impressions.

Dylan didn't do small talk. He didn't have the lightheartedness that allowed someone like Kyle to form quick, shallow, bonds. No one (other than Maria Rose and my other flirty cousins) would care that Dylan was cute. They'd just want to know if he was husband material. It took me weeks to realize just how solid a guy he was, that he wasn't just some lazy bum dropout. Unfortunately, my family liked guys they could size up in five minutes or less.

Still, I had a plan. Dylan would clam up in big, group settings; his strength was one-on-one. We had to get there early, so he could meet my family little by little as they rolled in, before they turned into a mob. I didn't tell him this, of course. Instead, I told him I wanted to get an early start to beat the holiday traffic. At 4 am, I gave up trying to sleep and treated myself to a hot shower in an attempt to calm my nerves. I picked up Dylan at 5:30 prompt. He got into the car and leaned over to give me a kiss, but when his lips were still a good six inches away, I blurted out, "What are you bringing my aunt?"

He stopped, still puckered. "Sorry?"

"What are you bringing Aunt Sofia?"

"Uh…"

I held his face in my hands as if I'd caught him sneaking Halloween candy. "You'll be a guest at an Italian woman's home. I don't care if you have to take out a second mortgage on one of your buildings, you're not showing up empty-handed."

I'll say one thing for Dylan, he knew when to hold his tongue. "Anything else I should know?"

"Let's say the soup is too salty for your taste. My aunt asks you what you think of it. What do you say?"

"Uh…"

"You're hopeless. Repeat after me, 'It's wonderful, may I please have some more?'"

Dylan rubbed my shoulder. "Take deep breaths, Amber. It's going to be fine."

"It wouldn't be so bad if it was at my house or Aunt Theresa's. But Aunt Sofia is hosting this year. I can already hear her calling up my mother, 'What kind of a man is this new boyfriend of Amber's? He comes into my house empty-handed and starts telling me how to cook soup? I know Amber is desperate to get married, but surely she could do better than this.'"

Dylan laughed. "Since when are you desperate?"

"In Aunt Sofia's eyes? The minute I turned 21 without a ring on my finger."

Dylan softened his gaze to a look of pure pity. "I promise to do my best not to embarrass you. Any other instructions?"

"The men will act like they're in charge, but don't be fooled. Most of them could care less who I wind up with as long as I look happy. The women rule the roost. They're the ones you need to impress."

Dylan blinked. "I need to impress them?"

"They're going to pick apart everything you do. Not the younger ones; my cousins are fine. To be safe, don't talk to any woman over forty without me." Part of me hated to stoop to this level, another part was desperate. "But you can't ignore them either or they'll take it as a slight. The women will gather in the kitchen and dining room. You'll come in with me, and I'll tell you what to say to each of them. After ten minutes, I stay behind, and you can go watch football with the men."

"You know I'm not such a big football fan, right?"

"You are today." I patted his cheek. "Football on Thanksgiving is a tradition or something. Trust me, you can watch the game, drink a beer, munch on some chips, and be largely ignored. That's your safe zone."

"Is there a team I should root for?"

"I don't know who's playing. Just cheer for whoever everyone else is cheering for."

Dylan rolled his eyes. "Your family sounds like a lot of fun."

"They're the best. I love my family. You will too. Trust me. It's just this first time. My family judge people quickly and are slow as molasses to change their minds. Make a good impression this weekend, and you'll never have to worry about them again. They'll come to love you for who you are. Eventually."

"But for now…"

"You give them nothing to find fault with, or you'll never hear the end of it."

As we reached the end of the four-hour drive, I quizzed Dylan. "Aunt Theresa."

"Very into her clothes. Be sure to compliment something she's wearing."

"Good. Aunt Viola."

"Obsessed with her grandkids, especially her three-year-old twin grandsons. Let her see me playing with them."

"Yes! You remembered the twins." I gave him a high-five. "Aunt Sophia."

"She's the worst cook among the sisters and is terribly sensitive about it. She's also hosting this year, so she'll have cooked the most. You'll snoop around the kitchen to find out what dishes she prepared, and I'll make sure to compliment them and ask for seconds."

"Grandma Maria." I thought with pride that I'd make a good drill sergeant.

"She's the matriarch. She'll take the longest to form her opinion. She can be swayed by her daughters, which is why I need to make good impressions with some of your aunts. But her sons won't say much, and she could care less what their wives think. It's rare she and her daughters disagree, but if they do, all but one will bend to her will."

"Which brings us to the last of her daughters, my mom."

"Your mom is too invested in your welfare to be impressed by empty compliments. She wants to see that I treat you well, that I'm attentive, and that I'm able to support a family."

I bit my lip. That last one was going to be a problem. I couldn't bring it up to Dylan without him explaining how well he'd prepared for his financial future, but my mother was never going to buy his crazy plans.

We were among the first to arrive. That was good. If Dylan made a good impression on whoever was already there, he could lay low, and the new arrivals would hear the gossip before they met him. That way, they'd already be positively disposed toward him. If the first impressions were bad, we'd need to hang out by the entranceway, maybe even be sitting and talking on the driveway. That way, each new person would meet him and form their own opinions before they heard about him from anyone else.

We parked on the street in front of the house. Dylan pulled a big bouquet out of the back seat. He'd spent $75 without a word of objection. I owed him for that one. Aunt Sophia answered the door and immediately enveloped me. Over my shoulder, I felt her eyes drifting towards Dylan. When we separated, he said, "I'm Dylan. Thank you so much for inviting me for Thanksgiving."

A little stiff, but not too bad.

"These are for you," he added, holding out the bouquet.

"Oh please, you needn't have brought me anything."

Yeah, right.

Dylan's eyes panned the foyer looking for something to compliment, but Lord knows Aunt Sofia didn't make it easy, with all those gaudy pictures of angels on the wall. "What a beautiful home you have."

"Why thank you, Dylan. Can I get you something to drink? We have coffee, tea, beer, and a pot of hot cider I just finished making."

"The hot cider sounds wonderful," he said. Smart move.

"Coming right up."

I gave Dylan a reassuring squeeze of his arm. So far, so good.

Dylan listened to Uncle Pauli's war stories. He wasn't much of a small talker, but that boy knew how to listen. And as long as he was listening, he couldn't put his foot in his mouth.

Then a miracle happened. Aunt Theresa went to plug in a second coffee maker to keep up with the demand. She'd found an old one in the basement, that probably hadn't been used since the last time Aunt Sofia hosted Thanksgiving. She had only halfway plugged it in when a pop echoed through the kitchen, and the power went out.

Aunt Sofia looked daggers at Aunt Theresa, as if it was her fault that Aunt Sofia still had that old piece of junk lying around. "And Joe just went out for more beers," Aunt Sofia said. "It could be an hour before he gets back and gets the power back on."

Dylan happened to be in the kitchen, getting himself a third mug of my aunt's hot cider. "I can fix that for you."

"Oh no, please. I don't want you to hurt yourself. Joe knows how to fix it. He'll see to it when he gets back."

I had to grab the moment. "Dylan knows all about electricity from maintaining the properties he owns, don't you, Dylan."

Dylan sent me a quizzical look. He and I both knew his job, rather than his properties, had trained him to deal with electricity. Fortunately, he was smart enough not to object. "Yes, that's right."

"Well, if you know what you're doing…" Aunt Sofia gripped his arm, and I could tell she was trying to feel his muscles. She always ogled the pimped-up Italian men in the underwear commercials. "Come, I'll show you where the box is in the basement."

Dylan followed her, and a moment later, the power went on. Aunt Theresa put a hand to her chest. "My, he is quite handy, isn't he?"

"Oh yes." I stood a little taller.

"Well, Dylan," Aunt Sofia said loud enough for all to hear. "I don't know what we would have done without you." I thanked the angels she didn't smack his butt.

"Good job," I whispered to him. "Now go disappear and watch football with the boys before you do anything to screw it up."

Trouble started around 3 pm.

Neither my parents nor Grandma Maria had arrived. I sat with my youngest sister Josephine, hearing about her latest boy problems when she broke off her diatribe about Chad and laid a manicured hand on my knee. "Don't look now, but Dylan is talking to Aunt Sofia."

What was he doing? He knew the plan. He'd made a strong first impression; now he just needed to blend in and watch football. How hard was that? What kind of guy couldn't be trusted to watch football on Thanksgiving?

Breathe, I told myself as I made my way as quickly as I could without drawing everyone's attention. But by the time I reached them, it was already too late.

"You know, there's nothing to be embarrassed about being a dropout," Aunt Sofia was saying.

Why? Why did Dylan have to tell her he'd left school? Was it so hard to tell people about his real estate investments and shut his mouth about that stupid Cash Machine? Didn't he realize that no one would grasp his logic during a two-minute holiday conversation? I grabbed Dylan's arm, in a way I hoped would look affectionate, but gave him gentle tugs to indicate we needed to get away from this conversation. And fast. But once Aunt Sofia had her hooks in someone, she wasn't one to let go.

"Two of my boys were also dropouts. Eddie, Lord bless his soul." She gulped down a cheek-full of wine. "He was never from the thinkers, if you know what I mean. At least he tried. Unlike Jimmy." Aunt Sofia's face fell. "Jimmy could never keep it in his pants, if you know what I mean. If that boy went to class twenty times during his two years in college, it would be a miracle. $60,000 we spent sending him to school, and all we got out of it were headaches and a paternity suit."

I pulled Dylan's arm even harder, but the guy worked with his hands all day. He was solid as a mountain. And apparently as thick as one too if he wasn't getting the hint.

"But what's your excuse?" Aunt Sophia smacked his face in a way only an Italian would call loving. "You seem bright enough, and obviously, you're not one of those guys who just thinks with your hormones, or you'd never go for a girl like Amber." She nudged me so hard I lost my balance. "The boys just looking for a good time usually wind up with her cousin, Maria Rose."

I swear, this woman has no filter.

Dylan rested his hand on mine, which was still gripping his bicep for dear life. "Maria Rose. Was she that tall blond one you introduced me to?"

"Oh no," Aunt Sofia said. "You're thinking of Maria Victoria. That Maria's out of your league. Maria Rose is over there." She pointed to my cousin, who, despite the chill November weather, wore a mini skirt and tank top that barely held her in.

When she saw us staring at her, Maria Rose smiled flirtatiously and waved to Dylan.

My aunt forced Dylan's face back towards her as if to imply he was looking where he shouldn't be (even though she pointed him there). She didn't even whisper when she added, "You'd think she'd at least insulate her breasts for winter…"

Dylan gulped, but otherwise let the comment go. "There are a lot of Marias in your family."

"All named after my mother, of course. I'm the only one without a Maria, and that's just because I had all boys. But you chose well, Dylan." She pinched my cheek so hard, my whole head shook. "Maria Ambrosia has a special place in my heart. She'd be the spitting image of my dead sister Isabella if she wasn't so flabby in the thighs."

I tugged Dylan's arm harder this time, no longer worrying about subtlety. He finally got the hint and followed me away. There was nowhere we could talk privately inside with relatives everywhere, so I dragged him out the front door and toward the car. I had steam bulging out of every orifice, but Dylan had the audacity to giggle the entire way.

"Maria Ambrosia?" he asked once we were out of earshot.

"Ugh." I smacked his chest, which was so hard, I bet he didn't feel a thing. I wanted to leave a bruise. "Didn't I tell you to lay low and watch football with the guys?"

"You also told me to be attentive and complimentary to your Aunt."

"Only when I'm with you. I told you not to talk to any woman in my family over forty without me present." I threw my hands up in exasperation and paced wildly in front of him. "Why'd you have to go telling her you dropped out of school?"

Dylan's composure grew stern. "I did drop out of school, Amber. I'm not embarrassed by it. I still say it was the smartest choice I ever made."

Poor thing. He was doing the best he could, and here I was raging at him. I still felt like a fiery engine but tried to keep myself from blowing. "I know Dylan, but your reasoning is complex." I adjusted his shirt collar and removed a cracker crumb from his chest. "It's not the sort of thing my family will process over snippets of holiday conversations. Keep things simple. Just tell them you're in real estate. You own several apartment buildings, and you're looking to invest in several more." I grinned my sappiest, most pitiful smile. "That's simple. They can understand that."

"I work on a remodeling crew, Amber." His voice remained calm, but I could feel the frustration rising in his chest. "I don't feel the need to hide what I do. I'm sorry if it embarrasses you."

"It doesn't embarrass me because I know why you do it and what you're hoping to build. But my family won't get it. Not initially. Just like it took me a long time to get it." In some ways, I still didn't fully get it. I took a deep breath.

"Even your aunt said it's nothing to be embarrassed about."

I shoved him in the chest. "And then she compared you to her two loser sons, one of whom still lives at home at 31, and the other who's working as a janitor. The only reason she told you not to be embarrassed is because she assumes that anyone dropping out of school ought to be embarrassed. Otherwise, she wouldn't try to placate you. But as much as she tries to sound magnanimous, she'll be singing a different tune when gossiping with her sisters. Couldn't you just sit with the guys and have a good time?"

"Football isn't my thing. Besides, if I want a good time, it sounds like I shouldn't be with you at all." He bobbed his head and batted his eyelashes. "Perhaps I should call Maria Rose."

I punched him in the arm. "Some good times are worth waiting for, you know."

"I thought so as well. But something tells me that Maria Rose won't care that I'm a dropout."

I ran my hand through my hair. My family wouldn't get Dylan, not right away. All I wanted was for them to like him, and over time, they'd come to see what an amazing guy he was. But I was so focused on them, I'd hardly thought at all about him. He always seemed so tough, so resilient. I figured he'd roll with all the coaching. But what had I conveyed? That I was embarrassed by him. That I didn't want my family to see the real Dylan. That I didn't think he could represent himself or share the things that he cared about.

I looked up at him with tears running down my face. I owed this amazing man an apology. I ought to stand proudly by his side for the rest of the holiday, then take him home and show him the affection he deserved, show him he could have a good time even with me. A great time even, because with me, it would be real, and I would make it all worth the wait. But before I could say a word, a voice called out behind me.

"Amber?"

I'd know that voice anywhere. Dad. Of all times to show up. I turned to see my father, my mother, and Grandma Maria all watching us. I quickly wiped the tears from my cheeks.

"Amber, is everything all right?" My father said.

"Mom, Dad, Grandma Maria, I'd like you all to meet my boyfriend, Dylan." I took his arm again, but he gently drew it away, not fully out of my grasp—he'd never embarrass me as I'd embarrassed him—but enough so that I knew.

"Pleased to meet you, Dylan." My father held out a hand, but his gaze was guarded. Nothing provokes an Italian man more than seeing his daughter cry.

Mom looked right past him. "Amber, is that your car? Were you in an accident?" She grabbed my hand. "Are you OK?"

The car. The stupid car. I'd gotten so used to the dent I barely spared it any mind. How could I be so dumb? It would have been so easy to rent a new car for the drive.

"I'm fine, Ma. I bought the car that way." I hugged her. "I'll tell you all about it later."

I kissed Dad and Grandma Maria on both cheeks, and we all walked back into the house. All my careful planning had blown up in my face. How could I repair the damage either with my family or with Dylan?

I'd tried to be the dutiful girlfriend and stay by Dylan's side the rest of the day, but the situation spiraled out of control. My parents wanted to talk. They wanted to hear about the car and especially about the guy. I told them everything, but I didn't do a good job of explaining. Like I'd told Dylan, these weren't concepts I could convey in sound-bites, especially to those predisposed against them. After walking in on us in the middle of a fight, they'd heard Aunt Sophia blab, "I have to tell you, I'm surprised your bright daughter's dating a college drop-out who's working some manual labor job. Maria Rose, that's one thing, but our Maria Ambrosia? I would've thought she'd want a guy with ambition." I was done for.

Dad was a trial attorney, and cross-examination was his specialty. He asked me clear, pointed questions, and I didn't hold back. They learned Dylan didn't own a car, had never once taken me out to eat, and lived in some basement apartment. I explained that he owned the entire building he lived in, as well as two others. I told them how great he'd been to me, and though they nodded without interruption while I rose to his defense, everything I said fell on deaf ears. Dad's sister, Aunt Vicky, used to invent all sorts of excuses for her abusive husband, and it took Dad years to convince her to finally walk out on him. My excuses now would have no more impact than Aunt Vicky's did all those years ago, because nothing I said would shake his first image of us together: the two of us fighting while I cried in the driveway.

Then they found out about the house I'd bought. The one closing in three weeks. The one I'd invited Dylan to move into with me. My mother elbowed my father. Dad stepped closer. "It's been too long since we've paid you a visit. There's more going on in your life than we've understood in our recent calls." He patted me on the head the way he did in middle school. "That's very exciting news about buying a house. We'll come see it for ourselves."

I swallowed hard.

"Before you close," Dad added. My heart fell to my knees.

We'd originally planned to stay the night, me at my parents and Dylan at Aunt Sofia's, but we decided to make the long drive back home instead. I apologized to Dylan profusely on our way back, but he, like Mom and Dad, didn't want to listen. We drove in eerie silence. To try to break the tension, I said, "When I was with my parents, you seemed to be having a fairly intense conversation with my cousin Lorenzo."

For the first time on the drive, a smile came to Dylan's lips. "He asked if I needed money to buy a ring."

That was the final proof I needed. Everyone in my family was convinced Dylan was a loser who couldn't get it together. "He actually offered to give you money to buy me a ring?"

"Give? Oh, no, no. Lend. 'Very reasonable terms,' he said."

CHAPTER 11

CORNFLOWER BLUE

A tense peace settled between Dylan and me, and it stayed that way for almost an entire day.

I called him early Saturday morning. "We need to get going on the house."

"What house?"

"My house. *Our* house." Images flashed through my mind of all the details that needed fixing, not the least of which was the stench. "The Death Trap on Haber. We need to start working on it." My heart raced to keep up with my thoughts. "Now!"

"Amber." Dylan's voice had that groggy morning waver. "You don't close on that place for another three weeks."

"And my parents will be here in two weeks! They're going to want to see it." My fist tightened around the phone. "What do you think they'll say when they walk in and smell rotting corpses?"

"Look, Amber, you can't just—."

How could he be so calm? "Come over. Please just come over. I'm freaking out."

Dylan promised to come. I hung up the phone but couldn't sit still. My mind was racing. I needed to do something to put myself at ease, and nothing calmed me like cooking. I put on some Nora Jones and sang along as I prepared french toast, scrambled eggs, a green salad, a pot of coffee, hot chocolate, and fresh orange juice. I actually squeezed orange juice. I would have kept going had Dylan not arrived.

"You look freezing," I said. He was all bundled up, jacket, scarf, hat, and nonetheless stood there shivering. "I'm so sorry." I reached out to welcome him in. "I should have come to get you. I wasn't even thinking about the weather."

"It's OK. A nice brisk ride gets the blood moving." He took off his gloves and rubbed his hands together. One look in the kitchen set his eyes aglow. "You cooking for an army?"

"I'm anxious. When I'm anxious, I cook."

Dylan's eyebrows danced. "I'll have to make you anxious more often."

"What would you like first?" I bounced from one end of the kitchen to the other. "Coffee? Hot chocolate? Or do you want to dig right in on the french toast?"

"I'll tell you what I want." He removed his hat, jacket, and scarf, then took me in a bear hug. For the first time all morning, I exhaled. I sank into his chest and listened to his heart, which still pumped loudly from his bike ride. "I know you're freaking out, but we'll get through this." He laid his lips on my hair and whispered, "We can get through anything together."

My shoulders shook, and tears filled my eyes. "I wanted to buy this house and fix it up. Then I'd bring my parents out here to see it and tell them how they'd never believe how awful it seemed when I bought it. And they'd say, 'you're kidding, it's so nice now.' And I'd say 'that's because the house had great bones, a solid foundation, and great architecture, but it had broken windows and smelled of rotting corpses, and was filled with trash. I needed to be able to see beneath the surface, to find the beauty in it, and bring that out.' And they'd say, 'If that's the case, then you've done a great job, Amber, because it's certainly beautiful now.' And they'd say how proud they were, and they could see that I'm on a healthy track with my life, and I'm no longer their little girl who needs looking after.

"But now they're going to come and see this house filled with trash that smells like the dead, and they're going to say, 'We think you've gotten in way over your head, Amber. What happened to you that you're driving a dented car and buying a broken-down house? We always wanted better for you, and frankly, we thought you'd want better for yourself. And we know why you're doing it. You've lost your mind over that dropout boy who's swayed you with his crazy ideas.'"

Dylan still held me tight. "Then what will they say?"

"They'll tell me to pack my bags; that they'll be taking me home because I've clearly shown I can't be trusted to live on my own."

Dylan released his grip and held me at arm's length. He stared into my eyes, and I knew he was about to say exactly what I needed to hear to make everything OK. Instead, he said, "I'm hungry. Let's eat."

So we sat down to eat, and as we gorged ourselves on the feast I'd prepared, everything did start to feel better. "We don't need to fix up the entire house, but if we can just get in there and get rid of the garbage and take care of the smell, maybe my parents won't flip out when they see it."

"Bad idea, Amber." Dylan shook his head. "One of the rules of real estate is that you never want to mess with a property before it closes."

"Why not?"

"Because there are still a million things that could go wrong."

"What could go wrong?"

"What if the owner decides she sold for too little? She's signed a contract, but we can't exactly force her to sell. Yes, there are penalties if she backs out, but they're not always so easy to enforce, especially if she says we made changes to the property."

"I just want to clean it up." I wiped a puddle of coffee that had dribbled onto the table. "We're not going to make any big changes."

Dylan made the voice of a witch preparing a stew. "What if that rotting corpse you're always complaining about is her mother, and we accidentally throw away the body?"

I laughed. "The smell is probably from animals coming in through the broken windows and doing their business."

"And you'd throw away her animal feces collection?"

"What if we just opened the windows and aired the place out?"

Dylan poured himself some hot chocolate. "It could rain through the window and warp the floorboards. Who knows what can happen? If you don't mess with the status quo, you don't give her any reasons to back out."

"After you sign, you never go into a building?"

"I'll go in and take measurements. I'll have an architect or a contractor look the place over. I'll start putting plans together and maybe even place orders for cabinets or appliances." He topped his drink with a pair of baby marshmallows. "But I won't change a single thing, and I won't commit any money I can't get back."

"You think going in there, removing trash, and scrubbing the place down will cause the deal to fall through?" I buttered my umpteenth slice of toast. Perhaps if I got fat enough, my parents wouldn't recognize me; then they wouldn't take me away.

"Remember, it was the grime and the smell that drove away other potential buyers. The owner could never be bothered to deal with it herself, but if we take care of it for her, she might start to see the value in the place."

"What if Jade says it's OK?"

"You want to ask Jade?" Dylan closed his eyes, and I could tell he was working hard not to roll them to the back of his head. "Be my guest. Call Jade."

So I asked her. "If you want to give me my $5000 up-front and take all the risk on yourself, you go right ahead." Jade's voice got bar-brawl feisty. "But if you're planning on paying me only when the deal closes, you stay the *hell* out of that house."

"You know," I said, "if you told me I could go in, I might have invited you over for breakfast."

"$5000 buys a lot of cereal. Don't mess this deal up." Without so much as a goodbye, Jade hung up.

"What am I going to do?" My head fell into my hands. "My parents are going to hate this place."

Dylan rubbed my back. "What if we only show them the outside and pictures of the interior? We can say we can't enter until after closing. At least that way, they won't get the smell."

I sat up and faced him. "My father can smell a lie like a hound smells blood. Never mess with that man."

"What do you want to do?"

"I don't know." I bounced in my seat like a whiny toddler. "Distract me. Get my mind on something else."

A hike would've been good—the exercise would've released anxiety. But it was cold and rainy, so Dylan and I spent the weekend playing games and cuddling on the couch, watching movies. He wanted to get romantic, but I couldn't go there. Not now.

Things would have been different had Thanksgiving not been such a disaster. Had my family embraced Dylan, I could've let myself fall into his arms. But they were all convinced I'd wound up with a loser, and now my parents were coming to prove it.

I know I shouldn't be so influenced by my family's opinions. Plenty of women could care less if their family approved of the guy in their life—hell, half the reason Maria Rose ran around with bums was to antagonize her folks—but I wasn't like that. My parents had looked out for me my entire life. Was I going to blow off their opinions now?

The next weekend arrived without any new ideas on how to ward off the impending disaster. The weather dropped below freezing, and then below zero. I offered to pick Dylan up Saturday morning, but he'd had to deliver appliances the day before for a remodeling job, so he had the company van for the weekend. He came by with groceries, and we spent much of the day cooking. I taught him how to make ravioli, and while I made the sauce, he made a thick, brown bread, which tasted delicious even though it didn't go with the meal.

Sunday, I had a lunch date with Libby and our friend Kara, who'd recently gotten engaged. I got into my car at noon and turned the key. The car made this sound like an 86-year-old man climbing uphill with a refrigerator on his back. I tried again. Same thing. I called Dylan in a panic. "My car won't start."

"I'll be right over."

It was a good thing he had the van. Five minutes later, he pulled up. "Show me what's wrong." I turned the key and let him hear the car gasping. "It sounds like the battery. When was the last time you drove it?"

"Friday, home from work."

"Pop the hood." I searched around until I found the release button. Dylan took one look and shook his head. "Cold can be a killer for batteries, especially when you haven't used it in a couple of days. Fortunately, I've got jumper cables in the van."

Dylan pulled the van around so it stood nose to nose with my car. He was good with his hands, but not terribly knowledgeable about cars. Dylan had to look up how to jump a car; he knew doing it wrong could fry out the electrical system. At first, I let Dylan figure it out. I bit my tongue so I wouldn't say a single word, but I couldn't help pacing like a crack addict itching for a hit. After checking my watch for the umpteenth time, I jumped in and tried to help as best I could, even though I probably only slowed Dylan down.

Finally, we were all set. He revved up the engine on the van, and I turned over the Honda. It started right away. "Give it some gas," Dylan called. I did, and the engine roared to life. "You'll want to let it run as much as you can," he said, but I was already off.

I arrived forty minutes late to lunch, apologizing profusely.

"Did your mascara break or something?" Libby pointed to my hands. I looked down to see my fingers coated in car grease. My pants weren't looking too good, either.

"Yeah, well…" I said. "Car trouble."

Kara yanked a bunch of napkins and handed them to me. "What did you expect buying something that old?"

I didn't know what to say. I just stood there and shrugged like an idiot. The napkins weren't doing much; they stuck to the grease and tore as I rubbed.

"Excuse me." I scurried to the bathroom, pumped half the bottle of soap into my palm, and scrubbed my hands until they stung. Black guck still lined the insides of my fingernails, but at least I wasn't a total embarrassment.

Libby and Kara were well done with their waiting-for-Amber-to-show-up coffees and had already ordered by the time I sat down and hid behind my menu. Dylan's diatribes about unnecessary spending rang through my ears, so I quickly ordered the cheapest dish at the cafe.

"Chicken fingers?" Kara asked. "Missing middle school, are you?"

"Come, on, Kara," Libby said, "I'm sure Amber's just trying to be frugal. You can't expect her to order the seared tuna while she's dating Dylan, can you?"

I squirmed in my seat. "I can order whatever I want. It's not like I'm his pet or something."

Libby's hands went up in self-defense. "I'm just saying."

I grabbed another napkin and started folding it into origami. "I like chicken fingers. They remind me of my Grandma Mona."

Kara's head tilted towards her shoulder. "Wasn't she the amazing Italian chef?"

"Yeah. She makes a mean chicken parmesan." I shrugged, my eyes still glued to the messed-up napkin concoction I had going. "It's basically chicken fingers."

From the edge of my vision, I saw Libby and Kara eyeing each other. My pathetic retort hadn't swayed anyone. Better to change the subject.

"So." I finally faced Kara and offered my most enthusiastic impression. "Tell me about your wedding plans."

Kara laid her hand on mine "We're thinking of a destination wedding."

"Really? Where?"

"Aruba. We figure we'll get married next December when everyone's got vacation. But who wants to get married when it's an igloo outside?"

"Everyone will fly out to Aruba?" I could imagine Dylan's reaction. *You want me to spend all that money to attend your friend's wedding? Think about the flights and hotels…*

The waiter arrived with our drinks. I'd gotten water, but Kara and Libby had each ordered rum and coke.

"Yeah." Kara sipped a bit of her drink. "We can get one of those group rates, you know?"

Still, Christmas break is the most expensive time to fly. There was Dylan's voice again, pointing out all the financial pitfalls. Kara was just trying to make a fun weekend for everyone. "I bet the water's beautiful there," I said.

Kara nodded. "The brochures look stunning! We're talking to this travel company that makes packages including hotel and food and everything."

"Ooh." Libby dangled her cup in the air. "Does that mean open bar?"

She and Kara toasted to Aruba, but all I could hear was *cha-ching cha-ching! You gonna pay for that on a teacher's salary? Good thing you got all that money from your grandma…* I wanted to smack Dylan, and he wasn't even there, yet his voice kept ringing out in my head. Kara and Libby were my best college friends. I wasn't going to let money get in the way of that. "Sounds so fun," I said, "like the weekend of a lifetime."

"Yeah," Libby said, "you only get married once, you know, so you might as well make it count."

Dylan pipped in again, but this time with Aunt Sofia's high pitched squeal. *Once? You know, fifty percent of marriages end in divorce. And debt is a massive contributor to that.* "Shut up!" I said.

"What?" Libby and Kara both eyed me with confusion.

"I mean, shut up. You know, like 'I can't believe this'll be so great!'"

Libby perked right up. "I'm even thinking of not telling Kyle and making the whole weekend a surprise." She and Kara squealed like schoolgirls, and I half-heartedly joined them.

I was already feeling the heartburn from my lunch when we headed out to the parking lot. Kara had given Libby a ride there, and I offered to take her home and stop at the fabric store to pick out curtains along the way.

"It kinda smells like… what is that?" Libby sniffed around the passenger seat like Fido on the prowl. "I know! It smells like my great aunt Alice. Her house oozes that funky combination of cold cream and tattered books."

I shivered as if from the frigid air. This was Libby's first time in the gray Honda, and that definitely didn't sound like a compliment. "Well, the couple who had this car was really old, so maybe—."

"Yeah. You know what's even worse? The smell of new car. Some people claim to like it, but to me, it just smells like plastic and chemicals."

I knew Libby was trying to make me feel better, but I *loved* the new car smell. If fresh starts had a smell, that would be it.

It smells like a freshly dug hole in your bank account.

"Yeah." I grinned. "I'm just saving up to—."

"I know exactly. You've got Dylan on the brain." *If she only knew.*

I shoved my keys into the ignition as though it were a knife cutting into flesh. Rather than a rumble, all I heard was click-click-click. I turned the key again and again, but that clicking sound kept coming back.

"I think it's dead," Libby said.

A sour taste filled my mouth. "It's the battery. Dylan jump-started it this morning."

Libby lay her hand on my arm. "You've barely driven this thing, and it's giving you problems already?"

"Yeah… well…" My head fell onto the wheel.

Libby got that cheery voice she used when she wanted to make everything OK. "Whatever," she said, "let's just figure out how to get out of here. Want to call Dylan to come jump it again?"

"No. I can't have him rescue me all the time. Besides, he said I should drive it a bunch, and I didn't. I just came over here."

Libby patted my back. "He can't expect you to drive around in circles when you have somewhere to be. I mean, we waited for you for almost an hour."

It was just 40 minutes Libby, chill out.

"Oh!" Libby's voice lifted my head enough that I could see where she was pointing. "I bet they could help us."

The new car handled beautifully. Over four inches of snow had fallen over the past three hours, but the all-wheel drive cut right through it. Despite the freezing temperatures outside, the heater made the cabin downright balmy, and the radio blasted away with crystal clear surround sound. The best thing was the color, my favorite cherry red.

I drove straight to Dylan's, bracing myself for what was to come. He was outside, shoveling the snow off his walk. I flashed my lights at him and lowered my window. As he watched me drive up, confusion tightened his face. "What's this car?"

"Come in and sit." I offered my best smile and patted the seat beside me. "It's nice and warm in here. And we need to talk."

He put down his shovel and came around to the passenger's side. A blast of chilly air hit me as he climbed in. "Did your car fail to start again?"

"Yeah." I turned away from him. "We couldn't get it going after lunch."

"It needed to run longer."

I shrugged. "I'm sure you're right, but I was late."

"So what's this? A loaner?"

"Sort of."

Dylan's eyes narrowed. "You didn't buy it, did you?"

"No. Not yet."

"What's going on, Amber?"

"The place we had lunch was right next to a car dealership." I started fidgeting with the heat controls. "When the car wouldn't start, the guys from the dealership came over and took a look. They said the car still had its original battery, almost a decade old, and it's a miracle that it lasted this long."

"Why didn't you just have them replace it and be on your way?"

"They're doing that now."

Dylan dropped his head in an attempt to catch my gaze. "It doesn't take very long to replace a battery, Amber."

I picked at my cuticles, a habit my mother said to never do in front of a guy, but I couldn't help it. "I know, but while the mechanics worked on my car, the salesman showed me around. They still had this one lying around from last season's models. They offered me a deal on it, plus they'll give me $2500 for my car, which is more than I paid for it, and not even charge me for the battery."

"So let me guess, they talked you into taking an extended test drive while figuring out how to drag out your battery change for as long as possible?"

"Pretty much."

"You're considering this, aren't you?"

My face grew hot. "The lease terms are good. And you never know how many more problems a ten-year-old car is going to serve up."

"This isn't just about the car, is it, Amber?"

I swallowed back tears. "No."

"You're terrified of your parents' disapproval, aren't you?" He brushed my hair behind my ear, but I shrugged him off.

"Yes, but it's not just that either."

"What is it?"

"Both Kara and Libby were going on and on about their weddings and honeymoons. Karen's ring is so elegant, nowhere near as flashy as Libby's." I turned the wheel back and forth as I spoke. "They both seemed so light and normal and happy. It struck me how I might never have that with you."

"The happiness or the ring?"

"The lightness. The normality. And the ring. We've never talked about it, but you'd never get me a ring, would you?" I still couldn't face him, but I searched his expression from the corner of my eye.

Dylan's eyes bulged. "Do you have any idea what Libby's ring cost?"

"We never talk about those things. I'm sure Libby doesn't even know herself."

"She probably doesn't. But *I* know. That ring cost Kyle $15,000. You think he had the cash for that?"

I so didn't feel like going into this. "He probably financed it."

"Exactly." Dylan's tone grew heated. "So this $15,000 ring will end up costing him $25,000 at least. That's the type of future where you can only keep your head above water if you never stop working for money. You must realize by now that I'm building us something far more stable and lasting."

"I do." Despite my best efforts, a tear slipped out of my eye and ran along the ridge of my nose. "I've worked hard to poke holes in your plan, and I can't. Your numbers are solid."

"But?"

"But I can't just run my life on numbers." I closed my eyes and shook my head. "Everything with you is so serious. We watch every dollar spent. When's that going to change?"

"In three years we'll—."

My hands shot up. "I know. In three years, we'll move into the next phase of your Cash Machine. But will our lives be normal then?" I finally mustered the courage to face him. "My gut tells me some things will never change. Do you see yourself buying a new car in three years?"

"Yes, I expect to get a car when phase one ends."

"I didn't say a car. I said a *new* car."

Dylan tried a boyish grin. "It'll be new for me."

"I'm right, aren't I. You won't buy yourself a new car in three years. You won't buy yourself a new car in 33 years, will you?"

"No, Amber, I won't." Dylan gritted his teeth. "The depreciation on a new car is just too high. I value money too much to throw it in the toilet that way. In three years, I might buy myself a car like you drive now. In ten years, I might buy a car that's half that age. And in twenty years, I'll probably buy cars that are one to three years old, cars that are still in like-new shape, but which no longer have new car price tags."

"So I'm right. We'll never have a normal life, will we?"

"Amber, the normal thing is to be up to your neck in debt." Dylan smacked the dashboard. "The normal thing is to work like a slave your entire life. The normal thing is to stress out when your daughter needs braces because you're already spending everything you make, and you don't know where you'll get the extra money. I see no appeal in being normal. You think these high-end new cars are being sold to millionaires, but you're wrong. Most of them are being sold to people who, if they got laid off tomorrow, would be broke in six months. Those who are truly wealthy don't live paycheck to paycheck; they spend their money wisely and build solid foundations for their future."

"And the ring?" I studied my bare fingers. I'd decided as a girl I'd never wear a ring of any kind until I got engaged. I wanted that diamond ring to be the first, to be special. "You'd never get me one of those either, would you?"

"Do you know that diamonds are not even a particularly rare stone? Their crazy prices come from the De Beers family restricting their supply and marketing the hell out of them. That diamond that Kyle is going to spend over $25,000 paying off will probably not fetch them $7500 if they ever need to sell it."

Dylan pivoted to face me, but I couldn't look him in the eye. "A diamond is not a sign of love; it's a sign of conformity to a nonviable system. If you feel like you need to play along for the sake of appearances, I'll get you cubic zirconia, which will look the same. But after all that you've learned these past few months, I'd hope you'd proudly walk around without a ring, and tell anyone who asks about it: 'My love for Dylan is real. I want to build a future with a solid man, and I no longer want to play society's backward money games. I'd rather use the money to buy a house that can provide for my family for decades, then walk around with an expensive-as-hell non-rare stone on my finger!'"

Dylan was shouting by the time he finished. It was the first time he'd raised his voice to me since that first date on the hike. I deserved it; I knew I did. Everything he said was right. Technically. He was that solid guy, and he'd sacrificed so much to build that solid future. He deserved a woman equally strong in her convictions, who would stand by his side every step of the way.

"I'm not the woman you want me to be." My lips trembled as I struggled to get the words out. "I don't want my life to be so heavy. Are society's values screwed up? Of course. But I don't have the strength to be constantly fighting back. I can't bring my parents to a house that smells like death. I can't have my friends waiting on me for lunch and then running over to an auto dealership because my pre-dented car won't start." By now, a mixture of tears and snot blubbered all over my face. "You need an extraordinary woman, Dylan. And I'm not. I'm very, very normal. I want normal things like a nice car, an engagement ring, a beautiful wedding, a romantic honeymoon."

I grabbed a tissue from my purse and sloppily blew into it. "I was willing to kill myself hauling garbage out of that house to make it look to my parents like I'd gotten a decent property, but the truth is, I don't want to buy a house where I need to haul garbage. If they see the house as it is now, they'll say it might be a good investment for someone, but it's just not right for a girl like me. They won't say this because they're narrow-minded, they'll say this because they know their daughter." All the hope I had for "us" slipped right out of me in one long, sad exhale. "This house is not what I want."

Dylan's voice quieted to match my own. "Then why did you buy it?"

"For you." I searched his eyes. They had that 'Why do girls have to be so confusing?' look. Didn't he know, deep down, why? "Because it's what you want. And I wanted to make a life with you."

"And now?"

My heart felt made of paper, and I'd just ripped it up into little pieces. "You're a great, great guy, Dylan. You're going to make some amazing woman very happy someday. But I don't think I'm the right girl to go on this journey with you."

"So that's it, then?"

"Almost." I reached out and took his hand. They felt cold and stiff and unsure. "I want you to do me one last favor."

"What's that?"

"I want you to buy the house. You can do that thing you were talking about. What was it? The cold thing."

Dylan spoke with a lifeless, quiet voice. "The BRRRR."

"Right." I tightened my grip around his hand, as if trying to convince both of us that everything would be just fine. "You can do it. I know you can. I believe in you so much. You said yourself this house would be perfect for that strategy."

Dylan released his hand and grabbed my shoulders, as if trying to wake me out of some stupor. "Amber, buying this house will completely change your financial picture. Even if you don't want me, take it. It will bring me comfort to know that something good came to you from this relationship."

"Dylan, there was so much good here. But I don't want the house. I'm asking you, I'm begging you, as a favor, take it. If you don't, I'll back out on the deal anyway, and I'll lose thousands of dollars, a giant chunk of the money Grandma Mona left me."

Dylan motioned as if to argue, but I lay a finger on his lips. "If you take it over, there will be no breach of contract. You can pay me back for what I've already spent on the inspection and the title search, and I'll be right back where I started. You'll wind up with a great property at a great price, and you'll do that BRRRR thing, and build your Cash Machine that much faster. You have the money to do that, don't you?"

"I do," Dylan said, but his head kept shaking in disagreement. "I can borrow against my other properties. Is this really what you want?"

"To thine own self, be true, Dylan." I nodded, and my chest fell in exhaustion from trying too hard, wanting so much, but feeling like I'd failed not just Dylan, but also myself. "I'm not made for the kind of journey you're walking. I want my normal life back."

"Very well." Dylan gripped the door handle. "Then may it bring you the love and happiness you desire." Dylan climbed out of the car, shut the door, and didn't look back.

Still feeling the tingle of my now ex-boyfriend's hand in mine, I drove back to the dealership to sign the paperwork for my new car.

When my parents heard I'd broken up with Dylan, backed out of the house deal, and bought myself a new car that didn't look like it had been through a demolition derby, they cancelled their trip. It was too bad. I could have used someone's shoulder to cry on.

Somehow, driving my new cherry red Chevy didn't give me the satisfaction I'd imagined, nor did shopping with Libby and buying myself a beautiful winter coat.

Weeks passed. Dylan closed on the house. I knew he did because his attorney called to ask for some of my paperwork. I could have mailed them, but I decided to bring them to Dylan in person.

Every time I checked my phone to see if he'd messaged, I reminded myself that breaking up had been the right move. Dylan's path had diverged from mine the moment he dropped out of college, and I was only fooling myself by believing otherwise. I was a normal girl and needed to find myself a nice, normal guy. Shouldn't be too hard, right? If they're normal, then by definition, there should be a ton of them out there. Still, before going over to Dylan's new house, I put on his favorite blue dress and did up my makeup.

I buzzed downstairs, and Dylan let me up. He was working on the second-floor apartment, the one that would have been *ours*. The first thing I noticed was the scent of powerful antiseptic and fresh paint. The windows had been replaced, and sunlight shone through, making the apartment feel bright and airy.

"It's amazing how much you've done in such a short time." I sounded so nonchalant, despite the rabbits thumping in my chest.

Dylan offered a polite nod. "Not much, really, but odor is one of the easiest things to fix."

I gave Dylan one of my warmest smiles. The one that said I'm sorry. The one that said, with one word, I can be yours again. But Dylan was ever the stoic. He'd never learned to chase. He'd never learned that girls don't mean everything they say during a hysterical rant.

For a moment, our eyes locked in a dance of memory and sadness and longing.

Should I tell him? Should I come out and tell him that I'd just caved under pressure, but that deep down, I believed in him, believed in what the two of us could build together? Or had that ship already sailed?

All I could say was, "I have the paperwork for you."

"You can just put it on the counter. I'm covered in paint."

I'd paid little attention to what he was doing, but then I noticed a massive tub of paint by his ladder, which leaned up against the arches. The very arches he promised me he'd paint cornflower blue. He'd laughed at my choice, saying it wasn't practical for a rental, but he'd do it if that's what I wanted. Now they glowed a very practical off-white, the same color he painted all his walls.

I knew then Dylan would move on. He didn't make emotional choices, he made practical ones. And in my stupidity, I'd convinced him I was not the woman he needed by his side for this journey.

CHAPTER 12

TICKET TO RIDE

I hibernated like a bear in winter. I ignored my friends' invitations for girls' nights. I even blew off my family and spent Christmas alone with a pint of ice cream. Chocolate ice cream. With dark chocolate chunks. Of course.

Just before New Year's, Libby showed up at my house, forced me to clean up, shower, and get into something "befitting a woman and not a wildebeest." She sat me in front of the mirror and did my nails and makeup. "You're not going to get over this if you don't move on. We're going out tonight. I know you've been blowing off Kara's calls about her New Year's party."

"Libby, I —."

Libby pointed a finger at me. She wasn't even a teacher, but she had that bossy finger thing *down*. "I don't wanna hear it. I've worked for a month planning this party, and I did it at half my normal rate because it was for Kara. There's no way my best friend isn't showing up. Now close your eyes so I can get some sexy eye-shadow-action on you." I followed orders, and Libby stroked my eyes with her powder collection. "Listen. Kyle's bringing this friend…"

"Woah." I pulled back. "Makeup's one thing. A guy…."

Libby forced my head closer and gave me a look that said sit still. Or else. "We're going to take it slow. This isn't a date. All I'm asking is that if Kyle approaches you with a guy, don't run for cover, OK?"

I couldn't have exhaled louder if I was running sprints. "Fine."

Libby mentioned nothing more about the guy. I knew Libby well enough to know she did this for only one reason: to drive me nuts. Finally, as we were driving to the party early so Libby could help set up, my restraint broke. "Who's this guy?"

"Well, well, look who's perking up. Could there be life after Dylan after all?"

She knew how to drag things out. "What's his name?"

"Anthony. He's a client of Kyle's."

Anthony? The Italian? I didn't know whether to turn a pale green or a flushed pink. "You mean the guy who asked me to dance at the Halloween gala?"

"Oh… You remember him?" She looked at me expectantly, waiting for me to say more, but I wasn't going to give her the satisfaction. I crossed my arms and stared out the window.

The party was in the Warehouse District, a new venue in the industrial zone. Vintage-style Edison bulbs cast a golden hue on the concrete floor. Every other yard of wall showcased paintings that reminded me of Rembrandt, but with a bluesy edge. A portrait of an elderly couple on a porch swing drew me in, capturing their love, their years together, the joy and sadness and sweetness of life in its winter years.

"Don't tell Kyle I know it," Libby whispered, coming up behind me, "but he's planning on getting me a Ricardo."

"That painter that everyone's been talking about?"

"Yep. He's the artist behind everything you see here. I made a deal between him and Kara that she'd hang his stuff at her party. He gets the exposure, and she saves on decor."

"Nice."

"In any case," Libby's shoulders inched up to her ears, and she quietly squealed, "I'm excited to have a Ricardo hanging in my living room."

"You can still afford that with all the costs you're putting into the wedding and house?"

"Amber," Libby lay her hand on my shoulder and spoke in a tone somewhere between caring and patronizing. "It's not like we're going to burn it for firewood. Kyle thinks his paintings could be a great investment."

It really could be. Ricardo was making quite a name for himself across town, but had yet to burst onto the national or international art scenes. I leaned in to read the slip of paper under the painting before me. The painting was entitled *Swinging Seniors* and had a price tag of $20,000. Of course, even if it did skyrocket in value, it wouldn't be a cash flowing investment. To get a return on the painting, they'd need to sell it, and I couldn't imagine Libby parting with a painting she loved. Even if she could, they'd be locking up a ton of cash in the meantime.

When did I start thinking this way? It was like I had Dylan's voice playing in my head. Why couldn't I be happy for Libby? "His work is stunning," I said.

Libby leaned in and whispered. "And Ricardo is already over 60."

"So?"

She shook her head as if she couldn't believe my thickness. "You know what happens to artists' works when they die, don't you? The prices go through the roof."

"60 is hardly on death's door."

"The point is, he's not going to live forever."

"I suppose if you ever run on hard times, you could always knock him off."

"Amber!"

"I'm going to get myself a drink." Something told me it was going to be the first of many before this night was through.

An hour later, Kyle approached with Anthony, who stood a full head taller than himself. I had to admit his strong chin and sharp brows were something to look at. He would have appeared even more handsome if his skin didn't have the slightly pasty look I assumed came from long days in front of a computer. "Anthony, you remember Libby's friend Amber."

"How could I forget?" Anthony held two drinks in his hands and extended one to me.

I accepted it with a smile and a soft, "Thank you." As I promised Libby, I didn't run for cover, but I couldn't think of much to say either. Not that I could have said much over the blasting techno music anyway. I'd need to scream in his ear to be heard, and his ear was too high up to reach. Claiming he wanted to get to know me better, Anthony proposed to Kyle that we double date that weekend. And to my surprise, I accepted.

Saturday night found the four of us together again. Anthony liked to talk. A lot. Between him and Kyle, I never had to worry about the conversation entering an awkward lull. But Anthony was also considerate. He opened the passenger door of his midnight blue Porsche for me before squeezing his giant frame into the driver's side. When we arrived at the restaurant, Libby and I went to the little girl's room while the hostess escorted the guys to a table. By the time we'd returned, they were deep in shop talk.

After hearing them go back and forth on a few deals they were working on, I finally broke in. "You know, I'm not even sure what venture capital is."

Anthony gave me a polite smile. "Think of us as gasoline."

"Toxic and smelly?" I asked.

The question jarred Anthony out of his polite smile, and he let go a loud laugh before recovering his composure. "Imagine a field with a thousand small campfires burning." His hand panned through the air, as if laying out the whole scene. I felt certain he'd given this description before. "We hunt out the best ones and throw gasoline all over them."

"Won't all that gasoline just cause them to burn out faster?"

"Oftentimes, yes. But if even one out of ten turns into a forest fire, you'll hardly miss the heat from the campfires that burned out."

Somehow, I couldn't picture this guy either camping or hauling gasoline. He seemed too much the urban type. "The analogy is cute and all, but I'm trying to understand it on a practical level. You find companies you like and throw money at them?"

"It's not just money. We also bring expertise. We'll usually take at least one seat on the board to weigh in on strategic decisions."

I grabbed a breadstick covered in black sesame seeds and took a small nibble, even though I was so hungry I wanted to scarf it down. "Still, most of these investments fail?"

"About 75%."

I took another bite and chewed over what seemed to be an insane financial proposition.

"I think it's even higher than that," Kyle said.

"Am I missing something here?" Libby asked.

"Let me clarify." Anthony spooned a handful of olives onto his plate. "Let's say that each of these is a company. How many do we have here?"

"Eight," Libby said, picking up the ninth one and popping it into her mouth. She'd always been crazy for olives.

"OK, so these six are probably going to fold." Anthony took the hint and spooned them onto Libby's plate. He stuck his fork in another. "This one is gonna do OK, maybe make a profit. If we're lucky, we'll be able to get our money out." With his knife, he pushed the olive off the fork onto Libby's plate.

"You've got one left," I said, "that's the one you're hoping strikes gold?"

"Exactly. This little sucker turns into an olive grove so gigantic it would blow away any Sicilian. One Facebook or Google makes up for hundreds of duds."

I finished off the last of my breadstick. Something still wasn't sitting right with me. "And you don't care that businesses might get run over in the process?"

Kyle laughed. "Amber, you don't get the start-up world. It's not like they're taking over some nice mom and pop grocery store that's been in the family for fifty years and running it out of business."

"Exactly," Anthony said. "The guys we invest in want to go big. Some of them are serial entrepreneurs, who start one company after the next. They don't want to build some nice, small business. They're usually in emerging fields, and it's a race to see who's going to control the space. Win the race, they're billionaires. Lose, and they take their lumps, learn what they can, and look for the next opportunity."

"The idea of building nice, reliable sources of passive income just doesn't exist in your field?"

"Passive income?" Kyle leaned in to whisper in my ear, "Sounds like someone still has Dylan on the brain."

I blushed, but Anthony came to my defense. "Don't be so quick to laugh her off. The fact is, we're not looking for good, steady profits from the individual companies we invest in. But we are from our portfolio as a whole. With an iron in so many fires, the successes and failures tend to balance out, and our overall success is more consistent than you'd think. But it's a long-term investment for those looking to grow their wealth, not meant for those needing monthly or even yearly returns."

Then Anthony did something I wasn't expecting from Mr. Loudmouth Venture Capitalist. "Enough about my work. Tell me about your job, Amber."

Anthony spent the next two weeks traveling on business, but he called me twice, once from France and once from Germany. We planned to get together the weekend after that, but he was pulled away last minute to Austin, Texas, to work on the terms of an acquisition offer.

So it was already late January by the time we went out on our first one-on-one date. What Anthony lacked in availability, he made up for in style. For the first time in my life, I sat in box seats at the symphony. Afterwards, he took me out for dinner at a swank Greek restaurant in the Arts District.

"Didn't you just love that Vivaldi piece?" I asked him.

Anthony picked up a menu. "Which one was the Vivaldi?"

"The last piece they played." I decided not to add that it was Four Seasons, Vivaldi's most famous work. Grandma Mona used to melt over that one.

"Oh yes, it was quite nice." Perhaps I'd embarrassed him, for he was quick to add, "There's only one classical music piece that I can identify by name."

"What's that?"

"The 1812 Overture."

"I guess it's hard to miss when they bring out a cannon."

"Precisely. Violins are too subtle of an instrument to distinguish one piece from another. But a cannon. Now there's an instrument that commands attention." Anthony gave me a self-effacing grin. "Speaking of commanding attention, the octopus here is to die for."

I scanned the menu for the octopus and cringed when I saw the price. Anthony mistook the cringe, for he added, "I know many people find the idea of eating octopus revolting, but once you get over the image of all those legs and suckers, you'd be shocked at how good it can taste when made right."

"You're talking to a traditional Italian here, Anthony, not some squeamish Valley girl. If it swims in the sea, I've eaten it." I read the description: *grilled octopus served over santorini fava with caramelized onions, roasted red peppers, and capers.* No matter how good that sounded, there was no way I was going to order the most expensive item on the menu. "The Haloumi salad also sounds quite good." And quite cheap, only a third the price of the octopus. "I haven't had Haloumi in years."

"I'm not sure I've ever had it. What is Haloumi?"

"It's firmer and less salty than feta, best served grilled."

"Sounds interesting. I'd like to try that." He lowered the menu. "What do you say we split that and the octopus?"

Now he was talking. As long as he was the one ordering the crazy expensive dish, I'd gladly eat my half. Anthony ordered for the both of us. "Anything to drink?" the waiter asked. "The house Assyrtiko would be perfect with your selections, sir."

"Sounds wonderful." Anthony didn't even ask the price. "We'll take a bottle."

The waiter returned with the wine, poured a bit into Anthony's glass, and waited. Anthony took a quick sip and nodded, without doing any of that swirling it around or sniffing stuff. My gut told me that in a blind taste test, he probably couldn't tell the difference between a twenty-dollar bottle of wine and a hundred dollar one. But his attention wasn't really on the wine; it was more on me. "What do you think?" he asked when I took my first sip.

"Delicious," I said, partly to be gracious and also because it was true. "This is the first Greek wine I've ever had. I like the hint of rosemary."

"Oh?" Anthony raised an eyebrow. His face told me he was doing his best to look interested, but I could probably drop a sprig of rosemary into the glass, and he wouldn't notice. So I decided to switch to a subject I knew all successful men found interesting: themselves.

"So tell me about that business deal you had last week in Austin."

His energy perked right up. "It's an AI company. That's artificial intelligence."

"Yes, I know. Just last week, I assigned my students a project on AI and how it affects their lives."

"Don't you teach fifth grade?"

"Sure, but there's a huge push to get kids interested in science and technology. This assignment was inspired by one kid in particular, Mikey. He's one of those kids who's so bright; he spends most of his days bored in class. He's convinced that someday he's going to build a robot that can paint masterpieces."

"He might be right. We almost invested in an AI last year that can write poetry."

"Really? I wouldn't think venture capital guys would be so interested in poetry."

Anthony held up his glass. "*That man that hath a tongue, I say is no man, if with his tongue he cannot win a woman.*"

"You know Shakespeare?" I asked.

"Only a couple of lines. My father's family is from Verona. Pa says no respectable Hofer can go out into the world without knowing at least a few lines from *The Two Gentlemen of Verona.*"

Our meals arrived. Anthony had the waiter place the octopus in front of me. I dug right in. Perhaps with a bit too much enthusiasm.

"Sorry for doubting you. You definitely eat octopus like an Italian."

I wiped the sauce off my chin. "You date many Italian girls?"

"You're the first since high school." A bit of Italian-American accent crept into his voice.

Under this spit and polish, did there still dwell a neighborhood Italian boy? "What do they call you at home? Anthony or Tony?"

He winked at me. "Tony, of course."

"When did you make the switch?"

"When I started my MBA. Anthony sounds more professional."

"What do you think of yourself as?"

"Tony. Anthony's my out-in-public, professional name. Tony's my private, at-home name."

I cut into the octopus, avoiding Anthony's gaze. "What do you want me to call you?"

"For now? Whatever you want." Anthony reached over and forked a piece of octopus for himself.

"For now?"

His enormous brown eyes were soaking me up. "Yeah. For now, we're just getting to know each other. There's no pressure."

"But eventually?"

"Look, I've dated plenty of women over the years. But I've always known that when I get married, it will be to an Italian girl. For now, it's only our second date. There's no commitment, no pressure. But I want my wife to call me Tony."

"Is that why I'm here?" I grinned uncomfortably and reached for my glass. "So you can see if I'm that Italian girl who might call you Tony?"

"Of course. When Libby first told me about you, she said you were only interested in relationships that could lead somewhere. She said this like it was a warning, that I shouldn't get involved with you unless I was serious."

That Libby, always watching out for me. "And it didn't scare you away?"

"Just the opposite." His eyes were still on me, and the halloumi salad sat untouched. "That's what I'm looking for as well. I'm sick of just living out of my suitcase."

"Does that mean you're thinking of leaving your job?"

"No way. I love my work. But I no longer want to come home from a business trip to some empty apartment. I want a real home."

"And a family?" I knew what he was going to say—he was an Italian after all—but I still wanted to hear it.

"It wouldn't be a home without a family." Anthony finally broke the tension by digging into his salad. "This loomy stuff's not bad."

I pressed my lips together as I reached over to jab at some greens and a cube of cheese. "I like the salty chewiness of it."

"Could you make something like this for us sometime?"

I let that last comment slip by unanswered. "You really think I'm the one you'd like to build a family with?"

"Who knows? It's only our second date. But I like what I see so far. Didn't Libby tell you what I said after we met?"

"No." I couldn't believe that Libby would hold out on me!

"That you remind me of my mother."

By the time Libby's wedding arrived on a beautiful April afternoon, I'd been dating Anthony for over three months. Technically. But between his work hours and business trips, we'd gone out less than ten times in that period, so we were still not so serious that I would have brought him as my date to a wedding. Especially one where I was Maid of Honor. But as a friend of Kyle's, he'd been invited on his own.

Even so, going as his date wouldn't have been so bad had it not been for one thing: the Best Man. I hadn't seen Dylan since I dropped off the paperwork at The Death Trap on Haber. I don't know what I expected from Dylan. Was I thinking he was going to ride his bike to the wedding? That he was going to show up in his work clothes? Whatever it was, I'd grown so used to my story about his austerity, that I wasn't prepared to see him drive up in a newish car, wearing a perfectly presentable tux. Granted, both of them were rented, but they were hardly an embarrassment either.

Still, you couldn't compare his Ford to Anthony's Porsche. Heads turned when Anthony, in his Armani tux, came around to the passenger side, opened my door, and escorted me out in my bridesmaid dress.

Dylan barely made eye contact the entire wedding, and if he saw me coming, he'd quickly make his excuses and leave. I always considered him to be tough, as someone who could take anything and keep chugging forward. And I was right. He was tough. But he still felt pain. Watching him slip away from me like an eel the entire weekend, I knew I'd hurt him badly. That pain wouldn't stop him, but it must sting something awful.

Still, there's only so much a Best Man can avoid a Maid of Honor. Libby wanted a traditional wedding, so at the processional, I walked down the aisle alone, just before the flower girls and the bride herself. But at the recessional, the Maid of Honor and Best Man are paired together. Of course, the recessional is much faster, and all eyes are on the bride and groom. Still, Dylan didn't meet my eyes as he extended his arm. I took it for the short, fast walk back up the aisle. At the end, I just managed to whisper, "Dylan, I'm so sorry," before he let go of my arm and disappeared.

I took off toward the lady's room, tears streaking my mascara as they ran down my cheeks.

CHAPTER 13

JARRED AWAKE

The trill of my phone jarred me away from the stacks of tests I was grading in the teacher's lounge. I saw my mother's name on the Caller ID. She never called me in the middle of the day.

"Ma?"

All I could hear was my mother's sobbing.

"Ma, are you all right?"

"We'll be all right, with time."

"What does that mean?" My heart thumped in my chest. "Ma, what the hell is going on?"

"Your father…" Her voice rattled, and I could imagine her lips shaking as she spoke. "He had a heart attack. Collapsed right in the middle of a cross-examination."

I dropped my pen, grabbed my purse and booked it out of the lounge. "How is he?"

My mother exhaled slowly. "He's stable. The doctors have him on oxygen and are monitoring his heartbeat."

I raced down the hall toward the principal's office. "Where are you? I'm coming now."

"St. Jude's. On Weston Avenue." She broke into tears again. "Cardiac wing. Third floor."

I swallowed hard, trying to keep my emotions in check as I pushed open the office door to tell the secretary I was leaving. "I'm coming, Ma. Just hold on for a couple hours. I'm coming."

My father and I never really got a chance to talk in the hospital. I'd held his hand while he lay in bed, but between the drugs and the attention from the doctors and nurses, there wasn't much chance to interact. That first day, I was there more for my mother, giving her a shoulder to cry on, relieving her at my father's bedside so she could go home to sleep. The next day, two of my aunts came to be with my her, and I decided to go back to work, knowing there was little I could do.

Four days after the heart attack, on Friday afternoon, my father came home. I drove out to spend the weekend playing nurse. I found Pa in the den watching college basketball and stopped in my tracks when I saw a stack of papers on the coffee table next to his pills and cup of tea. Legal briefs. Dozens of them.

"Pa, what are you doing?"

"Watching the game. Taking it easy." He looked weak and old. When did that happen? "Good to see you, Amber." He put his hand on the arm of the couch and tried to push himself up to hug me.

"No, don't get up, please." I sat down on the couch and hugged him there.

"I'm not so bad off, honey." He gave a brush of his hand, as though swatting an annoying fly. "The doctors say it was mild. Like a warning shot across the bow."

"I see you're taking the warning quite seriously." I picked up a couple of briefs, then let them drop hard on the table. "Taking it easy, eh?"

"Well, this could hardly come at a worse time." He rubbed my back the way he always did when I was stressing over a test. "We're right in the middle of a big case."

"You're always in the middle of a big case."

"The judge gave us a postponement due to the circumstances, but I've got clients depending on me."

I held my father's hand and tried to catch his eye. "You've also got a wife and kids depending on you. You think any of us will be served if you work yourself to death?"

"Oh, let's not be so dramatic." Dad's posture stiffened. "The doctors have prescribed a regimen. I'm following their instructions. See, I'm watching the game, and there's not a nacho in sight."

"That's what they think got you? The nachos?"

"Nothing's got me yet. Just a bit of a setback. I'm not as young as I used to be. I need to take better care of myself, and I will. But the heart attack didn't kill me, so don't ask me to start living the life of a dead man. I've got responsibilities, and I intend to fulfill them."

"You're not going right back to court?"

"No, I'll need surgery in a few weeks. Until then, I'm to stay off my feet as much as I can. But I can still run point from here, and I'll brief my associates on how to handle the case without me present. Now, are you going to watch the game with me or not?"

I snuggled next to my father and kept silent, but I couldn't focus on the game.

Three weeks later, I sat in a hard, plastic chair in the waiting room while my father went in for surgery. Only my mother was allowed to accompany him. I wanted to be there when he got out and didn't mind waiting alone. Unfortunately, I wasn't alone. Aunt Sophia came to lend support.

Even at the hospital waiting room, she wore mascara as thick as lacquer. "I do hope your father can get himself back on his feet and return to work soon," she said.

"I don't." My knee was bouncing. I tried to stop it, but it was too skittish. "He puts too much pressure on himself at the firm. He should take it easy and get his health in order. I was kinda hoping he wouldn't go back at all. He's 60. That's not too early to retire."

Aunt Sofia gave an exasperated sigh, probably the same sound she made each time her son Jimmy got fired from another job. "Retirement at 60 is a luxury, Amber."

My eyes narrowed. "He's worked 35 years as an attorney, almost 30 of those as a partner in his firm. How could he not afford to retire?"

"You kids are so naive." My aunt shook her head. "Your father's been raising children for 35 years. He's put four of you through college. He's already paid for two weddings, and he's no doubt hoping to pay for yours as well. Look how he's raised you. You all had a nice home, exotic vacations, cars when you turned 16. Where do you think that money came from?"

Numbers flashed in my mind. Four college tuitions, two weddings, four cars, vacations, braces, tutors, swimming lessons, private school for my older sister when she was having learning issues. Raising the four of us could not have been cheap. But still, my father made a good living. I didn't know exactly how much, but he never raised a word of complaint about money. "I'm sure he put something away for retirement each year."

"Of course he did. But look how long people are living these days. If he gets his health back, he could easily live another 30 years. Even if he doesn't, your mother could. You think he's saved away enough to provide for all that by age 60? You must be dreaming."

"Are you just guessing?" My head tilted. "Or do you *know* this?"

"A bit of each. Your parents have more saved away than we do, but not by a lot. For our retirement, Joe figures he'll have to work another fifteen years. And that's assuming Jimmy ever moves out and learns to provide for himself."

Fifteen years? Uncle Joe was almost sixty himself, and the only time I ever saw him exercise was when he got off the couch to get himself another beer. Could he really work well into his seventies? Even if he could, there was no way I wanted my father to do so. "How long do you think it'll be until Pa can retire?"

"If your folks hope to maintain their current lifestyle, I expect he'll need another decade at least."

Could my father live another decade at the rate he was pushing himself? He'd always been Mr. Dependable, the one who planned ahead, who had everything laid out and in order. How could he have set aside so little for his own future?

The following Tuesday, my father returned home with strict orders to rest until he was ready for physical therapy. No amount of begging on my part could convince him to lay off his legal briefs. I helped my mother prepare a slew of meals she could store in the freezer and got back to my classroom. If the kids were left too long with a substitute, they'd turn into wild animals, and I was too exhausted to play queen of the jungle.

Fortunately, we had a distraction that Wednesday. Sam, an engineer working in artificial intelligence, came in to make a presentation before the class. Anthony had arranged the whole thing, of course. Anthony's firm had made a sizable investment in Sam's company, and when Anthony called, they were more than happy to send out a techie for a few hours. Sam brought in a robot that helps blind people navigate spaces. My students got to see the robot in action, ask it questions, and put stumbling blocks in its way.

Mikey was the most enthusiastic kid in the room. "Seego, how cold is it outside?" he asked.

The robot "thought" for a moment and responded, "It's 47 degrees with a chance of rain. You should wear a coat and have an umbrella ready if you plan on going out."

"And what's the safest way for me to get from here to the door?" Mikey asked.

Seego's voice was slightly stunted and metallic. "You are four yards, two feet, and 3 inches from the door, but there are obstacles in the way." It then gave him detailed instructions as he made his way around desks and between backpacks until he reached the door.

"So, what do you think?" Sam asked.

"AI is awesome," Mikey said. "I want to make something like Seego one day."

I gave Mikey a proud teacher grin. "It must be exciting to make something that can help the world."

"Well, yeah. I guess there's that too."

"That too?" I bent to his level and rested my hands on my knees. "What else were you thinking, Mikey?"

"It'll make me rich!"

While the kids surrounded Sam and asked him all sorts of questions, my mind drifted to my father. He was the first Romano to graduate college, much less become a lawyer. My grandparents were so proud of him. I bet they thought he was going to make it big. That he was going to be rich.

An image of my father lying in his bed, his skin sunken and pale, flashed before me. The briefs looked like a ball and chain around his ankles. I always thought we were well to do, but now it seemed my father was trapped in debtor's prison.

And it was killing him.

Dad was all I could think about as Anthony and I walked into Mako, a new Asian fusion restaurant in the arts district. When we sat down, the host handed us menus folded into perfect origami cranes.

"Anthony, can I ask you something personal?"

He stopped unfolding his menu and looked up. "Sure, babe, what's up?"

I took a deep breath. "Well, I know you make a good living."

He laughed. "That's putting it mildly."

"But…" My throat suddenly felt dry, and I had to take a sip of water before I could continue. "How much are you setting aside for retirement?"

"Retirement?" His eyes narrowed, but only a bit. "Amber, I'm only 32, and I love my job. Why are you thinking about retirement?"

"Just curious. I assume you've put some away, right?"

Our drinks arrived, and Anthony sipped his scotch. "Well, I make my 401(k) contribution."

I knew this was the most unromantic way to spend our first time together since I left town to help my parents, but these questions burned for answers. "What about savings? How much runway do you have?"

"Runway?"

"If tomorrow you decided to quit, how long could you keep up your lifestyle before you ran out of savings?"

Anthony's eyes scanned the ceiling as he made some mental calculations. "A few months, I guess." He rested his huge hand on mine and squeezed softly. "But don't worry, I'm not quitting."

"I know you're not."

"What's bothering you, honey?" His other hand joined in, as though he were trying to overshadow my jitters with his calm. "Does this have something to do with your dad?"

I nodded and swallowed hard to hold back tears. "I'm worried about him. I'm starting to realize he doesn't have as much money saved away as I thought."

"I see. And you're worried the same thing could happen to us?"

"Well…," I shrugged. "Couldn't it?"

"Amber, I make significantly more money than your father."

"I know." I forced myself to hold his eyes. "But you also spend more. As you said, you only have a few months of savings."

"I've also got a hell of a lot more work years ahead of me." He handed me my glass, nudging me to drink some and relax.

I sipped my sake, and it burned its way down my throat. "And more expenses ahead as well. My father's already put his kids through college and paid for two weddings."

"I assure you, you don't have to worry. All you asked about were retirement and savings, but I have plenty of other investments."

"You do?" I brightened at this.

"Sure. I have equity in my fund, which means I own a small share of each deal we do."

"Yeah?" My shoulders relaxed, and I could breathe fully for the first time that night. "That's the basis for your Cash Machine?"

"My Cash Machine?"

"Your source of passive income."

"I mean, I share in whatever payouts the fund makes, but it's not what you'd call a passive income."

"Why not?"

"No one gets involved in venture capital to eke out a small return. The objective is growth. Virtually none of the companies we invest in are profitable. The last thing we want to do is erode their cash by forcing them to pay out dividends."

"So then when do you make your money?"

"When we exit. Some of our companies go public, others are acquired. Either way, we can wind up with a huge cash payout. Most of the money will be paid out when the fund closes after 7 to 10 years." He finished unfolding his menu. "I'm starving. Why don't we order something to eat, then you can grill me some more."

I opened up my origami crane, but the words on the menu were a blur. Dylan and Anthony had such different perspectives on investment. To Dylan, growth was a secondary objective; income was his priority. Anthony put growth first. They were both smart guys. Why the difference?

Anthony called the waiter over, and I forced myself to focus on the menu. My appetite had gone down since my father's heart attack, so I quickly ordered a salad and returned to the debate in my head.

I watched Anthony as he ordered his tuna maki, and it hit me. The answer was simple: Dylan and Anthony's investment priorities were different because their goals were different. Anthony wanted a life of riches, and no matter how much he earned, he fully expected to be working for the next three or four decades, accruing more wealth. He wouldn't know what to do with himself otherwise. Dylan's goal was financial independence, the freedom to *not* work. His model was all based on creating predictable income because as soon as his passive income reached his cost of living, he could do whatever he wanted with his life. But for Anthony, there would never be enough. In his field, those who had ten million wanted a hundred million. Those who had a hundred million wanted a billion.

When the waitress left, I jumped right back into my questions. "So because you're investing for growth, that's why you bet on long shots?"

"Exactly. It's high-risk, high-reward investing. My firm had one investment a couple of years ago that paid over one hundred times our investment."

"But it has a lot more investments that go bankrupt, right?"

"Well, sure, but that's how the game works. When you hit, you hit big. Though when you spread all this risk through so many investments, it balances out into a fairly steady return."

"And how long will that return last?"

"Theoretically, it can last forever, as long as we keep opening new funds and picking winning companies." He shook his glass and downed the rest of his sake.

In other words, it could dry up overnight if they failed to pick winners. And even if they continued to pick well, weren't there factors outside of their control? I'd been doing some research since my father's heart attack, mostly while I couldn't sleep at night. I knew that when the dot com bubble burst in 2000, it wasn't just one or two companies that went under, the entire sector dropped. The same thing with real estate in 2008. "Aren't there companies you could invest in that make good, predictable returns?"

"That's not venture capital. Companies like that are low-risk and low-reward." He looked at me like I'd suggested he trade in his Porsche for a Chevrolet minivan. "My fund would never get involved in something like that."

"What about outside the fund?" I busied myself trying to refold my menu. "Is that anything you'd ever consider getting involved in yourself? Buying into businesses that offer a steady income each year?"

"With what money?"

I shrugged. "Why not the same money you use to invest in your fund?"

"I don't put any money into the fund. I get a share as a principal in the firm."

Oh. "And if you ever leave the firm?"

"Well, some of my equity has already vested, so I'd keep it if I left tomorrow. But most of it requires me to stick around. Again, you don't have to worry about me going anywhere. I love my firm, and I assure you the feeling is mutual."

I wasn't about to be pushed off that easily. "What about investing the money you do get?"

"You mean my salary? That goes into paying for my apartment, car, theater tickets, and our dinner tonight. Speaking of which…"

Our waitress arrived, loaded with dishes.

We dug in silently, but my mind kept racing. The romaine lettuce in my salad got me thinking about Rome, which got me thinking about Italy, which brought me back, of course, to my family. To my father. Anthony's work hours were even more than my his. If Anthony didn't have a retirement plan past his measly annual 401(k) allocations, he was headed for trouble.

"What would happen…" I pushed bits of salad around on my dish, "if you were to live on half as much for a while and put the rest into building passive income sources?"

"Half as much?" Anthony's fork fell onto his dish with a loud clunk. "I work awfully hard to afford the lifestyle I have. You want me to work just as hard and skimp on the lifestyle?"

I offered him a smile and sweetened my tone. "Think theoretically for the moment. What would happen if you invested half your income into passive income sources?"

"Like what?" Anthony's hands balled up.

"I don't know. Maybe real estate?"

"What would happen is that our standard of living would crash."

Anthony had said, '*our* standard of living.' Commitment didn't scare this guy. Just the opposite. Everything he ever said about his firm reinforced how committed he was to staying and building his career there. And while he'd never yet told me he loved me, and he certainly hadn't voiced anything close to a proposal, I knew he was committed to me as well. So I echoed his language. But despite his obvious discomfort, I didn't back off. "But our long term financial stability—."

Anthony reached over and put a hand on my arm. "Look, I know what's happened to your father has shaken you up. But you don't need to worry so much about our future. We've got a solid financial foundation to build upon."

I nodded, not wanting Anthony to think I doubted him. But the truth was, if he, like my father, ever found himself unable to work, he would be gasping for air within a few months. Perhaps by age 60, he'd be in a more stable situation, but perhaps not. Anthony had more expensive tastes than my father, and I saw no indication that those tastes would lessen as we aged. He didn't just want the best for himself, he also wanted it for me, and I was sure he'd want it for our kids. For all my wanting to be with a guy who could provide a solid financial future, was I deluding myself into thinking Anthony's fat salary and flashy life meant he was capable of that? Maybe the song was right. Maybe all that glittered wasn't gold.

CHAPTER 14

TRAINING WHEELS

I came home from work on Monday to find two things waiting for me. The first was a giant bouquet of red and white roses leaning like so many supermodels against my doorframe. The after-dinner dancing must have compensated for the during-dinner inquisition. A note said, "We can get through anything together. Tony." He wanted me to call him Tony, but somehow I still couldn't shake Anthony.

Behind the roses, taped to my door, was an unstamped envelope. Inside was a letter from my landlord letting me know my lease was up in two months, and she'd be happy to renew with only a 5% increase in rent.

I trimmed the stems of the roses and arranged them around the apartment. They filled all three vases I owned, and I needed to use a pitcher to contain the overflow. I loved this apartment, with its exposed brick walls and tall windows, the kitchen where I regularly made magic happen, the bedroom with its plush down quilts perfect for snuggling into with a good book (though where, alas, no magic had ever happened). The roses brought additional color and life to the place.

I looked again at the renewal notice, and couldn't help wondering how much longer I'd live here. The apartment's simple elegance was such a far cry from both Anthony's luxury and Dylan's austerity. I had told Dylan when we first started dating that my apartment was a non-negotiable; I wasn't going anywhere. But beautiful as it was, I no longer felt that way.

Was it because Anthony had been hinting about my moving in? I thought about it. A lot. Especially because his apartment was so stunning, with views of the river, and the building had a full gym and private indoor swimming pool. And Anthony treated me like gold. But, no, I wasn't ready for that yet. I wasn't even ready to spend the night with him, much to Anthony's chagrin.

I couldn't fully articulate the difference, but something had shifted in me since my father's heart attack. It was time to take a step forward into the next phase of my life, a phase where committing myself to a new, year-long lease no longer made sense. I picked up my phone, but I didn't call Anthony. I called Phil.

A half-hour later, I sat down across from Phil's desk with a hot cup of tea. "Such a pleasant surprise to hear from you, Amber. What can I do for you?"

I'd already told Phil over the phone that I wanted to keep our meeting confidential, that I didn't want him telling Dylan about it. "I want a house hack with training wheels."

"Training wheels?"

"Doing renovations scares the hell out of me. Being a landlord scares the hell out of me. Buying a house…"

"Scares the hell out of you." Phil laughed easily, which allowed me to relax a bit. "I got it. You want a safe property, a good value—."

"Right, it doesn't have to be a great value. No diamonds in the rough." My hands crisscrossed in the air. "No rough at all."

"What about neighborhoods? Last time you were willing to look at C neighborhoods and above. Is that still the case?"

I gripped my teacup, and felt its warmth seep into my fingers. "You know, Phil, that's part of what I mean by training wheels. I know a house hack can be a great investment, but first and foremost, it's going to be my home. I'd rather take a worse investment for a better location."

"Where do you want to live?"

"Someplace with character and buzz. I love the Historic District, and I'm down in Little Italy at least twice a week as it is. Someplace like that."

"Anywhere else?"

I took a sip of the tea. "You know what I liked? That very first property you showed me."

"The triplex near the hospital? Can't blame you. That was a great house."

"But it's gone?"

His head tipped to the side with either sarcasm or pity; I couldn't tell which. "A house like that? In this market?"

"I know. Of course, it's gone. But I like that whole thing you were saying about the short-term rentals to the doctors. I could see myself doing that."

"And duplexes are out, right?"

I shook my head. "That was when Dylan was calling the shots. A duplex sounds great to me."

"Any other conditions?"

I remember the abject fear I'd felt with the idea of my parents entering The Death Trap on Haber. I felt stupid saying it out loud, but I added, "My father needs to approve."

"Not a problem. Is he local?"

"No, but if he needs to get down here in a hurry, he will."

Phil showed me five homes, none of which were *it*. Three were in neighborhoods I didn't want to live in, and two were overpriced. Then a week later, I received an urgent call from him at work. "Can you come meet me right now?"

"I've got class in twenty minutes."

"Can someone cover for you?"

"Is it that urgent?"

"Oh, yes. Forwarding you the listing. Call me when you're on your way."

I ran down to the principal's office and told her it was an emergency. When she pushed for details, I said, "I'm sorry, but I can't go into it." I'm sure she assumed it was my father again, which was fine with me. I'd feel like an idiot telling her it was a real estate shopping emergency.

I called Phil from the car. "So what's the big rush? Did this place just go on the market?"

"No, it's been on for three months. It started too high, so last month they lowered it. Then I'm guessing their exclusive period with their agent expired, because last week they relisted it as 'for sale by owner' and lowered it again. At the time, I thought they were asking a fair market value. I even considered showing it to you, but it wasn't in the areas you wanted."

"You pulled me out of school to look at a property that's been at the same price for a week, in not such an ideal area?" I was starting to wonder about Phil's judgment. "Where is it anyway? I don't recognize the address."

"It's in Little Havana, just three blocks from Little Italy."

I stopped at a light and pulled up the listing on my phone. It was a cute brownstone. At least that part he'd gotten right. "Hardly my favorite neighborhood, though I guess three blocks isn't too bad."

"Forget about the three blocks. This is where you want to be now." I could almost hear him bouncing in his seat.

"But it wasn't last week?"

"Correct."

"What's going on, Phil?"

"The city planning commission just voted this morning on their new light rail expansion, the blue line. They were looking at three possible paths, and most everyone thought they were going to vote on the one that ran along Southview. But they went with one of the alternatives instead. They're planning a stop a block from the house. That line will go straight downtown into the financial district."

I turned left on Charley Avenue. "Won't that take years to construct?"

"Three at least. But smart money is proactive, dumb money is reactive. Before long, this area will be packed with new restaurants, cafes, clubs, all catering to the young professional scene. Little Havana was already starting to gentrify, but now it's going to explode."

"Three years sounds like a mighty slow explosion."

"Amber, you'll be lucky to get this place at this price three hours from now. By the time the news hits the morning papers, forget about it. I just hope no one beats us there."

The light in front of me turned from green to yellow. Normally, I'd stop, but this time I gunned the car forward. My sporty little coupe shot through just as it flipped to red. My old dented Honda couldn't have done that. Perhaps this car hadn't been such a frivolous purchase. "Be there in a few."

Phil met me at the car. "Don't say a word about what we talked about earlier. When you look through the house, even if you love it, remain calm and indifferent."

"Isn't that dishonest?"

"Amber, in investing, information is money. The more you know, the better you do. They've priced their house based on the best information they have, and you're bidding based on the best information you have. I assure you, no one in this business puts all their cards on the table."

"So if the owners knew there was toxic waste seeping into the property, they wouldn't have to tell me? It's just *caveat emptor*, let the buyer beware?"

"Of course they'd have to tell you. There's no way you could know what's going on inside their house. But disclosure isn't a two-way street. The light rail plans are part of the public record. Besides, we're just making our best guess as to what's going to be in the future. We could be wrong. The city could cancel the plans next week, or the neighborhood might never catch on the way I expect."

"But you don't think so?"

"Amber, if I wasn't showing it to you right now, I'd be showing it to another one of my clients. There's a reason I've spent so much time tracking the light rail plans."

"Come in, come in," a short, dark woman called from the door. "I'm Susanna," she said with a thick Cuban accent. "My husband Pedro is out, but he should be back soon. Unfortunately, our tenants are away, so we won't be able to show you the other apartments today."

"You don't have a key?" Phil asked.

"We do, but our arrangement with them is that we give them at least 24 hours' notice before showing their place. I know I certainly wouldn't want people traipsing through my home if I hadn't had a chance to clean. That's why I suggested coming to see the house tomorrow."

"I completely understand," Phil said as we stepped into the house. "But today worked much better for us. We appreciate you making the time."

"Real estate is so funny. Either you're not interested, or you want it yesterday. When we first put the house up, we only got a smattering of interest, and then a little bit more each time we dropped the price. Then today, we've already had three calls. My next showing is in an hour."

Not if Phil had his way. I smiled at Susanna as I stepped inside. "You have a lovely home."

"It's in the historic register, you know. It's over a hundred years old, but, of course, it's been redone several times since then. And we've brought the plumbing and electricity up to date."

"Are these moldings original?"

"Oh yes, all the woodwork is."

"It smells like chocolate chip cookies." I couldn't help but think of the contrast between the scent of this house and The Death Trap on Haber.

The woman giggled. "My mother used to say, 'Always warm up the engine when selling your car, and always have something baking when selling your house.'"

"I do hope you aren't just trying to entice me with the smell."

"Well, it never hurts to present a house well."

"I mean, I hope I'll at least get to enjoy a cookie."

"Dearie, I've been trying to sell this house for three months. You make an offer, and I'll bake you an entire cake." She guided us towards the kitchen, where she pulled out a fresh tray of cookies from the oven (oatmeal raisin with giant chocolate chunks). Most of the newer kitchens I'd seen were larger than this one but also looked like they were planned by interior designers who couldn't separate an egg. In Susanna's kitchen, the spatulas and ladles hung within easy reach of the stove, a mixer as old as I was stood neatly tucked into the corner, and a needlepoint on the wall read 'La Cocina es el Corazón de la Casa,' which Susanna told me translated to 'The Kitchen is the Heart of the Home.' There was no question I could work my magic in here.

"Why are you selling?" I kept my voice unenthusiastic, yet sweet as Susanna's cookies. She wasn't the only one who could warm up an engine. "It's clear you've put a lot of love into this place."

"Pedro retired last month, and we're going to live near our daughter and grandkids in Arizona."

"How long did you live here?"

"38 years. Raised all three of my kids right here."

"What can you tell me about the neighborhood?"

"Oh, we love it here, though it's been through its ups and downs. When we first came here from Cuba, it was mostly young families like ourselves. Then things started getting a bit run down. I won't lie to you, it wasn't always the safest area, but in recent years that turned around. More and more young people like yourself seem to be moving in. There are even whispers of the new light rail line possibly coming this way."

At least she knew about that. As she showed me the upstairs, I considered this whole situation with the light rail. I was sure she hadn't heard the announcement with the finalized plans. If I didn't share what I knew, wouldn't that be taking advantage of her? As I bit into the last chunk of cookie, I realized that if I didn't use that information, one of the other two buyers who called today no doubt would.

What if I told her about the new line and allowed her to raise her asking price? Of course, that would screw over Phil, who put tons of time and maybe money into tracking major city works so he'd be able to give his clients the inside track. My insides twisted like a pretzel.

We were heading down the stairs when the front door opened, and a gray-haired man wearing a cap came in. "Hello there."

Susanna helped him remove his coat and hang it on one of the wooden hooks by the door. "Pedro, this is Amber. Just showing her around the house."

"Too bad you couldn't come tomorrow." He took off his cap and hung it on the hook. "I'd love to show you the other side."

"I saw the pictures you posted online. The two sides are a mirror image, right?"

"That's right." Pedro patted the wall as if it were a beloved pet.

"Then I don't need to see it in person. Can you tell me about the tenants?"

"Lovely family." He offered a simple smile, one that told me he had nothing to hide. "Three kids and a dog. Been here five years already."

"Any reason to believe they'll leave any time soon?"

"I'd guess they'll be here until their kids are all grown, which is at least a decade away. The guy's an electrician, works for the power company, so he's got good, steady work. Sometimes fixes things around the house when we need a hand. Wife's a bookkeeper part-time. Never had a moment of difficulty with them."

Wow. I loved the idea of not having to search for tenants or deal with problematic ones. The house had the charm I was looking for. It was a ten-minute walk from my favorite part of town, an even shorter drive to work, and according to Phil, this was bound to become a hot neighborhood. This was it. But what the hell did I do now?

Fortunately, Susanna's timer went off, and she went to fetch a second batch of cookies. Pedro excused himself and stepped into the bathroom. I gave Phil a jerk of the head. "I want it. What do I do?"

"Make them an offer."

Being the diligent little student that I am, I had read dozens of blog posts about how to negotiate a real estate purchase. One piece of advice that kept coming up was that real estate agents get paid on commission and therefore have no strong incentive to get you the best price. Still, Phil wasn't a Cynthia who helped clients once then never saw them again. He dealt with investors, some of whom bought multiple properties per year. I couldn't imagine him screwing over a client to pad his commission by a few hundred dollars. It wasn't in his personality, and it wouldn't be good for return business. I decided to trust him. "Can you handle the negotiation?"

"Do you have a price in mind?"

"You seem to think it's worth the asking. So I'm happy with whatever you can get."

"Will do. Just know, a 'for sale by owner' property is not as straightforward as one sold by an agent. One of you will have to pay my commission."

"I thought commissions are paid by the sellers."

"Normally, they would have paid their agent 6%, and the agent would have split that commission with me. But now they have no agent in place, which is probably why they dropped the price. They figured they'd pass the savings onto the buyer and have a better chance of making the sale."

I wasn't about to let a few thousand dollars dissuade me from the deal. "You get the best price you can. If I have to pay the fee, I will."

Five minutes later, the four of us sat down. Susanna placed the plate of steaming chocolate chunk cookies right in front of me, as if hoping they'd sweeten the deal. I guess she knew a sucker when she saw one. Fortunately, I had Phil negotiating for me, and he didn't look twice at the cookies.

"Amber and I have other homes we were planning on seeing, and I know you have others coming to see yours. But the fact is, Amber quite likes your house…"

"It really is beautiful." I grabbed another cookie. "And these are delicious!"

"While Amber may find a house she likes better if she keeps looking, and you may find a buyer willing to offer more if you keep showing it, my experience is that it's best for everyone to get a deal done right now if possible."

"We'd love that," Susanna said.

"Here's what I propose. Your latest price was $190,000. We are willing to offer $175,000 now. There's also the matter of my fee. Normally, when you list with an agent, the seller's agent splits the fee with the buyer's agent. Now that you're selling it yourselves, it's less straightforward. Sometimes the seller picks up the 3% fee for the buyer's agent, and sometimes the buyer does. In this case, I suggest the two of you split it, 1.5% each." Phil finally grabbed himself a cookie and leaned back in his chair. "Take a moment to discuss if you like."

Susanna turned to Pedro and nodded. Pedro said, "We listed it at $190,000, knowing we'd need a little wiggle room. Our absolute lowest price was $180,000. If you're willing to do that, Amber, we've got a deal. And we'll be willing to split Phil's fee, as suggested."

"Amber," Phil said, "is that acceptable to you?"

I pretended to think it over rather than leap across the table and crush Susanna and Pedro into a bear hug. "Yes. There's just one thing we need to add."

"Oh right, Amber wanted her father to approve before committing. Is it OK with you if we put that as a condition in the contract?"

I'd forgotten all about that condition about my father. "I just meant that Susanna promised me a cake."

It only took fifteen minutes for Phil to complete all the paperwork around the offer, but I was restless the entire time. Three phone calls came in before we signed. Two more interested buyers called Pedro to view the house, and I got a call from Anthony. I told him about the house and forwarded him the listing so he could see the pictures himself. He hadn't been thrilled a few weeks earlier when I told him I was looking to buy a property. He didn't understand why I'd been looking to buy when things were going so well between us, but then he seemed mollified when I explained that it was for investment. Now he listened silently as I went on and on about how excited I was about the house.

After the contract signing, Phil left, and Susanna walked me through the house again. She told me which rooms each of her kids grew up in. She shared about the time they'd been robbed and had the back door broken in, but quickly added that they'd replaced it with a high-security door, so I shouldn't worry about that. She seemed to want to download the house's memories, to make sure I knew just how special a place I'd be getting. Or, at least, how special it had been to her.

About half an hour into this tour, the doorbell rang. I thought nothing of it until Pedro came in trailing Anthony. He held a bottle of champagne. "I hear congratulations are in order."

He popped the cork, and the four of us drank our champagne out of clay mugs that Susanna had made herself. This felt so different from buying The Death Trap on Haber. This place felt like a home. If not forever, at least for now. I'd even left off the provision about my father needing to see it. I didn't need anyone to tell me this was the right house for me.

I continued to see Anthony just about every weekend he was in town, though he didn't always know when that would be. I learned not to be bothered by canceled dates. He sent me flowers at least once a week and bought me small gifts: a box of Godiva chocolates, a cashmere scarf for the night we went to an outdoor concert, a pair of pearl drop earrings, which were not at all my style, but which I wore anyway to please him.

Other than the weekends, though, Anthony was never around. He worked crazy hours, and he'd call me from different cities around the world, wherever he happened to zip off to for work. He called me more when he was in some exotic location, as if wanting to impress upon me how important his work was. Or, more likely, how important he was.

Dating a traveling workaholic left me plenty of free time. As smoothly as the house purchase was going, I wanted to make sure I didn't make any major blunders. I listened to podcasts while cooking for myself (I did think once or twice about inviting Anthony over for dinner, but never actually did) and read books in the evening before bed.

I started by learning about real estate, but there was less to know than I feared. OK, there was actually a ton to know, but since most of the strategies concerned identifying and selling properties, neither of which I needed, it made the subject more manageable. Plus, my property needed little renovation, and I had long-term tenants, so those were two more subjects I didn't have to worry about.

My biggest debate was whether to go with a 15 or 30-year mortgage. Had someone asked me the difference between the two, I would have guessed the 15-year had a monthly payment almost twice as high as the 30-year loan. But of course, that's because I, like most people, underestimated the power of compounding growth. My mortgage payment for the 15-year would be $1331 a month versus $912 for the 30-year. As the monthly payments were only 45% more on the 15-year, it seemed a no-brainer to cut the payment period in half if I had the money. And for the first time in my life, I fully expected to have more than enough money available at the end of each month. Why was I suddenly feeling so flush? It was simple. I would be collecting at least $850 a month from my tenants (that second apartment was worth $1000 or more a month in the current market, but Pedro and Susanna had only raised the rent once since the tenants moved in), and I would be saving more than $1000 a month on my own rent. Together, that would give me more than enough to pay the $1331 monthly mortgage payment on the 15 year-mortgage.

But it turned out that my no-brainer wasn't as simple as I thought. I was making myself a zucchini frittata when I heard one podcaster explain that a 30-year mortgage is better because you can always pay it down faster if you want to, even to the point of keeping it on a 15-year payment schedule. So any month when you have extra cash, you pay down a bit extra. But if there's ever a month when you find yourself tight on cash, you just make the minimum 30-year payment. Whereas, with the 15-year mortgage, you'd have to come up with the higher sum each month or else find yourself in default.

Another night, I was watching a video by a woman who pointed out that interest rates on the 15-year mortgage were lower, usually by about a half a percent. At first, I didn't understand why it would have lower interest until she explained that banks need to hedge their bets. There's less predictability over a 30-year period than there is over a 15-year period. Since no one knows what interest rates are going to look like in the future, and the banks are tying themselves to a rate now, they need to charge more for the longer loan.

But what ultimately got me to go with the 15-year term had less to do with math than with psychology. Dylan had shown me how I, like most people, tended to spend nearly every dollar I made each month. If I had the option to pay the bank $400 less, I'd probably wind up just blowing an additional $400 each month on clothes, nights out, and other non-necessities. So I liked that the 15-year gave me less flexibility on my payments.

Emboldened by my mortgage decision, I decided to dig deeper into the psychology of money. Not everyone had Dylan's discipline, but I discovered numerous tricks us mortals could employ to get the same results. Once I started reading up on these, I was able to implement several of them with just a phone call and a few clicks of the mouse.

First off, I set up a Vanguard ROTH IRA, a retirement account that was the exact opposite of my 401(k). The 401(k) was funded with pre-tax money, and I'd have to pay full income tax on anything I pulled out. The ROTH IRA was funded with post-tax money and grew tax free. I was allowed to deposit $6000 a year into the ROTH, but knew there wasn't a chance that I'd save up that much on my own. So I set it up to take money out of my account automatically each week. It came out to be just over $115 a week to make my maximum IRA contribution. With my lowered housing costs (plus Anthony picking up the bill on so many of my nights out), I'd probably never miss that money, provided that I never got used to having it.

On one of Anthony's long trips to Germany, I spent yet another Saturday night alone. To feel some of that German spirit, I settled down on the couch with a beer and chocolate covered pretzels while I read one of my new investment blogs about a program called Save More Tomorrow. The concept was simple. Since most people have a hard time cutting back on expenses, it's difficult persuading them to save any of their current earnings. So why not convince them to start a savings plan that only kicks in once they get a raise? Some companies offer this as a service. They have employees agree to give a portion of each raise put into a long-term investment plan. Since it's taken out of the paycheck before it ever reaches their greedy little pockets, there's little temptation to spend it.

My school didn't offer such a plan, but I found it easy enough to set up for myself. The raise I received when I completed my Masters in Education came out to $80 a week. I decided to devote all this to savings. So I opened up a Vanguard investment account that drew that $80 out of my account each week.

I had both Vanguard accounts, plus my 401(k), going into index funds. None of this was a huge amount of money, of course. The sums were so small that six months earlier I wouldn't have bothered. It didn't seem like it was enough to add up. But now that I was wrapping my head around the power of compounding, I knew it would.

A new guy and a new multi-unit house. My parents had heard that story before, and they were more than a little nervous to hear it again. Another visit was planned, but this one didn't caused me little stress.

Susanna was more than happy to let me bring my parents by the house before closing. "It will give me an opportunity to bake that cake I owe you." Anthony was thrilled to be introduced to the family as my boyfriend. Given that he was a good looking Italian boy on a killer career path, I had little fear of facing parental disapproval.

My parents drove in on a warm Saturday afternoon in early June. Anthony and I met them for lunch, and we all easily fell into a familiar Italian-American banter. Anthony spent ten minutes singing the praises of his late Grandma Regina, who I'd never heard of, but who clearly impressed my mother.

Then we headed over to the house. My father drove, since my parents would hardly have fit in the back of Anthony's Porsche (though my mother seemed eager to try). It was a week before closing, and I was starting to have sleepless nights thinking about all that could go wrong. But other than Susanna's unfortunate choice to make vanilla pound cake, the viewing of the house went off without a hitch.

"That really is a great house, Amber," my father said over dinner. "Sorry if I questioned your judgment."

I didn't tell him that my judgment on the last house was begging to be questioned.

"Are the two of you planning on living there together?" my mother asked.

Anthony almost choked on his bruschetta. Eager as Anthony was to move our relationship forward, he'd have to fall on some mighty hard times before he'd consider moving into that house. My mother saw his discomfort with the question but failed to understand the reason behind it. I decided that wasn't such a bad thing. "Ma, please. We haven't been dating all that long."

Anthony sent me a quizzical look, which my mother also missed.

"Of course," my mother said. "I'm glad to hear the two of you are taking your time."

CHAPTER 15

VEAL SCALLOPINI

I used to dread the first of the month: the day my rent came due. There had to be enough money in my checking account to send out the payment. But Pedro had been right; my new tenants were an absolute pleasure. Not on the personal level, we never got past a polite hello. But the husband was handy enough that he never came to me with problems, and on the first of every month, the wife slipped the rent check under my door. She got it to me first thing in the morning, often before I was dressed for work, and I had a little dance that I'd do each time in my pajamas. Just like that, rent day went from being one of my most stressful to one of my favorites.

While my first foray into being a landlord was ridiculously easy (truly the house hack with training wheels I'd asked for), I knew I couldn't count on it staying that way forever. If I was going to own a property and start managing it, I'd eventually need to learn what I was doing, and better I should find out now than to wait for the inevitable crisis to arise. Dylan, for all his shrugging off formal education, always emphasized how much he'd learned in seminars. I found one on managing real estate finances. That sounded perfect.

The seminar cost $100 for the day, which sounded steep to me since all I was going to do was listen to some guy lecture. Of course, I'd blown more money than that on entertainment dozens of times without blinking an eye. And then there was the cost of my Masters. When I broke down how much my education cost, I was probably spending $100 every time I stepped into class. Why did it seem like so much more now? Probably because there was no shiny diploma to show for it, no automatic raise at the end, and I couldn't roll the cost into some educational loan I could pay off over 20 years.

There were about 300 people in attendance. Many arrived in business suits, but there were also plenty of people in blue jeans, more the Dylan types. I'd brought a notebook and a big thermos of coffee. I was ready to go.

The speaker, John Hopton, jumped right in. "The crazy thing is, most everyone puts a ton of effort into making money and minimal effort into learning how to handle it. Many of you probably fall into that category as well. Or did. By the time you leave here today, every single one of you is going to know exactly what to do with your money."

"This is what 80% of people do with their money." He wrote the word *Income* on a whiteboard. "They make money, and it goes directly into their personal bank account." He wrote *Personal Account* and drew a line from income to account. "Now, every time they pay bills, whether it's their rent, a business expense, or taxes, it comes directly from this account.

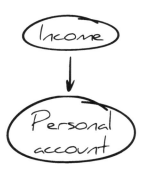

"What's the problem with this approach? Simple. The account never has enough money. Oh sure, you manage to stumble along from paycheck to paycheck. The checks you write rarely bounce. And if you need a little extra cash, no problem, you put that dinner with friends on your credit card, and you buy yourself a month to pay. All this more or less works OK. Until April 15 comes around, and you get slammed with taxes. What happens then?"

Nervous laughter filled the room. Clearly, this was a problem many could relate to.

"There's not enough cash sitting in the account." John's face waxed melodramatic. "You start to freak out, so you let the credit card bill go unpaid this month. Maybe even take a little advance. Suddenly, you find yourself paying 18% interest for months as you work to get your way back to even.

"This is why, for those of you who work regular jobs, your taxes are taken out of your paycheck. Everyone from businesses to the government understands you can't be trusted with your own money. So employees don't get stuck in the same way. Not because they're smarter, but because the entire system is set up to stop them from catastrophically ruining themselves.

"But if you're in this room, odds are that at least some of your income isn't coming from a job. And this is where the self-employed screw themselves. They often have no more money know-how than their employed friends, but they don't have a system designed to be idiot-proof. If that's you, you need to build that system for yourself."

One skinny lady in the front of the room called out, "How am I supposed to do that?"

"The first step is to incorporate. I want everyone to repeat after me, 'I promise that within thirty days of leaving this seminar, I will open a Corporation or Limited Liability Company, if I don't already have one.'"

Three hundred voices echoed his words.

"Good, because if you've got income outside of a salaried job, a corporation will save you money. Once you incorporate, open a business bank account and direct all your business income there. As soon as money hits the account, divide it three ways." John wrote 'business account' then drew three arrows from there, one going right, one left, and one down.

"First, put a third into a tax account." John wrote T.A. after the right-hand arrow. "Most of us falsely believe when we get a check for $10,000 that we have $10,000. Wrong. If we're lucky, we have $6600, because the federal government's going to take a third. I say if we're lucky, because some live in states that pile on additional taxes, leaving them with only $5000. So don't fool yourself; this money isn't yours. That doesn't mean you have to prepay it the way most employees do; that's just giving an interest-free loan to the government. Stick it into a safe, interest-bearing account, and forget about it until taxes are due."

John wrote B.E. after the left-hand arrow.

"Another third of your income should cover business expenses. Bill as many expenses to your corporation as you can reasonably get away with. If you drive for work, buy your car from your business account. Why? Business expenses are paid pre-tax, which means you'll get an extra 30% bang for your buck.

"The third chunk of your income goes into a personal account." He wrote P.A. below the bottom arrow. "Here's where you pay for rent, food, clothes, investments, etc. Now when you spend from here, you never have to worry about not having enough money because you've already created a solid system to protect your corporation's and the government's shares."

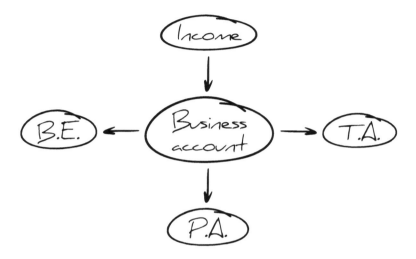

I scribbled notes as fast as I could, noting all those pointers about accounts. His words seemed pretty clear to me, but a guy in the row ahead of mine stood and called out, "I don't get any of this." The guy looked to be in his early thirties, with slicked-back hair and a thick Brooklyn accent.

"I'm sorry, sir, am I going too fast?"

"Too fast? No way. Far too slow."

The lady next to me told Mr. Slick to sit down, but John took it in stride. "I'm sorry, I'm not following. What is your name?"

"Vinny."

Vinny. Of course, he had to be Italian. I can't count the number of times I've told people I was Italian, and they asked me if my family was in the mafia. I rolled my eyes every time. My father was an attorney, my mother a social worker, and despite my cousin Lorenzo's offer to lend Dylan money for a ring, there wasn't a legit loan shark, hitman, or drug runner in my extended family.

Yet Vinny looked like an extra from every mafia movie I'd ever seen. Even his name sounded like it was chosen by a screenwriter for some low budget mob flick. His designer suit was sharp, too sharp for this conference. His hair was combed back, his cologne, which I could smell from my row, was undoubtedly expensive, and it looked like he wore a Rolex.

"So Vinny, what's your question?"

"I'm trying to figure out why you're yapping to these fine people about paying taxes." His hands were so animated, I would have known he was Italian from a mile away. "Why not prepare them to not pay taxes?"

"You're still young, Vinny, so I don't blame you for holding onto the dream of getting out of paying taxes. But like they say, there are two things that none of us can avoid, 'Death and Taxes.'"

John's comment got a polite laugh from the crowd, but not from Vinny. "Yeah? Well, neither one of 'em has caught up with me yet."

Grumbling came from around the audience. John still kept his patience; he was a pro on stage. "I get it. When you're starting out, taxes can sting. And if you're small and savvy enough, you can keep them pretty low for a while. But I'm telling you, Vinny, this is not a long-term strategy. By the time you're earning what I am…"

"How much you wanna bet I make more money than you do?" Vinny gave a self-satisfied grin. "And you know what my taxes were last year? Nada."

At this point, the audience had enough of Vinny. A few people openly yelled at him to shut up.

"If you don't mind, Vinny, I'm getting the sense people want me to continue with my talk." Quite a few cheered at this statement.

"Mind? No, I don't mind at all. If these fools want to learn how to pay more taxes, they deserve what they get. For me, it's clear I'm not going to learn anything worthwhile here."

The woman next to me said, "Good riddance."

Unlike the rest of the crowd, I wasn't offended by Vinny's style. Hell, if I couldn't handle overly slick Italian guys, I'd never make it through a family reunion. Like everyone else, I'd thought what John had to say made sense. I appreciated the idea of opening a corporation and dividing up my income into clear buckets. But I had to admit, I was intrigued by Vinny. What if there was a better way? Was he really able to skip out on taxes entirely? Now that I'd brought my housing costs way down, taxes were my number one expense.

Vinny exited the hall alone, accompanied only by dirty looks. After a moment of picking at my cuticles, I went with my gut, gathered my things, and followed.

By the time I exited the auditorium, Vinny was already leaving the building. I ran ahead and only caught up with him after half a block. "Vinny!" I called.

He turned, then his face grew puzzled as he saw me chasing after him. "Who are you?"

"Amber. Maria Ambrosia Romano." I had a hunch that if he heard my full name, he'd treat me more like family than like some crazed woman following him down Lincoln Boulevard. "I was sitting behind you in the seminar just now."

"Ah, good to see there's at least one other person smart enough to walk out on that guy."

"I'd…"

"Take a minute to catch your breath." He gave me a once over.

I regained my composure. "I'd love to hear how you manage to pay so little in taxes."

Once again, he looked me up and down. "How about I buy you lunch, and the two of us talk it over?"

I'd been hit on by enough Italian guys growing up to know that the only way to handle them was straight on. "I've got a boyfriend, Vinny."

"Oh."

"But I'd love to sit with you and pick your brain."

"Well, you know I've got a rule I tell everyone wanting my advice."

"What's that?"

"If you're buyin', I'm talkin'."

So now he wanted me to take *him* out to lunch? Other than my dates with Anthony, I hardly ever went out to eat anymore, choosing to cook for myself to save money. Then again, what I was saving on eating out was only a fraction of what I spent each year in taxes.

He saw me hesitate. "I promise you, for the price of a meal, you'll learn ten times as much as you would from sitting down with some $400 an hour tax attorney."

How much did I have to lose? "OK, let's do it. How about this place over here?" I pointed to an Italian restaurant on the corner that had a sign in the window advertising their business lunch special.

"You can take a jar of Ragu off the shelf at the supermarket and make better pasta than these guys. If you want Italian, I've got a much better place."

We were only a few blocks from Little Italy, close enough that I'd walked to the seminar that morning. Vinny led us straight to Giovanni's, a restaurant I'd loved the two times I'd gone there. Once had been with my parents, the other time with Anthony, as I couldn't afford to go there on my own. I just hoped whatever Vinny taught me would be worth it.

As we were seated, I had to reassure myself this was worth the investment. "You really pay nothing in taxes?"

"Nada. It's my private screw you to the government." His middle finger shot up like a rocket to the moon.

"You hate the government that much?"

A waitress came over with garlic bread and menus. I ordered chicken parmesan, the cheapest entree. But Vinny went all out. He ordered the veal scaloppini, a bottle of white wine, and three appetizers that he said were for the table. This guy's tax advice had better be good.

Vinny waited until the waitress left, then leaned in and lowered his voice. "My mamma raised me and my two brothers by herself. Nobody worked harder than my mamma, and the woman was as honest as the day was long." His finger hit the table for emphasis. "But then those bastards from the IRS come knocking on her door and start demanding five years' worth of receipts from the little store mamma ran out of the basement. She didn't know you had to keep stuff like that. Mamma lost the house, and we had to move in with my Aunt Cecilia. I can still remember the look of humiliation on her face. I swore then I'd never give the government a dime."

"You're not afraid of getting audited?"

He leaned back and smiled so big, his lips practically brushed against his ears. "Not a bit." The waitress came over and filled Vinny's cup with wine. She tried to stop when the glass was half full, but he waved her to keep going.

"Look, I know you're angry, but it's a stupid game you're playing. My aunt got audited once. She said it was one of the worst experiences of her life. Sooner or later they're going to come after you."

"Sooner or later? Are you kidding? I make a million dollars a year and pay zero in taxes. There's no sooner or later with a guy like me." He downed half his glass. "There are few guarantees in life, but here's one I'll swear by. Your pal Vinny will get audited every year of his life."

"But you said—."

"I said I wasn't afraid of audits. That's the difference. I'm sure your aunt skimps a little bit here and there on her taxes like most Americans." He flicked his hand in disgust. "Worse, she probably chucks her receipts in the garbage like my mother, never thinking she'll need them again. An audit for her is like a root canal every day for a year. But I know they're coming. I learned that lesson as a kid. The bastards never find a thing."

"How do you manage that?" I pulled out my notebook.

"You ever seen the tax code? It's over five thousand pages long." Vinny pointed right at me, displaying a fat ruby ring. "You know how much is dedicated to these tax brackets the politicians are always yappin' about?"

"How much?"

"Less than one percent."

"So what's the other 99%?"

"Exemptions, Deductions, Exclusions."

"Basically, loopholes?"

"That's what the Democrats call them."

"What do Republicans call them?"

"Incentives. If the government wants you to do something, they incentivize you with a tax break. They want you to buy an electric car or put solar panels on your roof, Bam!—Tax break. They want you to give to the poor, Bam!—Tax break. Most people look at the tax code like it's a bunch of penalties, instead of understanding what it is."

"Which is what?"

Vinny glided one hand along the other. "A roadmap for how to make money and keep it."

"Is that how the IRS looks at it?"

"Nah. The sadists at the IRS look at it as their own private whips and chains. They go around the country, beating up the innocent and ignorant with it. But they're not it's true masters. They can't be."

"Why not?" I took a sip of water. With the bill Vinny was heaving on my shoulders, I couldn't afford a beverage.

"If you had a roadmap for making a fortune, would you spend your life wearing a cheap suit and pushing papers all day long? Not a chance. The masters of the code are all on my side, living large."

"You make yourself sound like a leech."

"That's what the Democrats call me."

"That doesn't bother you?"

"Nah. They're a bunch of hypocrites. Not one of them pays a dime more in taxes than they think they have to, but if someone else is better at playing the tax game than they are, they jump up and down and call them leeches."

"What do the Republicans call you?"

"Savvy."

I had to laugh. "So I take it you're a Republican?"

"Never bothered voting. You could say I'm lacking in respect and admiration for our civil servants on both sides of the aisle."

"But that doesn't stop you from using their incentives."

"Damn straight." Vinny snapped his fingers. "They make the rules. I play the game."

The appetizers came. I helped myself to a piece of prosciutto. If I was paying so much for it, I might as well enjoy it. "So let me see if I've got this straight.

You claim to know this 5000-page tax code better than the IRS, and you use that knowledge to legally make a killing and pay no taxes."

"You've mostly got it. I'm sure the IRS agents acted all high and mighty when browbeating your poor aunt, but they're still bound by the law. I don't even bother going to the audits anymore. But my paperwork is airtight. My accountant sites chapter and verse on why each deduction is legit." Vinny reached for a slice of bruschetta. "The auditors crawl out of there with their tails between their legs."

"You said I've mostly got it. What am I still missing?"

"I don't know the 5000-page code. What's the point? There are a million anal details in there I'm never going to need. I only know a handful of the most powerful provisions. I use the same few rules over and over until I owe nothing."

This is what I came for. The idea of combing through a two-foot thick legal document had less than zero appeal to me. Even if it was a roadmap to fortune, I'd never get through it. But a few, ultra-powerful rules I could handle. I clicked my pen open. "What are they?"

"The Holy Grail of loopholes is depreciation." Bits of tomato flew out of Vinny's mouth, but he didn't seem to care. "You know what that is?"

"That's the amount something goes down in value, right?"

"You got it. Except it's a myth."

"How?"

"Say you buy yourself a car for business. According to the government, it depreciates evenly over five years. Meaning a $20,000 car should be worth $16,000 after one year, and after five years the government says it should be worth nothing. That's a load of crap. You'd be lucky as hell to get $16,000 for it after the first year, but after five years, it still might be worth $5000 or more."

I thought of the 9-year-old car I'd briefly owned. It hadn't been expensive, but even with the dented side, it was hardly free. "So you're saying there's platonic depreciation, and then there's actual depreciation."

Vinny tugged at his collar. "I'm Italian, not Greek. What the hell do you mean by platonic depreciation?"

"There's an assumption and then there's the reality, and they're not the same."

"Now you're talking my language. They're nowhere near the same. But for purposes of taxes, we use whatever number the government gives us, whether it's accurate or not. Remember, they make the rules…"

"And we play the game."

"You got it. So back to our car example." He served himself some arugula salad. "If your business is making $50,000 a year and you depreciate the car at $4000 a year, then you pay taxes on $46,000 for each of those five years."

"So it's not that you reduce your taxes by $4000, you reduce your taxable income by $4000?"

"You got it. So maybe you save $1000 or $1500 on taxes." Vinny picked up a sliver of parmesan and popped it into his mouth. This guy wasn't classy, but I wasn't here to date him, so I didn't care.

"OK, so you get some financial advantage if the government thinks something is tanking in value, but is that enough to make a killing on? Even if the car didn't go down a full $4000, it probably still went down by the $1000 or $1500 you're saving out of pocket. So how does that help?"

"Ah, but what if it's not going down in value? What if it's going up?" He jabbed a slice of prosciutto with his fork and laid it on his plate. "Let's say you bought a classic car for $20,000, and after five years, it's worth $25,000. Then you'd be saving on taxes and making money at the same time." Vinny grinned as he cut into the ham.

"So is that what you're into? Classic cars?"

"Please. The classic car market is tiny. There's a much bigger arena where I make my dough."

"What's that?" I asked.

"Real estate."

"Real estate depreciates?"

"You got it. Over 27.5 years for residential and 39 years for commercial. Don't you love those numbers? It's like they drew them out of a hat."

I grabbed a piece of prosciutto before Vinny finished it off. "Don't properties usually go up in value?"

"You got it. That's what makes depreciation the Holy Grail of loopholes. I can be making a killing on a property and still owe zero taxes on it. Better yet, I report it to the IRS as a loss and use it to offset other income."

"What if the IRS catches you doing this?"

"Catch me? I rub their noses in it. It's not like I'm making this stuff up." His voice boomed. "I'm using their freakin' laws."

"I'm not getting the numbers here. If I take the cost of an investment and divide by 27.5 years, I can deduct less than 4% a year. It doesn't seem like that big a deal."

"It's 3.63% to be exact, and the math gets worse before it gets better because the land the property is on doesn't depreciate at all."

"So how are you saving all this money?"

"You ready to be blown away? You seem to like numbers, so let me walk you through a deal I did a couple of months back. I bought a building with 14 apartments for $1,200,000. You know how much it cost me out of pocket?"

"How much?"

Vinny leaned in and whispered. "Nada."

"How'd you manage that?"

"OPM, baby!" Vinny downed the last of his wine. "Hey, beautiful," he called to a passing waitress passing, "can you fill me up?"

I forced my eyes not to roll. "What's OPM?"

"Other people's money."

"Who'd pay for you to buy a building?"

"$1,000,000 came from the bank at 4.85% interest. Most only get 70-75% on a building like that, but I'm a good customer at my bank. I got seller financing for $150,000 at 8% interest, and for the final $50,000, I took out a private money loan from a guy I know at 10% interest. So it didn't cost me a bent penny."

I scribbled the numbers into my notebook. I was missing something, and I wanted to be able to go over the numbers again later. "What does that have to do with depreciation?"

"The land was worth about $200,000, so I acquired $1,000,000 in depreciation for nothing."

"Wait, you can depreciate what you never spent?"

"You got it. Other than the land, you can depreciate it all, whether the purchase money came out of your pocket or not."

I took out my phone and pulled up the calculator. I divided $1,000,000 by 27.5 and got $36,364. "You're telling me you can make over $36,000 a year on this property without owing any taxes on it?"

"A hell of a lot more than that." Vinny served himself the last of the salad. "The building brings in an income of about $150,000. From that, I can deduct maintenance costs, property management, repairs, even the interest on the loans. After all that, I'm left with around $50,000 a year. Not bad for a building that costs me nothing."

"I still don't see how you can avoid paying taxes. If you're making $50,000 and depreciating $36,000, isn't there still $14,000 left of taxable income?"

"You're a smart cookie, you know that? Just how serious are things with this boyfriend?"

"Very," I said, making sure Vinny didn't get any ideas.

The main dishes arrived. Vinny breathed in the steam coming off his veal. "I love this place. They're the only ones who know how to prepare veal like my mamma."

I took a bite of the chicken parmesan. It was good, but my face hardly bore the signs of elation on Vinny's.

Vinny took ten bites before he looked up from his veal. "Sorry, what was the last question?"

"How can you avoid paying taxes if you have $50,000 of profits on the books and can only depreciate $36,000?"

"Ah," his eyes lit up. "When I buy a building, I wind up with a lot more than just walls and ceilings."

"Like what?"

"Like furniture, lighting, appliances, cabinets. Most people lump all that stuff together with the building costs. But if you separate it, that other stuff mostly depreciates over 5 years, instead of 27.5. That's called a cost segregation.

"To keep the numbers round, let's say the land was worth $200,000, the building $800,000, and all that other stuff $200,000. Now what's my depreciation? Plug that into your phone and see what you get."

I was already entering it. The $800,000 still depreciated over 27.5 years, so that gave me $29,090 for the building component. For the next bit, I didn't even need my calculator. $200,000 divided by 5 years is $40,000 a year. Adding those together, I got "$69,090. Wait, but that means you have more depreciation than you're making."

"Exactly." He rubbed his hands together like a movie villain. "So not only does the depreciation knock out the entirety of my $50,000 in profits, it knocks out another $19,000 from other properties."

This sounded too good to be true. "You can use depreciation from one building to offset income from other sources?"

"You never appreciated the beauty of depreciation before, did you?" Vinny took a bite of his veal, showing an almost indecent amount of pleasure.

"You ever worry about having too much depreciation?"

"Absolutely. The total amount I get is fixed. It's not like the IRS will send me a check if I have more depreciation than income, so I don't want to waste it. I keep a close eye on how much depreciation I need. I only do cost segregations when I have enough income to offset. If I didn't have enough when I bought this last building, I could have let the entire $1,000,000 depreciate over the 27.5 year period. Then, if there came a year when I needed more depreciation, I could retroactively separate out the furniture and stuff." Vinny popped a scallop into his mouth.

"You don't need to do the cost segregation when you buy?"

"Nope. And in the year you do the segregation, you get to pile on all that extra depreciation from the years you missed. Using our numbers, the segregation gave us an additional $33,000 a year in depreciation for the first five years. Let's say I didn't need that deduction in the first two years, so I waited until year three. In addition to the $33,000 coming to me that year, I can add $66,000 from the two years I missed."

"You'd be able to offset almost $100,000 worth of income?"

"Ain't it great?"

"But it's not like the segregation increases your depreciation, you just use it up faster."

"The total is the same, but why wait 20 years to get my money?" It was hard not to get distracted by the piece of veal on the end of his fork. "The cash I have in hand now I can use to buy more properties. It's compounding at a mad rate. Besides, once the higher levels of depreciation are used up, I can always do a 1031 exchange."

My chicken was getting chewier by the minute. I couldn't believe how many tricks this guy had up his sleeve. No wonder he didn't flinch at the price of Veal Scallopini at Giovanni's. "What's a 1031 exchange?"

"I sell my current building and use the profits to buy a more expensive one. Just like that, I've acquired a truckload of depreciation."

"You don't pay taxes on those gains?"

"Nada."

"So the downside is that you can't take profits on the first building? You have to reinvest it, right?"

"Downside? I don't work with downsides." He cut another piece of veal. "After I make the exchange, I refinance the new building, and take that additional money right back in my greedy little pocket in the form of a loan."

"And that's not taxed either?"

"Of course not. In the government's eyes, it's borrowed money, not profits." The waitress arrived with more wine, and Vinny winked at her. "Thanks, Doll."

"So if you're making a million dollars of income, you must own a lot of buildings?"

"Almost twenty, but not all this size. I don't get anywhere near a million dollars in annual depreciation. But depreciation is only one tool in my belt. I like to live large, and I make sure that just about every dollar I spend is a legit-business expense. That means I spend my money pre-tax."

"How?"

Vinny spread his arms wide. "Take lunch today. We're talking business, aren't we?"

"You told me *I* had to pick up the tab."

"My mamma raised me to be a gentleman and a sexist. She'd chew my head off if she heard I had a lunch meeting with a nice Italian girl and stuck her with the bill." He winked at me. "This is on me."

"Wow. Thank you, Vinny."

He lowered his voice. "You're wishing you'd ordered the veal now, aren't you?"

"Well, you do seem to be enjoying it." I quickly added, "But the chicken parmesan is very good."

"Sure, it is." Vinny hailed the waitress. "I want you to pack up this lady's chicken parmesan to go and bring out another plate of veal scaloppini."

The waitress reached out for my plate, but I stopped her. "You can take what's left of the chicken when you come back with the veal." I took another bite. Now that I was no longer paying for it, it tasted a hell of a lot better. "How is this a business expense for you? You're giving me all this free advice. It should be an expense for *me*."

"Real estate is all about networking. So when two investors go and spend the entire meal talking shop, it's a business expense. You might think you're getting all the benefit, but who knows? Three years from now, you might come across a hot property that's out of your price range. You'll walk away, but later that day, you'll pass a bistro and see a guy sitting outside eating veal scaloppini. Suddenly, you'll think, 'this property is perfect for Vinny.' You give me a call, I close the deal, and I make a million dollars."

"You're full of crap, but I appreciate it anyway."

"Don't laugh it off; that's how this business works. I find most of my properties through referrals."

"Well, in that case, I thank you for the meal, and I thank your mamma for raising a gentleman."

"My mamma's the best." He brought his fingers to his lips and kissed them, Italian style.

"With all this money you're making, I assume she can lay easy these days."

"Actually, she's overseeing the renovation of a building I bought in Hawaii."

My fork dropped onto my plate, making a loud clang. "You put her to work?"

"I put her on the beach. Trust me, my mamma knows she doesn't have to lift a finger on that property if she doesn't want to. But she learned her lesson with the IRS, and she knows the power of deductions."

"And she doesn't have to do any work?"

"Get this, the IRS says that only half of each day needs to be spent on business for the entire thing to be considered a full business day. You know what they consider a business day? Eight hours. The lazy bums. So she spends four hours and a minute each day on the property, overseeing the construction, or out shopping for furnishings, then she clocks out and spends the other twenty hours doing whatever she wants." He counted the items on his fingers, relishing the jab he was making at the IRS with each one. "Her first-class ticket, her penthouse suite, her convertible rental car, all her meals, they're all legit deductions."

"All of it?"

"Mostly. Her meals are only 50% deductible, but she'd have to eat anyway. The rest, I can deduct every red cent."

My veal arrived, and it took only one bite to see why Vinny was so obsessed. If I ever came across a hot property out of my price range, there was no question I'd refer it to Vinny. Just for the veal alone.

My mouth was too busy to ask any more questions for a while. But when I was halfway through my veal, I said, "I'm still trying to get my head around this. You're saying I don't have to pay taxes? It makes no sense. Say I have a job paying $80,000 and I—."

Vinny threw up his hands. "Whoa, stop right there. If you're planning on being a salaried shnook, the government's got you by the balls."

I wasn't so worried about the government. If they could find my balls, they could have them. I was far more worried about Vinny. My eyes shot over to the second wine bottle, now empty. I'd had half a glass, so he'd drunk the rest. The dessert menus arrived. I wouldn't ordinarily impose on Vinny's generosity but ordered the chocolate soufflé, which takes a notoriously long time to make to give him time to sober up.

"Fine, so let's say I'm not a salaried employee. Let's say I'm making $80,000 working for myself."

Vinny crossed his arms in a giant X. "Wrong. Now you're doubly screwed. You'll be paying 15% self-employment tax on top of your income tax."

"What's self-employment tax?"

"Social Security and Medicaid."

"Don't I already pay that?"

"If you're working a job, you pay half, and your employer pays half. Once you're self-employed, it's all on you. By the time you add it up, you might pay more in Social Security tax than you do in income tax."

"That can't be."

"No? Not only does the government take 15%, but they still make you pay income tax on that 15%. They're taxing your taxes. Then, if Social Security is still around by the time you're old enough to receive it, they'll tax you on your distributions too. All so they can supposedly invest it for you at some lame rate of return. And the more you put in, the lower percentage of it they pay you back."

"Why would they pay you back a lower percent?"

"Because it's not an investment, it's a safety net. The more you earn, the less Uncle Sam figures you need it, so your contribution gets redistributed to those who earned less. You're better off paying none of it. You'll make ten times as much investing it yourself if you know what you're doing, and you won't have to wait forty years to enjoy it."

I chewed over my veal and his words at the same time. "You talk about all this stuff as if it's optional."

"It is. If I don't have to pay it, neither do you."

"But you never showed me how. Back to my example. If I'm making a salary of $80,000, how do I avoid paying income and Social Security tax on that?"

"Say I cut off my finger in some construction accident." Vinny held out the finger with the giant ruby ring. "I'm rushed into surgery, and the doctor sews it back on. A few months later, I come back and complain, 'It still doesn't work the way it used to. Can't you do any better?' The Doc replies, 'Absolutely. Next time come to me first, and I'll show you how to not cut it off.'"

"I don't get it."

"Once you've earned your money on a salary, you're already screwed. There's only so much the world's greatest tax guy can do for you. You'd be better off seeing a priest." Vinny devoutly clasped his hands before his chest. "So don't come to me after you've earned the money and say, 'Vinny, how do I protect my money from the big, bad IRS?' You have to come to me first, before you've ever made the money. Then I can teach you how to earn it in a way they can't touch."

"Which is how?"

"Passive income. Self-Employment tax only applies to active income. Also, all those things I told you about depreciation offsetting your other income, most of that also applies only to passive income. To escape the grips of the IRS, you need to take your active income and use it to build up passive income sources."

This was starting to sound like Dylan-talk. "What do you consider passive?"

"If you have a business, for your work to be considered active, it has to be regular, continuous, and substantial."

I wrote down his words, but despite being plain English, they sounded like jargon. "Regular, continuous, and substantial?"

"I know. You can just picture those jerks fondling their thesaurus, can't you? There are like seven different tests to determine if your business qualifies. But if you work in it less than 500 hours a year, and all the work isn't falling on you, it's likely considered passive."

"You work less than 500 hours a year in your real estate ventures?"

"Real estate is a special category. The type I do, buying homes and renting them out, is almost considered passive by definition."

"But what if my business isn't in real estate and it requires me to work more than 500 a year? Am I stuck paying 15% self-employment tax? I know you couldn't stand the speaker today, but he was pretty insistent that we should all open corporations. Wasn't that to protect us from taxes?"

"If it's not passive income, I can't get you out of all the taxes on it. But I'll give John that much, having a corporation can help. Back to your example of making $80,000 a year. If you report that you're self-employed, the government will want self-employment tax on all of it. But let's say you form a corporation. Then on your taxes, maybe you'll claim that you took a $40,000 salary, and you made another $40,000 in profits."

"How does that make a difference?"

"You only pay self-employment tax on wages."

"Which is why passive income doesn't pay it."

"You got it."

"So why not call it all profit?"

"If you pay yourself too little, the IRS will be all over you like hemorrhoids on my Uncle Freddie's ass. They'll reclassify all the distributions as wages, so you'll pay self-employment tax on all of it. Then those leeches will slap you with penalties."

"So how can I know what's a good amount?"

"What would you reasonably pay someone else to do your job? If the job market demands you pay $50,000, then you better declare $50,000 as wages, or else you're begging for trouble."

"Because if I don't, they'll get the entire $80,000?"

Vinny nodded as he worked at his teeth with a toothpick. "They might. You try to get away with too much, you give the bastards power. Learn the rules, follow the rules, and they've got nothing on you."

"Even as you pay next to nothing in taxes?"

"In my case, nothing at all."

The desserts came. After one bite of soufflé, I felt well rewarded for looking after Vinny. Then my mind started reeling with everything I'd learned, and I grew annoyed. "You don't feel bad at all about not contributing your fair share?"

"I contribute more than my fair share. Just not through the bloodsucking government. You have any idea how many families in my old neighborhood only have food in their fridge because of the help they get from good old Vinny? My money does a hell of a lot more good there than funding an overpriced drive shaft on an aircraft carrier." His speech was coming steadier and his vocabulary less vulgar, so I assumed he was sobering up.

When the check came, Vinny took a picture of it with his phone.

"What are you doing?" I asked.

"You think a year from now when my accountant is going through my expenses that I'm going to remember what this bill from Giovanni's was for? The trick to beating the IRS at their own game is to document everything, the sooner, the better."

He typed on his phone, then spun it around for me to see. Beneath a shot of the receipt and the price was a caption: *Lunch during John Hopton's real estate finance seminar. Networking meal with fellow investor Amber Romano.* "You think the IRS will ever get into a pissing contest with me over this expense? Not a chance, it's too well documented, too easy to justify. They only bully people like my mamma, who wasn't anal enough to keep track of each expense."

"But she does now?"

"Damned right. My family might not be the world's fastest learners, but once we get a lesson, we never forget it."

"You don't ever think it'll make economic sense for you to pay some taxes?"

"Economic sense? Perhaps. But I'd rather spend two dollars avoiding taxes than give one dollar to the government."

"That's insane."

"Is it? My vendetta has led me to uncover dozens of loopholes. It's saved me a fortune."

I sat back, my soufflé gone, my head feeling like it was about to explode. I truthfully hadn't followed everything Vinny had said at lunch, and I was probably going to have to study my notes like a school kid. But I got enough to realize how narrow my perspective on taxes had been up until now. "All this is going too fast for me."

"Catch up!" He stood up. "Don't ever expect the world to slow down to your speed."

CHAPTER 16

GREAT EXPECTATIONS

"**Y**ou're not going to believe this house," Anthony said as we rolled our luggage towards our gate. "Tahoe's incredible. Skiing in the winter, boating and hiking in the summer."

Anthony's mentor Leonard, one of the partners in his firm, invited us to his mountain house for the long Memorial Day weekend. It was our first trip away together. "So he's got two big homes, one here and one in Tahoe?"

"I don't know if I'd call the one in Tahoe big. It's more like a chalet. But the view is unreal." He stretched out his arm, setting the scene for me. "Imagine the sun coming down over the mountains and reflecting on the water. It'll take your breath away."

"That must have cost a pretty penny."

"What he paid is nothing compared to what it's worth now. There's a reason I worked so hard to impress Leonard when I first got to the firm. I wanted to work on his projects to learn from the best. The guy rarely makes a poor investment. This little chalet has probably quadrupled in value since he bought it. It's become quite the asset."

It was only an asset on paper, I thought to myself, but it must be costing them a fortune to maintain. Still, I bit my tongue, knowing this would only annoy Anthony. Instead, I said, "It's awfully nice for him to have us over."

"Sure is." Anthony caressed my cheek. "That's really what all this money is for in the end, isn't it? Getting to share it with family and friends."

Anthony had asked his question rhetorically and didn't wait for an answer. But it got me wondering: what was money for?

"Flight B168 to Tahoe is now open for boarding," a flight attendant announced.

Anthony filled the silence during takeoff with chatter about his latest trip to Germany, where his firm was investing in a robotics company. I barely paid attention while images flashed through my mind: Dylan's Crypt, Libby's new house, my father in his hospital bed, Anthony's Porsche. Money was at the center of all this, but did that bring me any closer to understanding the true purpose of money? Did I even get the basics, such as how much I should make, should spend, should invest?

A flight attendant bringing us drinks interrupted Anthony's flow. I took advantage of the pause and blurted out, "Anthony, what's your approach to taxes?"

"Where'd that come from?"

"I met this guy this week. He's also Italian, actually."

"Met him where?"

"At a seminar. Though he walked out after a half-hour, and I followed to pick his brain. We wound up getting lunch."

"Oh yeah? Where'd you go?"

"Giovanni's."

"Giovanni's?" Anthony gave me a look. "Who picked up the bill?"

"He did."

"Let me get this straight. You went out to lunch. With a guy. At the best Italian place in town. And I'm supposed to believe you talked about...taxes?"

"Oh, don't get all jealous on me. Vinny asked me out, and I made it very clear to him that I was taken." I put my hand on Anthony's arm. "Besides, there's no way I'd date this guy." I held my hands out like a shield. "He wears enough hair grease to support a salon for a year."

Anthony relaxed a bit when I insulted Vinny. "Taxes, eh?"

"Yeah. It's cool stuff." Just having the chance to talk this out with someone who understood finance would help me digest it. "The guy doesn't pay a cent in taxes despite making a killing in real estate."

"Amber, honey. I hear you're all excited. And I get it. For a teacher who doesn't make much, taxes are a painful hit."

"Exactly!"

Anthony put down his soda and patted my hand. "But it's time to stop worrying about your current financial challenges, and start thinking about where you're headed."

"Oh?" I pulled my hand away. "And where am I headed?"

"To Tahoe for one. This weekend you're going to get a glimpse at the life we can build together. Trust me, a guy like Leonard spends next to no time worrying about his taxes. He hires the best tax attorneys and accountants in the state, and he leaves everything in their hands."

"But Vinny kept telling me that there's only so much any of these tax specialists can help after you make your money."

"Are you saying I should change my profession so I can earn money in some tax-sheltered way?"

"No, of course not."

"Look, Amber. I've met people like this Vinny. They shoot themselves in the foot. They get so myopic about saving on taxes that they miss out on killer opportunities."

"Like how?"

"Like when I was trading stocks after college. I knew guys who bought these plodding, loser stocks, but they still insisted on holding them for over a year to save on taxes. What's the point? For me, I preferred to find something that was on fire, get in, make my money, and get out. Did I pay more in taxes than they did? Absolutely. But who cares? Even after paying my taxes, I still made two to three times what these other guys did. For me, taxes are just a cost of doing business."

It hit me then how unfair I was being. Anthony was willing to take on the burden of making a great living for both of us. Was I going to second guess how he spent it or what tax strategies he preferred? I knew I'd been a bit of a cold fish lately. I took his hand in mine and leaned over to kiss him. "I'm so excited," I said, making sure to play up the enthusiasm in my voice. "I've never been to Tahoe before."

"You're going to love it." Anthony gave me the biggest smile I'd seen on his face in weeks. "Trust me."

Anthony had called Leonard's Tahoe house a chalet. I didn't have the first clue what distinguished a house from a chalet. After getting the grand tour from Leonard's wife, Heather, I wondered if the term chalet referred to a five-bedroom wooden mountain house with an entire wall made of glass to show off views of the lake and surrounding mountains. If so, you could put me down for one.

Initially, they'd put the two of us together in the guest room. But when I told Heather I'd prefer a room of my own, she had her housekeeper Juanita make it up for me.

Leonard took Anthony out to the deck. I sat on a barstool at the counter while Heather glided through the kitchen, gathering up ingredients. "I'm obsessed with this drink. We first had it at the last partner's retreat. Now it's a must in my house." She pulled strawberries and basil leaves from the fridge and pulled down a bottle of bourbon from a top cabinet.

"Were you a dancer?" I asked.

"Yes. How did you know?"

"Your posture and the way you move."

"I did six years with the American Ballet Company." She laid everything on the counter in a neat row and pulled her perfectly highlighted hair into a bun. "I stepped down when I got married. And, of course, I've never moved the same since having kids. These days, I feel like I stomp through the house with the grace of a water buffalo."

"I have several aunts who could take pointers from a water buffalo. Trust me, you move nothing like them."

Heather held out a knife and cutting board to me. "I hear you're quite the whiz in the kitchen."

"You heard that from Anthony?" Other than bringing him a handful of fresh chocolate chip cookies on one of our dates, I'd never actually cooked for him, despite his many hints he'd like me to.

"Well, from Leonard, but it's the same thing. Of course, the only thing Leonard can cook is barbecue. Funny how when it's outside over fire, cooking suddenly becomes a man's job."

"Indeed. Though my father also made a mean Caesar salad." I minced the basil with the chef's knife, drawing appreciative looks from Heather. I could never match her grace on her feet, but the kitchen was my wheelhouse. "How often do you come out here?" I asked.

Heather washed off the strawberries. "As much as I can."

"In the winter, too?"

"Winter's our favorite. The skiing's great. Ever since my daughter Jenna first started racing competitively, we had to come out just about every weekend so she could be on the team."

"Really? Leonard can get away that often?"

Heather laughed. "As the wife of a venture capitalist, you never schedule your life around your husband's availability. He shows up when he can, but we have to make allowances. Without his work, we'd never have this lifestyle."

I'd always hated it as a kid when my dad was in the middle of a case and had to work weekends. "Where are your kids, anyway?"

"Jenna boards at a ski school in Vail. Collin's off on a sailing trip with his buddies." She cut the greens off the strawberries and threw them into her blender. "The recipe calls for sugar, but a beekeeper delivers liquid gold to my door." She poured a stream of honey onto the strawberries.

"You don't look old enough to have your kids out of the house."

"Don't let your eyes fool you. A little nip here, a tuck there, and ten years disappear in the blink of an eye. But the kids aren't all that old themselves. Jenna's fourteen and Collin's sixteen."

My parents never let me or my siblings get that far from home at those ages. "It doesn't bother you having them away?"

"Are you kidding me? I worked for years getting them this independent." Heather poured the blended strawberry mush into a saucepan and stirred it over the stove. Her jeans and cashmere blouse were casual but clearly didn't come off the sales rack. Everything about her looked relaxed and easy, as though she didn't have a care in the world. I bet she never had to worry about her sauce burning on the stove. Juanita probably looked over that while Heather sipped her wine and did whatever rich ladies did with their time.

But something tugged at my insides. I scanned the house, the mountain view, the orange light of the setting sun glinting off the lake. It didn't feel anything like the Memorial Day weekends I grew up with. I'd spent the previous one at my parent's house. Both of my sisters came in with their families. It was an unusually warm day, so Donny, Johnny, and little Marie chased each other around with water guns. Jack sprayed the grill so much, he put out the fire, and my father got so mad he tackled the kid to the ground and tickled him to pieces. The other children piled on top of the pair, and they all rolled around the yard like puppies. Melissa and Bobby were doing the typical 'I'm too cool for my family' stance, smoking what I hoped was only tobacco behind the garage and checking their phones every two minutes.

This place felt so...quiet.

"This smells so good!" Heather took the strawberry syrup off the stove, ran it through a sieve into a pitcher, and threw in a couple of ice cubes. "The key ingredient," she held up her pointer finger, "is bitters. But I don't use that junk they sell in town." She grabbed an unlabeled mason jar from the liquor cabinet. "The bartender at the Ritz Carlton gave me a private lesson. My bitters have juniper berries, mint, and rose hips, all which grow wild here in the mountains."

Heather placed the pitcher, some glasses, a box of crackers, and a round of brie onto a serving tray, and led me out to the deck.

"That girlie drink again?" Leonard asked as soon as he saw the pitcher. He turned to Anthony. "This pink thing's just a sweet dressing over my favorite bourbon. Why don't we put some hair on our chest with the real deal?"

"Whatever the boss says," Anthony replied with a grin.

"Two bourbons coming right up." Heather leaned in toward me on her way back inside and whispered, "More for us."

I sat next to Anthony, feeling like an intruder on the men's conversation. Rather than sit in awkward silence, I blurted out, "It's beautiful out here."

"Sure is," Leonard replied. "You can credit the Almighty for the view, but Heather for the house."

"She designed it herself?"

"Hardly." Heather stepped back outside with the two bourbons. "I just touched it up a bit."

"If you could call a gut job a touch-up," Leonard said.

"Anyway," Heather continued, "I'm no designer. But the guy I brought in is fabulous."

"And fabulously expensive," Leonard added. "I had to fly him in from San Francisco."

"Don't listen to a word he says," Heather said to me. "He feels honor-bound to bemoan the cost, but the truth is there's nowhere in the world where he's happier, and he wouldn't have the house any other way. Am I right?"

"Happy wife, happy life," Leonard replied.

They both seemed as comfortable in this exchange as a worn-in shoe, and I suspected they were going through the motions of a debate they'd had dozens of times before. "Do you see yourselves moving out here year-round when you retire?" I asked.

"Retire? Who would want to retire from the greatest job in the world?" He winked at Anthony. "I'll be playing VC roulette till they carry me out feet first."

By the time the moon was overhead, Heather and I had finished the cocktail, and the men were on their fifth bourbons. Leonard and Anthony toyed around on the putting green at the edge of the property like drunken sailors.

"So how serious is this?" Heather nodded in Anthony's direction.

"I'm still trying to figure that out." I reclined on my chair with my feet up.

"Well, if you want to be with a guy who's going somewhere, you couldn't do better. I've only seen Leonard take a few guys under his wing like he has with Anthony, and all the others made partner."

A guy who was going somewhere. Was that what I wanted? "I have no doubt Anthony will be a financial success."

"So what doubts do you have? Is he not good in—"

Even with nothing but liquor and a handful of crackers in my belly, I was so not going there. "He's a good guy. He'd take good care of me. And our kids. I know he would."

"But something is holding you back."

Heather looked so elegant bathed in the moonlight on her deck in the mountains. She looked born for this life. Would she understand my hesitation at all? Part of me wanted to blow off her questions with pat answers. After all, I didn't know this woman, and anything I said was likely to reach her husband's ears and then Anthony's. On the other hand, who else could help me understand what it would mean to be married to a venture capitalist as she could? "I'm struggling with the lifestyle," I admitted.

"I'm not surprised. I used to struggle as well."

"Really?"

"Sure. I mean, I grew up comfortable, but nothing like this. When I was dancing, I lived four girls to a two-bedroom to get by. I used to think there was something romantic and enlightened about being poor."

"Not anymore?"

"Fortunately, two of my best friends got married before I did and quickly disavowed me of that belief."

"What happened to them?"

"One married a school teacher. They do OK, especially now that their kids are older, and she's back to work, but money is a constant stress for them."

"And the other?"

"Her marriage only lasted three years, but she managed to have two kids in that span. Her ex disappeared on her; I don't even think he's still in the country, so she gets nothing for child support. She's had to take on a part-time job in addition to her full-time job, and she still barely has enough to provide for herself and her kids. Don't tell Leonard, but I slip her a bit of money every month."

"So the romance over poverty…"

"Left in a hurry when confronted with reality," Heather said. "I realize now how immature a belief that was. Think about it, do you want your kids learning from an overwhelmed teacher in an underfunded school? Or do you want them learning from the best, with a small student to teacher ratio, in a school with top-notch facilities? I'm not one of those parents who buys BMWs when their kids turn 16, but I want them having the best teachers, coaches, and equipment."

The school comment hit home. As good as a teacher as I tried to be, there was only so much attention I could give each kid when I had to deal with 30 at a time. And little though I liked to admit it, the biggest trouble makers got the most attention. The best kids, the ones engaged and eager to learn, could advance far faster with a more present and less frazzled teacher.

"Don't you get lonely with Leonard working so much?"

"Look, growing up, my dad was home by 5:30 every night. We ate together as a family, and he and my mom watched TV together until bedtime. I get that vision. I do. But…"

"But what?"

"But you adapt. You build a life that works for you."

"You don't mind being alone so much?"

"Amber, I'm only alone when I choose to be. I know you're picturing it as lonely, but that's just because right now it's only you and Anthony, and when he's gone, it's just you. But it's not going to remain that way."

"Because you've got kids?"

"Kids are part of it. But no matter who you marry and what he does, recognize you'll still have your own life. You'll go to the gym, have lunch with friends, and pursue whatever passions you have. For me, I'm still dancing, and I love the theater. With time and money in abundance, you can design the life you want."

"Well, sure, when the kids are grown up like yours, I imagine you have plenty of time."

"I have more time now, no question, but with a guy like Anthony, you'll have time even when they're little. I told you about my two friends. Both used to complain about how exhausted they were. One friend used to complain incessantly about how early her kids woke up."

"Your kids slept in?"

"I have no idea. By the time I woke up, they were dressed and ready for school. We ate breakfast together without all that early morning stress."

"Does Leonard ever resent the fact that he works so hard while you have it so easy?"

"Are you kidding? I make sure that when he's here, he feels like a king in his palace. Not that men are so hard to satisfy. As long as I keep his bed warm and his belly full, he's thrilled."

"And you don't miss Leonard when he takes these long work trips?"

"Honestly…" Heather cupping her hand around her mouth as if telling a giant secret, but the men themselves were so drunk, loud, and far away, she would have had to scream to be overheard. "In some ways, I prefer it when he's gone."

"Really?"

"Sure. When he's here, I have to make sure Juanita has dinner ready on time. I've gotta watch football. I've gotta listen to all that VC chatter and pretend I care about the latest financial crisis in Kuala Lumpur." She rolled her eyes. "Plus, he misses me so much while he's gone..." Heather's eyebrows shot up. "I'm well rewarded when he returns."

I finally made it to my bedroom after midnight. Skiing posters covered the walls, and a bookcase overflowed with trophies. A package with a purple bow lay on the bed. Inside, I found a skimpy red nighty. Still dressed, I held it up against me and looked in the mirror. It was my size. Not that it covered much of me. You'd have to double the amount of material to properly blow your nose with it.

I hadn't laid down the law with Anthony quite as clearly as I had with Dylan, but I'd still avoided any real intimacy. That wasn't difficult, as Anthony was ever the gentleman. He'd never pushed to come in when dropping me off after our dates. But this was something different, this was a weekend away together. He told me how important it was to him that I meet his mentor. He told me how this trip, more than anything we'd done so far, would help me understand the type of life that he and I could build together. And so far, he was right. My conversation with Heather had left me plenty to think about. But I also knew in my gut that this trip was something more, that he'd come to think of it as a romantic getaway.

I should have been crystal clear that I was not yet ready for commitment, which meant that I was not yet ready for intimacy. I knew from experience that once sex comes in, my brain leaves the station. But I hadn't been clear. I hadn't stood my ground. I'd bitten my tongue so as not to push him away. I saw him getting rankled when I asked for my own room, but of course, he couldn't visibly protest in front of his mentor. Had his brains been stronger than his hormones, he would have caught on then that it was not the right moment for this gift. But gentleman though he was, at his core he was still a guy. He expected me to put this skimpy thing on, and then he expected to come in for a visit.

I immediately locked the door to my room. Then I changed into my sweatpants and t-shirt and slipped into bed. Sure enough, not ten minutes later, I heard a hand try the door. No knock, no nothing. He jostled the knob, found it locked, gave up, and walked away.

The next two days were jam-packed with activities. Saturday, we sailed on Leonard's 34-foot catamaran. On Sunday, Heather and I went for a hike while the men golfed, then we met them for lunch, followed by an outdoor concert. Anthony was pleasant and affable as always, but there was a coldness about him, a distance that hadn't been there before. I continued to lock my bedroom door at night, but it wasn't necessary. He didn't try the knob again, at least not that I heard.

It wasn't until Monday that we were alone. Or almost alone. Leonard and Heather had an earlier flight home than we did. So after long, gracious goodbyes, we found ourselves in the house with just Juanita, the housekeeper.

Anthony, who'd been so amiable in front of our hosts, grew sullen. We'd all had casual drinks earlier, but now Anthony served himself a double scotch. I didn't know what to do, so I left him on his own and went to pack. When I returned to the great room, I found him staring out the window, but the look on his face told me he wasn't taking in the view.

"All this isn't good enough for you, is it?" His eyes locked on mine. "The house. The yacht. All of it. Somehow it still isn't good enough for you?"

I didn't know whether to approach him or keep my distance, so I just stood awkwardly in between. "What are you talking about? I think it's all wonderful."

"Oh, I see." He drained his scotch. "Then it's me that isn't good enough?"

"Anthony, I think you're a great guy."

"Then why did you lock your door Friday night?"

My hands twisted around each other. "I told you early on, I don't want to get intimate until I know—."

"Until you know this is going somewhere. Yeah, I remember." The muscles in Anthony's jaw tensed. "Yet, somehow, even after six months, you're not sold."

"First of all, six months with you is only like a month with a normal guy since you're hardly ever around." My right hand squeezed around my left fingers. "Secondly, this is a choice I'm trying to make for life, so I'm damned well going to take my time."

"Still," Anthony stood to face me. "After everything I've done for you."

"Everything you've done for me?" The squeeze got tighter. "What's that supposed to mean?"

"I take you out to all the nicest places in town. I buy you gifts. I call you when I'm on trips. But what do you give me in return?" He refilled his glass. "Nothing. You don't give me any affection. You don't even cook for me."

"Anthony…"

"And that's another thing. I told you to the business world, I'm Anthony. But my real name, the name my family calls me, the name I want my wife to call me, is Tony." His Italian accent came out in full force as his voice grew agitated. "But you always call me Anthony, like you're telling me you never want to get too close."

"That's not why…"

"Heather appreciates all Leonard does for her. When he's here, she treats him like a king. I promise you, she's never locking the bedroom door." He stepped forward. A mixture of hurt and anger colored his expression. "But whatever I do for you is never enough."

"Enough for what?"

He stamped his foot. "For you to give anything in return."

"So that's what this weekend was about? So you could show me just how good the Anthony gravy train gets? So you could show me you're headed for big things? Because you think if your star gets bright enough, I'll want to come along for the ride?"

"Isn't that why you keep asking me all these questions? What retirement planning I've done? What my tax strategies are?"

"You think it's because I doubt you?" Now it was my turn to get loud. "I just want to understand what's going on."

"Why's that so damn important? You think my mother ever pried into my father's tax strategy? You think she ever second-guessed his retirement plans?" Scotch spilled from his glass. "She married a good guy who promised to take care of the family, and she left it in his hands. And she was *appreciative*."

"Yeah? You know what that sounds like?" I gritted my teeth to hold back hot tears.

"What?"

"It sounds exactly like my mother. But then at 58 years old, she gets a message that her husband is lying on the floor of the courtroom because his heart stopped after working himself to the bone for 35 years. And rather than just taking care of him and encouraging him to stay home, she has to help him get healthy as soon as possible so he can go back to work." My voice rose to a feisty pitch. "So he can keep killing himself. Because if he can't somehow crank out ten more years, neither of them can retire. At least not without taking a huge hit to their lifestyle, which they refuse to do because they've grown so used to pampering themselves, they can't imagine going without!"

"Pampering?" Anthony's hands flew up in exasperation. "So that's why you're so unimpressed by all this? You consider it pampering?"

"Unimpressed? How can you say that?"

"Because you don't feel even the slightest desire to give anything in return."

I'd also thought about how little I gave to Anthony. Why didn't I ever feel like cooking for him? Why did I hold back from intimacy? It's not like with Dylan, where I doubted his ability to provide for a family. So what was my hesitation? "You're right. You are. And I'm finally ready to make a real change."

Anthony looked up, with the first glimmer of hope in his eyes. "Yeah?"

"Yeah. I'm finally ready to call you Tony."

"Great." Anthony rolled his eyes. "Way to make my day."

"You know why I called you Anthony until now?"

"Why?"

"Because I'd never actually met *Tony*." My hands dug into my hips. "But here he is, out in the open at last."

"What the hell's that supposed to mean?"

"It means Anthony is all spit and polish. It's the face you put out to the world. And as much as you wanted me to call you Tony, so far, you've only shown me Anthony."

"And now?"

I studied him like a model on a runway. "Now I'm starting to see beneath your shiny exterior. The Italian accent is finally coming out in your voice. You know what the difference is between you and Vinny?"

"What?"

"He doesn't try to impress anyone. He says whatever he wants because he doesn't give a damn what anyone thinks. But you, you're so busy kissing ass that the real you never comes out."

"That's not fair, Amber."

"Isn't it? If you were so pissed about me locking my door Friday night, why did it take you two days to say anything?"

"I didn't want to make a scene. I figured I'd wait till we were alone."

"We're not alone." I pointed towards the kitchen. "You don't think Juanita hears every word of this?"

"That's not what I mean."

"It's exactly what you mean. She doesn't count because she's the help. But before a partner, you have to put on the perfect face. You want to know why I haven't gone all gaga over you?" Only as I was shouting the words did I realize how true they were. "Because I've never met the real you. Until now. And let me tell you, Tony is hardly making a strong impression."

"So that's it? You're ready to kick me to the curb?"

"I'm not the one who raised this big stink. I'm just trying to take my time. To figure out what I want. And the more I understand what you want, the more I question whether it's for me."

Anthony puffed out his chest. "What do you think I want?"

"Some pampered Queen who dotes on her King. Some Italian version of Heather, who will dutifully await your return from Singapore with a bowl of hot fettuccine and a roll in the hay."

Anthony grinned. "Sounds pretty good, actually."

"I'm sure it does. To you."

"Would such a life be so bad? We'd have family, kids. We'd live well. We'd have help. We'd have a gorgeous home. Amazing vacations. Why do you spit on all this? Isn't financial stability worth something?"

"Of course. But to me, financial stability doesn't just come from earning more so you can spend more. That's why I kept asking you about retirement and taxes." Only then did I realize how much Dylan's perspective had made its mark on me. "I'd rather have less but build a more solid foundation."

"All this is solid." Anthony knocked against a wooden beam. "Do you have any idea how many businesses Leonard owns a part of? How much property he owns? He's ten years younger than your dad, but if he had a heart attack tomorrow, his family would be set for life."

"Anthony, you keep trying to show me how high you can climb up the corporate ladder, as if I doubt how far you can go." I could see where we were headed, and it knocked the fight out of me. "Maybe the problem is, I'm just looking for a different ladder."

"What does that mean?"

I approached him, trying to soften the blow. "I mean, I want a guy who can provide, but I don't think a guy who can provide ten times as much is ten times the man. I'd rather have one house with a guy who will be home each day and play with his kids, than two houses and a guy who's gone all the time."

"So that's it then? I'm not what you want?"

"I don't know. I'm still trying to get my head around it." I took his hand. "I think one reason I haven't offered to cook for you was that I was afraid of what happened Friday night, that if I had you over for dinner, you'd get all kinds of thoughts about dessert."

He stared at my hand, and his head hung low. "I probably would have."

CHAPTER 17

UP IN FLAMES

I stepped out of the terminal in the Ecuadorian backwater and hailed a cab. It took me two flights to arrive, a direct one to Quito, the capital, then a puddle jumper here, to the middle of nowhere. The cabbie told me it would be an hour trip to Vilcabamba.

I settled in the back and pulled out my phone. One new message caught my eye. It was from the dealership where I'd leased my car. They'd taken a picture of me standing in front of my red coupe on the day I signed. Now they sent me a note congratulating me on my second anniversary, no doubt hoping I'd think fondly of them the following year when my lease was up. How ironic.

After our trip to Tahoe, Anthony had another two-week business trip, this time to Sweden. He didn't call me once while he was gone, which I could have easily brushed aside as being due to the time difference. But I knew better. Our big fight was forcing him to rethink things. Everything was percolating in my mind, too. So many emotions were bouncing around in my gut that I lost my appetite, which was saying a lot—food was usually my comfort go-to.

On the one hand, Anthony was the perfect guy: handsome, successful, Italian. He was a gentleman in a world were those were hard to find. A voice in my head told me I was nuts to let him go. He wasn't one of those guys afraid of commitment. Just the opposite, he dated me because I so perfectly fit his picture of a future wife. He'd buy me a palace and treat me like a queen.

Yet, for all its glamour, the life we saw in Tahoe lacked the coziness I craved. I wanted the intimacy of a family that spends tons of time together and works like a team.

Anthony's sheen fizzled in my eyes with each passing day, so there were no butterflies when his name showed up on my phone. He'd just gotten back, he said, and invited me out to dinner. No show. No concert. No after-hours party. No asking me to cook him dinner. We met at the Olive Garden, an insult to any Italian worth his shirt.

The conversation was as pasty as the food. We parted on polite terms. Not angry, not passionate, not distraught. Polite. That pretty much summed up everything. I felt sorry for Anthony. There was a time I'd dreamed of exactly what he had to offer, but things had changed. I couldn't be the wifey of some high flyer. Not anymore.

A year and a half later, I was still alone. A series of bad blind dates and short-lived relationships made it abundantly clear that whatever I was doing wasn't working. That's what brought me to Ecuador. I needed to get away, to come to a place where I could get full clarity on what I wanted and how to get it.

My body had begun to defrost as soon as I'd gotten off the plane. The cabbie took me to the vacation rental I had my cousin rent for me under her name. The owner stood outside, waiting for us, looking both tanned and relaxed. He came down a brick path and walked directly to the trunk to get my suitcase. By the time he slammed the trunk shut, I was already standing at his elbow.

"Hello, Dylan."

"Amber!" For a moment, he looked at me like I was an alien who'd dropped from the sky. "What are you doing here?"

My heart was fluttering so fast it made everything shake inside. "I came to recover something I'd lost." I searched his face for a sign. Was he happy to see me?

But Dylan was speechless. Never one to force out words when none would come, he took my bags and carried them in. The house had a sizable kitchen, a single bedroom with a full bed covered in a tent of mosquito netting, a comfy couch, and stunning views all around. Still, it had that unlived-in, vacation rental feel—not at all like a home.

A bottle of white wine with two wine glasses stood on the table, a welcome gift from the owner to the renter. Since I *was* a paying renter, I took the bottle and opened it. "Care for a drink?" I filled two glasses, then carried them out onto the deck, where we had an amazing view of the sunset over the valley.

He accepted a glass from my hand, but his expression was still blank with shock. "What are you doing here?"

We sat facing a forest canopy, filled with trills of tropical birds at sunset. I gripped my wine glass and gulped the rest of it down. "I came to beg for another chance."

"Amber, look—."

My chest clenched. "You don't have to give me an answer right away. I rented this place for two weeks." I looked down and licked my lips. "But I do at least hope you'll show me around. If you're not too busy."

"Busy? Not down here, no."

"Excellent." I feigned a yawn. I didn't want to have this talk with Dylan right now. I wanted him to stew over it first. "I'm exhausted from my trip. I think I'll head to sleep early, but I'm dying to get into these mountains. How about you take me hiking tomorrow?"

"Hiking?" Dylan's eyes darted around, uncertain. Was he nervous about reopening his world, his heart, to me? "Sure. What time?"

I knew his favorite time of day. "When does the sun rise?"

"Just before 6 am, but it starts getting light around 5."

That was awfully early, but I wasn't going to flinch. "5 am it is. I'll be waiting."

By 5:30 the next morning, we were on the trail, hiking to a place called Yamballa. Dylan taught me about the plants and birds that surrounded us. I hadn't brought up our relationship again, nor did he, but I could see he was enjoying himself.

I stretched my arms up over my head. "So how is it that you're able to come out hiking on a moment's notice?" We'd stopped to snack on green mango with lime and salt that Dylan had prepared. "Shouldn't you be off working two jobs? Or is your decade of deprivation already at an end?"

"I decided to end it early when I moved down here a year ago. Of course, that was partially your fault."

His words stung. "I'm so sorry I hurt you, Dylan."

Dylan laughed. "I'm not talking about you breaking up with me."

Oh. "Then, what was it?"

"Two things. One, you made me realize I was already financially independent. I'd been so focused on hitting an extreme goal, that I hadn't stopped to see just how far I'd come. I wasn't yet making enough to support a family, but I'd already been living on less than my passive income."

"And the other thing?"

"You encouraged me to leave my job and BRRRR instead." Dylan bit into a piece of mango and puckered from the sour taste of the lime. "I was hesitant to do it, but when I agreed to take that house from you, I had no choice. I would have lost more money letting it sit empty than I'd been making from my job."

"You quit to work on The Death Trap on Haber?"

"You should see it now—it's no longer a death trap. When I finished it, I was able to refinance it and get more than my investment back. Then I took that money and repeated the process."

"You must be doing great on the Haber house." I guess I could no longer use my old nickname.

"I am. Real estate has gone crazy these past two years. You ever regret giving it up?"

I swallowed and looked him straight in the eyes. "Yeah, but I regretted giving up the guy more." An awkward silence filled the air. The tension was broken when a fly landed on my nose, and I had to swat it away. "But you didn't answer my question. What are you doing down here?"

"I'm living the life. I was financially independent in America as long as I kept my lifestyle meager, but after we broke up, living in The Crypt lost its appeal, and I didn't yet have the means to quit and live well in the States. But it's a different story here. We're right now in the Valley of Longevity, where people live longer than almost anywhere in the world." He stretched his arms out over the valley. "It's gorgeous, it's spring all year round, and it's dirt cheap compared to the US."

"So you decided to move here and live off the revenue from your Cash Machine."

"That was my intention, but it hasn't worked out that way."

I shouldn't rejoice at his difficulties, but part of me was glad he was still struggling. "So reality finally caught up with you? Living on your passive income hasn't turned out as easy as you thought?"

Dylan shook his head. "No, it's the other way around. I intended to live on the passive income from my Cash Machine, but I haven't had to tap into it." He had an ease and confidence I hadn't seen back home, where he seemed like a square bum in a world created for round corporate pegs. "I've never exactly been lazy; I just didn't want the pressure of having to work."

"What have you done?"

"For money? A variety of things." He pointed down the mountain with the mango in his hand. "That house you're staying in is one of two vacation rentals I own. There are quite a few tourists around here, and periodically I'll work as a guide for a day or two. I've also been coaching people remotely on how to build Cash Machines of their own."

"And what do you do not for money?"

"There's a village close by building a small school."

"Putting your construction background to good use?"

"You could say that. I'm not doing any hardcore construction, but I volunteer my time here and there to help them out."

"Sounds like a pretty good life."

"Pretty good." Dylan started us hiking again, covering the last stretch to a lookout just before sunrise. "But, I'll admit something was missing." Dylan took my hand.

"Does this mean you're giving me a second chance?"

He faced me with a glint in his eye. "Yes, Amber. You've got your chance."

I grabbed him, pulled him in tight, and kissed him just as the golden glow of the sun flooded the morning sky.

We stayed at that lookout for over an hour, then started our return through the valley, hand in hand.

Dylan shot me a look. "What will your family think about you getting back together with your bum of an ex-boyfriend?"

"I'm not one bit concerned about them."

"No?"

"Remember how in college you frat boys used to joke that a girl who started the night a '6' would be a '10' after four drinks?"

"Not our finest hour."

"Yeah, well, that's sort of how my family works. When I was 22, they thought their precious daughter deserved someone with more than just an undergrad degree. By the time I was 25, undergrad was fine, but a college dropout, no way."

"And now?"

"Now I've got another two years and another failed relationship under my belt. They're getting ready to accept any guy with a job."

Dylan helped me over a log that cut across the muddy trail. "You do realize that I'm unemployed and living in South America?"

"The problem with you, Dylan, is that you never learned spin. You are not some unemployed hippy backpacking through the Andes." I put on my best British broadcaster voice. "You're a real estate magnate who owns homes on two continents and lives off the fruits of his success."

Dylan let go of my hand. "You're back to me wanting to spin the facts to impress your family?"

"I'm just telling you the facts as I see them. But you tell my family whatever you like." I stepped on a boulder to be as tall as Dylan, grabbed his shirt, and pulled him close. "I have no intention of asking their opinion this time around."

When we got back, Dylan took me out to lunch at a place with a stunning 360-degree view of the valley. It felt so strange, sitting with him in a restaurant. When the waiter came, Dylan ordered in perfect Spanish. I had no idea what he was saying, but it sounded delightful coming off his lips.

Five minutes later, the waiter returned and laid three small plates before us. "You ordered appetizers?"

"I figured you'd be hungry after the early morning hike." Dylan cut himself a piece of plantain. "I sure am."

I was ravenous actually, and it wasn't long before we'd emptied all three plates. Fortunately, just as I finished the last empanada, the waiter returned.

"Is that steak?" I asked in a tone that was embarrassingly loud and accusatory.

"I'm sorry. Did you want something else?"

"What happened to not eating out? What happened to living simply?"

"Amber, this entire meal is the cost of a burrito at Chipotle."

I felt almost betrayed. What happened to the Dylan I knew? "But—." It felt like my mind had turned to glue. "What about your Cash Machine?"

"Building a Cash Machine is like rolling a boulder down a hill. It takes tremendous effort to get it going, but once you get it rolling on its own, it will keep building momentum without you." He cut off a piece of steak. "Now I get to reap the rewards."

After lunch, we went back to Dylan's house. His place was no larger than my rental, but it had the coziness of a home. "This is what I need," I said, "a fully stocked kitchen." Copper pans hung from a rack over the island, and the drawers were full of chef knives, ladles, and everything else I'd need.

"I'm afraid you'll find the selection of Italian cheeses at the local market rather limited."

"I didn't come down to Ecuador to cook Italian. I want to eat like the locals." I tugged at his shirt. "Let's go to the market. I want at least one of everything."

"Let's do it." Dylan grabbed his keys and headed for the door, but I hesitated. "There's one thing we should do before we go."

"What's that?"

"It's winter break, so vacation rentals are probably in high demand now, right?"

"Yeah. So?"

"So you should relist the place I rented. I won't be needing it."

I learned a few things that night:

One: I like sweet plantains far better than the green, savory ones. Take a sweet one, top it with shredded coconut and local cinnamon, bake it for a half-hour and prepare for a bit of heaven to melt right on your tongue.

Two: That crap they sell in South America that looks like angel hair is anything but. Avoid it at all costs.

Three: Ecuadorian hot chocolate tastes a hundred times better than the Swiss Miss I grew up drinking.

Four: I caused two people needless suffering when I refused to allow Dylan to touch me our second time around.

Dylan's strong hands never rushed as they massaged away two years' worth of stored up tension. I don't remember falling asleep that night, but I will never forget waking up the next morning in his arms, roused from my dreams by the cacophony of birdsong that fills the valley at sunrise.

I'd been so eager to hit the mountains that first day, but today, I felt no desire to go anywhere.

A week into my stay, Dylan and I headed to a local craft market. "What are these dolls I'm seeing everywhere?" I pointed to a paper mâché man tied to the front fender of a car. "I didn't notice them when I first got here."

"They're effigies."

"You're not serious. Actual effigies? Like voodoo doll type things?" We walked past a bench with life-sized representations of old men sitting arm in arm.

"Oh yes. See that one?" Dylan pointed to a paper mâché doll stuffed with T-shirts and painted with salt and pepper hair, red lips, and brown eyes. He wore a dress shirt and slacks that must have come out of someone's closet. "You'll see a lot of him. He's the president of Ecuador."

"Wow, people must hate the guy."

"Actually, it's considered an honor to be burned in effigy on New Year's Eve. People aren't saying they want him to die, just to burn off the bad decisions and sins of the previous year, and start the new year fresh. You'll even see tons of people making effigies of family members."

We came up to a store with hundreds of masks on display. "Not that one." I pointed one out. "Batman was an orphan, remember?"

"Yeah, you'll see a bunch of superheroes and cartoons too. It's all part of the fun."

"And then they do what? Burn them at New Year's?"

"Yep. At midnight, you'll see bonfires all over the city." Dylan put on a mask of Donald Duck. "Want to get one?"

I bent over laughing. It felt good to be playful with Dylan. Last time around, we'd spent too much time talking about Cash Machines. "You should make yourself an Amber doll."

"That's OK. I have no desire to burn you."

"You won't be burning me, remember?" I tapped him on the chest. "You'll just be burning away my poor decisions that kept us apart all this time. What do you say? I'll make one of you too. It'll be fun."

"You have a problem with my decisions?"

"Absolutely."

Dylan took off the mask. "Like what?"

I grabbed his cheeks and shook him. "Like letting me go."

Dylan turned away and put down the mask. "Amber, you dumped me."

"Yes." I pointed at him the way Grandma Maria used to do when she got all bossy with Grandpa Lou. "And you're going to burn up that horrible decision of mine. But just because I dumped you didn't mean you had to give up on me."

"I couldn't force a relationship on you, Amber."

"Would it have killed you to fight for me a little? Couldn't you see that I was hysterical and acting irrationally? Didn't you notice what I wore the day I came to the house to bring you the paperwork?"

"My favorite blue dress." At least he wasn't totally clueless.

"Exactly." I reached for his arm, but it stayed stiff, unmoving. "Couldn't you see that I wanted you to take me back?"

Dylan's eyebrows shot up. "I'm supposed to gather that from what you wear?"

"What do you want me to do, hold up a sign?"

"It would be nice. There's nothing wrong with communicating your feelings."

"And there's nothing wrong with fighting for what you want." I headed towards the edge of the store, to a display of art supplies. "I'm going to buy myself some paper mâché and burn away that wussiness of yours. We're going to start this year on a whole new foot."

Dylan's paper mâché skills blew away my own. I built a doll that was somewhere between Dylan and He-Man. But his Amber doll looked eerily similar to me (would it have killed him to make the butt trimmer than reality?). So what did we do with these dolls? We acted like the Ecuadorians, strapped them to the roof of Dylan's Jeep, and drove them around wherever we went.

On December 31, a day hardly anyone was working, we hit our first traffic driving through our small Ecuadorian town. I leaned out the window and couldn't believe my eyes. "Tell me those aren't prostitutes soliciting the drivers ahead."

"They're not prostitutes soliciting the drivers ahead." Dylan held a straight face, but his chest shook just enough to make it clear he knew something I didn't.

"What are they?"

"They're widows."

"Widows? They don't look like widows to me. Those skirts look way too pink and way too short to—." My mouth fell open. "Has that one got a beard?"

We inched forward, and suddenly five figures surrounded the jeep. Men wearing miniskirts, tight sweaters, and bras stuffed with socks danced, gyrated, and grabbed themselves in wholly inappropriate places. I couldn't help but giggle. "Why are they doing this?"

"They're the widows of the effigies we're going to burn tonight. They dance at the street corners for donations." Dylan took out a bunch of coins and passed them out to the widows, one of whom was rubbing up against our hood.

"You've moved to a bizarre place."

Giant bonfires sprouted up all over town as we counted down the final hours to midnight. Live music was everywhere, and Dylan and I walked through town, carrying our effigies, and taking in the air of celebration. Dylan bought me a pod the length of my arm. "What the hell are these?" I asked.

"Ice cream beans."

"Ice cream beans? You're joking, right?"

"Go on, try them." Dylan took the pod, which looked like a vanilla bean only a thousand times larger, and twisted it open. I pulled out the white, fuzzy fruits from within. I sucked off the fuzzy fruit layer, which looked and felt like caterpillar slime—sweet, delicious caterpillar slime, mind you—then spit the giant seeds into the gutter.

When midnight hit, Dylan threw his effigy into a bonfire. Much as I didn't like the fat butt, I was bummed to see Dylan's beautiful Amber doll go. I prayed it would burn all my sins and poor decisions away and give Dylan and me a brand new start. I kissed my He-Man Dylan doll on the cheek (for even when Dylan made poor decisions, there was never anything malicious in him) and threw it into the fire. A few seconds later, its features distorted, then burned up. That was the old Dylan, the cheap Dylan, the one who resigned himself to a life of deprivation. Let him go with the old Amber, the one who wanted to impress her family with her choices rather than listen to the calls of her heart. That Amber was no more. It was a new year, a new start, and a new me.

Dylan drove me back to Quito for my flight home. We arrived in the exhaust-filled bustle of the capital on the morning of my last day. Dylan insisted there was a mountain we had to climb.

"Normally, when I think of mountain climbing, I expect to use my legs," I said as we rode the teleferico, a cable car up the side of the mountain.

"Don't worry, this only gets us to 13,000 feet. We still have plenty of climbing to do when we get off. We won't hit the peak of Ruku Pichincha until well past 15,000."

From the top of the cable car, we could see Quito laid out before us, an expanse that seemed to go on forever. Dylan pointed out the snow-capped cone of the Cotopaxi volcano in the distance. I wrapped my arms around him. "This country is breathtaking."

Dylan grabbed my hand, and we hiked several miles of gradually rising trail. Just below the summit, the trail grew too steep to walk, and we had no choice but to climb our way through the mass of cliffs and boulders leading up to the peak. Dylan kept pausing to pull me up the harder stretches, his strong arms easily taking my weight.

I jumped up and down when I reached the top, pumping my arms. Dylan just sat on a boulder and pulled a thermos from his backpack. "I brought us a little treat."

"Ooh, is that a final dose of hot chocolate? You do know the way to my heart, don't you?" I kissed his cheek, then sat beside him. "These have been the best two weeks of my life."

"I'm so glad you came down here to chase after me. May these two weeks be only the beginning."

Something in his words caught me. "A new beginning for our relationship, you mean?"

"Our relationship, our amazing life down here, our—."

"Dylan, you do realize that I fly back home tonight?"

"Well, sure. Temporarily. You came down here to rekindle things between us." He removed the hair that had blown across my face and ran it behind my ear. "I assume you weren't just looking for some two-week fling?"

"Of course not. But this isn't our home." I met his hand and wove my fingers between his. "I came down here to bring you back."

"Ecuador is my home now, Amber."

"After all we've had these past two weeks, you're not going to come back with me?"

"After all we've had these past two weeks, you're going to leave?"

We sat in silence, the air between us filled with tension, with confusion, with all the feelings I'd hoped we'd burned away at New Year's. How could I get him to understand our logical next step?

"Dylan, come on." I tried to smooth things over by rubbing his hands between my own, ignoring how tight they'd become. "You know we can't just...live here."

"Of course we can. We're fully financially independent down here. We can stay for the rest of our lives and have everything we need."

"But, Dylan...this isn't my life."

He gripped my knee. "It can be."

I searched his face. The man of my dreams was slipping away. Again. "You're really not going to come back with me?"

"You're really going to leave?"

He'd been too grounded in numbers before, and now he was up in the clouds. "Dylan, come on. I've got a job."

"Amber, I'm retired." He rubbed my shoulder, working away at the tension forming there. "You can be as well."

"I'm 28 years old. What the hell would I do in retirement?"

"I thought we'd build a family together. You always said you wanted the option to not work when you had kids. Is this so different?"

I turned towards the horizon. "It sounds like a dream, Dylan. But it's time for me to return to reality."

"If you can live it, it's not a dream." Dylan's fingers touched my cheek ever so gently, and goosebumps ran down my neck. "We can live this, Amber. Who says reality needs to be drudgery? There's nothing more real than dollars and cents. I've studied the numbers. We can make this work. Forever."

"Can't you also make it work back home?" I faced him again, my voice growing into a pleading tone I knew was beneath me. "You said you're not even drawing off of your Cash Machine down here because you've got other income coming in. With that other income and your revenue from your Cash Machine, won't that be enough back home too?"

"What income? Guiding tourists into the mountains of Ecuador? Kind of hard to take that with me. And the vacation rentals? The numbers on those only make sense if I'm here to run them."

"But you said you were coaching people in building Cash Machines."

Dylan waved that away. "I do that a couple of hours a week. That money goes a long way in Ecuador, but hardly amounts to anything back home."

"Couldn't you ramp it up?" I squeezed Dylan's hand to a deep shade of purple.

"Maybe, but I'm not looking for a career. It's fun having a couple clients, but to be bound to a business to support myself? No, thank you."

"But you lived so frugally in the States." Was I whining? "You were financially independent before."

"As long as I lived on the cheap, yes. But what am I supposed to do? Go back to not eating out? To not having a car?"

"Why not? You did it before."

"It's not so easy to go back. That's why I started this journey so young, before I got used to having luxuries in my life. I'm now at a point where I don't have to deprive myself. Why should I go back to living like a pauper?"

I popped up. I had a perfect solution. "What if you came back and lived with me? Your cost of living wouldn't be that high."

"What would I do with myself all day? I'm hardly ever bored here. I hike, I raft, I interact with a constant stream of new visitors, and I volunteer building a school. Back in the States, I wouldn't know what to do with myself if I wasn't working. And I'm not going to live like some leech, letting my girlfriend support me."

"Can't you do more of that BRRRR thing?"

Dylan shook his head. "It's getting harder and harder."

"Why, because the real estate market's been doing so well?"

"Exactly. The cost of houses in our area has almost doubled since I bought that quadruplex. Meanwhile, rental prices have increased less than 5%. Cash flowing properties are harder to come by."

How did we get back to talking about money and real estate? "What if you just came for a few months until we figured things out?"

"I'll make you a deal. I can see you not wanting to quit in the middle of the school year. I'll agree to come back with you until school gets out if you agree to quit at the end of the year."

"And you expect that I'd move down here?"

"Why not? It's a fabulous place to live. Though if you don't like it, there are dozens of other countries we could choose from where we'd still be financially independent."

"I don't know, Dylan." An image of my father in his hospital bed popped into my mind. "I don't want to leave my family."

"Amber, you hardly ever see your family. We could return to the US a couple of times a year. You might have more time with them if we come for a few weeks each visit."

"I know, but there's something about having them close by." I shrugged. "When my father had a heart attack, I was able to be there on a few hours' notice. I couldn't do that from Ecuador."

"So you never want to be far from home, just in case someone needs you? I thought you were done letting your family decide your path?"

My body curled into itself. "Can we just not talk about it anymore?"

"Then what are we going to do?"

I swallowed back tears. "We're going to spend one last, fabulous afternoon together. Then tonight, you'll drive me to the airport."

"And then?"

"We'll have to let the future figure itself out."

Needless to say, the afternoon was not fabulous. We climbed down Ruku Pichincha in silence, and when we boarded the cramped cable car, Dylan stared through its glass bottom the entire descent.

CHAPTER 18

ONE WIMP

On my flight back home, I cried through an entire bag of tissues. My time in Vilcabamba had been a dream, but I wasn't up for the long-distance thing, not at my age, not with a guy who didn't know if he'd ever return to the States. Part of me wanted to say the hell with it, pack my bags, and follow Dylan. Why not have a bit of adventure? But I couldn't just drop everything and move to Ecuador—I wasn't that kind of girl.

For two weeks, I chewed my nails down to the painful pink. What if I'd made the wrong decision? What if I'd lost him, yet again, because I was too scared to step out of my comfort zone? What if I never saw him again? I didn't sleep much. I even let my students run around like chimps at the zoo and resorted to the time-honored teachers' shortcut for classroom control—showing them movies.

Seventeen days after my return from Ecuador, my phone rang.

"You told me to call you if I was ever in the States," Dylan said.

I'd been driving home from work and immediately pulled over. "You're here?"

"I am." I could feel the smile in his voice, almost feel his breath against my cheek.

"You didn't come back for *me*, did you?" I asked as innocently as I could.

"No, but I came back because of you."

His response fell short of the *yes* I'd been hoping for. "Isn't that kind of the same thing?"

"No. During your visit, I realized I'd been away for too long. I'm not keeping my finger on the pulse of the market. I've got an itch in the back of my mind telling me I should sell one or more of my properties while the real estate market's high. I booked meetings with Phil and a few other guys to figure out my next steps."

How could someone who was so damned strategic be so clueless about what to say to a woman? "Couldn't you have done all that over the phone?"

"I could. But you get a feel for a place when you're in it. Besides, I've never actually sold before. There will be all kinds of tax questions I'll need to answer. I need to network to find the right advisor."

Why must he sound so dry and calculating? Underneath all that logic, was he as heartbroken as I was? It's not like I was waxing poetic, either. The least I could do was help Dylan, even if only as a friend. "I think I have just the right guy for you."

"Let me see if I get your gist." Other than breaking in to order dinner, Vinny had sat silently listening to Dylan's story for an entire fifteen minutes, probably a personal record. "Your property values have gone through the roof, but since rental values are as stuck as a constipated mule, you're getting a piss poor return on your money. Is that right?"

I giggled, but Dylan kept a straight face. "Yes."

Vinny's wine arrived, and he swished it around his glass as he spoke. "You could use your equity to buy more properties, but at current purchase prices, they wouldn't cash flow, so they'd be sinkholes."

"Right."

Vinny sipped his wine and nodded in approval. "You could stay the course since your passive income's only gone up, but you want your money moving at a sprint, not a limp."

"Right, and because I accelerated the depreciation on my properties, I've used up much of my tax benefits. That was fine as long as I was adding properties, but pretty soon, I'm going to get hit with taxes."

Vinny's eyebrows went up. If there was anything he was sensitive about, it was taxes. "What are you thinking?"

Dylan fidgeted with his napkin. "Well, I could sell some properties…"

"But your portfolio has gone through the roof, so if you're not stuffing your cash into new properties, you'll get walloped on capital gains. To boot, you'll be stuck with a giant hunk of cash you don't know what to do with." Vinny leaned back in his chair and shook his head. "Sitting cash is just a recipe for trouble."

"How come?" I asked.

"Cause it's hanging around the corner like a red-light whore, and as easy to pick up and spend."

Dylan blushed. He ignored Vinny's comments and continued with his concerns. "If I had a decent enough place to invest, I could just refinance and get the appreciation of the properties in hand…"

Vinny tapped the table. "And you wouldn't owe any taxes on them since you don't pay tax on borrowed money. The problem is that you'll start owing interest on that cash, and right now, interest rates are higher than your rates of return, so what's the point? Plus, if the market does go down, you'll be in danger of having your properties underwater and taken by the bank."

"Right." Dylan nodded at me. The fact that Vinny picked up everything so fast showed him my recommendation was spot on.

Vinny took another sip of wine. "So, what can I do for you?"

"Am I right to be nervous about the real estate market?"

"Absolutely. Growth has been nuts. You see it in every boom; banks give away money without a care. Why bother doing credit checks when everyone's rakin' it in? So what happens? Simple supply and demand. The pool of buyers gets bigger, so the prices go through the roof. Eventually, prices get too high for deadbeats to make mortgage payments. Banks get more cautious. Now they're rejecting even guys with decent jobs. The pool of buyers gets smaller. Plus, everyone was building like crazy during the boom, so there's more housing stock to go around amongst fewer buyers. Prices crash."

I broke into the conversation. "That's what you think is going to happen?"

"Guaranteed it's going to happen. The question is, when? Timing these things is always the trick."

A hot loaf of bread arrived on a cutting board. I cut each of us a slice, then topped mine with herb butter. The crust was flakey, the inside warm and chewy, and the butter melted over all of it. "When do you think the downturn's going to happen?"

"It's already beginning. Interest rates are creeping up, which is an early warning sign. My bankers are telling me they're rejecting more and more applicants."

"Are you selling?" Dylan asked.

"Me? No way. I rarely sell."

"Why not?" I asked.

"I make my money when I buy. That's the beauty of the buy and hold strategy. Cash flowing properties make money in good economies and bad. As long as rental prices stay up, I don't worry about the sticker price. Not to mention that I'd get taxed to hell and back, both on my profits and on repaying all the depreciation I've deducted over the years."

I swallowed my bread. "I thought you avoid taxes if you reinvest the profits?"

"You can with a 1031 exchange. But to do that, I have to find another, more expensive property to put my money in. But that property is likely going to be just as inflated, and there's a huge transactional cost to buying and selling."

"The problem is," Dylan said, "I depend on the equity in my properties to make future investments. If prices go down, I'll lose my equity and my leverage along with it."

"You're skittish about losing money. I hear that. Just remember, markets bounce back."

"So you think I should just hang on to what I have?" Dylan asked.

I expected Vinny to give a quick 'yes,' but he didn't. "Tell me more about your properties. Do you have any that you've lived in for two out of the last five years?"

"Yeah, the last quadruplex I lived in."

"If you insist on selling something, that's the one."

Dylan nodded, but I was confused. "Why does that matters?"

"Up to $250,000 profit on that place is tax-free."

"$250,000?"

"And that's only because he's single. Had he been married, he could have taken up to $500,000."

I felt an immediate stab of guilt. Had I stood by his side a couple of years ago rather than freaking out and dumping him, we could have taken advantage of the full tax savings. But of course, he wasn't the only one who could use that tax law to his benefit. "I've owned my duplex for over two years. Should I sell too?"

"Look, Dylan's got a bunch of properties, and he's paranoid that the market is going to crash. If he's looking to hedge his bets, it makes sense to sell the one that's tax-protected. You're in a different situation. All you've got is the duplex, and it's also your home."

I knew how much having a home meant to Vinny, especially after losing his as a kid. "But if the market's going down…"

"That's a big if." Vinny cut himself another slice. "Dylan thinks it will. I'm inclined to agree. But no one ever knows these things for sure."

Dylan jumped back in. "My quadruplex has gone up a hell of a lot more than $250,000."

"Count yourself lucky."

"What do I do with all the money?"

Vinny pretended to rub his eyes. "It's quite the sob story: too much money and no clue what to do with it."

"I know, I'm hardly deserving of pity."

Vinny waved that away. "I've never bought that crap that big money problems are less important than small money ones. The fact is, those with money contribute a hell of a lot more to the world than those without, so there's no reason they shouldn't stress over it."

Dylan ripped little pieces of bread, making crumbs land on his plate like confetti. "So what do I do?"

"First off, your timing's good."

"How's that?"

"It's January. You've got over a year to figure out what to do with your profits before you'll pay any taxes."

"I hear that."

"Next, the fact that you're in Ecuador opens up some opportunity. Do you make any active income in the US?"

"A bit. I've been coaching people online."

"And you pay US income tax on that?"

"I'll have to start soon. So far, depreciation has knocked out my active income, but when my depreciation plummets, I'll lose that ability."

"I thought depreciation only applies against passive income?" I asked.

"If your active income is low enough, and mine is *super* low," Dylan pointed at the ground, "then deprecation can even offset active income."

Vinny picked up his questioning. "How long are you planning on living in Ecuador?"

Dylan shot me a look. "I'm not sure. Why is that important?"

"The foreign earned income exclusion."

"What's that?" I asked.

"In most countries, when you stop living there, you stop paying their taxes. But Uncle Sam demands his protection money regardless of where you live. But remember what I told you about our lovely tax code?"

He'd told me dozens of things about our tax code, but I had a hunch where he was going with this. "If you use it right, it's a roadmap for how to make money and keep it."

"Bingo. In this case, if you live out of the country and *earn your income* out of the country, you get to exclude over $100,000 a year of that foreign income from US taxes." Our garden salads arrived, and Vinny dug right in.

"But even if Dylan can somehow transfer his income to Ecuador," I asked, "won't he just pay taxes there instead?"

"Very good, Amber. Which is why Dylan will do best if he can earn his money outside of the US *and* Ecuador. I take it Ecuador won't tax your worldwide earnings, will they, Dylan?"

"No. Just what I earn in Ecuador, and even there the first $9000 or so is tax-free. But if I'm working with US clients, the foreign earned income exclusion won't help, will it?"

"Like anything else, it depends on how you structure it." Vinny jabbed at a tomato and popped it into his mouth. "I've got a buddy who can set you up with a corporation out of Belize."

"How will that help?" I asked.

"Easy peasy. The client pays the corporation for the coaching, the corporation pays Dylan a salary for doing the coaching. Bingo, Dylan's income comes from Belize, which last I checked wasn't in either the US or Ecuador. Bye, bye taxes."

My eyes narrowed. Vinny told me everything he did was above board, but this sounded shady. "So the client has to send the money off to Belize? Won't that make some of them suspicious?"

"Absolutely not. The Belize corporation sets up an LLC here in the States."

"What's that?"

"A Limited Liability Company. Basically, a US company."

I crossed my arms. "So you're going to create an offshore company, then have it own a US company?"

"Exactly. That way, the LLC banks in the US no problem, and clients pay the US company. Any work Dylan does will be as an employee of the Belize company. He'll draw his money from there."

"And this only works if he lives outside the US?"

"Exactly. He needs to be out of the country for at least eleven months a year."

I jabbed at my salad. "I'm not a big fan of this plan."

"Look, it's not the only way to go. But if he's already beaching in Ecuador, might as well protect him from the IRS's grubby fingers. And if he sells US properties, he could reinvest overseas."

I chewed on the last of my salad as I processed this. How did the oh-so-great real estate market suddenly become a trap? "Is foreign real estate investment an option? It seems a lot less profitable without the crazy depreciation laws we have in the US."

Vinny waved that off. "You and I might think the US policies are nuts, but that doesn't mean the rest of the world's governments agree. In my experience, they all operate on one guiding principle."

"What's that?" Dylan asked.

"Monkey say, Monkey do. Most loopholes in the US exist everywhere else too. Will it be exactly the same? Nah, instead of depreciating a house in 27.5 years, some will depreciate it in 25 and others in 30. Don't write off investing internationally, but plan on doing your research first."

Part of me had been hoping I'd catch Vinny, that he'd realize that foreign investment wasn't such a good idea. What was I thinking, that he'd admit his mistake and advise Dylan to stay here with me? I'd have to suck all this up like a big girl and face reality. "Are you still buying real estate, Vinny?"

"Not with the market this high. Cash flowing properties are a thing of the past."

"So what are you doing with your money?"

"Oil exploration."

"Oil?" I couldn't help but laugh. "Seriously?"

"Oil gets mad subsidies. Over 70% of the cost of a well depreciates in the first year. And unlike real estate, this depreciation offsets unlimited active income." Vinny wiped his mouth with his napkin. "Then there's depletion."

"Depletion?" I asked.

Vinny pointed to Dylan's untouched plate. "If Dylan continues to ignore his salad, what's going to happen to it?"

"The waitress will clear it away."

"What if there is no waitress. What if it sits here till Tuesday?"

"It will go rotten."

"Exactly. The lettuce will be inedible by morning. The tomatoes and cucumbers will take a little longer, but they'll go too. Eventually, even the croutons will be disgusting. That's depreciation. Dylan's got a ten-dollar salad that will deteriorate until it's worth nothing. Ah, but could that ever happen with my salad?"

"No way. You eat it too fast."

"Exactly. Each bite I take depletes what is left until it's all gone."

"The tax code treats depletion like depreciation?"

"It can be even better. If I buy $100,000 of real estate, by the time I've depreciated $100,000, it's gone. Bye, bye depreciation."

"You get even less because the land doesn't depreciate," I said.

Vinny shot me a wink. "You've been paying attention. But depletion is different. I get to deduct 15% of my gross profit every year. So if I take out $10,000 in oil, I can deduct $1500. And I can keep doing this till I'm worm food. If I'm still pumping black gold out of that hole 100 years from now, I'll still get my 15% depletion credit every single year until the oil runs out."

"Do you have to choose which tax benefit you want?" I asked. "Depreciation or depletion?"

"Oh no, you get them both."

"That would never happen with Dylan's salad."

"Very true. Isn't the tax code great? I'm telling you: Disney couldn't create a better fairy tale."

Technically, Disney got his fairy tales from Grimm, but I wasn't about to correct Vinny. Besides, our dishes finally arrived. Vinny, of course, had gotten his veal scaloppini, but I couldn't bank on him covering the tab this time, so I got the chicken. Dylan still hadn't touched his salad and told the waiter to hold off on his dish. After a bite of chicken, I asked, "You're diverting your real estate profits into oil to keep them from getting taxed?"

"Anything to keep them slimeballs from getting it." Vinny made a gesture I'd rather not describe.

Dylan finally managed a bite of his salad. "What do you think about my situation?"

"You want my honest two cents?" Vinny cut into his veal and chewed a few bites before continuing. "You know what your problem is? You've gotten lazy."

Dylan's hand curled around the napkin on his lap. "You think I ought to still be working full time?"

"I don't mean physically lazy. You think I care if you lounge in your hammock sipping piña coladas all day? The fact is, you got intellectually lazy. You're a one-trick pony. Your strategy was to spend nothing and put your cash into rental real estate. As strategies go, it was a good one. For a while. But now you're priced out of the market, and you desperately need a strategy update."

The muscles around Dylan's jaw clenched. "You think I should have been diversifying all this time?"

"Nah. Diversification is a highway to mediocrity. Virtually everyone who's ever made it big had one focus. Still, when your one thing stops working, you're stuck."

Dylan slumped in his chair. Vinny had him pegged, and it hurt. "What should I be doing?"

"Step one, stop thinking of yourself as one of those beggars on Staton Ave."

"Look, Vinny, I barely have enough income to squeak by in the US these days."

"Someone did a great job drilling into your head that the number one thing is passive income. Good. But just because it's number one, don't think it's the only thing. Fact is, while you've been sipping margaritas…"

"I thought they were piña coladas?" I said, trying to lighten the mood.

"Whatever. Without Dylan doing a damn thing, he's become a millionaire, which means he's accredited."

"What does that mean?" I asked.

"You ever heard of a company doing an IPO?" Vinny asked me. "You know what that stands for?"

"Initial…" My shoulder inched towards my ear. "Public Offering?"

"Bingo. You ever stop to think what those words mean?"

I bit my lip. "It means they can start selling stock to the public."

"How'd they raise money before?"

"Privately, I guess."

"Which means a private company can have shareholders?"

I thought back to Anthony's early investments in companies. "Yeah."

"So why couldn't this company sell the shares to the general public before their IPO?"

"Because they weren't listed on an exchange?"

"Nah, that's just circular reasoning. Let me put it this way. Think of an IPO as a GSO. A General Shmuck Offering. Once it goes public, any shmuck is allowed to buy shares. Before it goes public, only select people are allowed to invest. These privileged few are accredited investors."

"Why limit it?"

"Our lovely government is afraid big bad companies will pull the wool over the eyes of us helpless lambs." Vinny held his hands over his eyes. "So they make companies go through a million hurdles before they can IPO."

"I think I get it. If investors are savvy enough, the government's not afraid they'll get ripped off, so they let them buy shares before the IPO?"

"In theory. In practice, it's a load of crap." He cut into his veal.

"Why?"

"Because you know how you demonstrate your investing expertise to the government?"

"By taking an exam?"

Vinny slapped the table. "Yeah, right. Like a driver's test? I'm afraid that's a bit too logical for the dunces on Capitol Hill."

"How do they decide?"

"It's all based on how much money you have. If you've made $200,000 or more two years in a row, you're basically accredited. Married couples are good at $300,000."

"But Dylan doesn't make that much." I turned to Dylan, who was finally finishing the last of his salad. "Do you?"

"He doesn't need to," Vinny said. "He fits the other test."

"Which is?"

"If I got my math right, your net worth, ignoring your primary residence, is over $1,000,000. Am I right?"

Dylan nodded. Something about Vinny's chatter had finally gotten him hopeful. He waved over a waiter to bring him his chicken parmesan.

"Why don't they count your primary residence?" I asked.

"You're looking for logic from those crackpots in Washington?"

"Oh come on, they're not that bad. They must have a reason."

Dylan broke in. "It makes sense. First of all, a primary residence isn't normally income-producing, so it's not money that's working for you. Secondly, if you get into financial trouble, they want you to have enough cushion to get out of it without having to sell your house."

Vinny shrugged this off, like he did with any comment crediting the government with half a brain. "In any event, Dylan is terrified about losing money, which is why he's frozen like a popsicle in the Arctic." He nodded toward Dylan. "I don't believe you'll go into oil or any one of a hundred other investments you don't know a damned thing about because you don't want to risk losing your precious money."

Was Vinny trying to break Dylan? If so, it wasn't working. Dylan sat up, suddenly defensive. "Is that such a bad thing?"

"Nah. Like Warren Buffet says, the first rule of investing is don't lose money. But you also don't want your money sitting in some bank earning loose change."

"What about index funds?" I asked.

"The stock market has shot straight up along with real estate. Odds are, they'll tumble together like Jack and Jill."

"So what are you recommending?"

"Here's the thing. When Dylan was poor, he had to figure it all out on his own. The big shots in finance wouldn't talk to him. They couldn't, according to law, because he wasn't accredited." Vinny relished his last scallop with a groan that belonged more in a bedroom than a restaurant. He leaned across the table with a sly grin. "Now, Dylan, it's a whole new ball game. You're worth over a million, so you can start swimming in a bigger pond. You'll still be a small fish, but you can finally start investing with the killer whales."

"And that's a good thing?" I asked.

"Mostly. It's not without its perils. It also means you'll be swimming with bigger sharks."

"Meaning what?"

"They'll come at you with slicker sales pitches. It can be harder to tell the genuine investments from the shysters who smell blood in the water. But it also opens a world of opportunity."

Dylan asked, "How do I tell the good deals from the bad?"

"It sounds like when you first started, you learned everything you could. You did well. But the game's changed, and your financial position's changed. If you're going to start selling properties, you gotta get back into the school of life."

The next day, Dylan drove over to my place, where I was cleaning like mad. If I was going to put my duplex on the market, I wanted it to shine.

Dylan asked for a tour of the house. "You did all the design work here yourself? It's so cute."

"Beats covering the entire place in off-white paint, doesn't it?"

"For living in, definitely." His head did that I'm-not-sure-about-that shimmy. "But for practical upkeep—."

"Yeah, yeah, I know. But there's more to an apartment than practicality. Come on."

I led Dylan into the garage, which I'd converted into a short-term rental. "You have no idea. Adding a few flairs has done wonders for attracting tenants."

"Who do you rent it out to?"

"Mostly corporate types here for conventions. Right now, I'm getting the ones who want to be in a quaint part of town close to restaurants and cafes. But once the light rail is done, it'll only be three stops from the convention center. That was my main motivation for fixing it up." I sat on the plush sofa and leaned against one of the African pillows that brightened up the space. "I'm going to miss this place."

Dylan nestled next to me. I should have pushed him away—he was only in town for a visit. But his warmth felt so good, I couldn't help but fall into him. "You don't need to sell it, you know."

"Yes, I do."

"Why?"

"Dylan, when we first started dating, I was over $10,000 in debt. Through implementing the strategies you taught me, I got myself completely out of debt and started building up some assets. You know what I now have?"

"How much?"

"About $8,000 in the bank plus a little more in my ROTH IRA plus my 401(k) from work."

"It sounds like you're doing pretty good, considering where you started."

"True. But if I can make $250,000 tax-free right now…," I wrote the number on my pad and circled it. "I'll make more than 30 times my current savings in one shot. I can't pass up on that opportunity."

"The money is still yours; it's just in the house now."

"Right, and if the market tanks tomorrow, all that equity will just disappear."

Dylan rubbed my shoulders. "Why is it so much easier for you to let go? You love this place; it's written all over your face. My properties are just investments, yet I'm struggling to part with them."

"Trust me, I hate letting go."

"Then how can you do it so easily?"

"It's not easy. But…" My head fell. "Did I ever tell you what happened to my father?"

"You mentioned a heart attack."

"Right, that was two years ago. He got it from working crazy hours under intense pressure."

"I'm so sorry to hear that, Amber." He ran his fingers along the base of my neck.

"I haven't gotten to the bad part yet. He was barely out of the hospital before he was right back to work. I wondered why he didn't retire, take it easy."

"Amber, there are people who just wouldn't know what to do with themselves if they weren't working."

"That's not the answer I got." My face grew hot with the memory. "He couldn't afford retirement. But with another $250,000…"

"You're going to give all that money to your parents?"

"You know why my parents can't afford retirement?" Guilt cut into my chest. "Because of me and my siblings. Paying for our braces, paying for college."

Dylan lifted my face to meet his. "I met your dad. There's no way he's going to accept a penny of that money."

I shrugged. "Even so, I have to try."

"I admire your resolve. Next to you, I feel like a wimp." Dylan's head shook slowly as he spoke. "I so hate risk. I figured out a way to put my money in a place where it will be working for me rather than me working for it. Now I need to find a new place to put it or suffer losses. The uncertainty is killing me."

"You'll figure it out. I know you will." I rested my hands on his face and held it still. "You've got a lot more knowledge in this head than you give yourself credit for."

"I suppose you're right. The truth is, I'm not entirely clueless. I've read plenty of books and listened to podcasts in areas other than real estate. Nothing Vinny said last night about being an accredited investor was new to me. I just lack first-hand experience."

"Yeah?" My eyebrows shot up. "You understood what Vinny meant by the killer whales?"

"Sure, there's no big secret there. He meant hedge funds, venture capital, private equity. Funds that are only open to accredited investors."

"You'd consider going into venture capital?" The idea that Dylan could wind up investing in Anthony's firm felt wrong on so many levels.

"Right now, I'm just trying to understand my options."

"Would you make more in those funds?"

"Not more than I made when I house hacked. Not a chance. But I'll make more than I'm getting now. My current returns, relative to the value of my properties, are pathetic. And there are other advantages."

"Like what?"

"Like it's no longer my headache." Dylan rubbed my temples. "Have you ever heard of a professional tenant?" I shook my head. "I had one of those my second year in real estate. Total nightmare."

"What is it?"

"A professional tenant is someone who isn't paying rent, but also refuses to leave. It can take months and cost a fortune getting them out."

"Don't they have to pay you back?"

"Legally, yes. But they're usually broke, so good luck getting anything out of them. I had a period of three months when I still had to cover all the costs of that apartment, without any rent to cover them. Then I had to pay a lawyer to get an eviction order and have the sheriff throw them out."

I was missing something. Again. "What does this have to do with being accredited?"

Dylan took the notebook and pen out of my hand. "Let's say I wanted to invest in real estate through a private equity fund." Dylan drew a little house complete with chimney and smoke. "Instead of buying a place with a couple of rental apartments, I might own a small share of a 400-unit apartment complex." Now he drew an enormous high rise. "What would happen then if a professional tenant moved in?" In between his house and high rise, he drew a hobo stick man.

"Wouldn't it be the same process of getting him out?"

"Identical. The same lawyers, sheriffs, unpaid rent. Except this time, I'd never hear about it. The unpaid rent from that one apartment would be balanced out by the other 399. Getting rid of the tenant would be someone else's problem. At worst, it would be a footnote in my quarterly report explaining why distributions went down by $100."

"What about when Vinny said diversification is a highway to mediocrity?"

"Mediocrity is not always a bad thing. When I started, I grew my net worth by 50-100% per year, but I also busted my butt, took all the risk, and lived like a pauper. These funds are more likely to return 8-12%."

"And the risk?"

"Like Vinny said, there are bigger sharks in the water. Still, if you diversify across industries and across funds to protect yourself against the unexpected, the risk is pretty low."

"This is where professional investors put their money?"

"No. Professional investors run these funds, and their returns are far higher. They raise money from wealthy people who don't want to be bothered learning the ins and outs of every investment, who want no hassles, no headaches, and steady, predictable returns."

"No hassles, no headaches, and steady, predictable returns." I sank into the couch. "Sounds like the perfect recipe for a guy who wants to lie in his hammock sipping margaritas."

"I prefer piña coladas."

"You know, I'm surprised at you." I took his hand in mine. "One of the things you kept emphasizing when teaching me this stuff was that you could figure out whatever you needed to know. The information is out there; we just have to sift through it."

"You're right. Count me in." Dylan rose to his feet. "But even before then, I should put The Crypt on the market. On that house, I won't take such a huge hit on the taxes."

"And I'll put this place up. Should I call Phil and ask him to list them both?"

While Dylan looked up real estate listings online to get a sense of the market, I called Phil. When I told him why I was calling, he just said, "You too, eh?"

Uh oh. "Are a lot of people trying to sell?"

"The inventory is going through the roof. Especially since all these new buildings are finally getting their certificates of occupancy."

"Are we too late?"

"Not at all. Prices keep rising, despite the additional inventory. Just know that houses aren't moving as fast as they were a few years ago."

My chest clenched. "How fast were they moving?"

"If a house was well priced, I'd get multiple offers the day it opened. Everyone was afraid they'd miss out if they didn't jump."

"And now?"

"The pool of buyers is smaller, as fewer people can afford the current housing prices, and those who can afford it are growing wary of a market correction. But so far, the drop in interest has only slowed the growth, it hasn't reversed the market. I still think we can sell your place within a couple of weeks as long as the market doesn't plummet before then."

"And if the market reverses?"

"While the market is skyrocketing, buyers get paranoid of being left behind, and they trip over each other to put in offers. When things shift, the opposite happens. Buyers get afraid of overpaying and are more likely to wait for it to bottom out."

"You think we have some time before that happens?"

"No idea. All the warning signs are flashing. But there've been plenty of false alarms before when the market continued its upward trajectory."

I took a cue from Susanna and made over three pounds of cookie dough for the open house. I added extra vanilla so the scent would spread. I placed freshly cut flowers everywhere. Phil suggested I not be home when the buyers arrived, but I couldn't bear to leave. So I took a book and sat on the loveseat to highlight the coziness, and I baked batch after batch of cookies.

Of course, I couldn't read a word of my book and was relieved whenever anyone wanted to ask me questions. About anything. But mostly just agents saw it the first day, and they directed their questions to Phil.

The new light rail stop would be operational within three months, so the neighborhood was hot, just as Phil predicted it would be. The first offer came in three days after the listing was put up, and it was a low ball. I was debating countering, but Phil told me to hang tough.

The next weekend brought a flurry of activity. Agents who had come on their own were back with clients. Cookies came out of the oven at thirty-minute intervals. It was a good thing I'd made so much dough in advance, as there was no way I was going to dirty my spotless kitchen during the showings.

At the end of the weekend, we had three new offers. By the time Phil finished negotiating, the highest bid came in $280,000 over my purchase price.

"So all that except for $30,000 will be tax-free?"

"You won't pay income or capital gains tax on any of it," Phil said. "After you deduct improvements made to the house and my commission, you'll be just below $250,000 in gains."

So I did it! Even after paying Phil's commission, I'd have almost exactly $250,000 to do whatever I wanted with. I knew where I wanted it to go. The question was, would it be accepted?

"I've got news," I said to my parents over Sunday dinner at their house.

"Oh?" My father's eyebrows shot up.

I bounced in my seat the way I did when I'd come home with a 100 on a test. "I sold my duplex."

"Really?" My mother stopped grating parmesan over her fettuccine. "But you loved that place."

"I did, but it was time to move on." I served myself another beefsteak tomato with mozzarella.

"Where will you live?" she asked.

"I'll have to find an apartment." I shrugged as if it was no big deal, but the reality was that I had no clue where to go. I hated the idea of leaving my home.

My mother's head tilted further in confusion. "But why?"

"I was able to get out $250,000, tax-free."

"That's wonderful, Amber," my father said. "At your age, that will set up a great nest egg."

I shook my head. "I want you to have it."

My parents looked at each other. "Amber, we appreciate that," my mother said, "but we can't take your money."

"It's not mine. It's yours. I'm paying you back for the money you put into my education."

"Amber, that money was a gift." My mother laid her hand over mine. "You pay it back by giving to your own kids. We don't want it."

"Amber," my father said, "does this have anything to do with my heart attack?"

I nodded, and tears flowed down my cheeks. "I know you didn't have enough to retire on. I thought, if I could help…"

"That I'd retire on your money? And what would I do with myself all day?"

"I don't know." My voice sounded so young, so scared, like when I'd cry over not getting invited to a sleepover in middle school. Why did visiting my parents always do that to me? "Golf?"

"I enjoy my work. I enjoy interacting with my colleagues and clients. I appreciate the thought, but even if I had more money, I wouldn't leave."

"But, your health…"

Dad kissed my forehead. He looked right into my eyes and said, "My health is doing much better. I'm going to the gym twice a week. I've cut back on desserts."

Recognizing that I wasn't going to win this one, I changed tactics. "What about your house?"

"What about it?"

"You're living alone in a five-bedroom. The market is high right now. If you sold, the first $500,000 in profits on the house would be yours tax-free. You could downgrade to a one or two-bedroom and put that extra money into your retirement. That way, when the time comes, you'll be prepared."

What I was thinking, but didn't say, was when the next heart attack hits, he wouldn't be forced back to work.

"It's funny you mention that," my mother said. "We've been discussing downsizing for years, maybe moving downtown where your father will be closer to work, and we can enjoy the city life. But we were afraid you kids would miss having the house you grew up in."

I studied the flowered wallpaper in the dining room. I *would* miss this house. I had so many memories here. But I was more concerned with the memories I wanted to create in the future, memories of my kids bouncing on their grandfather's knees. I wanted my kids to have him in their lives for a long time to come. I'd talk to my siblings and make sure they'd be supportive. I flashed them my biggest grin and kissed my father's cheek. "Sell it. It's a good time for it. Moving downtown sounds like a great idea."

In the end, Dylan's fear of loss won out over Vinny's advice to hang on for the long term. He decided to hedge his bets and sold three of his six properties, allowing him to clear $1,050,000 in post-tax profit. It was a windfall, yes, but at the same time caused him stress. Money only contributed to his Cash Machine when it generated passive income, and he wasn't sure what to do with it now.

It's not that he couldn't find cash flowing investment opportunities. The very opposite was true. There were thousands of new investment opportunities open to him now that he was an accredited investor. The question was, how to best choose between them? And most of these funds required him to commit his money for five to seven years, which he wasn't comfortable doing.

Short term, he dropped his cash into a money market account, where it earned him a bit of interest, yet was liquid enough he could access it any time he wanted. But it wouldn't generate enough passive income for the life he wanted in the US, so he planned to return to Ecuador.

The problem with Dylan and myself was that one of us was a wimp, totally afraid to take life by the horns. But which one of us? Was it Dylan, because he chose Ecuador for its low cost of living and his income tax exemption? Or was it me, because I was afraid to leave home and dive into a life of adventure with him?

In many ways, it was the perfect time for me to go. I was about to lose my home, and I had serious money in the bank for the first time in my life. But I couldn't bring myself to give up everything I'd known for life in the jungles of Ecuador. So when the time came for Dylan to leave, I sent him off with a goodbye dinner and a platonic hug. I then stood in the driveway on a frigid, wet night and watched the only man I wanted in my life drive off for the airport.

CHAPTER 19

ENEMY NUMBER ONE

L et's recap:

I had no Dylan.

I had no house.

I had over $250,000 in the bank. Most would consider that wonderful, but it scared the hell out of me. It wasn't until that money landed in my account that I understood what Vinny meant when he said 'sitting cash is just a recipe for trouble.' Dylan had told me early on, 'Money is potential. It wants to be used. If it's just sitting there, it burns a hole in your pocket.' This money was my nest egg, and if I didn't treat it with care, all I'd have left were pieces of broken eggshell.

I had to invest that cash somehow, but I had no idea where. And I didn't have Dylan's luxury of being accredited. So all the big boys in finance wouldn't even talk to me. I had to figure this one out on my own.

Real estate was bound to go down. The same was true of the stock market. As Vinny said, they rose together and would probably fall together. And there's no way I'd dump all my precious money into an oil well like Vinny. The risk of hitting a dry well was just too high, and oil felt like such icky business. I couldn't turn to Dylan. Besides the fact that he'd chosen some South American backwater over me, he was just as frozen as I was. So where did that leave me?

I already felt the draw of all that money when I went looking for a new apartment. My brain kept telling me I could afford more than my teacher's income justified. It nudged me about the pile of cash *just sitting there*, saying, 'what's the harm in using a little bit to subsidize your lifestyle? You work hard. You deserve it.'

"What a load of crap!" I yelled back, weirding out the landlord of an unnecessarily extravagant place downtown. I wasn't about to wind up like my parents, who at age 60 still didn't have sufficient savings to retire. I was determined to grow my $250,000, not shrink it.

I wanted to put the money back into real estate once the market bottomed out. Unfortunately, the market Vinny and Phil predicted would go down refused to cooperate. The number of properties changing hands continued to drop, but the prices kept rising.

That sucked for me. Three months after selling, my house was worth ten thousand dollars more than I'd sold it for. I'd left all that money sitting on the table. At least it had turned out well for my parents. They got their house on the market in time to catch the wave. Considering how much their area had appreciated and the fact they'd owned their home for over thirty years, they had no problem pulling out over $500,000 tax-free.

They got themselves a sweet two-bedroom downtown, close to my father's office and the theater district. They ditched one of their cars, which further reduced their expenses, and my father walked to work on good-weather days, which was great for his health. Their second bedroom doubled as a guest room and home office. They'd considered buying, but I talked them into renting while the market was still so high. While they knew it made sense to downsize and were enjoying city life, my mother was nonetheless heartbroken about never being able to host the holidays again.

As for me, I wound up renting a beautiful one-bedroom for $200 a month above my budget. Of course, the $250,000 had whispered in my ear, telling me I could afford it. The smarter move would have been to get a larger apartment with roommates, but I couldn't bear to go back with living with others at this point. The next time I lived with anyone, I wanted it to be my husband.

"Dylan, why'd you have to go and leave again?" I yelled into my beautiful, empty apartment.

As the end of the school year approached, I realized I couldn't have the $250,000 sitting in my account any longer. My car lease was coming due in another six months, and I found myself craning my head whenever I passed a dealership. It would be so easy to drop $30,000 into a gorgeous new car (that the money kept whispering I deserved), and my nest egg would continue shrinking.

Up to now, I'd only invested my money in real estate and the stock market, both of which I feared would soon drop. Fortunately, Big Brother knew what I needed before I did. My social media feeds were suddenly filled with *get rich quick* schemes and seminars. One that caught my eye was "How to Buy Businesses: The Best Investment You'll Ever Make." It was a two-day seminar set for the coming weekend and cost $250. The business world was something I knew nothing about. If I could learn about a great new way to invest, wasn't that worth 0.1% of my nest egg? OK, I knew that was a dumb way to think about my money, but that's what having so much cash in the bank does—it justified everything. This time, the justification worked (as Big Brother knew it would), and I decided to take a flyer on the seminar.

I arrived early and, like the nerdy schoolgirl I've always been, sat in the front row. There were only 30 of us in attendance, and Shakti Patel came on stage without any of the preamble I'd seen at larger seminars. She straightened her razor-sharp suit and cut right to the chase. "Small businesses typically sell for between 2.5 and 3 times their annual profits. If that's the case, what is the annual ROI, your Return on Investment, when purchasing a business?"

That was a simple math problem. I just had to divide the purchase price by the multiplier. I raised my hand, and Shakti pointed to me. "33% to 40%," I said, then thought better of it. "Wait, that can't be right."

Shakti's eyes gleamed, and I could see she was pleased by my discomfort. "The math is spot on. Do you mind coming up here?"

I stepped forward sheepishly.

Shakti asked, "What's your name?"

"Amber."

"So Amber, tell everyone what's bothering you."

"Well, I keep hearing that on the stock market, a business with a price to earnings ratio of 15 to 1 is considered a good value. But you're saying it should be around 3 to 1."

"Very good, Amber." She shifted her posture to face the whole group. "That's a key difference between small, private businesses and large, publicly-traded ones. If the returns were the same, then why would anyone buy a small business? It's so much easier to log into your brokerage account and buy stocks. The fact is, as businesses grow, their valuations increase exponentially." Shakti wrote down these different categories on a huge whiteboard. "A mid-sized business, with revenues of $15,000,000, might be worth 5 to 10 times its annual profits, and a large business could easily be worth 15 times profits. Which should already give you a big hint for one way to make money with small businesses. Have you figured that out, Amber?"

I studied the categories and numbers on the whiteboard. "You could buy multiple small businesses and aggregate them?"

"Excellent. Say you buy dental practices. One practice will go for about 2.5 times its annual profits. A conglomerate of fifty practices might go for 10 times their annual profits. So if all you do is buy 50 practices and put them together into some giant company called Dental Deals, you'll quadruple the value of your investment. But let's assume you don't have the resources to buy 50 businesses, you're looking to buy just one. What return can you hope to get on your out of pocket costs?"

"33% to 40%," I repeated.

Shakti shook her head vigorously. "Not even close."

"But you told me my math was spot on."

"Your math is spot on, but your assumptions are way off." Shakti faced the crowd. "Can anyone see the flaw in Amber's assumptions?"

A guy in the back raised his hand. "She's assuming she's buying the entire business in cash."

"Exactly." Shakti offered him a thumbs up, then turned back to me. "You conflated two numbers, Amber. Your ROI is your return on the entire purchase price. But unless you buy the business in cash, and almost no one does, your cash-on-cash return will be much higher." She erased the board and held her marker at the ready. "Let's take a look at some numbers to make it more real. Our fictional business, Cheap Chinese Crap Incorporated, CCCI for short, does $2,000,000 a year in revenue, with profit margins of 25%. Amber, you've done well with the math so far. What would our annual profits be?"

I blushed at the attention. "$500,000."

"And let's say that CCCI is selling for 2.8 times its annual profits. What would the cost of the business be?"

I bit my tongue as I did the calculation. "1.4 million."

"So if you had $1,400,000 sitting around, you could buy the business with a check, but you'll get better returns if you don't. How much do you think you'll need out of pocket to buy this business?"

Someone in the back called out, "$1."

Many in the room laughed, but not Shakti. "$1 is the most common amount businesses are sold for. Of course, you're usually only able to buy a business for $1 when it's distressed. In tomorrow's class, we'll talk a bit about how to identify and buy distressed businesses, but for today, let's assume CCCI is a good, healthy business.

"If you're selling a business, the more interested buyers you have, the more money you'll normally get. Since few buyers want to pay cash, sellers, on average, will carry 50% to 70% of the purchase price. In other words, they'll be willing to loan you the majority of the money you need to buy the business. So let's say the board at CCCI agrees to offer 60% seller financing, payable over eight years at 8% annual interest."

She passed the whiteboard marker to me. "Amber, you're our math wiz, will you do the honors of tracking our numbers?"

I wasn't such a math wiz, but I *was* a school teacher, so I felt right at home. I walked up to the whiteboard and wrote:

CCCI Purchase Price: $1,400,000
CCCI Seller Financing: -$840,000
Total needed to buy: $560,000

Shakti looked over what I wrote. "That all looks good so far. At this point, you'd only need a little more than one year's worth of profits in pocket to buy the entire business. But you might not have $560,000 lying around. Fortunately, the business probably has some assets. A bank might not be willing to finance the entire purchase price, but they'll lend you money against those hard assets. So let's call that another 20%."

I added that to my list.

CCCI Purchase Price: $1,400,000
CCCI Seller Financing: -$840,000
Bank Financing: -$280,000
Total needed to buy: $280,000

"Our picture is looking better, but I'm sure some of you are about to say 'But Shakti, I don't have $280,000.' That's OK. Let me ask you, is there anyone here with cash they'd like to invest who'd be happy to get a 20% annual return on their money?"

I raised my hand as did five others. "Look around the room," Shakti said, "those are all possible investors. You can afford to give out fantastic margins because our business makes $500,000 in annual profits. So you can borrow the majority of that 280 grand from private investors. They won't own any shares of the company, but they won't need it. It's a safe investment for them because they're putting their money into an already profitable business, and they'll get a fabulous return until they're paid off. You'll rarely get *all* the money you need from private investors, because everyone feels safer if you have skin in the game. So let's say private investors put in 15% of the purchase price. Amber, what does that leave us with?"

I wrote it all in.

CCCI Purchase Price: $1,400,000
CCCI Seller Financing: -$840,000
Bank Financing: -$280,000
Private Investors: -$210,000
Total needed to buy: $70,000

"In our example, we only need 5% of the purchase price to buy this business. True, the business still has tons of debt, but it's very manageable debt because its profits are so high."

A college kid in a T-shirt and jeans said, "How is the debt so manageable? It's over a million dollars?"

"It's worse than that." Shakti's face brightened at the challenge. "It's 1.33 million, and some of that is at an extremely high-interest rate of 20%. I'm sure those numbers sound intimidating to those not used to leveraging debt. But bear in mind the annual profits are half a million dollars. If it was me, I'd pay off the entirety of those private investor loans in the first year to get that 20% interest off my books. Believe it or not, you can pay off those high-interest loans, plus make minimum payments on the rest of your loans, plus pay yourself over a hundred thousand dollars all in the first year. After that, you can give yourself a nice fat raise and still pay off all the debt within five years."

Murmurs filled the crowd.

"So, back to you, Amber. What would your cash-on-cash returns be on your $70,000 investment?"

My eyes widened. "Are you saying my first-year salary would be more than my total investment?"

Shakti nodded. "Those who don't mind carrying debt a little longer can make double or even triple their investment money in first-year salary alone. And when the debt is fully paid off, you'll own a 1.4 million dollar company outright plus have a salary of $500,000 a year.

"Of course, that's assuming you keep the profits the same. If you're skilled in business and can grow the profits, then both your annual salary and the business valuation will scale accordingly.

Shakti's eyes scanned the room. "Bear in mind the opposite is also true. If you don't know what you're doing in business and are hoping for a passive income source, you may be in for a nasty surprise. Because if you can't maintain profits, all this falls apart.

"Now, with that warning, let's dig into the details of how to find a business and negotiate the purchase."

I learned an absolute ton from Shakti's seminar, but the one thing that burned brightest in my brain was her warning. This was not some turnkey, passive money scheme. Buying a business offered a fabulous opportunity for someone who knew what they were doing, but for me, I'd be way over my head. And even though I raised my hand when Shakti asked who had money to invest and wanted a 20% return, did I know enough to tell a good deal from a bad one?

The more I thought about it, the more I realized what I had to do. "Desperate times call for desperate measures," I muttered to myself as I got in my car and drove to the bank.

Is there a more fearful investment in the world than the Certificate of Deposit? Well, gold, I suppose. Dylan once told me he hates gold, because "unlike businesses or real estate which create value, gold just sits there looking shiny. If Chicken Little ever decided to invest, he'd probably buy gold because gold is hoarded by all those who think the sky is falling. When the world's governments and banks collapse and the streets are ruled by gangs of post-apocalyptic marauders, your gold will still be sitting there, shiny as ever."

Still, gold does have intrinsic value, which means whenever public trust in our financial system tanks, gold prices rise, and over the long haul, gold's value normally keeps pace with inflation. Which brings us back to the even more pathetic Certificate of Deposit. CD return rates were often lower than inflation, especially when you factored in taxes owed on the gains. That meant the longer you left money in a CD, the more its buying power eroded. In exchange for receiving these paltry returns, you had to commit to keep your money in the CD for a set period of time or face financial penalties.

Vinny told me the first rule of investing was 'don't lose money.' I had expected this business buying seminar to expose me to a new way to *make* money. What it did was open my eyes to how much I didn't know, and how many ways there were to lose my precious little nest egg. Buying a business seemed like a great idea. In the future. For Amber 2.0. After she got herself a business education. For now, it was way too risky an investment. In the meantime, easy access to my cash was nothing short of dangerous.

Unsure what else to do, I asked at the bank about getting a CD. Interest rates were going up, so I hoped I'd get something decent. But returns were still pretty pathetic. Vinny or someone like him could have suggested a more lucrative plan, but I wasn't focused on making money as much as keeping it far from its biggest enemy: me.

So I took my nest egg and tied that beast down for a full year. I didn't only strap down its arms and legs. I invested the whole lot.

Well, just about. First, I made my ROTH IRA contribution, which I'd never gotten around to doing. I got in just under the wire for the previous year's $6000 and added this year's contribution as well. I'd take care of next year's after the CD matured. Unfortunately, I couldn't do the same with my car money. By the time I could access my cash, my leased car would be well out of my hands and back at the dealership. I'd learned my lesson: this time, I was buying used all the way, but I was no longer so dirt poor that I needed to go dumpster diving. I decided that given my improved circumstances, $5000 was a reasonable budget for a used car.

Still, I wouldn't need that car money for another five months, and my greedy little fingers would be itching to spend that too. Fortunately, my bank let me have dozens of connected accounts for no extra charge, so I created a new one called *Car Money, Don't Touch*. Then I created another account called *Emergency Fund, Use Only in Case of Unemployment or Wedding*, and I dumped a full three months' worth of living expenses in there.

I left my primary checking account with less than $2000 in it, just enough to keep up with my rent and credit card bills. The rest of my funds, which came to just under $235,000, I locked safely behind the fortress of a one year CD. I knew it was a crappy investment, but at least it was safe, and I'd be charged a painful, slap-on-the-wrist fee if my grubby hands tried to touch it.

You think it's hard waiting for a pot to boil? Try waiting for the real estate market to crash. The bastard just kept going up. I suppose it didn't matter all that much—I had a one year lease on my apartment and so much money tucked into my CD I couldn't buy anything even if a deal came available.

But I was still antsy to get my finances under control. Even with the overpriced apartment, I was doing well. My credit card debt days were over, and an end to car payments was on the horizon. I was also eating out less. Mind you, that wasn't exactly a money-saving strategy. It was because I hated going out alone, and since I was no longer dating anyone and most of my girlfriends had gotten married, I lacked opportunities to blow money at restaurants.

So how could I take my financial circumstances to the next level? Passive income was a dead-end for now. All my investment money was locked away in my CD, awaiting some future opportunity. Cutting expenses didn't interest me—I'd made as many improvements there as I wanted to. That left one big untapped area: active income.

With all the financial changes I'd made, one thing had remained a constant: my job. Was it time to switch? I loved teaching. I'd never planned on staying a teacher forever, but I had expected to teach until I had kids of my own. One thing was certain: I was not about to go back to school to retrain for anything new. I'd spent enough time and money in degree programs.

I thought of my friend Stacey. She taught with me for my first two years and left for some tutoring gig. Last I heard she was making more money than even the senior teachers in my school. She was still teaching, but had moved to the business side of education, and ever since Shakti's seminar, I'd been itching to start learning how businesses worked.

"So, you finally decided to leave the grind?" Stacey said when I called her up.

"I haven't decided anything yet. I'm just exploring options, including picking up a couple of tutoring hours after school."

"Well, let me tell you, going out on my own is the best thing I've ever done."

"How so?"

"I love teaching but hate classroom control. It's amazing how one kid who doesn't want to listen can suck so much of your energy that the rest of the class gets cheated."

"Tell me about it!" My shoulders tensed just at the thought of Brodie, who terrorized every girl in my class. "How do you deal with those kids now?"

"First of all, I rarely get those challenges. Since my energy is focused on one kid at a time, they don't need to act out for my attention. But periodically, I still get one who won't listen."

"What do you do then?"

"I drop 'em. Let someone else discipline them. I have enough business that I only work with kids I like."

"But if a kid is struggling to learn…"

"Look, Amber, I'm not saying no one should work with them. But as a school teacher, I taught whoever they gave me. I had no choice. Now the work I do is private. I get so drained dealing with one tough kid that one hour feels like three. So I don't do it. There are people out there who do wonderful work with difficult kids. They say there's nothing like getting through to a kid who no one else can reach. Me, I hate it. That's the thing about being in the private sector: we make our own rules."

"What are you teaching? Whatever the kids need?"

"That's what I did at first. I taught math, English, whatever. Then I got trained in cognitive skills development. That's all I do now. It pays better, and there's more work than I can handle."

"I bet that took some serious training."

"Not really. I started looking into it when all my coworkers were telling me that I needed to get my master's degree. The masters was two years and $30,000. To get certified to teach cognitive skills took less than a month and cost a fraction as much." Stacey exhaled. "Let me tell you, the work pays so much better. And when I've taught a kid how to think, their performance improves in all their subjects. It's a no brainer."

I got that same reluctant feeling as when a salesman tried making his product sound too perfect. "How could you learn all that so quickly?"

"I also used to think a month seemed fast, but truthfully, I could train you to do it in a week."

"Really?" Despite my hesitation, what did I have to lose? "Would you?"

"Well, that depends. Your timing couldn't be better, but there's no point in talking about practicalities until you know what you're dealing with. Why don't you come observe my client sessions tomorrow afternoon?"

Stacey had been teaching third grade before she left Jenkins Elementary, so I was expecting to see her working with little children. But as she went through her sessions, I saw kids as young as five and as old as sixteen. They all wanted to learn how to think better, concentrate longer, and have an easier time in school as a whole. Stacey's techniques mostly involved playing games with her clients, but in-between sessions, she explained how each game targeted a different aspect of brain development. That was almost as impressive as the checks she received from parents for $100 an hour, five times what I made at Jenkins.

"You learned all this in a month?" I asked as we sat snacking on roasted nuts between sessions.

"It's a completely different paradigm, Amber. In a master's degree, they teach you mountains of theory so you can design your own curriculum. This company I trained with spent years developing and testing their curriculum. They've already honed their methodology, and their tools have been proven to work." She leafed through her binder and showed me exercises and notes. Every page bore the company logo.

My chin fell into my hand. "Sounds like McDonald's for education."

"You're not far off. It's a franchise model, so they need to give you a system that's easy to learn and replicate. That's the magic of McDonald's too. They didn't become the world's most popular restaurant by making the best burgers."

"So how did they do it?"

"McDonald's built a phenomenal system."

"Being in the McDonald's of education hardly sounds inspiring. It seems formulaic." I grabbed a cashew. "Does this stuff work?"

"That's the best part. The results are incredible!" Stacey pulled a chart on one of her students from her binder. I could see how far this girl's test scores progressed from session to session. "The fact they've created a system doesn't take away from the quality of the education. It's the opposite. Think about it for a moment. How do teachers at Jenkins get paid?"

"Mostly by their years of experience and the highest-level degree they've received."

"Exactly. I'll never forget the summer before my second year teaching. The other third-grade teacher was Mrs. McGillicutty, whose teaching style was as antiquated as her hairdo. Meanwhile, word got out about me, and tons of parents called the principal's office asking to switch their kids from her class to mine. So which of us do you think was paid more?"

"McGillicutty, obviously. She had her Ph.D. before you were born, so I expect she made twice what you did."

"The free market isn't that way. No unions decide what we get paid. You earn more by producing more. If this company couldn't demonstrate spectacular results, their franchise never would have taken off. But they're thriving all across the country, and referrals are my number one source of new students. Parents are so happy with the changes they see in their kids, they can't help but brag to their friends. Trust me, these techniques are far better than anything I was teaching when I was trying to figure out my curriculum from scratch."

I fanned out a deck of cards with strange symbols Stacey used with a student struggling with concentration. "So how does this work? You pay the company to train you in their methods?"

"They offer certifications to both individuals and franchises. Either way, each time you work with a client, they get a small cut."

"Which are you? An individual or a franchise?"

"Funny, you should ask. That's why I said your timing couldn't be better. I was an individual for three years, but lately, I've been so overwhelmed with demand, I decided to buy the franchise, giving me exclusive rights to teach this material in our county."

"So I can't do this even if I wanted to?"

"Of course you can, you'd just do it through *me*. The franchise allows me to hire and train my own staff."

"Oh, I see. What would the salary and benefits look like?"

Stacey had a nice laugh as she headed over to the office kitchenette. "Salary and benefits? Oh no, Amber, you're still in the teachers' union mindset. With me, you wouldn't even be an employee, you'd be an independent contractor. If I provide you with a client, you'll get 50% of what I make. If you get the client directly, that jumps to 75%."

"But what if I don't fill up?"

Stacey came back with a glass of lemonade for each of us. "Then, you make less. But being an independent contractor also gives you flexibility."

"How?"

"Say you don't have enough work from me, and someone comes to you for tutoring in English. I have no problem if you take them on." She took a sip of her drink. "It's just not summer without ice-cold lemonade, eh? I spiked it with a shot of something special. Couldn't do *that* in the classroom, could I?"

I had to admit the sprig of mint and extra kick were just perfect on a hot afternoon. "So if I tutor some kids in English, what cut would you take?"

"Nothing. They'd be your client, and my business doesn't offer English tutoring. Now, if you wanted to use my office space to teach them, you're welcome to rent it at the rate of $10/hour."

"Do I pay rent if it's one of your clients?"

"No, the office expenses come out of my cut."

This would be a good addition to my current income. Of course, the money would be even better if I quit teaching and did this full time, but then there'd be a catch. "You offer no benefits?"

"None. But bear in mind, the money covering your current benefits doesn't just drop out of the sky. That's value you create, yet it skips your pocketbook to fund benefit packages for your coworkers. Rather than you paying for someone else's maternity leave, all that money goes straight into your purse."

"But if I ever need maternity leave..."

"You'll use that extra money you saved up to cover yourself. It's not like you have to quit teaching to try this. You're still getting your benefits from Jenkins. Summer's coming up, so it's a perfect time to explore your options while still having a safety net."

Using the summer as a trial wasn't a bad idea. "Is there enough work for two?"

"Truthfully, I'm not bringing in enough for both of us at the moment. But I'm not trying so hard. Once I filled up from referrals, I stopped putting out the word. I have enough work now for about 20% of your schedule, and between my advertising and your own referrals, I expect we'll soon cover the rest."

I drained the last of my lemonade. "This can really make me more than teaching?"

"In my first year, I made double my teaching salary."

I decided to dip my toe in the water. The last weeks of school, I trained with Stacey whenever we could. By the time Jenkins rang their last bell, I was ready to take on my first student.

The first thing I noticed was how good it felt to not be a disciplinarian. I also wasn't working well into the evening developing curriculum.

What surprised me most was the interaction with the kids. I thought I'd miss out on connecting with my students, but the one-on-one time was so much nicer than the thirty-on-one interactions I'd grown used to. The job felt so much less stressful, and money flowed in.

Stacey billed our time out at $100/hour. $10 came immediately off the top to the parent company. Of the remaining $90, I got half because all my initial clients came from Stacey. Still, $45 for an hour of teaching was double what I made at Jenkins. And if I could somehow bring in my own clients, I'd get $67.50 per hour. If I ever got myself up to full-time hours at that rate, I'd crush my teacher's salary, even taking benefits into account.

By my second week tutoring, I was convinced enough to give notice at Jenkins. Wouldn't you know it, not two days after quitting my job, who should call?

Dylan.

Of course.

He'd taken Vinny's advice to heart and was investing out of the United States. He decided to spend the summer biking through Europe, and he wanted me to come along. We would mostly be touring, he said, but he'd also schedule meetings with Private Equity firms to learn about new investment opportunities. Having already started working with five different students, I had to turn him down. But my stomach flopped with insecurity. Would my answer have been the same had I still been teaching at Jenkins and had the summer off?

Stacey gave me about a third of my clients that summer. The rest came from tapping into my network at Jenkins and circulating word amongst friends from my master's program. What used to be my two quietest months of the year filled up fast.

I still got to be creative in my handful of tutoring gigs in math and English, but Stacey's clients bored me after a while. Still, that wee bit of boredom was outweighed by the reduction in my prep work and the gain in my take-home salary. I charged my private clients $80/hour and decided to give Stacey her $10 to use the same space throughout the day.

I also began my own advertising after doing a little back of the envelope calculation. On Stacey's program, it took ten meetings for a student to complete the curriculum. If she found the client, I'd get $45/hour, or $450 for the entire time we worked together. If I found the client, I received $67.50 per hour or $675 total. That meant if I could bring in a new client for less than $225, it made sense to do my own advertising. Of course, learning advertising also took time, but I enjoyed both the challenge and the opportunity to learn a practical business skill in a low-risk environment.

By the time September rolled around, I was delighted I wasn't returning to the grind with my colleagues.

CHAPTER 20

SILVER LINING

During my final few months teaching at Jenkins, real estate prices just kept going up, which isn't too surprising, as spring is normally the hottest sales time of the year. At the market's peak, my house would have been worth a full $30,000 above my final sale price. In theory, at least. The boom's endless energy was finally running out, and few homes sold at all. But even as the stagnant real estate market entered the slower summer months, buyers and sellers remained in a standoff like two cowboys in an old western. Sellers couldn't accept that their properties were worth less, so they refused to lower the prices. Buyers, meanwhile, awaited a correction. I ran into Phil one afternoon sitting in a cafe with little work to do; sales volumes had ground to a halt.

Eventually, banks resolved the standoff, but not in their favor. Years of writing shaky mortgages finally came back to haunt them. To make the loans more affordable, banks wrote these mortgages with two years of sub-prime interest. At the end of those two years, interest rates jumped dramatically, and so did monthly payments. Defaults went through the roof, which led to foreclosures, which led to banks suddenly owning real estate.

Banks aren't in the real estate business, so unlike the pool of sellers holding onto their properties waiting for prices to rise again, banks sold foreclosures for whatever they could get. By the time fall came around, enough sellers feared the longer they held to their guns, the more value they'd lose, and the selloff began in earnest.

It didn't take long before property values sank enough for buyers to want to get back in the game. By Thanksgiving, the slide could have been over. But banks that had no problem lending money when the market was roaring now clammed up. You'd think they'd want to end the slide as fast as possible, but by rejecting so many loan applications, the pool of buyers couldn't grow large enough to stop the downturn.

I watched with giddiness the entire time. The market's fall meant I could get back into real estate, the area I felt most comfortable investing. The combination of my higher earnings and the $240,000 in cash I'd be getting back from my CD (slightly higher than the $235,000 I put in), meant I'd be well-positioned for a mortgage, even with the stingiest of banks.

Or so I thought. For as Vinny had warned me, the real estate and stock markets that had risen together also fell together. The nation's economic confidence deflated like a giant balloon. Spending slowed. Decreased spending led to layoffs. The stock market took a huge hit just as the holidays approached, a time when money is generally tight even when the economy is booming.

Just when I thought I'd be sitting pretty to take advantage of the downturn, the financial crisis hit closer to home. The phone rang. It was Stacey. "I'm sorry, Amber. I don't want to ruin your holidays, but I thought it better not to wait to deliver bad news."

I closed the book I was reading and sank into the couch. "What's wrong?"

"I had three clients cancel this week alone, and my online ads have been so ineffective the past few months they're not worth paying for. Everyone is tightening their belts, and many consider us a luxury."

"But look at our results—."

"The results are tremendous, but $100 an hour is steep, especially compared to the free education these kids get in school. With our current demand, we only have enough clients to keep one of us busy. I need the clients myself, and I can't afford to spread them too thin." Stacey sighed. "I'm afraid I'm going to have to let you go."

I felt like I'd been punched in the stomach. Stacey had encouraged me to leave Jenkins elementary, and now she was cutting me out? "What about the clients I brought in the door?"

"I pay the parent company a monthly licensing fee for each person I keep on my staff."

"But I'm technically not even an employee."

"It doesn't matter. I still pay a fee for you. When I stop paying for you, I'll have to take your clients under my caseload. But you're right, you deserve something for your leads. So I'll pay you a 20% commission on any referral you've brought in."

That 20% was enough to cover my utility bills but not much more. "Do I get severance or something?"

"I'm afraid not. As you said, you're not even an employee. I'm sorry, Amber. New referrals have dropped over 50% in recent months. Everyone's panicking. Hopefully, it will turn around, and then I'd love to take you back. But for now, I'm not sure how I'm even going to keep the doors open myself. I'm so sorry."

Is there a more appropriate time to take stock than New Years?

Kyle and Libby hosted a party at their house, and Libby pushed me to come and meet some guy. I didn't have it in me to go through that again. So, while my friends were out partying, I sat alone on my couch. Well, not quite alone. A fire burnt in my awesome fireplace, and a paper mâché Amber doll sat beside me. It wasn't as beautiful as the one Dylan had made the year before, but at least it was slimmer in the nether regions.

I brought out a pad and pen and got to work. I drew a line down the middle of the page. On the left-hand side, I put *liabilities*. Where was I? I was unemployed. I was single. I had no car (my lease had just run out, and I couldn't bring myself to buy a new one until I knew where I stood financially). The economy was in the toilet and tanking fast, so my job prospects were slim.

There was one clear answer to my problems. Since my apartment lease was about to expire anyway, I could pack my bags and follow Dylan to Ecuador. I could lay low down there and spend next to nothing until the economy turned around. But if I ever did return to Dylan, I wanted it to be from a place of strength, not crawling back because my life had fallen apart.

"OK," I told myself, "get a grip, Amber. All is not lost. Let's look at what *is* working." I wrote *assets* on the right-hand side of the sheet. What did I have? Well, I had a lump sum of $240,000 about to fall in my lap when my CD matured. That gave me options. The other thing I had in abundance was time, the great benefit of being unemployed. Time and money and a down economy. Vinny would call that a recipe for success.

I thought of calling my greasy Italian friend and asking him for a play-by-play of what to do. But just like I didn't buy oil wells when real estate was high, I questioned whether I'd execute whatever crazy plan he suggested during the economic decline. I couldn't bring myself to call Dylan either, but I knew he'd tell me to learn whatever I needed to know to pull myself out of this. Every time Dylan said that, he'd been right.

Time and money and a down economy. What else did a girl need? I caught a glance at the clock and saw it was 11:59. I smiled at the memory of the widows dancing in drag on the streets the year before. I turned on the TV just in time for the final countdown: 10. 9. 8. 7. 6. 5. 4. 3. 2. 1.

I had to kiss someone, so I kissed the back of my hand. I turned off the TV, picked up my paper mâché Amber doll and threw it in the fire. I watched the doll burn up, much slower here than it had in the giant bonfires in Ecuador. As it burned, I pictured it destroying my poor decisions from the past, wiping out regret, negativity, stuckness, and the great big lie that I was a victim of my circumstances and couldn't work this out.

I watched until the doll was nothing but ash. Then it was time to get cracking.

The first thing I did was get on the substitute list for teaching. I hated living off of savings, and what was more, I had a huge bill coming due in a few months. I had spent more money than I should have when it was coming in easily during the summer, and I made the critical mistake of not taking anything out for taxes. Not only did I have the largest bill of my life waiting for me, I hadn't set aside anything to cover it. I was reminded of that first day I met Vinny, when the speaker John said the big mistake self-employed people make is not planning for taxes. Vinny had argued the smarter path was to plan *not* to pay taxes. But I hadn't followed either John's or Vinny's advice, and I left myself exposed as a result.

The next thing I did was get myself a cheap set of wheels. All the desperation had driven used car prices down, and I got myself a six-year-old Mazda with 78,000 miles on it for $4000 (and yes, it was red, thank you very much).

But my home was a far bigger hit to my pocketbook than my car. I thought about calling Phil (I loved working with Phil), but given that I was unemployed with a quickly eroding nest egg, every dollar counted. I trusted Phil to find me good deals, but I wanted great deals. Any house he brought me would have realtor fees built-in, plus, they'd be on the open market.

The one thing I had going for me was cash. If I bought low enough, I didn't need a mortgage at all, which put me in position to purchase a wholesale deal. As much as I dreaded doing it, I rang up Jade.

"Never thought I'd hear from you again."

Me neither. "I'm back in the market for a house."

"Last I recall, you were only half in the market."

I bit back the desire to get uppity and defensive. "I'm fully in this time."

"What are you looking for?"

"A house hack. Same as last time."

"Cash or charge?"

"I can go up to $240,000 in cash if need be."

"Well, well, well, look who's moving up in the world. Neighborhood?"

It felt good to not only understand Jade's jargon but to have quick answers. "C or above."

"Still need to be a quad?"

"I care less about the layout and more about the cash flow."

"You know, girl, we might just make an investor out of you yet."

I couldn't help but sit taller. "Do you also do foreclosures?"

"Foreclosures, pre-foreclosures, short sales, you name it. Some of these get complicated, but there's always a work around."

There went my expertise in real estate jargon. I pulled out my notebook and turned to my glossary section. "What's a pre-foreclosure?"

"Sellers hate being foreclosed on."

"I bet. It must suck to get thrown out of your home."

"Getting thrown out isn't the worst of it. The smart ones realize they're getting thrown out anyway, and know a foreclosure will wreck their credit rating and mean five years before they'll can get another mortgage."

"So they sell before the bank forecloses."

"Exactly. If they have any equity in the property, they're eager to sell."

"And a short sale?"

"Those are more complicated. The seller's got to get the bank to agree to take less than the amount they're due. In this economy, you'll get more of those 'cause banks realize they'll get screwed either way and foreclosing's an expense and a bureaucratic hassle."

"But why does the seller care? If they owe more than the house is worth, they wouldn't get any money out of the sale anyway."

"The black mark on their credit score doesn't sting as much from a short sale."

"Banks allow you to wholesale these deals?"

"Technically no, but if I cared about technicalities, I wouldn't be in this business. Banks won't allow me to assign the contract to someone else. So I form an LLC, sign the contract in the company's name, and you buy the company from me. No biggie. But I prefer pre-foreclosures anyway."

"Why's that?"

"I've never clicked with suits. I'll do some digging and let you know what I find."

Having all this time on my hands was good. In theory. In practice, I lounged around a lot, unsure what to do with myself. Even knowing I needed to move, I left the hunt to Jade. For a girl trying to get herself out of a financial jam, I read more pop literature than I care to admit. I was halfway through some trashy romance when my phone rang.

Dylan's name appeared on the screen for the first time since he'd asked me to bike through Europe with him the previous summer.

"I'm back, Amber."

"Let me guess, you're hoping I'm going to leap into your arms as if you hadn't disappeared on me all this time?" That wasn't fair, given that I was the one who dumped him, and my condition for getting back together was him moving halfway across the world. Still, the heroine in my romance novel had just been dumped by her arrogant, stockbroker boyfriend, and I was feeling particularly indignant at the moment.

"I'm not interested in going back to the way things were."

Oh. I'd been looking forward to hearing him beg. "Then what do you want?"

"Come outside."

Outside? Was he stalking me now? I stepped out onto the porch of my rental house, and saw it filled with daisies, my favorite flower. In the middle of the array stood Dylan, wearing a suit and tie. As soon as he saw me, he dropped to one knee. He opened a jewelry box, and there, from the guy who told me he'd never buy me one, was a diamond ring.

"I know you've always wanted one of these," he said with a wink. "Will you marry me, Amber?"

"Marry you?" Just who did he think he was? "No, I won't marry you. Get up off your knee, you fool." I crossed my arms. "You can't just show up on my porch, after all this time, and propose to me on the spot. For all you know, I could be living with someone, or dating, or…"

"Or run off with a lesbian biker gang?" Dylan stood, and a tingle ran up my spine. "You could have done any of those things, but you didn't."

I uncrossed my arms then crossed them again. "I'm going to kill Libby. She told you I was still alone, didn't she?"

"It's not like no one was interested. She told me about all the hearts you've broken. You've been alone for the same reason I have. Because you've never found anyone you like as much as me, just as I've never found anyone I like as much as you." Dylan stepped so close, I could feel his breath on my face. "We've both been alone for too long. Let's end this already."

I shifted from one foot to the other, too jittery to stand still. "That's your big romantic proposal. Let's end this?"

"Yes, let's end our suffering of trying to be apart."

"You can't just show up here like this and ask me to marry you."

Dylan's smile grew. "Apparently, I can."

My indignation melted as I looked into those deep, sincere eyes of his. "Well, my answer is still no. But you can come in if you like."

"I would like that."

He followed me into the house. I, of course, went straight to the kitchen. Dylan's presence always made me want to cook. "How about a glass of hot chocolate?"

"I thought you couldn't drink the American stuff after Ecuador?"

"I can't." I opened the cupboard and pulled out a tissue-wrapped disk. "This is Mexican. Interested?"

Dylan leaned against the counter with that smirk still plastered on his face. He was enjoying making me all flustered. "I'd love some."

I put the kettle on. "You bought me a diamond?"

"You told me you wanted one."

"You do realize those stones aren't even rare, don't you? Their value is artificially inflated."

Dylan lifted the ring from its notch in the box and twirled it between his fingers. "And like so many things that are artificially inflated, when prices come crashing down, they crash down hard. Especially the resale value. People are taking whatever they can get for them these days."

My eyes narrowed. "You didn't get me a used diamond, did you?"

"These things are millions of years old, Amber. Their value doesn't slide just because someone else has worn them."

"You did. What, did you get it on eBay or something?"

"It's not used, it's an heirloom."

I laughed in spite of myself. "What a load of crap."

"You were the one who told me I needed to learn spin."

"I swear, Dylan, you know less than nothing about romance."

"You sure you don't want it? I can get my money back for another two weeks."

"Get your money back." It was only then that I realized I'd been crying. "I'm just happy to have you back."

I stepped forward and fell into his chest. He wrapped those strong arms around me. I never felt as safe as I did in Dylan's arms. He might say and do all the wrong things, but he knew how to hold me in a way which said, 'don't worry, we'll weather the storm together, you and me.'

I whispered in his ear, "You really are back, aren't you?"

"I'm back. For good this time." He kissed my forehead. "And I'm going to propose to you once a month until you give in and say yes."

"Yeah?" I grinned and wiped my eyes. "You'll just keep coming back here with bigger and bigger diamonds until you finally win my heart?"

"Oh, no. Smaller and smaller gems. As this market shows, when people expect more in the future, they hold out. But when they fear loss, they sell for whatever they can get."

I pulled back and shot him a narrow gaze. "So that's what you're here to do? To instill in me the fear I'll be left with nothing?"

"No, I'm here to buy." Dylan's lips brushed my ear as he breathed, "In a big way."

"What are you buying?"

His voice sent chills down my neck, which made the next thing he said all the more surprising. "I'm hunting for something that used to be as rare as Bigfoot sightings. 2% rule properties."

Dylan took me out for dinner that night. At a restaurant with tablecloths and everything. This guy was getting classy. Later that evening, we headed to the beach and built a bonfire. He'd learned all about stargazing in Ecuador and wanted to share the night sky with me. It was frigid out, so he wrapped us in a pair of alpaca blankets he'd brought back.

"What's the 2% rule?" I asked, warming myself by the fire.

"That's when monthly rent exceeds 2% a property's purchase price."

"You used to tell me that 1% was good." I skewered a marshmallow and held it over the blaze.

"It was. I used to get that no problem when starting out. Then purchase prices skyrocketed." His hand shot up. "But rental prices didn't keep up, and they dropped to less than half a percent of my properties' value. That's when I gave up and moved to Ecuador."

"So now you're back and getting 2%?"

"I'm trying to."

"What type of neighborhoods?" I pulled the marshmallow out of the fire and blew on it.

"Even in this market, I can't do it in A neighborhoods. I might get lucky and find some in B. They definitely exist in D, but I won't go there." Dylan yanked a piece off my marshmallow.

"You've no desire to buy in a war zone?"

"None. I want my investments to eliminate headaches, not multiply them."

I bit right into the burning hot goo. "So you're aiming for C?"

"You got it. Good, inexpensive, working-class neighborhoods."

"And how will you find them?"

"There's a ton of foreclosures on auction."

"Have you ever done auctions before?"

"No, I was always afraid of them because you have to buy sight unseen."

I skewered another marshmallow. "What's changed?"

"My financial position. Before, I only had enough cash to buy one property at a time, and if that didn't turn out well, I'm be screwed. Now I can tolerate far more risk." Dylan took the marshmallow stick from me and held it over the fire. As much as I loved my marshmallows golden brown, in my impatience, I almost always burned them. But Dylan held the marshmallows far enough away and kept rotating the stick, allowing them to brown evenly.

"You're really here for good?"

Dylan nodded, his eyes fixed on the fire.

"You're not going to buy a few homes and go running back to Ecuador?"

"There's no need. Once I've bought and rented out my properties, I'll no longer need to live in some dumpy basement or a third world country to be financially independent."

I elbowed Dylan. "Already a couple of years ago, you could have made it work here financially. But you refused to come back with me because there was nothing for you to do here."

"There wasn't."

"What's different now?"

"Three things. One," he leaned over and kissed my cheek, "I'm itching to build a family with the woman I love."

"Don't go banking on anything, I haven't said *yes* yet."

Dylan ignored my feeble protest. "Two," he turned my head and kissed the other cheek, "with the market downturn, it's a great time to reengage."

"Markets go up and down, that won't last forever."

Dylan ignored this as well. "Three," I waited for him to kiss me again, but this time it didn't come, "I've finally found my passion. Something I can do with my life and not just count down the years to retirement."

"I thought I was your passion?"

"You're the one I want to come home to each night. But if I don't get my butt out of bed and do something meaningful with my days, our passion will be short-lived."

"What's this new passion of yours that I suddenly have to compete with for your attention?"

"Believe it or not, education."

"Education? From Mr. Dropout?"

"Remember Luther's two conditions?"

"Give to charity and share your knowledge."

"Exactly. Those two things came together in Ecuador. If you'll recall, I got involved with building a school in a nearby village. Even once the school was done, I continued to go there to teach English."

"So that's what you want to do? Be an English teacher? You'll need to finally get your degree."

"English was a big need down there, but up here, every school has English teachers. I want to teach kids to build Cash Machines, teach them about money when they're young, before they've made financial choices they can't undo."

"You think schools will pay you to teach about money?"

"They won't have to. This will be on a strictly volunteer basis."

"You're going to teach about money for free? Isn't that ironic?"

"Just free for schools. I still have private clients, and I'm thinking of giving seminars too. But my biggest passion is reaching kids young. Think schools will have me?"

"If you're not charging them? Are you kidding? Schools love bringing in meaningful programs; they just rarely have the budget for them."

"So they'll say yes?"

"I mean, maybe. If you build your presentation right. You should consult with someone who really understands education to build your curriculum."

"Like a teacher, perhaps?"

"No, teachers are too busy. An ex-teacher would be ideal."

"Perhaps someone retired?"

"No one too old. Some of these retired teachers still think the slide-rule is high tech. You want someone younger, who gets kids today."

Dylan leaned in. "You know anyone?"

"I'll have to give it some thought." I lay back on the sand. "You're really here for good?"

"You're not getting rid of me so easily this time." Dylan bent over me. "After all these years, I can now build the life I want. The life we want. Right here."

I finally got my third kiss. After that, there was no more to say.

CHAPTER 21

GOING ONCE

The next morning, I turned the last page on yet another trashy novel. I was so groggy, I had no idea what time it was, and was shocked to see 11:07 am on my phone's screen. I turned on the TV and flicked between talk shows and soap operas. No thanks. Hours in my day begged to be filled, days in my week itched to be scratched, but there was nothing for a jobless bum like me to do in the middle of winter. I hated to be the needy girlfriend, especially after we'd already spent so much time together, but I was ready to pull my hair out, so I called Dylan. "What are you up to?"

"Driving around, looking at properties." I could hear the sound of traffic on his end.

"You with an agent or someone?"

"Nope, just on my own."

"Want some company?"

So Dylan came to get me. He drove a hunter green pickup with a huge cargo bed. "What happened to that sporty little rental car you had last night?"

"I told you, Amber, I'm here to buy this time. It was criminal what I paid for this truck. I practically stole it."

I pulled loose a fleece blanket from behind my seat. It smelled like pine and Ivory soap, clean, but not like Dylan. "You sure the guy you bought it from didn't steal it?"

Dylan laughed. "You're pretty close. He repossessed it."

"Lovely."

"It's a buyer's market, Amber. The few people who have money are reluctant to spend it. A guy like me, with ready cash, can practically name his price."

"You don't feel bad taking advantage of others' misfortune?"

"You think if I hadn't bought the pickup, then the repo man would've returned it to the owner? He lost out when he bought more truck than he could afford. You buy something, you can't afford to pay for it, you lose it."

I got to thinking about myself lounging on the couch all morning. "But maybe he could afford it when he bought it, but then got laid off or something."

"That's possible." Dylan turned off the engine and faced me. "It's more likely he had no savings, no cushion to catch his fall."

"I just...I don't like winning on someone else's loss. It feels too much like Monopoly."

"If you can't handle that, you probably don't want to come with me today."

"Does that mean you're buying foreclosures?"

"That's right. The properties I buy in this down market will set the financial foundation for the rest of my life. Hopefully, for the rest of our lives." He ever so gently touched my cheek. "I want my dollars stretching as far as possible."

"I understand that. I do." I shrugged, and my head fell into his hand. "But it still feels like you're capitalizing on poor John Doe's misfortune."

"Let's say John Doe is about to lose his house. He's seriously in the hole with the bank, he's swimming in credit card debt, and has two years of back taxes looming over his head. He's strapped for cash and would benefit from selling his house at the market rate."

"Exactly, he could sell it to—."

"But nobody's buying. He's in so deep, the bank won't wait any longer for him to get his act together."

"So he'll lose his house either way?"

Dylan nodded. "If I didn't buy, you think John Doe would be better off? The fact is, buyers coming back into the market stabilize housing prices, which leaves struggling homeowners much better off."

"That doesn't help those who've already been foreclosed on." Why was I fighting Dylan so much? I was reminded of how, as a little girl, I wanted to give my friends identical presents to be perfectly fair to everyone.

"It can. Remember, we're buying these houses at auction. Auction prices are incredibly low right now because there's such a strong supply of foreclosed houses, and the number of buyers is so low. But the more people who bid on foreclosed properties, the higher they'll sell. When the sale price is high enough, a homeowner with equity can get money back."

I perked up. "They get the difference between what they owed and what it sold for?"

"Not quite. Foreclosures are expensive. There are bank fees and attorney's fees on top of the mortgage. Only after all that is paid do they get any money back. That's why if the homeowner has any equity, it's in their best interest to sell pre-foreclosure."

When I thought about it logically, I knew Dylan wasn't stealing people's homes. The owners had already lost them to the bank, and the more buyers there were like Dylan, the better off the banks and the homeowners would be. So why did it make me queasy?

He revved the engine and drove across town. We pulled up to a one-story house. An old rusted lawnmower lay in the front yard next to a broken bicycle, a ripped trampoline, and other pieces of junk. "You're not seriously interested in this place, are you?"

"That's what I'm here to find out." Dylan got out of the truck. I thought he'd head to the front door, but he instead went around to the side of the house.

I ran to catch up. "Aren't you going in?"

He squatted next to where the gutter drained out to the lawn. "I have no right to. It's not like the owners are selling it. It's being taken from them."

"So then what are you doing?"

"Just walking the perimeter." He stood again and continued towards the back yard. "I'm searching for signs of damage. Cracks in the foundation. That kind of thing."

We passed by a bay window that I assumed belonged to the master bedroom. I was so tempted to see inside. How could someone buy a house without knowing what was creeping around in there? What if there was a corpse in the living room? What if there was a corpse in every room? "Can we at least peek in?"

"I've never been the peeping Tom type."

"Oh, come on. Where's your sense of adventure? Real estate is boring enough without sticking to the law. Go on, give me a lift up." I grabbed the window sill and held up a foot for Dylan to hoist.

"As you wish." Dylan leaned over and cupped his hands. I stepped into them, and he easily lifted me high enough to get a decent look inside.

"This place is deserted, Dylan. There's junk everywhere, but no signs of life."

"That's good."

"Why?"

"No one to evict." Dylan's voice grew deeper, probably from the strain of holding me. "Do you see any signs of damage?"

"No, but I can't see much. You're really not able to enter?"

Dylan grunted and lowered me to the ground. "That's how foreclosure auctions work."

"But what if you get a house that needs major repairs?" I circled around to the kitchen window and put my hands on the sill.

Dylan hoisted me again. "You either suck it up or walk away."

Half the cabinet doors were off their hinges, and garbage was strewn throughout the kitchen. "You can walk away without having to pay?"

"No, I'd be out the purchase price." Dylan lowered me down again.

"And you're willing to risk that?"

"It's the risk that drives down the prices." Dylan kept eyeing the house's foundation as we circled around it. "Most houses don't have some major, hidden problems, and you make enough on the good ones to cover the losses on the bad ones. It's like a poker hand. If your cards say you have an 80% chance of winning, you bet big. You'll still have some losers, but if you play enough hands, you're bound to come out in front."

This sounded like Anthony and his bets on start-ups, though I don't think his VC firm would have invested in a company sight unseen. "If that's the case, then getting in a little extra-legal inspection seems like an ace up your sleeve."

"Not my style, Amber. Walking the perimeter is about as far as I'm willing to go."

At the next house, we didn't get so lucky. The yard was fenced in, and a Doberman paced behind it. "This place is definitely still occupied," I said. "What are we going to do?"

Dylan pulled out a drone from the back of his truck. "We'll just take ourselves a little video." He flew the drone up and over the house. The dog chased it, barking like mad, and jumping as if to attack, but the drone flew too high for its reach. Dylan got the shots he wanted, including a full inspection of the roof.

A woman poked her head out the door. "Rudy, what the hell you barking for?" Then she saw the drone, and her gaze landed on us. "Are you some more of those real estate agents? Bugger off! I'm not selling."

"She seems friendly enough," I whispered between tight lips. "Let's talk to her."

"You call that friendly?" He mumbled back.

I waved to the lady. "I said friendly enough. What's it going to cost us?" I approached the fence. "Sorry to bother you, Ma'am, but you do realize this house is being foreclosed on, don't you?"

The woman waved me off. "They've been threatening to foreclose on us for years."

"But now it's going up for auction."

"That's why you leeches have shown up…" Her words hit me like a punch to the stomach. I could see what Dylan meant about evictions. Even if he did win this place on auction, I wouldn't want to be the one charged with kicking her out of the house.

Dylan came over at 8 am. He'd offered to pick me up at 9 for the day's events, but I convinced him to come over for breakfast first. Nothing too fancy this time. Just pancakes and orange juice. With hash browns. And fresh jam. And coffee, of course.

"What's that in the pancakes?" he asked as we sat down.

"I made three kinds. Blueberry, plain, and chocolate chip." OK, fine, so I went a bit overboard. Can you blame a girl for wanting to cook for the man in her life? "Which would you like?"

"I'll start with blueberry, then have the chocolate chip for dessert."

I served Dylan two of the blueberry. "I can't wait. This is going to be my first auction."

Dylan poured himself coffee. "It's not that exciting."

"No?" I held out the maple syrup but then drew it back out of his reach. "Do I hear one kiss for the maple syrup? One kiss for the maple syrup? Do I have any bids?"'

"Two kisses."

"Two kisses to the man in the flannel shirt. Two kisses going once. Two kisses going twice. Sold to the man in the flannel for two kisses."

Dylan got up, took me in his arms, kissed me twice, and grabbed the syrup.

"And you're telling me that isn't fun?"

He drowned his pancakes in syrup. "You're a lot more kissable than the auctioneers at the courthouse. Trust me, it's not that exciting."

"Well, I'm excited, so don't kill it for me."

We arrived at the courthouse around 9:15 to find a crowd milling outside. "It's late already," I said, "I'm surprised they haven't opened the doors."

"Oh, they have. Court's already in session."

"Then what are all these people doing outside? Shouldn't they be in the auction rooms?"

"There are no auction rooms." Dylan splayed his hands out wide. "This is where it all happens."

"Right here? On the courthouse steps? I thought that was just an expression."

"Right here."

"Where are the auctioneers?"

"They're here. That guy in the blue suit is one. That woman's another. If you look around, you'll see at least five of them."

Once Dylan pointed out a couple of them, the auctioneers were easy to spot. All wore suits and read aloud off iPads. About forty others sat on the steps, talked on their phones, or chatted in small groups, not one of them paying attention to the auctioneers. "What are they reading?"

"Legal disclosures."

"No wonder no one's listening."

An assistant stood next to one of the auctioneers, holding up a whiteboard with the address of the property on auction. The rest of the auctioneers had no such signs, and Dylan had to ask around to find out which properties were being auctioned off. "OK, that's one of the houses I'm bidding on." He pointed toward a group of six milling around an auctioneer. "We might as well wait with the rest."

He sat on the courthouse steps, and I sat on the step below him. "If we're just going to be waiting, it's a shame for those hands of yours to remain idle." Dylan rubbed my shoulders, the response I'd been looking for. All in all, I could think of worse ways to spend my morning.

Eventually, the auctioneer said, "OK, we're about to start the bidding for 258 Geppart Road. All interested bidders must come forward to certify."

Dylan pulled identification and a check out of his pocket. "What are you doing?" I asked.

"Proving that I've got the funds to bid on the house."

"How do you do that?"

"Cashier's checks."

"But you don't know how much the house is going to sell for."

"That's why you come with a bunch of checks for different amounts. I'll need to put down a 20% deposit today, so before I'm allowed to bid, I have to show I have enough in ready funds."

Once everyone checked in, the auctioneer announced, "The opening bid on 258 Geppart Road is for $34,000. Do I hear $34,000?"

Two of the bidders threw up their hands and walked away. "That's it?" I said. "They're done, just like that?"

"The first rule of auction bidding is to know your maximum bid."

"But didn't they know the opening bid before they showed up?"

"No. You never know until they start."

"But we're still in?"

Dylan squeezed my shoulder. "Yes, we're still in." He leaned into my ear and whispered, "I've got 52 grand in cash I'm willing to spend on this place."

"Do I hear $34,000? Going once. $34,000, going twice. Final call at $34,000."

"Dollar over," Dylan said.

"The bid is now at $34,001. Do I hear $34,100? $34,100 going once. Going twice. Final call at $34,100."

"$34,100," a lady in a brown coat standing next to me said. I shot her a scathing look.

"I have $34,100. Do I hear $34,200? Going once. Going twice. Final call at $34,200."

"Dollar over," Dylan said.

"I have $34,101. Do I hear $34,200?"

Dylan was right. This got boring fast. It wouldn't have been so bad if people just cut to the chase like they do in the movies. If Dylan was willing to pay $52,000, he could have just said so, and either he'd win or he'd be outbid, but at least the damn thing would be over quickly. OK, I know that's stupid. I didn't want Dylan paying $52,000 if he could get it for $35,000, so I got that it had to move up slowly. But did it have to move so slow? If Dylan wanted to outbid someone, why not just jump in and do it? Each time the auctioneer called out *going once*, no one said anything. *Going twice* received crickets. *Final call*, and finally someone would pipe in, but often just for a dollar at a time. So we stood as the price slowly crept up. At $37,000, one of the bidders left. At $43,200, we lost another. At $48,000, one more dropped out, leaving just Dylan and the woman in the brown coat. At $52,000, Dylan said to me, "that's it, we're done."

"You're going to walk away and let her get it?"

"The number one rule of bidding on auctions is to know your price. $52,000 was my max. I'm done."

I'd never even seen this house, but I couldn't stand the idea of Dylan walking away a loser, especially after blowing 30 minutes in this auction. "You're just going to give up?"

"On this house, yes. But don't worry. I've got twelve more properties to bid on today."

Five of Dylan's auctions were postponed or outright canceled before they even began. On two more, the opening bid was beyond his maximum, so we walked away without a single bid. Dylan's first win came a little after noon. By this point, I was over fifty pages into Anna Karenina. I figured if I was going to spend so much time reading, I might as well pick up some classics to balance out the cheap romance novels I'd been binging on, so at 10:30, out of sheer boredom, I'd slipped out to a used bookstore on Beacon.

I shoved Anna in my bag and went to stand by Dylan when I saw he was one of two bidders left. When the other bidder dropped out at $62,000, I wrapped my arms around Dylan's waist and whispered in his ear. "What was your max amount on this one?"

"$78,000."

Not a bad bit of savings for a day. "Nice going."

Dylan pulled out a cashier's check for $15,000 and signed it over to the attorney. Oh yeah, it turned out that all the auctioneers were actual attorneys. No wonder the proceedings were so boring.

"I thought you only owed 20%," I said.

"I do, but that's the problem with pre-written cashier's checks: they're rarely going to be exact." Dylan bent over a clipboard to sign some papers.

"So you wind up putting down more than the minimum?"

"They'll mail me back the difference in a few days."

"So when do you close?"

"I have 30 days to pay the rest of the money."

"And if you don't?"

Dylan walked toward the next auctioneer. "I forfeit my deposit."

Late in the afternoon, a woman in her mid-fifties, dressed in a bold red suit, patent leather heels, and a Louis Vitton handbag showed up accompanied by an assistant and a suit who looked fresh out of law school. The attorney read the boring legal disclaimers, the assistant held a sign with the property address, and the woman worked the crowd, making sure everyone who mattered signed in to her auction. By the time she was ready to start, twenty or more bidders surrounded her, despite her starting bid of $650,000, far more than anything else that day.

"Do I hear $650,000 going once?" she called out.

"$652,000," shouted a man in a green jacket.

A corporate type upped him. "$655,000."

Bidders jumping up the bid? Not waiting for the final call? I stuffed Anna away again. This is what I'd come to see. Many of the other bidders stood by silently, not getting in. Some of them, I knew by now, were serious bidders, waiting for all the suckers to drop out before jumping in and stealing the show. Others, I suspected, were just like me, enjoying the excitement of an auction that finally moved and that wasn't run by some stuffy attorney mumbling legal disclosures. In less than five minutes, the bid had jumped to over $800,000.

"Come on, people," the auctioneer called, "the water's warm. Who's ready to dive in?"

I turned around to check on Dylan, who was now one of three bidders left in a different auction across the courthouse steps. I was having too much fun watching this one to track his, but something caught the corner of my eye. An auctioneer stood all by himself, which wasn't that unusual since these guys could read off disclosures forever. But this one wasn't looking down at his iPad. He'd looked up, as if checking for people.

I left the big crowd and went over to him. Even though he was alone, he was still making announcement after announcement, probably to fill some legal requirements. I got there just in time to hear him say, "As there are no bidders, this house will be…"

"Wait," I called out. "Don't close it yet."

He turned to me. "Are you interested in placing a bid, ma'am?"

"What's the opening bid?"

"Just $100." Even he sounded bored by this deal.

"What can you tell me about the property?"

"Just the address." He scanned the screen. "This auction is for the home on or near 278 Alpharo Street."

"On or near?"

"That's what it says."

"And you can't tell me anything about the house at all?"

"I can't tell you what I don't know, ma'am." The suit checked his watch. "This is my last house of the day, so if you're not going to bid, then I'm going to send this one back to the bank and—."

"Dollar over."

"What was that?"

"I'd like to bid a dollar over."

"Hang on. You're jumping ahead here. First, you need to be certified to bid. Can I see your identification and a cashier's check?"

I pulled out my ID. I didn't have a cashier's check. I could probably go and get one from Dylan, but it would be in his name, and I'd have to pull him away from his auction to do so. Instead, I showed the guy a $20 bill. "All I've got is cash. I hope it will do."

"It's not standard, but it is legal tender. OK, I certify you as a bidder. Sign here."

I signed the document and rubbed my hands together, ready for action.

"I hereby start the bidding at $100. Do I hear $100? Going once."

"Dollar over."

"I have a bid for $101. $101 going once. Going twice. Final call at $101. Sold, for $101 to this lady right here."

"Woohoo." I threw my arms around the startled auctioneer. I got several strange looks at that one, especially from Dylan, but I didn't care.

"Now, I'll need a deposit for 20% of the closing amount."

I handed him the $20 bill and fished an additional quarter out of my purse. "You can keep the change. No need to mail me back the five cents. Won't be worth the price of the stamp." I had no idea what I just did, but I was having fun.

"OK, I'll need you to sign here. You have 30 days to close, or you'll lose your deposit. Put your address down here, and I'll mail you all the pertinent details. Plus your check for five cents. If you don't want to cash it, you don't have to, but I need to follow procedure."

"You go right ahead then, if it makes you happy."

Behind me, the professional auctioneer called out, "You can't take it with you, sir, so no reason not to pony up the cash today. Do I hear $1,115,000?"

I couldn't imagine the house that would sell on auction in this economy for over a million, but could it be worth 10,000 times the one I just bought? I hoped not.

I skipped over to Dylan, where he was one of two bidders left. I grabbed his arm, but couldn't hold still and bounced up and down. "Do I hear $84,000?" the attorney called out. "$83,500 going once. $83,500 going twice. $83,500 going a final time."

"$84,000," Dylan said.

The other bidder threw up his hands. "That was my number. Good luck." He walked off, but of course, we weren't yet done. These auctioneers had to follow procedure.

"Do I hear $84,500? $84,000 going once. $84,000 going twice. $84,000 going a final time. Sold, to this man right here for $84,000."

"You did it." I hugged Dylan again, this time jumping right off my feet. He stumbled but caught me.

"That's two houses today. Not bad."

"Three, actually." I held up three fingers. "Two for you, and one for me."

Dylan's eyes narrowed. "Amber, what have you done?"

"Was that idiotic?" Dylan and I ate early bird specials at a diner across from the courthouse. Neither of us had eaten a thing since that morning's pancakes.

"I don't know." Dylan focused on his meatloaf.

I downed a load of fries. The more I thought about it, the more I feared I signed onto something scarier than I'd realized. "OK, now I'm freaking out. What's the worst that could happen?"

"The worst is that you pick up a ton of liability."

"How would that happen?"

"First of all, you don't even know if the foreclosure you just bid on was a first or second mortgage."

"I'm not following you." I opened my notebook and had my pen at the ready.

"Say a guy buys a house worth $100,000 with an $80,000 mortgage. Later on, he's strapped for cash and takes out a second loan against the value of the house for another $15,000."

My parents did something like that when three of us were in college at the same time. A pang of guilt turned my insides. "Is that like a home equity loan?"

"Yes. It's also called a second mortgage."

"I thought a mortgage was money you borrowed to buy a house?"

"A mortgage is any loan secured by real estate no matter what you use the money for." Dylan poured more ketchup onto his plate.

"OK, so bring me back to this guy. He's borrowing another $15,000 against his house. But that makes his loans almost equal to the value of the property. Risky, no?"

"To the borrower? Not necessarily. I've taken out plenty of HELOCs over the years."

"HELOCs?"

"Home Equity Lines of Credit. That's how I was able to buy The Death Trap on Haber. I borrowed against the equity in my other properties. Since I was acquiring another cash flowing property, I didn't mind leveraging myself. The bigger risk is to the second mortgage lender."

"Why?"

"Because they've taken a second position loan. Back to our example. Let's say this guy bought a year ago in a stronger real estate market, then loses his job and defaults on his $80,000 mortgage. The bank forecloses and can sell the house for only $75,000. Since they have the first mortgage on the house, they keep all $75,000. The other mortgage still gets wiped out, and the bank that lent him the $15,000 gets nothing."

I bit into another chewy chunk of meatloaf, feeling grateful I never grew up with the stuff. "That sucks."

"That's why interest rates on second mortgages are higher. They need to make more to cover the risk."

I dipped the meatloaf into ketchup and was surprised to find some improvement in the flavor. "What happens if John Doe is making the payments on his $80,000 mortgage but defaults on the $15,000 line of credit? You said they could also foreclose, right?"

"Yeah. Even a home equity line still has the right to put a lien on a house."

"What's a lien?"

"The right to repossess," Dylan said.

"But they don't have first rights...."

Dylan nodded. He was enjoying watching me put the pieces together. "Precisely. If the first mortgage forecloses, all later mortgages get wiped out. But if a later mortgage forecloses, the first mortgage still exists."

"Which means..." I dropped my pen. "Are you freaking kidding me? I might have just bought someone else's debt?"

"It's possible. That's why it's crucial to do a title search before buying a house at auction." He snatched one of my fries. I slapped his wrist, but he managed to eat the fry before I could grab it back. "By the way, there could be debt on this house that's not even owed to a bank."

I quickly forgot about the fries. "Then to whom?"

"The government. If these guys haven't been paying their mortgage, you think they've been paying taxes?"

The meatloaf sat even heavier in my stomach. "So now the government might come after me too?"

"Maybe."

"But even so, it can't be that bad, right? I mean, if I did inherit a mortgage or taxes, that means the debt is on the property, not the individual. So if I don't pay, worst case, they'll foreclose on the property again, right?"

"Even so, failing to pay it can still destroy your credit and make it nearly impossible to take out loans in the future."

This picture was getting gloomier by the minute. I flicked my salad around with my fork. "Anything else that could go wrong?"

"Oh yeah." Was he enjoying this? "The house could be in total disrepair and require more work to be livable than it's worth, but you might still have to pay taxes on it. The house could be a hazard. If it's dangerous, you won't be able to get insurance on it, but you'd still be liable if anyone gets injured."

"But it's private property. The only way someone could get hurt is if they're trespassing."

"Still doesn't protect you from liability."

"Oh man, I'm so screwed."

"Screwed?" Dylan laughed. "No, you're not screwed. At least I don't think so."

"Why not?"

"Because you didn't actually buy the house. You promised to buy the house within 30 days, but you don't own it yet."

"What happens if I walk away?"

"You lose your deposit."

"It won't be a black mark against my credit?"

"Not as far as I know."

This was why Dylan had so much fun spreading doom and gloom at my expense. "You mean that at worst I'd be out 20 bucks?" Even at his stingiest, Dylan would have considered that cheap tuition for a crash course in foreclosures. "I can live with that."

"And at best, you've acquired an asset basically for free." Dylan grabbed a few more of my fries. I guess my mood made him feel it was a safe play. It was.

"I might have done something brilliant?"

"It's possible."

I pumped my arms in victory. "What do we do now?"

"Everything we'd normally do before the auction. We'll take a look at this property, do a title search, and then decide if it's worth it or not."

"That doesn't sound too bad. What should we do first?"

"Let's drive over there."

They say that beauty is in the eye of the beholder. In this case, ugly was in the eyes of the auction winner. Because that's the first thing that hit me about this place. It was U G L Y.

It was a two-story house on a fifth of an acre lot, and the exterior was painted a color that I would generously call puke. It probably didn't look that way when the paint was fresh, but I doubt I'd been born then. The two front windows were boarded up and covered in graffiti. As soon as I saw that, my stomach turned. "Just how bad is this neighborhood? Is this what you'd call a war zone?"

"It's not the *worst* neighborhood in town."

"But it's still a D neighborhood?"

"D+."

"Then it's a good thing I've got my bodyguard with me." I wrapped myself around Dylan's arm, and he led me closer. "Come on, let's take a look at this thing."

We climbed onto the porch, and I tried the door, which was locked. "You know," Dylan said, "you don't own it yet, so you don't technically have the right to enter."

"You're not seriously telling me to walk away without getting a good look inside this place, are you? What do you think the odds are there's a back door?"

"You want to add breaking and entering to your list of misdemeanors?" Dylan wagged his finger at me. "What happened to the girl who couldn't bring herself to buy a dirty house?"

"That house wasn't just dirty, it smelled like the dead. And that girl has grown up. Besides, I'm not advocating breaking, just entering."

Dylan kneeled down for a closer look. "Foundation looks good."

"How can you tell?"

"There aren't any cracks in the concrete."

The back door was also locked. Just for kicks, I checked under the mat. Wouldn't you know it, there was a key. I unlocked the door and went in. My heart pattered just like it did when my sorority sisters and I snuck into Kyle's frat and stole their toilet seats. The house didn't smell good, but at least it wasn't putrid.

More graffiti covered the large living room and kitchen area. "Looks like we've come across someone's clubhouse."

"Not so unusual with abandoned houses in this neighborhood." Dylan brushed his fingers against a wall and rubbed them together. "At least the spray paint doesn't look new. There's a good chance no one's been here for a while."

"A good chance isn't good enough. If anybody's squatting here, I'd rather they run into you first." I stood behind him and pushed at his hips. "You head upstairs, and I'll follow."

Dylan climbed the stairs, and I stayed just a step behind him. He poked his head into each of the three bedrooms. "I wouldn't be surprised if people have slept here. But there's no one here now."

A spider landed on my shoulder. I brushed it off but still squirmed. "Let's get out of here. I've seen enough." We sneaked out the back door like private detectives, made sure the coast was clear, locked up, and scurried to Dylan's truck.

"OK, Mr. Real Estate Pro." I buckled my seatbelt. "What's your prognosis?"

"It's a dumpy house in a dumpy neighborhood."

"Do you think I should walk away?"

"Too early to tell. The house needs work, but I don't see water damage, mold, or foundational issues. It's got hardwood floors, which need to be sanded and refinished, but which are otherwise in decent shape. I'd say that it will cost between $10,000 and $15,000 to get it to the point where you could rent it out."

"And what will it rent for?"

"I'd guess $600 a month."

I wrote down these numbers in my notebook. "So even if it costs me $15,000 to fix up, that's a 4% monthly return on my investment. That's pretty good, right?"

"It's great. Remember, I'm in the market for properties that give a 2% monthly return."

"What would the cash flow be?"

"There's a rule of thumb that says your expenses, before your mortgage payment, is usually 50% of the rent. Here there will be no mortgage payment, so you might cash flow $300 a month."

$300 wasn't a ton of money, especially for the headache of fixing up a house and renting it in a run-down neighborhood. Still, considering I was unemployed, it felt pretty good. "So I did OK making that bid?"

"We won't know that until we check the title and see if anything is owed on it."

I forked over another $100 to Dylan's title search company (this house was starting to get expensive), who said they'd get back to me within two weeks.

For a guy who claimed to be financially independent and never had to work again, Dylan was busting his butt. "I'm only financially independent if my money is working for me," he explained as we drove around in his truck for yet another day looking at properties. "So yes, as long as we're in this crazy low housing market, I'm going to hustle to get my assets producing as much income as possible."

In the two months since Dylan's return, he'd bought six single-family homes, four multi-family homes, and an apartment building with ten units. Multiple work crews labored to get them into rentable shape. His years doing renovations as a crew foreman were paying off. He knew how to evaluate and hire workers, and his fluent Spanish meant he could hire qualified foremen others had passed over because of communication barriers.

I played a valuable role as a sidekick. I packed us a picnic lunch each day. "Where is this house? We've been traveling for a while."

"Another five miles or so."

"Is this another foreclosure?" I asked.

"Tax lien. They haven't paid property taxes in over seven years."

"You think it's abandoned?"

"I hope so." He turned onto a one-lane road. "If it's any of those separatists who feel taxes deprive them of their Constitutional rights, they're likely to defend their property with a shotgun."

Dust rolled over the windshield. "They could just be regular folks who've fallen on hard times."

"Maybe. But then why not sell when the economy was booming? Seven years is a long time to go without paying taxes."

Dylan pulled into a gravel driveway longer than a football field. Finally, a house in scary disrepair came into view. "Uh, Dylan, if that's the house, you might wind up wishing they were separatists."

"Why do you say that?"

"Because that looks like it belongs to the Addams Family."

"I'm more afraid of the separatists. They might shoot you, whereas Morticia will probably invite us in for a cup of tea."

"If she does, say 'no thank you, I brought my own.' I wouldn't trust anything served by that woman."

All joking aside, the house was clearly inhabited by neither separatists, monsters, or humans of any other sort. The previous owners might not have paid taxes in seven years, but from the giant hole in the roof in the east wing (yes, this house was so huge it had wings) and the broken gutters, I'd guess that no one had lived in it for ten or more.

Dylan pulled right up to the front of the house since there was no one around to object. The front door was locked, but great, big windows overlooked the surrounding hillsides. Unfortunately, they also started a good eight feet off the ground. "Let me climb on your shoulders. I want to get a look inside."

Dylan, always the dutiful boyfriend, bent over and allowed me to walk all over him. "You know I won't be able to hold you up for long," he grunted.

"Yeah, yeah. I dig the strong silent type, so keep your mouth shut and lift me up to the window." He stood up, and I grabbed onto the windowsill for a bit of extra support. "No freakin' way."

"What?"

"The largest room I've seen in my life. It's still furnished and everything. There's even a grand piano that's probably only good for firewood, but still. Whoever owned this house must have been rich."

"And whoever buys it needs to be even richer," Dylan replied. "My back is going to bust."

I lowered myself down and wiped off the dirt my shoes had left on Dylan's shoulders. "You're not planning on getting it?"

"Are you kidding? This place is a money pit. Just hauling away the old furniture could cost a fortune. It's going to need a new roof, and who knows how much water damage this place has suffered." He headed back to the truck. "And all that for what? The rental value on a place like this is minimal. There could be ten bedrooms here, which will all need renovating, but even large families seldom want more than four or five bedrooms, so adding more doesn't bring up the rental value one iota."

"Couldn't you turn it into multiple apartments?"

"It's probably not zoned for that." Dylan turned back toward the truck. "Besides, who would want to live in an apartment out here? Whoever moves this far out wants their own property."

"So that's it? It's a lost cause?"

"I'm afraid so."

I looked over my shoulder at the house. "How does something like this happen anyway? This must have been such a beautiful house. How can it suddenly be worthless?"

"It's not sudden. It's years of neglect."

"But that giant hole in the roof didn't just appear out of nowhere. Did a tree fall on it or something?"

Dylan followed my gaze. "Not this time. That giant hole probably started out as a tiny leak. That's what happens when you don't maintain a property."

Something clicked in my head. "If someone had been living here when that tiny leak developed, how much would it have cost to fix?"

"Not much. $500 tops."

"So for the lack of a $500 repair, the entire side of the house is garbage."

"I'm afraid so."

"So Vinny's wrong."

"Huh?" Dylan didn't follow the leap in my logic.

"Vinny said depreciation is a myth. He said real estate generally goes up in value not down, and that the government's rule that houses depreciate in 27.5 years is a total loophole. But this gorgeous house has probably been neglected for less than a decade and look at it now. The government has a point. After 27.5 years without maintaining it, I bet most houses really would be garbage."

"True. Real estate requires maintenance to keep up its value."

"But those repairs are a relatively minor cost compared to the value they create, especially when you factor in the tax savings. It's like the government created its deprecation rules on the assumption that you'll make no repairs. Then if you do take care of your property, it's treated as if you've created all this value. And in a sense, you have, because you've stopped it from falling apart. Such a shame about this place. It must have been something."

Dylan put a hand on my shoulder and turned me to face him. "You were hoping I'd get it?"

My eyes scanned the broad doors, the tall windows, the old tiles on the roof. They wandered towards the orchards in the back of the property, and the views of the hills beyond. It felt like an enchanted place full of stories and fairies and mystery. "Just for the adventure of buying a haunted house."

"Not happening." Dylan leaned in and kissed my neck. "But if you like, we can picnic out front."

"Sure, let's do that." It was a bright, sunny day, so even if there *were* any vampires in this haunted house, there was no chance they'd show themselves at our picnic.

Dylan threw down a blanket, and I brought out sandwiches, salad, and lemonade from my cooler. As I laid out the spread, I thought about how, technically, I should have been looking for work all these weeks, but I was so enjoying the days in Dylan's company. And who knows, on the off chance the house I bought on auction came back with a clear title, I'd perhaps make some money *without* working. Even so, a few hundred dollars a month in cash flow wouldn't make up for a lost income stream.

I was so caught up in my internal financial debate, I hadn't noticed Dylan, the lover-of-food, hadn't touched a thing. He was beside me, resting on one knee. He held yet another ring box, this one bigger than all the rest.

As Dylan had promised, his proposals had grown less and less grand. On Valentine's Day, he proposed with a ruby rather than a diamond. There was an emerald-studded ring in the next gift box, and then I got offered a measly sapphire.

"Amber, my love. Will you marry me?"

He opened the ring box, and the moment I saw it, I couldn't help but giggle. It wasn't quite the ring of my girlhood fantasies, with the perfectly cut, multi-faceted diamond, though it did hold some resemblance. I held out my finger, and he slipped it on. The ornament on top was gigantic, far bigger than the precious stones my girlfriends wore, but this stone wasn't precious, nor even a real stone, though it was shaped to look like one. It was a hollow piece of plastic, shaped like a diamond, one of those princess rings you get out of the dispensers at the entrance to Walmart.

This was the ring for me, for the person I'd become, the ring I'd wear with pride. I no longer cared that diamonds are forever. How many women still had their diamonds years after their guy had left the scene? The ring could be a piece of crap as long as it was given to me by a forever man. That's what Dylan was. He was the guy I could build a future with, who'd stand by my side even when times got tough. If only I could have done the same for him all those years before.

CHAPTER 22

THE WEDDING HACK

I'll admit, I was nervous when I called my folks to tell them about the engagement. All I could think about was their disastrous first meeting with Dylan. But a lot had happened since then, a lot of years had passed, and as my family kept reminding me, I wasn't getting any younger, so all I heard on the other end of the line were congratulations.

My mother even suggested the two of us start looking at wedding halls. Wedding preparations shoved any thoughts of finding a job out of my mind. For now, I could live off my emergency fund (the one marked only to use in case of wedding), and I was marrying a guy who'd put over a decade into building a strong financial future.

My mother, of course, wanted me to get married at her church, with a reception at their country club. But to her credit, she agreed to consider halls near me. I called places where my girlfriends had gotten married and booked appointments. Over two marathon days, she and I visited seven different halls. We walked the grounds, sampled the food, and even heard two wedding bands. That first night, my mother took Dylan and me to dinner, and the meal was all superficiality and smiles, as both Dylan and my mother bent over backwards to not say anything that would renew the tensions of years before.

The second evening, my mother drove home, and I went out with Dylan alone. My smile collapsed, and I was in tears before the appetizers arrived.

"What's wrong?" he asked.

"Everything is so damned expensive."

"How bad?"

"Really bad." I blew my nose into my napkin. "You ever watch that show, Shark Tank?"

"Yeah. So?"

"There's that guy who calls himself Mr. Wonderful. He's always investing in wedding stuff because he says weddings and funerals are the two occasions when people will spend just about anything. That's how it feels here. It's like everyone is charging a fortune for every little thing because they know they can get away with it. I so want my parents to get to the point where they can retire without my father having to kill himself or diminish his lifestyle, but this wedding's going to set them so far back."

"Amber, we're in pretty good financial shape, we can pay for the wedding ourselves if you like."

I shook my head. "You don't get it. I come from a traditional Italian family. Where I come from, people take out second mortgages on their homes to marry off their daughters. It's a point of pride. My father will insist on paying for it."

"How high do you expect it to get?"

"Given the size of my family and the level of luxury my parents are accustomed to, I'd be shocked if they pulled it off for less than $40,000."

Dylan looked like a deer in headlights. "What!"

"All the decent places charge at least $100 a head."

"How many heads can there be?"

"My family alone is over 200 people."

"How's that possible?"

"We're Italian, Dylan." My hands danced in the air as they always did when I was with my family (or talking about them.) "That's one of the reasons I was thinking of getting married here rather than near my parents. Every Italian within a five-mile radius is somehow related to us. By the time you add in my father's business colleagues and friends from the club, we'd be looking at 400 guests from my side alone."

By this point, all the blood had seeped out of Dylan's face. Even his Ecuadorian tan seemed to turn a pale shade of green. "My whole family," he said, "including cousins, is like twenty people."

"Dylan, let's get real. We've got all our college friends, my sorority sisters, my colleagues from teaching, your construction and real estate buddies..."

"Do we have to invite them all? Can't we elope?" Dylan tickled the back of my neck, which usually helped me relax, but now just made me cringe.

"Right. And have my parents disown me? I don't think so."

"Didn't you say your sister got married at your parents' club?"

"Yes, at their *country club* where they charge closer to $200 a head. That's the other reason I wanted to get married here. I thought we'd find some cheaper venues. A wedding there could cost us $75,000 or more." My shoulders shook, and I started crying again.

"Forty grand is a ton of money but not impossible. Do you know how much your parents have in savings and investments?"

"I know they pulled out a little over $500,000 when they sold their house, and I expect they have at least that in other investments, but they still say they don't have enough to retire on." I crossed my arms over the table and crumpled into them. "Frankly, I don't even know how much they need."

Dylan rubbed my back. "Breathe, Amber, we'll figure this out."

I felt the warmth of his hand sink into my skin. "Oh? Can you tell me how much they need to retire on?"

"I can make a strong guess. Have you heard of the 4% rule?"

I tilted my head towards him. "Another rule?"

Dylan moved his hand up to my neck, massaging away the tension. "If you invest your money in the market, you should be able to pull out 4% of the total each year, and the rest would keep growing at the rate of inflation."

"Not following you."

"So let's say someone retires with $1,000,000 invested and it's growing at 8%. That should produce $80,000 a year in returns, right?"

I nodded.

"But if they spend all $80,000, then sooner or later, they'll be in trouble."

"Why? Won't they still be able to take out $80,000 each year?"

"Yes, but as inflation goes up, the amount they can buy with that $80,000 will go down, and they won't be able to keep up the same lifestyle. But if they only take out $40,000 a year and add the other $40,000 to their investments, they should be able to keep pace with inflation."

"Which works as long as they're able to live on $40,000 a year. My parents probably spend over $100,000 a year, which means they'd need retirement savings of at least $2,500,000. I don't think they're anywhere close to that. And even if we do the wedding here and it only sets them back $40,000 as opposed to the $75,000 at the club, it will still be a serious blow to their savings."

"I'm sorry, Amber. I know this is hard for you. But I have some news that might help you get your mind off it."

I was not excited by the typical 'let's get the girl distracted and avoid the major issue at hand' routine. But much as it annoyed me, I couldn't deny it was effective. "What's that?"

"My title search guy called today. He tried to reach you but couldn't get through."

"I had my phone off while looking at halls." I sat up and wiped my face. "What did he say? Is there still a mortgage on it?"

"Nope. The foreclosure's on the first mortgage."

"So that's it?" I whispered, hoping not to jinx the news. "I get the place free and clear?"

"Not quite. There are some back taxes due."

"How much?"

Dylan took a paper out of his pocket, unfolded it, and laid it flat on the table. It was a statement from the IRS. At the bottom, it said, Amount Due: $3517. Adding the expense of renovations, this house would cost me less than $20,000.

"The Dump is mine?" Amazing how much buying a dump could brighten my mood. I was *definitely* not the same girl I was a few years earlier. "You said I'd be getting around $600 in rent?"

"Yes, but assume half of that will be lost to taxes, maintenance, and management."

"So I'd be making $3600 a year." I calculated the numbers in my notebook. "And if we're conservative and assume this place costs us a total of $20,000, that's an—."

"18% return on investment." Dylan finished.

My shoulders slumped. "It's not enough to pay for a wedding, though."

Dylan leaned into my shoulder. "Alternatively, you could flip the house and probably make $10,000 or more."

I shook my head. "My parents wouldn't accept the money anyway. I might as well keep the place and live off the cash flow it brings in."

Dylan held up his wine glass. "To your new dump."

I touched my glass to his. "To The Dump."

I closed on The Dump a week later. Dylan and I went to the house and toasted. I relished every sip of the excellent champagne. "This might be the first time anyone has spent more on the champagne than on the house itself."

Dylan held up his glass. "A testament to my taste in wine and your ability to spot a deal."

"What do I do with this place now?"

Dylan held up a finger. "First, pay off the taxes. No use buying a house and then losing it again." A second finger went into the air. "Then, hire a contractor to fix the place up."

The thought of hiring an outside contractor had never occurred to me. "You're not going to oversee the renovations?"

"Not a chance. You need a contractor from the neighborhood."

"How come?"

"We're in a high crime area. The locals will be far less likely to mess with the property if it's being renovated by one of their own. The same goes for the property manager. Get someone local who knows the territory and is respected by the neighborhood kids." Dylan pulled out his measuring tape, pencil, and pad. The town registry didn't have the schematics for this house on file, so we had to take our own measurements.

"You don't think I should manage it myself?" I grabbed the end of the measuring tape and backed into the corner. "I figured without having income these days, I could…"

"You invested in a D neighborhood, Amber. You're out of your league. Don't try to nickel and dime it around here." He wrote a number on his pad, asked me to stay in my corner, and headed to the perpendicular wall. "Self-management will probably only save you $50 a month. It's not worth the danger, the headache, or even the gas money."

Next, we measured the kitchen, including the countertops, refrigerator gap, and ceiling height. "You think I can trust the local contractors and property managers?"

"Don't build relationships based on trust. Base them on incentives instead."

"What do you mean?"

"Let's say the lowest bid comes in from a contractor at $10,000, and he asks for 50% up front. What do you do?" Dylan led me upstairs.

"Let me guess: giving him a check for $5000 is the wrong answer?"

"You're damned right it is." Dylan smacked the banister for emphasis. "This guy might have twenty jobs he's juggling. What's his incentive to work on yours if he's already got your money in his pocket?"

"Can't you put a completion date into the contract with some penalty if he doesn't finish on time?"

"Those rarely work. There are always so many moving parts in one of these jobs; the contractor can always blame someone else. He'll say the job was late because the city inspector didn't show up on time, and good luck proving it was his fault. Besides, you'd have to take him to court to enforce the penalty."

"So what do I do?"

"You supply materials, that's it. Then compensate him for labor costs as he expends it." Dylan and I pulled the tape across the hallway. "Everything else is paid at the end of the job. If you want to have a target date, rather than penalizing him for missing it, add a bonus for hitting it."

"Wow, I never realized how careful you had to be doing business in a D neighborhood."

"The neighborhood has nothing to do with it. I'd recommend the same cautions with any contractor."

"So how do I find these people?"

"Remember, real estate is all about networking. I'll ask around. With the market so slow, you should have no problem finding contractors to take your business at a good rate."

We squished into the bathroom, and I pinched my nose. "You think they ever flushed the toilet?" Cigarette butts were floating in cloudy, brown water.

"The contractor will take care of all that. They'll bring in a cleaning crew to sand, strip, and sanitize this place to death."

"Or back to life, as the case may be."

Jade finally came through with a triplex I could house hack. It was a cash-only deal for $170,000. I'd have to also pony up her $5000 fee, plus closing costs, and at least $20,000 to fix it up. My CD had finally matured, so I had enough money, if only barely. Still, I didn't know what to do. Did I blow all my cash when I didn't have a steady paycheck? In some ways, the purchase made sense. It would bring my rent down to zero. Combined with the fact I already owned my car, my taxes were almost nothing (because I had next to no income), and the place would bring in a few hundred dollars of monthly cash flow, so I'd probably be able to get by on the few hours of tutoring I still did each month.

Even though I'd have to buy the triplex in cash, once I fixed it up, it would be eligible for a mortgage. Of course, banks were being pretty tight these days, would they lend to someone without a steady paycheck?

Another problem with these dumpy houses: you could never be sure how much work they'd need. What if there was some sewer pipe issue that no one discovered until after closing, and I was suddenly out another $10,000? Where would I get that money? Dylan would probably give it to me, but until we were married, I knew better than to treat him like my piggy bank.

I'd learned that lesson years ago when my older sister first got engaged. My father told her over dinner one night, "You're not family until you're family. I don't care how much you're planning on building a future with this boy, until you're married, you keep your money separate from his." It had been good advice—that engagement got called off three months later—and though I had no doubts about my future with Dylan, I continued to heed my father's words.

In the back of my mind, I knew there was another reason I was hesitating. It was the same reason I waffled about picking a wedding hall and choosing a date, despite always hating the idea of a long engagement. I was still hoping to spend some of that money on my wedding, even though I knew my parents would fight me on it. It didn't seem right for my father to sacrifice his retirement and health for one night, especially when I could afford to pay for it myself.

I called Dylan and downloaded the whole dilemma.

"Buy the triplex," he said. "The numbers on it look good. If you can get it fixed up and financed before we get married, then it allows us to own two properties on primary mortgage loans, rather than one."

"But what about the wedding?"

"I've got thoughts on that…"

"Oh? Do share."

"Not yet. Just don't let your folks put a deposit down on anything without confirming with me first."

Dylan blindfolded me, spun me around twelve times, and helped me climb into the passenger seat of his pickup.

"Where are we going?"

Dylan kissed my ear. "If I wanted to tell you that, I could've skipped the blindfold."

We drove for about twenty minutes, then stopped. "Can I take off the blindfold yet?"

"Nope." He took me out of the car, spun me around again, then loaded me back in, and drove us for another ten. It was a good thing I hadn't eaten breakfast yet.

The last stretch of road was particularly bumpy, and I was relieved when we finally stopped. "Now can I take it off?"

"Nope." He helped me out of the car, walked me a good twenty paces, and drew off the blindfold. "Now, you can see."

I stood looking up at the Haunted House. "What are we doing back here?"

"This time, we're going inside." He pulled a silk bag out of his back pocket and handed it to me.

I opened the bag and peeked inside. "Garlic?"

Dylan had woven a necklace of fresh spring garlic, like the kind they sold at the farmer's market. He drew it over my neck. "For the vampires."

I bit my tongue to stop myself from asking what this was about. I knew enough not to ruin a good surprise.

There was a large gargoyle knocker on the door (of course). Dylan knocked three times. The door swung open, seemingly of its own accord. Candles lit the dark interior, illuminating what looked like a severed head on a side table in the foyer.

I didn't know whether to cringe or laugh. "You went all out."

"What's the point of buying a haunted house if you can't have fun with it?"

My hands went to my hips. "You didn't buy it, did you?"

"Not yet. But I tracked down the owners. No one's lived in this house for twenty years, since the old owners ditched it to retire down in Florida. They've long since passed away, so the place now belongs to their kids, who haven't been here since their parents died and couldn't be bothered to pay the taxes. They knew the government was eventually going to seize the place but didn't care. They'd have to dump tons of money into it to get the resale value to anything decent. So when I contacted them and told them why I wanted it, they were willing to let it go for next to nothing."

I wiped a cobweb out of my hair. "But you said it wouldn't be worth the money you'd have to put into it."

"True. As a rental, we'd never get that back."

My eyes narrowed as I faced my fiancé. "You don't mean for us to move in here, do you?"

"Maybe eventually." His face was all mischief. "But not now."

"Then why buy it?"

Dylan ignored my question. "Right this way." Dylan led me to giant double doors coming off the foyer. Just before he reached them, they opened on their own. At the same time, *Here comes the Bride* blasted out from the other side. Balloons hung from the chandeliers of the giant ballroom.

"Your parents might insist on paying for the wedding. But what if there's nothing to pay? What if you insist on getting married in the place where you got engaged, in a house that you and your fiancé own? Could they really object?"

I walked down the aisle to the music. The whole experience gave me chills. "But buying this place, even if it's just the taxes, has to cost a hell of a lot more than renting out a wedding hall. And that's before we've fixed it up."

"True, but that money would be ours, not theirs. And there are other ways we could make money on the property."

"Like what?"

"Like renting it out as a wedding hall."

The great doors to the ballroom slammed shut, and I jumped. "Or as a haunted house," Kyle said. I spun to see him dressed in a suit buttoned up over his head, like a headless butler. That explained the severed head in the foyer.

"Or as a place to hold seminars." Libby, dressed up as Morticia, came out from behind the moth-eaten blinds. "This is a great, old house. There are tons of things you could do in a space like this."

I turned to Dylan. "The renovation costs aren't going to be insane?"

"Yes and no."

"What's that supposed to mean?"

"One whole wing of the house, where the roof caved in, is a mess. We'd have to gut and rebuild the entire thing to make it livable. But the other wing and the central area with the kitchen and ballroom are in decent shape."

"Show me."

The four of us walked through the scary old mansion, which wasn't all that scary. The section where the roof gave out was filled with mold and water damage. But the rest of the house was charming, with a giant kitchen clearly intended to handle large parties. The appliances were rusted old dinosaurs, but with the right modifications, it really could be used to cater events, and the space was perfect for seminars like the ones Dylan wanted to run on building Cash Machines. But that would be for another time, far in the future. As we completed our walkthrough of the house, a more immediate plan formed in my mind.

"You said you haven't bought the place yet."

"The owners gave me two weeks to look around and bring an inspector if I want to."

"Bring the inspector. I've got an idea brewing about this wedding."

"What are you thinking?"

"Let's call it a Wedding Hack."

The inspection, of course, was a disaster, mostly because of the water-damaged wing, but also due to the outdated plumbing and wiring. Getting this place in shape would cost a fortune. However, the foundation was solid, and that was our biggest concern.

The purchase price was next to nothing, since the heirs were about to lose the place anyway. We sold them on our story of getting engaged on the lawn and wanting to be married in the house. We even promised to send them invites. They ate it all up, and the three siblings agreed to sell us the house in exchange for $1000 each. Dylan paid off the overdue taxes the day after we closed.

That night, I emailed out a Save the Date, which included the following statement:

In the old days, weddings were a cooperative affair. Friends and family would pitch in to send off the bride and groom. There were no fancy wedding halls, nor were guests expected to bring lavish gifts. Rather, each person contributed as they wished, and anything that may have been lacking in splendor was more than made up by the feelings of love and connection created by everyone working toward one goal. This is the feeling we wish to create at our wedding. So, we request our guests to abstain from bringing gifts and to instead contribute to the wedding itself.

Dylan proposed on the lawn of a stunning old house. Despite it's being abandoned and dilapidated, we fell in love with the place, decided to buy it, and hope to one day raise a family there. We can think of no better location to hold our wedding. Given the current state of the house, there will be quite a bit of work to do to prepare the location, the food, the decorations, and other important details. You'll find a link below to a sign-up sheet, and everyone who wishes to do so can choose the contribution that feels most natural.

We look forward to having you join us as we start our new life together.

Amber and Dylan

My parents were going to flip out when they saw the message. As soon as I hit send, I turned off my phone and went straight to bed. By the time they managed to reach me, it would be too late to change anything.

CHAPTER 23

THE SCOREBOARD

D ylan and his work crew wasted no time in making the two most important fixes to the Haunted House. First, they plugged the hole in the roof to keep the rain out. Next, they sealed off the moldy, water-damaged wing from the rest of the house. The house inspector suggested this. She said the cost of repairing the damage would be astronomical, but if we sealed this section off, it would stop the mold from spreading and still leave us with plenty of house to spare.

I didn't tell Dylan, but I had a plan for the vacant wing. Since it was a gut-job anyway, there was no reason we couldn't eventually turn it into a beautiful, modern townhouse. The wing had enough space for a kitchen, living room, office, and three bedrooms. We didn't need a gargantuan mansion, and I didn't want to give up on the income from renting the other half out for parties and seminars. But I'd come to love the property with its orchards and view. I wanted a cozy home, and eventually, this would be perfect for us. This was where I wanted to raise my kids, and when the time came, renovating the damaged wing could allow me to do just that.

Speaking of kids, Kyle and Libby took an evening away from theirs for a double date. Normally, I'd arrange these get-togethers with Libby. She still called me her best friend even though we hardly saw each other now that she had one kid and a second on the way. Yet, this time, Kyle called me himself, saying he had something to celebrate.

"Well, well, don't the two of you look the dapper couple," Kyle said when we walked into the restaurant.

"Don't the two of you look the pregnant couple," Dylan retorted. "Is that all sympathy weight you've put on, Kyle?"

"I thought it would be inconsiderate to allow Libby to grow rotund on her own." Kyle patted his stomach. "There's nothing wrong with having a bit of meat on your bones. One of these days, Dylan, you're going to realize that all those muscles make you look gaudy."

"Gaudy is a compliment coming from you. Is that a Rolex you're sporting?"

"Good eye." Kyle wrapped his arm around Libby as we followed the host to our table. "A little present from the little woman."

Libby patted his chest. "I got it for him when he made partner. They just announced it last week."

We were seated at a corner booth. Libby barely fit into a spot at the edge.

"Partner, eh?" Dylan raised an eyebrow. "I guess congratulations are in order."

"Spare your congratulations. You know what I want." Kyle put out his hand, palm up.

Dylan took out his wallet, removed a dollar bill, and held it out to Kyle, but when Kyle reached to take it, he pulled it back. "Not so fast."

"Come on, hand it over. A deal's a deal."

"Prove to me you've won."

"What are you two talking about?" I asked.

Kyle ignored me. "Do you have any idea what a partner in my firm makes?"

"In this economy," Dylan said, "I'd think you'd be on food stamps."

"Oh? Did I never tell you I switched to the bankruptcy division a few years back? In my firm, we have an *eat what you kill* compensation plan."

"That's gruesome," I said. "What does that mean?"

"It means not all partners get paid equally. The more money you bring into the firm, the greater a share of the pie you make. My clients helped us stay profitable during the down year. They had to transfer six associates onto my team from other divisions where there wasn't enough work."

A waiter brought us menus and a platter of homemade tortilla chips and dips.

Libby unabashedly grabbed a handful. "Kyle's contacts from his days dealing with start-ups have been a huge boon to the bankruptcy practice."

As I nibbled a chip, I wondered about Anthony. In good times, only a small percentage of his portfolio companies survived, and even fewer made money. What was happening now? Was he still able to pick out enough winners in this economy to balance out the rest?

The guys ignored the chips, their eyes still locked. "I haven't checked the scoreboard in a while," Dylan said. "What will you clear this coming year?"

"I'm a bit concerned about some of the other divisions dragging down the firm's profits. But if all stays strong, I should break a million."

Dylan whistled. "That's not a small amount of money."

"No, it isn't." Kyle leaned in, and his tone grew feisty. "Now give me what I'm due."

The boys continued to stare at one another until the waiter came back with our drinks and asked if we were ready to order. "Dinner's on us," Kyle said, "so get whatever you want. We're celebrating."

"You're treating Dylan?" Libby asked. "You never treat Dylan. You always said it was cheating."

"Not anymore. Not now that I've made partner."

I raised my wine glass. "To making partner."

"Screw the partnership," Kyle said. "I've known I was going to make partner since my second year in the firm. We're celebrating my victory over Dylan."

"You're 100% certain that dinner is on you?" Dylan asked.

"Absolutely. Go on and order whatever you want. We can all put on a little sympathy weight tonight. Just hand over what you owe me."

"Well, if you insist you're treating…" Dylan ordered a skillet steak, a bowl of chili verde, and a mesclun salad.

Libby turned to her husband. "You do realize that dinner is going to cost a hell of a lot more than the dollar you're getting?"

"Oh, hush." Kyle rubbed her back. "It's all about the bragging rights. I'm going to hold this over Dylan's head for the rest of his life."

"Really?" Dylan finally reached into the chips. "I'm not so certain."

"It's right there on the scoreboard in black and white."

"Hold this safe, honey." Dylan handed me the dollar and pulled out his phone. "I have to check something."

Libby held up both of her hands. "Will you boys finally tell us what all this is about?"

"Of course." Kyle kissed her on the cheek. "As soon as I collect my winnings."

Dylan shook his head. "My apologies, Kyle. It appears I've been a little lax."

"No harm done, little buddy, as long as you can admit it. Just hand over my winnings, and all will be forgiven."

"I meant I've been lax in keeping up the scoreboard." Dylan turned his phone around to face Kyle. "It appears I haven't updated my numbers since I moved down to Ecuador. I'll have to rectify that tomorrow."

"Don't give me that tomorrow crap." Kyle dipped his chip into the ultra-hot chili sauce. "Scoreboard or no scoreboard, you've always known your numbers down to the penny. Are you willing to admit defeat or not?"

"Defeat?" Dylan's lips formed a sly grin. "Oh, no. My position is far too strong to admit defeat."

"Will someone please tell us what this is about?" I said.

Dylan put his hand around my shoulder. "Just a little bet that Kyle and I made in Mexico."

Libby's eyes narrowed. "What kind of bet?"

"You see, Kyle thought—."

"I'm perfectly capable of telling my wife what I thought," Kyle said. "Dylan and I were the ideal test case: two guys preparing for solid, professional careers; one stays on the sane track, while the other decides to play Mexican fisherman. For some crazy reason, Dylan thought this would be a healthier career path."

"Kyle told me I was a fool. So I said, 'you wanna bet?'"

"Hell yeah, I wanted to bet. I bet him that by the time I made partner, my financial position would trounce his own." Kyle slapped the table. "And it does. There's no way he can compete with a million a year."

"Let me get this scoreboard thing straight." Libby grabbed another handful of chips. "You two have been sharing financial data this whole time?"

"We were supposed to. But as you heard, Dylan's gotten a little lazy over the years."

Libby glared at her husband. "You've been sharing all the details of our financial life with Dylan, and you didn't even ask me for permission?"

"Sometimes, privacy has to take a backseat to matters of science." Kyle kissed her hand. Libby shook her head but had become too used to Kyle's antics to mount a real protest.

"But isn't Kyle right?" I asked Dylan. "We don't make anywhere near a million a year, do we?"

"Not even close," Dylan said.

"Then Kyle won. Didn't he?"

"You see, Dylan? Even your fiancé can see sense. Be an honest fellow and give me my due."

"Absolutely not." Dylan popped a chip into his mouth.

"You're one stubborn bastard." Kyle's slowly shook his head. "Just like me. So how are we going to resolve this?"

"That's easy." Libby winked at me. "You two boys shared our private data. It's only fair that we get our revenge by getting to play judge and jury. Right, Amber?"

"Right." I slid over next to Libby. "Kyle, you brought the claim. You can make the first opening statement."

Kyle rose to his feet, stepping into full-on lawyer mode. "Your honors, I present to you a most simple case. It is a case of two men with very disparate incomes. One has reached the zenith of his career, becoming a partner at one of the most prestigious firms in town. The other has no career, and spends his days ridding his properties of roaches so he can rent them out for a few pesos more per month."

I refilled my wine glass; I was going to need it to make it through Kyle's speech.

"Yes, esteemed members of the jury, one man makes a million dollars a year, drives a Lexus, has a gorgeous 6000 square foot home, and belongs to the finest country club in town. The other makes only a small percent of that, drives a used pickup, lives in a home a fraction of the size, and proposed to his fiancé with a ring that came with a free gumball. I offer for your consideration that there is no comparison between the two men, and that the one making the million dollars a year is in a far greater financial position."

"Thank you, counselor," Libby said, "you may step down."

Kyle gave a half-bow and took his seat.

I'd let Libby have her fun with Kyle, but Dylan was all mine. "Dylan, how do you plead?"

"Uh, Amber," Dylan said, "you're confusing things. That's just for criminal cases."

"Who's the judge here, you or me?" I poured on my thickest Italian accent. "I've seen My Cousin Vinny. I know how these things work. The next word out of your mouth had better be guilty or not guilty, or else I'm holding you in contempt."

Dylan sighed. "Not guilty."

"That wasn't so hard, was it? Now move along with your opening statement. You're starting to bore me.

"It's very simple," Dylan began, but I wasn't done with him yet.

"You dare speak before this panel while seated?" I filled my wine glass for the third time. "Have you no respect for this court? Get to your feet, counselor."

"You are having entirely too much fun." Dylan stood. "Ladies of the jury, I present to you two men. One is very proud of his income, but if you listen closely, you'll detect something else beneath the pride: fear. He's a man running on a treadmill. While he's earning a million dollars a year, he can keep up with its ever-increasing pace. But disaster lurks one misstep away. The other lives without fear, for he has learned to control the treadmill's speed." Dylan bowed and sat.

"Thank you, Dylan," Libby said, "that was both short and pointless."

"Let's get to my favorite part," I said. "Cross-examination." I was my father's daughter, after all.

"Who gets to cross-examine?" Dylan asked.

"We do, of course," I answered.

"You can't be the judge, the jury, and the cross-examiner," Dylan said.

"This is my court; I can do whatever I want." I smacked my spoon against the table like a gavel. "And if I hear one more word out of you, I'll hold you in contempt."

"Fine. Ask away."

A waiter swapped our empty basket of chips for a full one, and Libby scooped up another handful. "Kyle already shared his income, so let's start there. Dylan, how much do you make?"

"I guess that depends on how you define 'make,'" he said.

Kyle snorted at this. "I think one lawyer in the room is more than enough. Just give us the obvious answer."

"I'm not salaried like you are, so it's not so obvious. I'm currently collecting over $40,000 a month in rent from my properties. After paying all expenses, that leaves me with about $10,000 a month."

"Then your income is $120,000," Kyle said. "Simple."

"Except it's not so simple. Almost half that money goes to paying down my loans. If I wanted to, I could slow the rate of repayment and pocket more cash each month. But would you consider that making more money?"

"What do you mean?" Libby asked.

"I take out 15-year mortgages on my properties. If they were 30-year loans, I'd pay less each month."

"But you'd have to make payments for twice as long."

"Correct. But my current income would increase."

"I'll give you that." Light flickered in Libby's eyes. She was starting to get it. "I won't credit you with the interest payments, but reducing the principle can count in your favor. How much is that?"

"Another $5000 a month."

Kyle jumped back in. "OK, so that brings your income to $180,000. It's still well below my million."

But Dylan wasn't done yet. "Well, hang on a second. Why are we counting the amount I'm paying down the principle? Isn't it because I'm building equity in my properties?"

Kyle crossed his arms. "Yeah. So?"

"So mortgage payments aren't the only way I'm building equity. Most of my equity comes from my properties appreciating."

"Oh, come on," Kyle said. "That's a stretch. Housing markets go up and down."

"I'm not talking about the appreciation that comes from normal market growth, like with your house. I buy properties from auction or wholesalers. Then I increase their value by fixing them up and renting them out. That's where my real equity growth comes from."

"Now we're getting toward the absurd." Kyle rolled his eyes. "Those are just paper gains, not money you can spend."

"No? Once I refinance a property, I can take most of that money back in my pocket."

"Only because you're borrowing against your properties. That's not income."

"I thought you said income was money I can spend?" Dylan jabbed his finger into Kyle's chest. "I can spend this. And it's actual value I created."

"I still say it's not income."

"Well, I'd argue with you, but you have a big ally on your side."

"Who's that?" Libby asked.

"The IRS. They also don't consider it income. So even though it's money in my pocket, it's not taxable. In fact, they're not taxing any of my real estate income."

I whispered into Libby's ear, and she nodded. "We think you're both right," I said.

"Oh come on, Amber," Kyle said. "You elementary school teachers think you can resolve disputes by giving each kid a sticker and a pat on the head, but there needs to be a winner and a loser here."

"Don't worry, Kyle, I'm not about to pat you on the head. We've decided not to count the increase in Dylan's property values as income."

"Now we're getting somewhere."

"Don't celebrate yet. It's not income. But the question before this court isn't who's got the biggest salary. If it was, you'd win. The question is, who has achieved the greatest financial position. And there's no question that all of that equity Dylan's amassing goes toward his net worth. Tell me, Kyle, what is *your* current net worth?"

"Uh, truthfully, I'm not sure."

"What do you mean you're not sure? It's right here on the scoreboard." Dylan held up his phone. "Despite your great big salary, you still owe $86,000 in student loans. You've got almost the same amount in retirement accounts, so those two cancel each other out. You lease your cars, so there's no value there. You've spent a ton on clothes, jewelry, etc., but you'd only get a tiny portion back if you had to sell. Most of your net worth is in your house. You still owe almost a million dollars on that, but even in today's lousy market, it's probably worth two to three hundred thousand dollars more than that."

"That's all we've built up?" Libby asked Kyle. But before he could answer, she turned to Dylan. "So…what's *your* net worth?"

"Over two million dollars."

A chip froze halfway to Libby's mouth. "How exactly?"

"That's what happens when you avoid bad debt, invest most of your income, and give it time to compound."

Kyle picked up a napkin and held it in the air.

"Are you waiving the white flag?" Dylan asked.

"It's not white, it's yellow. I'm calling a penalty." Kyle dropped the napkin on the table.

"Roughing the passer?"

"Unsportsmanlike conduct." Kyle held his arms out like a referee.

"For what?"

"For trying to distract the judges with this net worth crap."

"Net worth is not crap," Dylan said. "It's far more important than income."

"If we were 65, I'd agree. But I'm at the beginning of my career, not the end. Your net worth shot past mine the minute you dropped out of school and stopped taking on loans. But I consider all of that debt an investment, and now I start reaping the rewards. Hell, I haven't even received my first paycheck on my new partner salary. But I'll be making over a million a year for forty years. The reason I didn't live in a crypt and squirrel away dimes was because I knew this day was coming." Kyle got in Dylan's face. "Now, I'm ready to trounce you."

Dylan backed away. "I don't think you are."

"That's why we have these two beautiful, intelligent, discerning judges to decide for us."

"Trying to butter them up?"

"I'd never do such a thing. But ladies, let's not forget who's buying your dinner tonight."

I got the waiter's attention and held up the empty wine bottle. If I had to put up with Kyle's dross, I'd gladly add a refill to his tab.

Libby turned to me. "Dylan wins on net worth, and Kyle wins on income. So how do we settle this?"

"Well," I said, "like a wise man once told these boys on a fishing trip, it's not what you make that counts, it's what you keep. Perhaps Kyle's right that his net worth in forty years will dwarf the two million dollars that Dylan has now. But if I know my fiancé, his net worth is hardly going to stagnate for the next few decades either. So I'm wondering, whose net worth is growing at a faster rate?"

"You can quit your wondering, Amber," Kyle said. "You have any idea how fast a million dollars a year accrues?"

"I'd think very fast if you actually put away a million a year." I had too much experience with my father's lack of savings to believe that a large salary guaranteed a substantial net worth. "But saving has never been your forte."

"At a million a year, I can enjoy a few finer things and still save enough to create a giant nest egg."

"You can," I said. "But will you?"

"Why wouldn't I?"

The waiter brought our dishes and a new bottle of wine. Dylan and Kyle leaned towards their meals, but Libby said, "oh no, you don't. You guys aren't getting a morsel until we finish this." I guess she did know how to get back at her husband for his antics.

"I already see one tragic flaw in your plan, Kyle." I added guac to my burrito. Just because the boys couldn't eat didn't mean the judges had to suffer. "You think you're actually going to make a million dollars."

"Look, Amber, even if I'm short a million because the firm had a tough year, it's no big deal. The economy will pick up; it always does."

"I'm not talking about your salary on paper, I'm talking about what you take home. How big of a chunk will you lose to taxes?"

"Between federal and state taxes?" Kyle looked up as he did the math. "Probably half."

"Tell me, for the remaining half million, have you created a budget so you know exactly how much you can spend?"

Libby laughed. "Kyle is allergic to budgets."

"Have you decided what portion you'll invest annually?" I'd learned a few things over the years. "Choosing a percentage and taking it off the top, so you're not tempted to spend it."

"That I've done. As soon as I made partner, I upped my 401(k) contribution to $50,000 a year. That money gets invested before I ever see it."

"How are you investing it?" I bit into my burrito, which barely held together.

"Dylan convinced me to put it into index funds over mutual funds."

"That sounds like a solid move." I wiped the burrito sauce from my chin. "Anything besides your retirement accounts?"

The gap between Kyle's brows tightened. "Remember, you're supposed to be an impartial judge, not arguing your fiancé's side."

"Welcome to Amber's cross-examination. Just answer the question, counselor. Have you decided how big a portion of your take-home income you're going to put aside each year for saving and investing?"

Kyle's head fell like a boy caught skipping class. "Not really."

"That means no," Libby said.

"So here's my problem, Kyle." I gave up trying to eat my burrito by hand and went at it with fork and knife. "You want us to guess how much you'll invest each year. But most people spend virtually everything they make, no matter how high their income. And you've never proved that you're any different. So how am I supposed to determine how much you'll put away now that you have your big raise?"

"Even I can't spend a half million a year, Amber."

"I'm not sure you can't," Libby said. "You told me that once you made partner, we could get live-in help to assist with the baby and housekeeping. You also mentioned rewarding yourself with a new car and basketball season tickets. And we've discussed private school for the kids."

"Saving is like a muscle, Kyle," I said.

"If that's the case," Libby said, "you're kind of a weakling, honey."

"I've had enough berating from the two of you."

"That's the beauty of cross-examination."

"Look, here's what you need to consider…"

"If you're going to start a speech, let's move to closing arguments," Dylan said. "I'm getting hungry."

"Fine." Kyle recomposed himself and again rose to his feet. "Lost in all of this discussion of dollars and cents, is the bigger question of how money is best used. Will I spend money to get my kids a fabulous education? Absolutely. Will I spend it to bring in help when the baby arrives so my beautiful wife can sleep through the night and spend her days bonding with her children instead of doing the laundry? In a heartbeat. I will also spend it on vacations, nights out, and cars that don't have giant dents in the side and can survive a drive to lunch with friends without conking out."

That last line hurt. So much for buttering me up.

"All of that is included in what I consider one's financial position. It's the ability to use your money to enjoy life. If you can do that, while simultaneously saving for retirement and providing financial security for your family, I'd count you a success. If your only goal is to die with the most money, then I consider you dead already."

Kyle ceded the floor to Dylan. "I once told Amber that earning a living is like rolling a boulder. Those in debt must exert enough energy to provide for themselves and make the debt payments, so it's like pushing the boulder uphill. For those of us with Cash Machines, it's like rolling a boulder downhill. Many, including some at this table, have looked down on my lifestyle choices over the years, but I made them to get my boulder rolling. Each time I invested another dollar in my Cash Machine, it rolled a little faster. Each time I discovered a way to cut on expenses, learned a lesson about investing, or found a way to save on taxes, the slope of the hill got a little steeper.

"My boulder is now rolling so fast that it no longer needs a push from me to keep moving downhill. It took me over a decade, but I finally hit my goal: full financial independence.

"When I work one-on-one with a client or volunteer my time to teach about finances, I do it because I choose to, not because I need the money to live. When I buy a house on auction, fix it up, and rent it out, I'm choosing to invest my time so that my Cash Machine can grow even faster, so that I can live in greater abundance and be more generous with myself and others.

"Can I afford all of the fineries that Kyle treats himself to? Not now. Not yet. Not without eroding the base of my Cash Machine. But thanks to the magic of compounding, fueled by my understanding of investing, I'm getting there fast. And I'm getting there without having to sacrifice my time, my health, or my values.

"Kyle gave his definition of a strong financial position. Mine is the ability to spend my days doing what I most value without ever having to trade my time for money or live with financial stress."

Dylan faced his friend. "Kyle, I hate to say it, but you look like crap."

Kyle looked from Dylan to Libby. Her head fell. She didn't want to admit her husband had lost his youthful veneer. He faced me, hoping for some support, but all I could think about was Dad.

Kyle's shoulder's sagged. "Tell me about it. I don't have time to work out anymore."

"Yep, you're stuck in a bind." The energy at the table had changed. Dylan's voice no longer sounded competitive, but concerned. "You don't have time for yourself, but if you don't take better care of yourself, your career won't last 30 years, let alone 40."

"Make the time, Kyle," I said. "Don't wind up like my father."

Kyle didn't respond to me, but looked back at his best friend. "You've worked pretty hard this past year yourself, Dylan. You think you'll be able to slow down?"

"I worked hard because I saw an opportunity. I wanted to get in while properties were cheap. At this point, I've invested all I've got, and already prices are back on the rise. I wouldn't necessarily say I'm done buying. If the right opportunity comes and I have the funds, I'll jump back in. But for the moment, I'm no longer looking. I've got a wedding to prepare, a honeymoon to plan, and a family to build."

"You actually think you'll be able to live well on your Cash Machine?"

"I can't think of anything I need that I can't afford right now. And as time goes on, my income will keep getting stronger."

"Because you'll keep buying places?"

"Perhaps. But the rent on my current apartments should also continue to rise, and, in a few years, I'll pay off the mortgage on my first building, which will immediately increase my cash flow."

Kyle looked at Libby, both of their faces defeated, then returned his gaze to Dylan. "You've got everything figured out, don't you?"

"No, and I probably never will. There's so much to learn, I doubt I'll ever stop studying."

"Still, what you've done is no small thing. I'm not sure I fully grasped it until tonight." Kyle smacked his fist into his hand. "Crap!" He dug into his wallet and pulled out a dollar bill. "We don't need to hear from our judges. You have all the money you need and, even more importantly, the time to enjoy it. I can't compete with that. Take the dollar. You've earned it."

"We can still drink to you making partner." Dylan picked up his wine glass. "And I thank you for generously treating us to dinner."

Kyle scowled and lifted his glass.

CHAPTER 24

EVER AFTER

"**I** need a truck ASAP!" My cousin Regina shouted so loud I had to hold my phone away from my ear. It was two a.m. on the night before my wedding. Had you asked me five years earlier what I'd be doing at this hour, I'd have told you I'd either be winding down from a fabulous rehearsal dinner or getting my beauty sleep so I'd look my best the next day.

But there'd been no rehearsal dinner, just like there'd been no rehearsal. Both got scrapped in the frantic sprint to the finish line as we prepared the Haunted House for the wedding. The house no longer looked haunted, but it was filled with spirits tonight. Over twenty of us, a mixture of family and friends, were still going strong.

"Regina, what the hell are you talking about?" I shouted back. Before she could answer, I heard honking from outside. "Hang on, Regina." I put my hand over the mic and called out, "That's Uncle Fred with the pizzas. I need two guys to help carry them in." Aunt Delilah's sons Johnny and Frankie, who made flunking school an art form, dropped their paintbrushes and ran out. They'd each polish off at least a slice before getting the pies inside, but after working fourteen hours straight, they deserved it.

I returned to the call. "What were you saying, Regina?"

"I need a truck out at Collins Hall, and I need it now."

Collins Hall was one of the wedding venues I hadn't even considered because it ran a minimum of $200 a head. "What are you doing out there?"

"I told you I got this new waitressing gig, right? So I made sure to get this shift cause it's right before your wedding and they always leave the flowers, hundreds of gorgeous, beautiful, stunning, healthy flowers. Nobody takes them home. Crazy, right? And of course, these high-flyers didn't touch a single bouquet, not a one. Nobody even took the centerpieces. And they're freakin' roses, Amber, roses! Can you believe it?"

Regina wasn't the brightest star in our family's constellation, but she'd done good. I looked around the room. Who could I send? The open bed in Dylan's pickup took far too much wind. I spied Vinny talking to one of my cousins. Much as I appreciated him coming, he'd been more hindrance than help. Vinny couldn't work and talk at the same time, and since he was always talking, he was usually distracting someone else. But he'd arrived in a massive SUV. That'd be perfect. "Vinny! Can you drive out to Collins Hall ASAP to pick up flowers?"

He gave me a thumbs up. "You got it."

"OK, Regina, hold tight, someone's on the way."

I hung up and ran into the kitchen. My parents had, of course, flipped out when they learned they wouldn't be paying for the wedding. Though I'd won the first battle, the war stretched on. The next week, they'd insisted on coming out to the Haunted House. They agreed it had charm and beautiful grounds, but were appalled at the state of the kitchen. They insisted on replacing the appliances as a wedding gift, and I was too grateful for the offer to fight them. They favored buying new residential appliances but capitulated when Dylan found a deal on two-year-old commercial units at one of the many restaurants closing down due to the bum economy.

Twelve women chopped, stirred, and kneaded in all corners of the kitchen. They were, of course, all family. The last thing we needed was one of my non-Italian friends getting in the way, and besides, I needed Libby supervising the decorations with my sorority sisters.

Maria Rose chopped cabbage on the long counter by the sink. That girl was a terror with a chef's knife. I put my hand on her shoulder.

"What's up, Amber?"

"I need you to ride out to Collins Hall with Vinny. Regina's got a whole wedding's worth of flowers they're just going to throw away."

"Don't be stupid, Amber." She lifted the cutting board and slid the cabbage into a bowl. "If she's got that many flowers, you want as much space as possible to bring them back. I'd just take up space."

"Vinny doesn't know Regina. It's better if you're there."

She hacked the next head in half. "So give him her number. He's not an idiot, is he?"

No, he certainly wasn't. But I was starting to have my doubts about Maria Rose. "You'll be a big help there. Besides, you shouldn't be chopping with your broken finger."

She dropped the knife and faced me. "What broken finger?"

"The one I'm going to snap if you don't get your ass in that SUV." I pointed out the door, and she finally got the hint. All day I'd tried putting her together with Vinny, but she was too valuable in the kitchen and he too much in the way. A half-hour drive each direction was perfect, it would give him plenty of time to realize just how hot a property she was.

Maria Rose washed her hands, smoothed out her dress, and faced me. "How do I look?"

"Like an angel." And she did. She'd come here to work, not to turn heads, so for once, there was nothing ostentatious about her outfit or makeup, and she had a healthy flush from cooking in the hot kitchen. I kissed her cheek and whispered in her ear, "Be sure to ask him about his Mamma. Now go!" I slapped her butt, and she scurried out the door.

The deafening buzz of loudspeaker feedback reverberated from the great room. I shoved my fingers in my ears. "Angelo! Turn that crap down."

"Sorry, Amber." Angelo unplugged his electric guitar from the amp. "We were just testing the sound."

I relaxed my arms. "What are you testing it in here for? Aren't you guys setting up outside?"

"Well, yeah. But you know…," he shrugged, "in case of rain or something."

I stuck a finger in his face, "It is *not* going to rain on my wedding day."

His face turned stiff and pale. Poor Angelo. He was only 14, and the deranged bride routine was just too much for him. He backed away, but fortunately, his 16-year-old cousin Janine, the lead singer of the teen band that six of my cousins formed for the wedding, stepped in and took my hand. "No one's predicting rain, Amber, but it never hurts to be prepared. And we thought after all the old farts clear out, this room would be perfect for an after-hours dance party."

I pulled Janine and Angelo in for a teary-eyed hug. They were doing great, all of them were. Angelo squirmed out of my grasp, but Janine patted my back, saying, "It's going to be alright."

Across the great room, Libby pointed my way. Dylan came rushing over. "Come on, Amber, let's go."

"Go? Go where?"

Dylan took my hand. "Home. You need your sleep before the wedding."

"But there's so much to do here."

He pulled me toward the door. "And so many amazing people to do it. Libby will make sure everything gets done. Remember, she plans parties for a living."

"Yeah, right. She's a lawyer's wife for a living."

"She's still a professional." He yanked me toward the door. "You've done all you can for today."

I thought people would be angry at my leaving while they continued to work, but all I heard was "See you tomorrow, Amber," "You'll be great, Amber," and Libby's "Don't worry, we'll take care of everything."

With so many amazing spirits in the Haunted House, was it any wonder I wanted to make it my home?

Kyle rapped the side of his champagne glass with the back of a knife. Slowly, the crowd of 400 settled into something approaching silence. True silence was never heard among my family. To us, silence was the sound of the dead, not of a vibrant family celebrating life. It was hopeless trying to rein in the kids running and screaming on the lawn in front of the Haunted House. If the adults had to speak a bit louder to be heard, so be it. Janine dashed over to Kyle with her microphone, the same one she'd used to sing us down the aisle three hours earlier.

It had been a strange wedding by any account. The tablecloths didn't match, nor did the tables they covered, which came in assorted shapes and sizes. In fact, other than the centerpieces Regina rescued the night before, nothing matched, not chairs, plates, cutlery, glasses, or even the food. Had we ordered lasagna at a wedding hall, we would have gotten giant trays of the same bland noodles. Instead, I counted at least eight different lasagnas, dozens of pastas, and close to fifty salads. If anyone minded the lack of uniformity, they didn't mention it to me. For I had found my match, both in the man sitting by my side and in the crowd of family and friends gathered to see us united.

So what if we danced on grass rather than parquet? I'd rather dance barefoot than in heels any day. So what if our wedding band had yet to sprout facial hair? They played their hearts out, and what they lacked in polish, they more than made up for in enthusiasm. So what if there'd be no pile of expensive gifts awaiting us? We'd received something far more precious from our guests: they'd given of themselves to make our wedding a reality.

Kyle rapped his glass twice more, this time amplified by the microphone. He cleared his throat and said, "I can read on all of your faces the joy, excitement, and gratitude you've felt throughout this wedding. But for my wife Libby and me, one emotion takes precedence over all others."

Libby leaned into the microphone and said, "Relief."

"We've been watching this long, drawn-out saga from day one. And let me tell you, it was not always pretty."

As Kyle told the sordid details of my on-again off-again romance with Dylan, my mind wandered to some all-too-familiar ruminations. Since that fateful day I received Dylan's letter, I'd repeatedly wondered where I'd gone wrong. Had I been wrong to wash my hands of him back in college? Wrong to walk out on him seven years later? Wrong to not drop everything and follow him to Ecuador?

I'd beaten myself up over my choices so many times. But now that the doubt and uncertainty were over, now that we were finally united, I wondered, had I gone wrong at all?

If I had been Dylan's traveling buddy in Mexico instead of Kyle, perhaps things would have been different. Perhaps we could have come to one mind about our financial future. But Dylan was moved by Luther's words, not me. He had to investigate the path that spoke to him, and I had to be true to my own journey. Despite spending plenty of money, my head was not in finances at the time. I was hardly thinking about making a living, much less saving for retirement.

Seven years later, I'd matured in many respects, but still not so much in the realm of money. Sure, I paid my bills and made my 401(k) contributions, but that was about it. I started learning about building a Cash Machine, not because I saw a need for it, but because Dylan valued it. I tried to play the role of the dutiful girlfriend. But that could only go so far.

My second go-around with Dylan can be summed up in one word: *compromise*. Dylan initially talked about compromising with me, but I feared asking him to. Instead, I compromised over and over again. I drove an ugly dented car and bought a terrifying house from a woman who looked more at home on a street corner than in a real estate office. And why? To show Dylan that I was ready to go with him on his journey. But one-sided compromise isn't the foundation of a sustainable relationship. While everything Dylan told me made logical sense, it was still *his* journey, not mine. And forcing myself into a life I didn't love, even for a man I did, just wasn't tenable.

The part of the tale that wouldn't make it into Kyle's Best Man's speech was that everything shifted when my father had his heart attack. That's when all that information Dylan pumped into my head finally entered my heart. That's when I took my first true step in Dylan's direction. And I wasn't the only one who shifted. As Dylan's Cash Machine grew, he finally loosened his purse strings and moved towards me.

Had I learned more about money from the start, could we have made the relationship work a decade earlier? Perhaps. But that's not where I was. It wasn't *who* I was.

The crowd laughed, and I returned my attention to Kyle's speech. "So a trip that began with my best friend and I traveling together ended with me coming home alone. But at least I didn't return empty-handed. Oh, no, no, no. Like a modern-day version of the Pony Express, I came…bearing a letter."

The table with my college friends laughed loudest at this. They remembered this part of the story far too well.

Libby took the mic from her husband. "Amber remains my best friend to this day, but admittedly, our conversations have lacked the pluck they had before I got married. We used to sit up for hours talking about boys. Now I'd spend half the time talking about dirty diapers. She was even worse, though. She'd spend the other half talking taxes!"

Vinny leaned in and whispered something in Maria Rose's ear, no doubt bragging about how he'd set me straight on taxes. I could only see one of Vinny's hands above the table, and I guessed the other rested on Maria Rose's knee. I considered Vinny more than repaid for all the advice he'd given me over the years. A guy like Vinny needed a good Italian woman, and Maria Rose was certainly that.

I didn't relate to Vinny's vendetta against the IRS, but there was no question I respected his knowledge. I expected him to achieve levels of financial abundance in his lifetime far greater than anything Dylan and I would reach. Even so, I had no interest in walking his path. Dylan and I were financially free, meaning we now had enough passive income to support our family and build a life together without financial pressure. Working twice as hard for twice as much, or even ten times as much, had zero appeal for me. Vinny, on the other hand, would never stop. He'd never want to.

In thinking about all the people around me and all our journeys, it hit me how there was no singular path to financial success just as there was no singular path through life. Dylan wasn't wrong for dropping out of college, nor was I wrong for staying in. Kyle wasn't wrong for taking on massive educational debt, nor was Vinny wrong for maximizing tax benefits.

Still, that doesn't mean all financial choices are created equal. It's a little scary for me to remember that from leasing my first new car to renting my first one-bedroom apartment, I'd spent virtually zero time thinking about how these decisions would impact my financial future. I didn't even have the tools to analyze the costs, so I mostly made the same choices as my equally clueless friends.

That was Dylan's objection to school, not that it wasn't right for anyone, but that he'd found himself on a path without knowing why he was on it, without understanding the costs involved, and without a clear vision of what he wanted to achieve at the end. Once he took time off to understand his options, he decided he'd be better off leaving school, but he could just as easily have decided otherwise.

There are literally millions of paths regarding money, and each of us can choose the one that appeals to us most. But to make responsible choices, we need financial literacy. education.

Kyle raised his champagne glass. "And so, after many years, many trials, and many tears, the saga of Amber and Dylan's dating life has now, thankfully, come to an end. As you enter this next stage of your lives, may you continue to learn and grow together. I wish you a marriage filled with love, with happiness, with abundance."

I took Dylan's hand. No longer was I compromising for love. No longer was I on a blind path, hoping that if I followed the crowd, all would work out. I felt pure gratitude to finally be on my chosen path with my chosen man.

I want to bless you, Dear Reader, with success on your financial journey. If I've given you anything, I hope it's insight into some of the obstacles and opportunities you'll encounter as you forge ahead. Just know, this is not the end of your financial education. This book is not a blueprint for achieving wealth—it's more like a treasure map. You'll no doubt need more research before implementing these strategies, but I hope I've shown you where to dig.

My story is over, but this next leg of your financial journey is just beginning. Some paths you have to walk on your own, but remember, help is never far away. Resources, both free and paid, exist in abundance within the financial community. I'm sure if you're diligent in your search, you will have no trouble accessing all the information you need. To make your search a bit easier, I've curated and assembled my favorite tools and information sources at **BuildMyCashMachine.com**.

Want more of *The Cash Machine*?

Earlier drafts of *The Cash Machine* contained one chapter not found in this edition. This chapter, *Hard Money*, occurs right before the wedding. In it, Amber and Dylan learn many of Vinny's most advanced tactics.

We badly wanted to include these strategies in the book. So why did we cut the chapter? Beta readers felt it was too complex for the book and slowed the pace of the narrative.

In the end, we decided the book would be better without *Hard Money*. Of course, we still want to get the material into readers' hands. We love the Vinny character and the advice he gives in this chapter is powerful stuff, including a number of advanced techniques for those already in strong financial positions. We decided to make *Hard Money* a bonus chapter and give it free to our readers.

To read *Hard Money*, the deleted chapter from *The Cash Machine*, go to **BuildMyCashMachine.com/bonus-chapter**

ACKNOWLEDGEMENTS

This book is the product of the most intense research project we've ever done. We wish we could remember the names of all the bloggers, vloggers, podcasters, authors, speakers, etc., that we learned from, but we're not that conscientious.

We'll put a full bibliography of recommended sources on our website, **BuildMyCashMachine.com**. For now, we want to acknowledge and thank the following financial experts who most influenced us as we were writing this book, including: Robert Kiyosaki, Tom Wheelwright, Paula Pant, Josh Sheats, the Mad Fientist, Mr. Money Mustache, Brandon Hall, J.D. Roth, Kris Haskins, Dave Ramsey, Tony Robbins, Marie Forleo, and the entire crew at BiggerPockets.com, including David Greene, Brandon Turner, Scott Trench, Mindy Jensen, Matt Faircloth, and Joshua Dorkin.

Thank you to all of those who patiently shared their expertise, including Ari Lasky and Yonah Weiss on real estate taxes, Mark Chess (Moshe Chesed) on Venture Capital, Michael Perlin on fishing, Kayla Malo for teaching us a credit card trick for raising your credit score, and Ari Feinstein on real estate and financial independence.

A special thanks goes to Marie Fragomeni Garofalo and her twin sister Rose Fragomeni Gargiulo for advising us on all things Italian, especially the unwritten rules and dynamics of traditional Italian families. We had a great time laughing together reading out these scenes. If they sound at all authentic, it's due to them.

Thank you to all of our Beta Readers who gave us constructive feedback on the book, including: Beth Shapiro, Shimi Herman, Aryeh Lev Mason, Barbara Mason, Jessica Rhein, Shifrah Devorah Witt, Carlene Gunsior, Jamie Shakotko, Giovanna Tiberini, Jennifer Harter, Malka Sima Pais, Georgia Lima, Shalom Steinberg, and Noga Hullman.

ABOUT THE AUTHORS

Dave and Chana define their mission as "Learn, Grow, Teach." They see every moment as an opportunity to learn something new, grow from what they're facing, or share wisdom with others. They are passionate about personal growth, healthy living, and stories.

The Masons live in the funky Nachlaot neighborhood of Jerusalem, where they interact with tourists, adventurers, and spiritual seekers from all over the world.

Chana is a Vitality Coach, helping clients manifest their dreams and live healthier, more energetic lives. Learn more about her coaching and culinary tours at ChanaMason.com.

Dave is a Rabbi and the owner of Knobs.co, an online cabinet hardware store.

Chana is a gourmet vegan chef, and Dave is an avid ultimate frisbee player. Along with their son Aryeh Lev, the Masons enjoy books, games, and exploring new territory.

Their greatest wish is that you learn key lessons in this book, incorporate them into your life, and inspire others.

Also by
Dave and Chana Mason

Also by
Chana Mason

Also by
Dave Mason

Manufactured by Amazon.ca
Bolton, ON

11298488R00189